UNPACKAGED TOURS

UNPACKAGED TOURS

World Travels
Off the Beaten Track

Edwin Morrisby

TAPLINGER PUBLISHING COMPANY

NEW YORK

For Henriette Maria Maximiliana Barbara,
who unfortunately had to stay at home

First published in the United States in 1988 by
TAPLINGER PUBLISHING CO., INC.
New York, New York

These chapters originally appeared, in somewhat
different form, in *Quadrant* magazine (Australia)
and thanks are due to its editor, Peter Coleman,
for his generous help and support.

Library of Congress Cataloging-in-Publication Data

Morrisby, Edwin.
  Unpackaged tours.

    Bibliography: p.
    1. Morrisby, Ted.   2. Voyages and travels—1956–1978
  I. Title.
  G465.M68A3   1987   910.4   87-13207
  ISBN 0-8008-7939-2

Book design by Susan Hazlett Ryf

Maps designed by Kannegieter & Vogan, Sydney

Contents

List of Maps*

*Maps are provided for those islands, countries, or territories not easily found in most general atlases.

UNPACKAGED TOURS

1

Albania

THE LAND OF THE EAGLES

The Albanians have always appealed to the poetic imagination. Early last century Byron was quite taken with Ali Pasha of Tepëlenë and adopted Albanian costume—a white fez, embroidered shirt, sash stuffed with pistols, and a flared multi-pleated skirt. Edward Lear, who earned his living painting landscapes and only wrote poems like "The Owl and the Pussy Cat" for amusement, devoted a book to Albania (*Journals of a Landscape Painter*). It was something about their wild, lawless ways. Like the Scottish Highlanders they were hopelessly over-romanticised. As *Childe Harold* has it:

> Fierce are Albania's children!
> Their wrath how deadly! But their friendship sure.

The truth is that the Albanians were then, as now, a poor, backward, clannish, contrary people. But not one lacking in interest. Once, as the Illyrians, they had occupied most of the Balkan peninsula. Dalmatia is an Albanian word meaning sheep country, and some of the gods in the Greek pantheon (Nemesis and even Athena) have recognisably Albanian names. In prehistoric times the Greeks entered the peninsula from the north and, later on, the Romans conquered Illyria and turned it into an imperial province. Then, in the 6th

1

century, the Slavs entered the Balkans from the plains and marshes of the Ukraine and the Bulgars came riding out of the Central Asian steppes. In the end the Albanians were driven back into the crumpled knot of mountains in the southwest corner where they live today.

When the Turks invaded Europe in 1452, they quickly overran the Balkan lands and ruled them until the middle of last century except for Albania. The Albanians fought valiantly at first—Skanderbeg is one of the great heroic figures of the late Middle Ages—but, finally, they threw in their lot with their conquerors and went on to govern the Ottoman empire for them. Once again the Scottish parallel comes to mind.

Even Kemal Atatürk, founder of the modern Turkish state and victor over the Anzacs (Australian and New Zealand Army Corps) at Gallipoli, was of Albanian origin. But so were others. The Egyptian royal family, for instance, which is why King Farouk's bodyguards were always Albanians. And Sinan also, it is said, the architect who was responsible for many of the exquisite Turkish mosques, including the Sülemaniye, the most splendid in Istanbul. Indeed, one of Istanbul's really enchanting suburbs is called Arnavutköy, which means Albanian Village. The Albanians embraced the Muslim faith (they are the only European country that is predominately Muslim) and identified themselves completely with the Turks. When the Great Powers forced the Sultan to give them their independence in 1912, they were rather put out, to say the least of it.

In line with other Balkan nations they chose a German princeling as their king. When World War I broke out he promptly rejoined his regiment in Germany and that was the last they saw of him. After the war the Albanians offered the throne to a well-known English cricketer but, before he could assume it, one of their own tribal chieftains came down out of the mountains and seized power, first as president then as king. Zog was his name and, in Albanian, Zog means bird. A wily bird he turned out to be, for, when the Italians invaded Albania on Good Friday 1939, Zog flew the coop taking the Albanian treasury with him.

When I was a schoolboy in Australia and began to collect stamps, I quickly found out that our local fishmonger was an Albanian. He came from Gjirokastër in the south (later the scene of some memorable Greek victories over Mussolini's troops). And so, Zog and his queen Geraldine swam into my ken on stamps bearing the odd name *Shqipëria* (pronounced Sh-kyip-eria), which is what Albanians call their country. Popular lore has it that this means "Land of the Eagles" from the word *shqiponjë* or "eagle," but philologists claim that a more likely derivation is from *shqip*, the adverb "clearly, intelligibly," and the name means "Those you can understand." I resolved to visit them one day.

I had to wait a long time. World War II intervened. Albania was occupied by the Germans, who came to Mussolini's rescue after his attack on Greece faltered. Under Yugoslav guidance a Communist resistance movement developed and, when the war was over, Albania became, to all intents and purposes, a Yugoslav satrapy. Albania, however, took Stalin's side in the split with Tito and, when Khrushchev demolished Stalin's reputation at the Twentieth Congress of the Communist Party in 1956, Albania eventually broke with the USSR. So the Albanians wound up being at loggerheads with everyone in Europe. In a curious sort of way this suited them. Their only friend then was China, and China was sufficiently far away. Now they have broken with the Chinese. They are alone.

My first trip to Albania was short and sweet. The rift with Russia was still fresh in 1959 when I was a passenger on a Romanian ship from Yalta to Venice. We called at Durrës, the Albanian port, and after much discussion (in which I learnt the Albanian words for yes and no—*po* and *jo*—the latter being the more common), a few passengers were allowed to go to Tirana by bus.

Tirana is a jumble of old Turkish houses, cobbled or dirt streets, mosques, and statues of Stalin. There are more statues of Stalin in Albania than there are petrol stations. Right in the middle of the only square in the city—Skanderbeg Square—was a half-finished building. This was the House of Culture, began by the Russians. They had left for home without completing it, taking the plans with them.

Running off the Square was a broad avenue called The Boulevard. On it were all the modern buildings in Tirana: the university, parliament, the Hotel Dajti, army headquarters, government departments, and so on. They had been built by the Italians during their four-year occupation. The only traffic on The Boulevard was a solitary horse-drawn phaeton and a couple of men on bicycles. Nonetheless, a traffic policeman stood in the middle directing them. Although there were undoubtedly many ways to die in Albania, being run over seemed the least likely of all. I had just been reading Ilya Ehrenburg, the Soviet writer and journalist, and I remembered what he had said of Tirana: "I have been in many cities without a boulevard, but this is the first time I have been in a boulevard without a city."

After the break with the Soviet Union, Albania became even more remote—a sort of Tibet of Europe. Some years later in England, however, I noticed an advertisement in the *New Statesman* calling for the formation of an Albanian Society. I went along and managed to be elected to the committee (there were hardly enough people in any case).

Once on the committee I immediately suggested a film expedition to Albania "to show the fraternal British people the great advances made by the Albanian People's Republic." I happened to know that there was absolutely no film on Albania anywhere in the UK. So we drafted letters to the Committee for Cultural Relations with Foreign Countries in Tirana and sent telegrams to Enver Hoxha, the First Secretary, Mehmet Shehu, the President, and various members of the Politbureau like Misto Treska and Vito Kapo, whose names our chairman, a chemist from Essex, somehow knew. But to no avail. Tirana didn't even bother to answer.

In Turkey for the fiftieth anniversary of the Gallipoli landings, I called on the Albanian Embassy and was hospitably received with coffee, currant cake, and green brandy. I explained how important the Albanian Society was in England and asked them to transmit my application for a visa. They promised to do so but suggested I might be better off applying to Paris. (There were only three Albanian embassies in Europe then—in Italy, France, and Romania.) This got me thinking. A friend of mine, Jacques Vergès, was the editor of *Révolution*, a glossy magazine financed by the Chinese. He must be friendly with the Albanians. So, next time I was in Paris, Vergès and I went to the Albanian Embassy and made a formal application for permission to film there. Twelve months later the request was approved.

Albania has only one open border post. It is near Shkodër on the Yugoslav frontier. When we arrived in a Yugoslav hired car—late, I might add—we were met by a man who introduced himself in French as Monsieur le Directeur. We never found out what he was director of or why the Albanians had insisted on a land crossing. We could have flown from Bari in Italy, though the flights were erratic. Monsieur le Directeur had a bus and we set off almost immediately for Tirana, a six-hour drive over abominable roads. The sound recordist and the cameraman grumbled all the way.

That night we stayed at the Hotel Dajti and the following morning I asked whether we could meet the head of Albturist, the Albanian Tourist Bureau. Monsieur le Directeur said he did not know where his office was. I later learned it was in the hotel. I then asked could we perhaps meet the secretary of the Committee for Cultural Relations with Foreign Countries. He said he was out of Tirana. And so it was with everyone. Upon asking for a telephone book I was told that no such thing existed in Albania. In addition we were expressly warned not to film anything until permission had been granted.

Monsieur le Directeur was going to play it in his own obtuse way. Losing my temper with him would get me nowhere. So we went for a walk around the town. The House of Culture had been finished I noted. New also were the signs reading: *Rrofte Mau Ce Tung* ("Long Live Mao Tse-Tung").

There was very little for sale in the shops—soap, kitchen utensils, bread, cheap shirts in various shades of purple and red, a few books mainly about Skanderbeg and the inevitable speeches of Enver Hoxha, First Secretary of the Albanian Communist Party. I did notice *Aventurat e Hekëlbër Finit* (*The Adventures of Huckleberry Finn*) in the hotel and bought it as well as a book of Albanian folk songs.

That night, over dinner, Monsieur le Directeur said a decision had been made about us. We would go to a hotel on Durrës Beach, where there was a party of tourists—the first ever admitted to the country from the West. They were to be taken on daily excursions and we could accompany them.

Albania has probably the best beaches on the Adriatic, and midway along Durrës Beach, which stretches almost 10 kilometres south of the port, was a group of hotels, built to serve tourists from Eastern Europe. After the rupture with the USSR they were all boarded up. The Adriatik had been specially reopened for these Western tourists.

There were half a dozen English couples there—mainly fellow-travelling school teachers and a handful of French. We were all told that it was forbidden to speak to any Albanians other than our guide or to go anywhere without permission. Tourists were treated very warily in Albania.

For the next fourteen days we travelled all over the country. Albania is not very large—about the size of Switzerland—and the road system is somewhat limited. Still, we filmed in Krujë, where Skanderbeg held out against the Turks in the mid-15th century; in Berat, a medieval town of a thousand windows (many of which are stained glass ones in churches); in Sarandë, in the extreme south opposite the Greek island of Corfu; in Shkodër in the north; in Korcë, where Enver Hoxha had taught French; in Gjirokastër, the hometown of my boyhood friend, the Albanian fishmonger; in Tepëlenë where Byron had met Ali Pasha. Ali had complimented Byron on his "small ears, curling hair & little white hands" and kept stroking his knee. We saw Himarë, where they grow bananas, and Vlorë, where the long point of Karaburun divides the turquoise-tinted Ionian Sea from the sapphire-spangled Adriatic. We jostled market women in the last *souk* (covered bazaar) in Albania at Elbasan and filmed men in native costumes (worn, incidentally, by the Greek Palace Guards, or Evzones, who came originally from the Albanian-speaking parts of Greece). Albania must be one of the few countries in the world where what is called peasant costume is actually worn by peasants. We shot footage from the pine forests of the northern mountains to the rhododendrons on their slopes to the cotton fields and orange orchards of the coastal plain. We visited Lake Ohrid on the eastern border and the Shkumbin River that divides the country, separating the southern tribe of Tosks from the northern tribe of Ghegs (Zog was a Gheg, Hoxha a Tosk). We were taken to the Roman ruins of Appolonia and Butrinti, Byzantine churches and Whirling Dervish shrines (the headquarters of this Muslim mystic sect is in Albania), partisans' graves, oil derricks, and textile factories. In short, we went all over Albania, drinking the excellent brandy and less than palatable wine, eating goat's meat and tomatoes at almost every meal, meeting gypsy troupes and their dancing bears, seeing the guards on every culvert, every bridge, every road junction. Like Byron we were captivated by "places without a name and rivers not laid down in maps." The only two towns we had not been to were Durrës, the port, and Tirana, the capital. Inexplicably, they were out of bounds for tourists.

We had, unfortunately, aroused the suspicion of Monsieur

7

le Directeur. He had no English, so I translated his little speeches from French. While this was happening the camera-man and sound recordist would slip away and take to the back streets of whatever town we were in. Monsieur le Direc-teur had reprimanded me a number of times. I felt his patience was fast running out.

One evening at the Adriatik I heard German spoken. Drinking brandy at a table was a group of men, so I approached them. They were East Germans and initially cautious, but I was able to reassure them. I mentioned that I had had dealings with Gunter Richter, Director of *Deutscher Fernsehfunk*, the East German television service, and I dropped another name—that of Heinrich Eggebrecht. I had met Heinrich in Zanzibar. He was the Secretary of the Afro-Asian Solidarity Committee of the German Democratic Republic and constantly referred to Ulbricht, then the leader of the GDR, as "*der Walter—mein guter, alter Freund.*" Egge-brecht travelled in the West on an Australian passport. He had spent the war years in Australia as a refugee from Hitler's Germany.

The East Germans worked on a dredger in Durrës harbour and lived at a hostel on the beach. Once a week they were allowed to go to the Adriatik Hotel and have a few drinks. Apart from that they had no contact with anyone, not even with their Albanian workmates who, they said, would walk right past them in the street. One ruefully remarked that Durrës was the only port he had ever been where there were no prostitutes. For kicks, they said, they occasionally went up to Tirana, 50 kilometres away. It was forbidden but there was no problem about boarding the train—there were only three short lines in Albania at the time. The lower level of Albanian officials—the ticket collectors and guards—didn't seem to care. It was the clean-shaven men wandering around in open-neck shirts and cotton trousers that one had to be careful of. They were *sigurimi* or secret police. One in ten Albanians belonged to the *sigurimi*—three times the number in the armed forces.

I returned to our table and relayed this information to the camera crew. Three mornings later the cameraman and I got up at 4:00 A.M. and walked the five kilometres along the beach to Durrës. The sound-recordist was given a day off. We wore our oldest clothes and had not shaved for three days. The camera was in a carry-all. Either we were indistinguishable from Albanians or it was as the Germans had said.

We spent about five hours in Tirana and filmed almost everything. You can walk around Tirana in an hour, so we had plenty of time. We shot Enver Hoxha's modest two-storey house and the guards around it. They obligingly pointed their guns at us. We shot the cordoned-off street where the Polit-bureau live. This body had some overtones of the Mafia as nine of the members were related to each other and two, in addition, were husband and wife. We shot the parliament building, the military headquarters, a new housing estate, the old quarter, the statue of Stalin, the mosque, King Zog's former palace on the hill overlooking the town, the now-completed House of Culture, and literally dozens of posters reviling those enemies of the Albanian people—the USA, the USSR, Yugoslavia, and Greece. And, of course, portraits of an ever-smiling, ever-youthful, ever-watchful Shoqe ("Comrade": pronounced Shocker) Enver Hoxha. We also mugged a few Chinese wandering around, any number of *sigurimi*, and some shabby soldiers looking like battle-weary partisans. Nobody said a word to us.

After lunch we caught a train back to Durrës and did the same there, including in our footage the port installations. As evening fell we walked back along the beach to the hotel. As soon as we arrived we knew something was wrong. Monsieur le Directeur was waiting impatiently for us in the foyer. He wanted to know where we had been all day and we said we'd been on the beach. That was impossible, he replied, as searchers had been out looking for us. We shrugged our shoulders and said, "They didn't find us, that's all."

In our room we carefully packed our exposed film. Then we took the unexposed film that we had left and opened all the cans, taking good care to tear off the first six inches or so with the perforated stock number on it. We closed the cans, marked them up as if they had been exposed and put camera tape around them.

That night in the hotel there was a farewell party for the tourists. They were leaving the following morning. I asked a few of the English people whether they would take some film out for us, trying to sound as casual as possible. Most nearly collapsed on the spot, but one woman, the wife of a dentist, was delighted. It was, she explained, the nearest thing to James Bond that had ever happened to her. She carefully stowed our exposed film among her undies.

About nine o'clock the next morning, two hours after the tourists had left, a black Mercedes Benz drew up outside the hotel. It was the only one I ever saw in Albania, which had about two hundred motor vehicles—mostly trucks. Monsieur le Directeur told us that someone from Tirana wanted to see us.

Then began twelve hours of interrogation by the Albanian Secret Police. There were three of them and an interpreter. The name of the leader was Ded Gjo (I got him to write it down for me) and his rank was Colonel-General. They took it in turns to ask the questions, which were always the same. Had we ever been in Yugoslavia? The adjective attached was "revisionist." Had we ever been in Greece? The adjective attached was "fascist-monarchist." Did we speak Serbo-Croat? Did we speak Greek? Where did we go on the day we were missing? Whom did we meet? Whom did we talk to? Why were we in Albania? When I patiently went through the whole story of the Albanian Society, they said this was being looked into. When I mentioned Jacques Vergès and the Chinese connection, they said the visas had been issued to us "by administrative error." When I said that the film would show people in Britain how Albania was progressing, they replied that they considered a state of war existed with Britain. This was, no doubt, a reference to the sinking of a British warship in the Corfu channel by an Albanian mine after the war.

Every so often someone would bring in Turkish coffee and a glass of brandy. They offered us cigarettes (Albanian cigarettes are very good). Then they would begin again. Sometimes we would be harangued for ten minutes in Albanian with a lot of shouting and table pounding. The interpreter would get up, smile in an embarrassed sort of way, and then proceed to harangue us in English with exactly the same noisy gestures.

I kept on asking who had complained about us. Their answer was The Albanian People. When I pressed them they said the complaint was that we had filmed negative not positive aspects of Albanian life. I asked for a definition of negative and positive aspects of Albanian life. They had a little conference over this one and eventually said that filming a factory was positive but filming the workers coming out of it was negative because they would be wearing old clothes. Filming a new housing estate was positive but filming the old quarters of towns was negative. Filming Young Pioneers was positive, filming old women in baggy pants was negative.

Lunch came. They smoked incessantly, even when eating. Instead of using an ashtray they would lift the tablecloth and ash the cigarette underneath it. The interrogation dragged on. Finally Ded Gjo produced his trump card. We had been seen filming Albanian soldiers. This was strictly forbidden and carried a mandatory jail sentence of two years. (Ilya Ehrenburg had said that Albanian soldiers were for the most part barefoot so he also qualified for a jail sentence.) So that was that. It was no use trying to appeal to the British Embassy. There wasn't one. The cameraman at this stage broke down. I was worried that he would tell them where we had been and what had been done with the film, but he was shattered at the prospect of not seeing his wife again. The evening meal was a very gloomy one.

Finally they took us up to our room. Our unexposed film, made up to look as if it had been exposed, was confiscated. When I asked what they would do with it, they said they would develop it. Albania has a small film industry. We had been shown a film they had made—about Skanderbeg—at the hotel some nights before. I knew that if anyone put our film through a bath it would soon become obvious that it had never been exposed at all. I told them it was the latest American film and needed special hard-to-get chemicals to develop it. Otherwise there would be no image, nothing, just blank.

They considered this. Then they announced, "Albania can do anything the Americans can. We will be able to develop this film." They also confiscated our equipment. I insisted on a receipt and, in the end, they gave me one. We were told we were under house arrest. We were not to leave our rooms. They would decide what to do with us when they had seen the film.

Two days went by, two long days. The hotel staff averted their eyes when delivering our meals. They did not attempt to clean the room. The sound-recordist was stoical but the cameraman was sunk in apathy. We sat on the balcony most of the time and watched the few swimmers. Beyond them, about a hundred metres from the shore, the bright red and white motorboats of the *Policia Popullorë* patrolled.

On the morning of the third day Monsieur le Directeur appeared. We were to leave in half an hour. We were being deported from Albania. Because of our frankness with the secret police the equipment was being restored to us. I didn't dare ask what they judged frank about our answers—maybe the cameraman's tears. When I asked about the film I was told it was still being processed.

It was a hot day and the trip to the border took seven hours. We had to wait at the border post, sitting sweating in the bus, while our passports were examined. This took over an hour and I expected at any moment a telephone call from Tirana.

At last Monsieur le Directeur came out and shook hands. "*Lamtumirë*," the border guards said. "Farewell." Though in Albanian the word has a somewhat more sorrowful sound. "*Lamtumirë*."

Then the frontier gate was raised.

We had to lug our equipment across into Yugoslavia, going back and forth several times. The Albanian border post is right on the border while the Yugoslav one is 5 kilometres away. I had to walk to it and persuade the Yugoslavs in a mixture of Italian and broken Russian to send a truck to pick up our gear. They were understandably reluctant as they had been fired on before from the Albanian side when they approached too near.

The next day we met the party of English tourists by accident in Titograd. We knew they intended to tour the Dalmatian Coast and we had hoped to see them in Dubrovnik or Split. Now luck had smiled on us again and we collected the exposed film from the dentist's wife and took her out to dinner.

A year later in Belgrade I learnt from a friend of mine in Yugoslav Intelligence that visas for Western tourists had been suspended and the whole staff of the Adriatik Hotel replaced. Monsieur le Directeur had disappeared. It looked as if the Albanians had found out, after all, that they had been duped.

Since then Enver Hoxha has gone. So has Mehmet Shehu—in a shoot-out with Hoxha in the Politbureau. A new man has taken over: Ramiz Alia. He is making tentative moves to reestablish contacts with the West, even to the extent of ending the technical state of war that has existed between Albania and Greece since October 1940 and of linking the northern Albanian city of Shkodër by rail to Yugoslavia. No doubt tourists will be on their way to the Land of the Eagles again. It is, after all, a beautiful country. And the brandy is excellent.

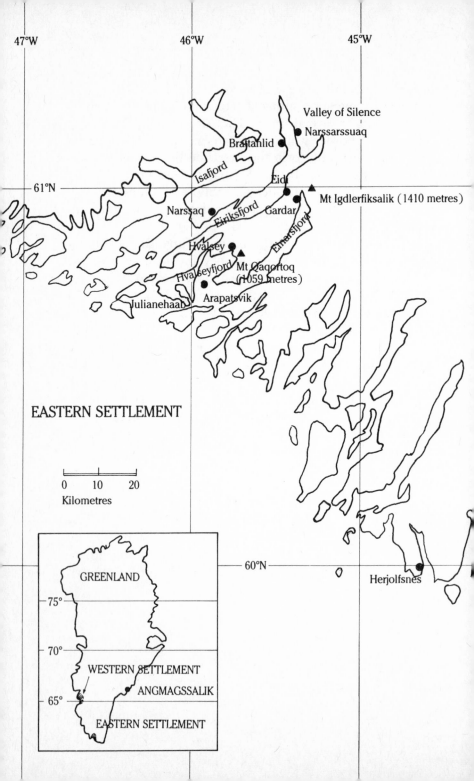

47°W · 46°W · 45°W

Valley of Silence
● Narssarssuaq
Brattahlid ●

Isafjord

61°N — Eidi
● ▲ Mt Igdlerfiksalik (1410 metres)
Narssaq ● Gardar ●
Eiriksfjord
Einarsfjord
Hvalsey ● ▲
Hvalseyfjord Mt Qaqortoq
(1059 metres)
● Arapatsvik
Julianehaab

EASTERN SETTLEMENT

0   10   20
Kilometres

GREENLAND

75°

70°

WESTERN SETTLEMENT
ANGMAGSSALIK
65°

EASTERN SETTLEMENT

60°N — ○
Herjolfsnes ●

2

Greenland

UNDER THE LODESTAR

"He called the country he had discovered Greenland, for he argued that men would be drawn to go there if the land had an attractive name." In this somewhat laconic fashion *The Greenlanders' Saga* explains how Greenland got its name. *He* was Eirik the Red—a red-headed, red-bearded, and often red-handed Viking. Eirik (usually spelled Eric) had been born in southwest Norway but was forced to leave that country for Iceland because of some killings. In Iceland he married but again became involved in blood-feuds and killed a number of men, as he said "to teach them some manners." The Thing (or Assembly) banished him for three years. So he decided to use the time profitably to explore some islands to the west that had been sighted by a ship a few years before when it was driven off course between Norway and Iceland. The islands were no more than skerries, but behind them lay Greenland.

A green land it was—in parts. Those parts were on the inner reaches of the fjords in the southwest. There, in summer, the grass is lush and thick. Buttercups and daisies grow in profusion, edible berries are everywhere with angelica, lyme grass, and bog cotton. In sheltered places there are thickets of deciduous trees—birch, alder, juniper, and dwarf willow. Barley can be cultivated in a good season, sheep and horses can spend the year round outside. But, more importantly, Eirik saw that Greenland was empty of people.

This was in the year 982. When Eirik returned to Iceland he found many to listen to his stories about the green land he had discovered. Ten years earlier Iceland had suffered the worst famine in its history. There were plenty of Icelanders with nothing and nothing to hope for. In the summer of 986 Eirik led an armada of twenty-five ships to Greenland. They ran into bad weather on the way—some ships sank, others were forced back—but fourteen got through. Perhaps four hundred people arrived. They took possession of land in the inner reaches of the 200 kilometres of fjord country Icelandic-fashion by throwing their high-seat pillars overboard and building their homes where they floated ashore.

As in Iceland, there quickly emerged a simple patriarchal society. Like Iceland the country was Christian from about 1000 A.D. and sustained in the same way a pastoral economy of isolated farmsteads. "It is reported," wrote the mid-13th-century author of the *King's Mirror*,

> that the pasturage is good and that there are large and fine farms in Greenland. The earth yields good and fragrant grass. The farmers raise sheep and cattle in large numbers and make butter and cheese in great quantities. The people subsist on these foods and on beef, but they also eat the flesh of various kinds of game such as reindeer, whales, seals and bears.

Like Iceland the colony was heavily dependent on Norway for many of its necessities—timber to build ships, wheat or rye, weapons and iron—and for all its meagre luxuries. In exchange it could offer furs, hides, a type of woollen cloth called wadmal, plaited ropes reputedly strong enough to take the pull of sixty men, and, more exotically, polar bears, walrus and narwhal ivory, and magnificent white falcons, a dozen of which were thought in 1396 to be adequate ransom for the Duke of Burgundy's son held captive by Sultan Beyazit of Turkey.

Today there are ruins of over three hundred farms, a cathedral, an Augustine monastery, a Benedictine nunnery, and sixteen churches which bear mute witness to the Viking colony. The most thickly settled part was called the Eastern Settlement and is in the district where Julianehaab now stands. Five hundred kilometres northwest was the later Western Settlement in the Godthaab district. In their heyday—the 14th and 15th centuries—these two settlements are estimated to have contained between 6,000 and 9,000 people. It all depends on how many were allotted to a farm. Some think twenty is the right figure, others thirty. Viking families were large—three generations generally lived together, and they had bondsmen and thralls. The uninhabitated and uninhabitable parts of Greenland provided the two settlements with excellent hunting and fishing grounds and with a constant supply of driftwood.

Yet sometime in the 16th century they all vanished. It is the largest number of people of European origin known to have disappeared without a trace. There are as many theories about this as there are scholars. For five hundred years the Norsemen had occupied and made the glittering subcontinent of Greenland their home. They had voyaged as far north as Latitude 76° and as far south as the coasts of Newfoundland. They had discovered America. They had traded regularly with Europe. What happened? This was the reason that brought us to Greenland—to film the localities the Vikings had lived in and to try to unravel some of the threads of the mystery.

Greenland is now a self-governing part of the Danish Kingdom, one of the last remnants of a once impressive empire that contained Norway, the Faroes (still a part of Denmark but also self-governing), Iceland, the Danish West Indies (sold to America in 1916 and now called the Virgin Islands of the United States), and a few trading posts elsewhere, like Christiansborg in Ghana, Tranquebar on the coast of Coromandel, and Serampore near Calcutta (all sold to the British last century).

The Greenlanders, who number about 54,000, are for the most part a mixed race—Eskimo and Danish mainly, but Eskimo and English or Dutch in settlements near the northern whaling grounds. They may also have some blood from the old Norse settlers. There are loan words in Greenlandic that can only have come from Old Norse. One is the word the Greenlanders use to describe themselves—*Kalaleq*. It is derived from the word the Vikings used for them—*Skraeling*. In modern Icelandic *skraeling* means "churl"; in modern Norwegian "weakling." The Norse view of the Eskimo.

Ninety-nine percent of these Greenlanders live along the west coast in scattered villages. The east coast is ringed with sea-ice and is far too inhospitable. There are a few small towns—the largest, and the capital, Godthaab, has 8,000 people. It was founded in 1728 by convicts—men from the prisons of Denmark, women from the houses of correction. Before they left Copenhagen they were lined up and married to each other. Australia was not alone in being so established.

If you don't count Australia, Greenland is the largest island in the world. Its area is 2,175,600 square kilometres, of which 1,833,900 square kilometres are under perpetual ice. This leaves about 350,000 square kilometres ice-free, and the bulk of that is given over to those saw-toothed mountains of Bishop Heber's hymn ("From Greenland's icy mountains"—number 358 in the Anglican hymn book) or rocky islets. So the area available to settlers was very limited.

> Men [said the *King's Mirror* in 1250] have often tried to go up into the country and climb the highest mountain in various parts to look about and learn whether any land could be found that was free from ice and habitable. But nowhere have they found such a place, except what is now occupied, which is a little strip along the water's edge.

What was true in 1250 is true today. Fishing remains the main occupation of the Greenlanders (cod, red fish, sharks, shrimp), with a little mining (cryolite and coal).

No roads connect the towns and villages. People get about in Greenland by boat or helicopter. There are only two commercial airports—one at Søndre Strømfjord, on the longest fjord in the world, which serves flights over the North Pole, and the other at Narssarssuaq in the heart of the old Viking country. There are two other airports, which are military—one at the American base of Thule in the extreme north and the other at Kulusuk on the east coast. This was my first introduction to Greenland.

I had been on a holiday to Iceland—a saga tour—in 1969. Back in Reykjavik I discovered that Icelandair was offering day trips to Greenland for $75, so I took one. There were only about half a dozen passengers in the ageing DC-6, and I later found out that Greenland gets perhaps five hundred tourists a year. The flight took two hours, but half an hour before we arrived we were over vast swathes of field-ice. The tops of icebergs could be seen towering above them, and as we approached land the ice became more and more compact, so it was difficult to see where the land-ice began and the sea-ice ended. Then we were over glaciers and fjords where the water was almost bright blue-green and icebergs floated serenely. We circled the township of Angmagssalik, the largest centre in East Greenland (there were only two) with a population of six hundred. Thirty kilometres to the east was the island of Kulusuk with an airstrip and a radar station, part of the American early warning system.

Half an hour's walk over soggy, mossy ground brought us to the village of Kap Dan. Here the people are pure Eskimo, still practising their ancient way of life to some degree, wearing their traditional clothes—seal-skin thigh boots, beadwork anoraks. There were plenty of kayaks drawn up on the pebbly shore (I only ever saw one kayak in West Greenland, the motorboat has replaced it almost entirely). Yet the kayak is, without doubt, the most ingenious of boats. Women make kayaks to measure for their husbands. It has to fit the owner like a well-tailored suit. Some of the kayakers obligingly rolled their boats for us but most were going about the serious business of preparing for the hunt—seals I guessed.

It was a bright, sunny day though cold. The village consisted of wooden houses all freshly painted red, blue, yellow, and black. Most were the same—rectangular with a loft. We were invited into several. In one a shaman did a drum dance, sang several songs, and banged his head against the wall of the house. In another I was offered a *tupilaq* for 100 krone (about $20). A *tupilaq* is a small figure carved out of a whale's tusk. It was a made-up monster, a kind of mannikin. Its purpose was to create evil, but it had to be animated by its creator or a shaman. Kap Dan is one of the few places in Greenland where *tupilaq*s are carved and, according to some, still used for sorcery.

What I had seen had whetted my appetite, and the next summer I was back in Greenland with a camera crew. Only this time it was to the west coast, to Narssarssuaq at the head of Eiriksfjord.

Narssarssuaq airfield was built by the Americans in 1941 as Blue West 1. It was a staging post for ferrying military aircraft to Europe as well as a base for convoy escort. The Danish Ministry for Greenland took it over in 1958. There is a hotel of sorts—the Hotel Arctic, which can sleep twenty-five. It is one of the only two in Greenland, the other is at Søndre Strømfjord airport. The Hotel Arctic is a converted former US barracks. The standard of accommodation is rough but comfortable. During the war there were 10,000 Americans at Narssarssuaq, and the remains of their occupation still litter the surrounds of the airport.

One such relic lies a little distance away—the hospital. It was the biggest war hospital in the world, with over 5,000 beds. No one went out of it alive. To this hospital were brought the basket cases—the men who were so badly injured or mutilated that they could never return home. Not only men from World War II but also from the Korean War. When they died their bodies were cremated and the ashes sent to their relatives accompanied by a note saying they had succumbed to their wounds.

The ruins of the hospital lie in a valley about 2 kilometres from Narssarssuaq. It is called the Valley of Silence. To get to it you have to climb a hill and descend the other side. Greenlanders won't go near the site.

On the brow of the hill is a spot where the men about to die were brought. There they were lifted out of their stretchers and given a last look at the wonder of the world. From this point you can see Eiriksfjord below, Brattahlid across the fjord from the airport, where Eirik the Red set his farmstead on rich pasture, and further down the fjord the great mass of Mt. Igdlerfiksalik soaring 1,400 metres (4,592 feet) into the air. If the story is true it is a poignant place.

Brattahlid, on the other hand, is an inviting location—green hillsides, a stream winding down to a plain by the shore. No wonder Eirik the Red chose it for his home. Greenlanders live and farm here, but what we were interested in were the ruins of Eirik's great hall and the first church in the New World. As luck would have it, Knud Krogh, the Danish archaeologist who had helped excavate these sites, was there.

Much of what I had read in the ancient records came alive as I stood in the foundations of the great hall (there have been second thoughts recently about whether this is the original hall or a later one). Here the first voyage of discovery to Vinland the Good was plotted by Eirik and his son Leif, here there were feasts with much storytelling, here a literature was created with the *Greenland Lay of Atli* as its most notable example, here Christianity first came to Greenland, here the first Greenland Thing or Assembly was held.

Eirik's wife was Thjodhild. When Christianity was brought to Greenland by Leif Eirikson, Thjodhild embraced it at once and had a church built. "Not over near the farm," according to *Eirik the Red's Saga*:

This church was called Thjodhild's Church and it was there she offered up her prayers along with those men who had adopted Christianity, who were many. Thjodhild would not live with Eirik as man and wife once she had adopted the faith, a circumstance which vexed him very much.

Eirik took coldly to the notion of abandoning his old beliefs.

In 1961 workmen were digging the trenches for a hostel at Brattahlid for children from outlying farms when they came across some skulls. The Danish National Museum stepped in and, over a number of summers, excavated Thjodhild's church and the surrounding graveyard. In it they found the remains of 144 people, undoubtedly the first settlers, probably many who made the first voyage to America. Among them must be Eirik, his son Leif, and his strong-willed wife Thjodhild. It is the largest number of skeletons from the Viking period ever found.

They were big, strong men and women. Most of the men were between five feet eight (172 cm) and six feet one (186 cm). The women ranged from five feet one and a half (156 cm) to five feet five (165 cm). At the verge of the churchyard the bodies lay more or less haphazardly while those in coffins were all close to the church. This was normal medieval practice. The finest coffin was only about 56 inches (143 cm) long. On the headstone runes had been carved: Ingibjorg's Grave. No father's name. No need. In a tightly knit community at the world's end they all knew the little girl. And loved her. She was buried in style.

Over the next ten days or so we explored Eiriksfjord thoroughly. At the head of the fjord on the same side as Brattahlid was a level valley leading to the aptly named Isafjord (it was full of pack ice at the time). We tramped 10 kilometres from one fjord to the other and came upon ruin after ruin—farmsteads and churches. Above us all the time a Greenland eagle slowly circled. When the Norsemen lived here this valley was thickly settled. Now it is deserted.

An hour and a half's journey down the fjord brought us to Eidi under Mt. Igdlerfiksalik. From here a forty-five-minute walk took us over a low ridge to Gardar at the head of Einarsfjord. This was the site of the cathedral in Norse times. The ruins of forty or more buildings cover the plain, and huge stones weighing 5 to 10 tons are piled up everywhere. The church itself—dedicated to St. Nicholas—was 90 by 53 feet (27 by 16 metres). It had stained-glass windows, an unheard-of luxury for this place and this time. Fragments of a bell have been found, and an old Eskimo story says that the bell was so big its sound could be heard at the mouth of Einarsfjord, 40 kilometres away. The skulls of walruses and narwhals have been discovered under the choir of the church. This raises an interesting question. Is it some survival of an ancient superstition or, at least in the case of the narwhal with its single horn, is it something to do with the unicorn, a medieval symbol of virginity?

There were also the ruins of a banqueting hall of 130 square metres, which could hold two or three hundred people, and of an enormous tithe barn. As well there is an irrigation system that still works and feeds water to all the fields. Clearly Gardar was a thriving place. But it, too, had been deserted. An Eskimo story describes the last resident of Gardar as a great hero called Ungortok (Yngvar). A splendidly bloodthirsty tale it is, too. The Eskimos were unable to kill him though he had slain many of them until they resorted to sorcery. Maybe a *tupilaq* was used.

One place we were eager to visit was Herjolfsnes. It is about 150 kilometres southeast of Narssarssuaq and on the sea—the only Norse settlement that was. In fact, it is at the threshold of the Viking area and was the first port of call for ships coming from Iceland or Norway. The reason we wanted to go there was because of the remarkable find in the churchyard.

Here bodies had been buried in their own clothes, not in coffins. And, because of the permanently frozen soil, many of these garments were preserved. They form the biggest collection of medieval costume known and prove beyond doubt that the Norse Greenlanders were in touch with Europe in the 13th, 14th, and 15th centuries.

The clothes were woven of wool and homemade. The colour was brown or brownish black and the style European. There are examples of the ankle-length surcoat of the 13th and 14th centuries. It was drawn over the head and worn with long stockings suspended from the waist. The men's surcoats were shorter than the women's. Otherwise there was no difference. But the most interesting finds were the cowls with liripipes, or tails, that hung down to the wearer's shoulders and were worn exaggeratedly long by the fashionable. This is the headdress of Dante and Petrarch, of Robin Hood and Chaucer. A person of high rank retained it on his head even when received by the King. The same applied to a thief when he was hanged. More than anything else the liripipe marks the man of the Middle Ages.

There were also some simple round caps, fairly high in the crown with a flat top. These were popular in the 15th century and can be seen in paintings of the Flemish school. Many of these garments were not owned by the common people in Europe but by the well-to-do. Altogether the finds point to a cultivated and prosperous community, not one on the brink of extinction.

In Copenhagen we had been given a letter by the Ministry of Foreign Affairs asking the Greenland government to render us any assistance we needed. One day an elderly Catalina flying boat turned up in Eiriksfjord. It had come from the Danish naval base at Gronnedal about an hour's flight away. I lost no time seeking out the pilot. He was quite agreeable to taking us to Herjolfsnes but had to consult his superior, who was at Narssarssuaq calling on the district administrator. But, when we found him, the superior officer was uncooperative. His name was Jørgen Bay-Schmith and he was an *Orlogskaptajn*—a War Captain or Commander. According to his card,

24

which I still have, he was President of the Danish Section of the Cape Horners. As I said previously, Denmark once held a fairly considerable empire, and the service where the greatest nostalgia for those days and those attitudes still remains is the navy. *Orlogskaptajn* Jørgen Bay-Schmith was not going to do a thing for journalists, even television journalists, plead as I might, show as many letters as I had, or try to get the district administrator to intercede on our behalf. It was all to no avail. So we more or less gave up on Herjolfsnes.

Until, a few days later, a small Grumman Mallard, a twin-engined amphibian, touched down at Narssarssuaq from Goose Bay in Labrador. It was being ferried to Europe via Greenland, Iceland, the Faroes, and Scotland by two Americans. They were delighted to help us out. But our luck had run its course. The sea at Herjolfsnes was too rough for the Grumman to land. We had to be content with some aerial shots. On the return flight the weather was fine so we took advantage of the opportunity and filmed all the fjords where the Norsemen had dwelt.

That night there was a party at Narssarssuaq and we went along. A mixed group of Greenlanders and Danes were drinking and dancing to a tape deck.

"You know," one of the Danes, who worked at the hotel, told us, "you can have any one of those Greenland girls. All you have to do is point your forefinger at her. A Greenland girl of twelve knows as much about men as her mother. But be careful. They all have gonorrhea. Greenland has the highest incidence in the world. They say it's because the machines that dispense condoms, which are required by law at all dance halls, freeze up during the winter."

We thanked him for his advice. All the early explorers had commented on the Eskimos' permissiveness. None had mentioned venereal diseases. That had to wait for the coming of the Danes.

To give the story a flavour of present-day Greenland we also filmed in Julianehaab and Narssaq, the two largest towns in the region—though they are hardly large by European standards. (Julianehaab, a two-restaurant town, has about 2,000 people, and Narssaq, a one-restaurant town, about 1,000.)

Julianehaab is gaily coloured detached wooden houses set on rocky outcrops. There are a few small service industries, one or two modern concrete block buildings, a cinema, telephones, piped water and main sewerage, though they have problems with the latter during the winter.

Narssaq is similar but here you have a fish cannery and an abattoir. There are some 20,000 sheep grazing the upper reaches of the fjords—the old Viking country. Both towns had their quotas of women pushing prams, youths with ghetto blasters, and old men sitting in front of their houses smoking pipes. In Narssaq old women often sat beside them scraping and working seal skins.

There was one Norse ruin that we still had to see—the best preserved of all. It was the church at Hvalsey. Getting there presented no real problem. We had to take a boat down Eiriksfjord to Eidi, cross the narrow neck of land between Eiriksfjord and Einarsfjord, pick up another boat, travel about 50 kilometres down Einarsfjord and Hvalseyfjord. All this took time, and it wasn't until the early afternoon that we arrived at the wide mouth of Hvalseyfjord. We made our way past the island of Arapatsvik, which divides the fjord into two arms, and headed towards the pyramidal peak of Qaqortoq at the head of the eastern one. The water of the fjord was so blue it was almost black. Small pieces of drift ice floated gently by. The sides of the fjord were green hills running up to the foot of the 1,000-metre mountain (3,280 feet).

The boat crew dropped us ashore. They wanted to go to Julianehaab and make some purchases. It was only 20 kilometres. They said they'd be back in three hours.

The church commands an excellent position on a slope bounded towards the north by rocks and about 50 metres (164 feet) from the shore. It faces east-west and behind it is a great hall with farm buildings and enclosed areas.

The stones of the church wall were laid in mortar. This makes it very different from the other Norse churches in Greenland and accounts for the fact that these walls are still standing. In the other churches the stones were placed directly in layers of clay. When the roof went and the clay became water-soaked, the stones slid out of position. The Hvalsey church, however, is of dry masonry with lime mortar, which keeps the stones in position. The ground plan of the church is almost a double square—53 feet by 26 (16 metres by 8 approximately). The east and west gable walls are about 20 feet (roughly 6 metres) high and the side walls about 13 feet (4 metres more or less).

In this church in 1408—on the first Sunday after Holy Cross Day, which is September 14—a wedding took place. The bride was Sigrid Bjornsdattir, a girl from Hvalsey, and the groom was Thorstein Olavsson, an Icelander. *Sira* (Rev.) Pal Halvardsson officiated. The banns had been called on the three preceding Sundays and a nuptial mass was read. After the marriage the young couple went to Iceland. Later it became necessary to attest the legality of this marriage, and there are no less than three quite detailed documents concerning it. Two were made out by persons at the wedding, including the crew of an Icelandic ship held up at Hvalsey by pack ice. This is the last record we have of Norse Greenlanders alive and well. Then silence and darkness.

The day drew on. We had finished filming. There was no sign of the boat. For a while we sat outside the church on a stone bench and watched the ice floes in the fjord. It became chilly so we went inside.

We were warmly clad—parkas, heavy trousers, and *mukluks* or fur-lined Eskimo boots—but the church was musty and the dirt floor damp. The sun had long since set, though there was still plenty of thin light. And midges. We smeared ourselves with repellent. It was highly unlikely the boat would return now. We would have to stay where we were.

I curled in a corner of the church, my face pressed to the sour soil, and fell into a fitful sleep, waking every so often because of the cold. On one occasion I thought I saw a light outside the church reflected in the sky. It was dark and after midnight. I assumed the boat's crew had come back and were looking for us with torches.

I went to the door and peered out. On the south side of the church, maybe 10 metres away, were a group of men who appeared to be monks with their backs to me. They were in long habits and had cowls. The men were watching a pile of wood that was blazing strongly. In the centre of it was a man lashed to a stake. I could smell the burning wool of his garments and see that his hair was alight, but I could not hear a sound. No crackle or hiss from the flames, no screams or cries from the man. At one side some more men held a woman, who was on her knees. I could see her anguished face. I turned to call the others and, when I looked again, there was nothing. I didn't sleep the rest of the night.

Early next morning the boat appeared. The crew were very sheepish. "Too much *akvavit*," they said and sadly shook their heads.

Shortly afterwards we left Greenland. We had filming to do in Iceland and Newfoundland, where the only authentic carbon-dated Norse site had been discovered at L'Anse aux Meadows near Belle Isle Strait.

Later we went to Oslo and met Helge Ingstad, the Norwegian explorer and writer who had discovered this site. Quite accidentally, in the course of the conversation, he mentioned that he had once spent a night at Hvalsey and had thought he saw an apparition. He would not say what it was. We would laugh at him. I did not tell him my experience.

In England we interviewed Arnold Toynbee about his theories as to why the Norse Greenlanders had disappeared and also Professor Gwyn Jones, the leading British authority on the Vikings. I told Gwyn Jones what had happened at Hvalsey. He got out *The Icelandic Annals*, turned to the year 1407, and read the following:

> A man in Greenland named Kolgrim was burned for lying with another's wife, who was called Steinunn and was the daughter of the lawman Hrafn. She married Torgrim Solvesson. Kolgrim enticed her with the black arts and was later burned in accordance with the law. The wife was never afterwards in her right mind and died within a short time.

He closed the book. "That took place at Hvalseyfjord."

Afterwards I went through all the notes I had made before going to Greenland in case I had read of this occurrence but forgotten it. I could find nothing, though it is briefly commented on in a footnote in Gwyn Jones' own book *The Norse Atlantic Saga*, which he gave me when I interviewed him.

One explanation of hauntings is that an event, usually a horrifying event, leaves a printout or a negative on matter—the walls of a room, for instance—by rearranging the molecules much the same way as a tape-recorder records sound by rearranging magnetic particles on the tape. And, like tape, the event can be played back, given the right equipment or circumstances.

Did the fact that the walls of Hvalsey church, almost alone of the buildings from this period in Greenland, remained virtually intact have anything to do with this phenomenon? It is a mystery, but no greater mystery than the total disappearance of the Norse Greenlanders.

The Danish National Museum has excavated many of the Norse farmhouses and, in one of them, the remains of a man were found lying in a passage. A last occupant, alone in his big house (it had fifteen rooms) with no one left to see to his proper burial? Is this how the Norse Greenlanders finally met their end?

About the year 1541 a merchant ship trading between Hamburg and Iceland was driven off course to Greenland.

They entered one of the southwestern fjords and observed that the land was inhabited, so they went ashore. There were boathouses and booths very similar to those in Iceland. By one of them they found the body of a man, clothed in a coat made of homespun. On his head was a well-made hood and at his side a knife that was much worn and honed. They took it as a souvenir. After that nothing.

Greenland, the most remote of medieval outposts, is a gloomy and forbidding place. The sagas that tell of Greenlanders do not leave the impression of a light-hearted community. Freydis, Eirik the Red's daughter, in an act of treachery causes the deaths of two Icelandic brothers. Then, when no one else will kill the five women of their family, she takes an axe and does it herself. When the wife of the Greenland farmer Thorstein the Black dies of the plague, her ghost walks again, and every timber of the house creaks as the corpse gets back into its bed. Her powerful husband needs all his strength to get her coffin out of the house. There are murderous feuds, use of the black arts, famine. It is not unexpected that something macabre happened to them. But what did?

There was a worsening of climatic conditions towards the end of the 13th century with more pack ice. This brought the seals and the seals brought the Eskimos. We know the Eskimos reentered Greenland sometime in the 14th century. There are many Eskimo legends that tell of bloody clashes between the two races. The same climatic conditions made contact with Europe more difficult so the settlers became isolated. In any case Europe was losing its taste for their trade goods—English woollen cloth was finer, elephant ivory from Africa was better, Russian furs were more readily available, falconry was going out of fashion except among the Muslims.

The Western (the more northerly) Settlement was at an end by 1342. How this came about is not clear. Bishop Hakon of Bergen in Norway had sent a priest to find out what was going on—the tithes had not been paid for some time. He reported: "When they arrived they found never a man, either Christian or heathen, merely some wild cattle and sheep."

The next year we find Bishop Oddsson of Skalholt in Iceland saying, "The inhabitants of Greenland of their own will abandoned the true faith and the Christian religion and joined themselves with the people of America."

Two centuries later the same thing happened to the people of the Eastern (southern) Settlement but the same comment was not made. Yet, to many authorities, it all rings true. The Eskimos were much better adapted to the Arctic than the Norsemen. The Eskimo lived on, by, and with the land. The Norseman, like all Europeans, tended to live against it. In this environment it was easier to be a hunter than a farmer. There is some disputed evidence of European-type house sites in the Ungava Bay region of Canada, virtually opposite the Eastern Settlement, and Canadian Eskimo legends tell of the *Tunnit*, a strong white people, who built these and intermarried with the Eskimos.

Others, like Knud Krogh, believe the explanation lies in the deterioration of the weather and the gradual dying out of a rural population. Until, in the end, no one was left.

A few cautiously suggest English pirates might have had a hand in the decline of the settlements. They swarmed into Icelandic waters in the 15th century, plundering, raping, and carrying people off to be sold as slaves to the galleys of the Barbary Coast or Moorish Spain. Bristol was the chief marketplace. Records exist of Greenlanders being sold there, and Eskimo stories relate that ships with sails attacked the Norse farmsteads and churches.

There is another candidate for this role—the Basques. The Basques had been whaling in the Bay of Biscay for centuries when, sometime during the 13th century and for no known reason, the whales left. The Basques followed them north. They were off the coast of Newfoundland in 1372 and, a little later, Baffin island. There is a Basque tradition that they were in touch with the people of South Greenland. If this is true it can only mean the Norsemen as the Eskimos had not fully occupied the southern part of the country until the 16th century.

There are other theories. The Greenlanders went back to Iceland. There is no documentary evidence for this and the Icelanders meticulously kept records. The Black Death wiped them out. Maybe. They were killed off or absorbed by the Eskimos. Despite the occasional clashes between the two races there was no reason for a head-on collision. The farms of the Greenlanders lay well back at the head of the fjords, where the sea froze late and the ice was never safe. This was of little use to the Eskimos, whose hunting was concentrated on the headlands, islands, and sea-ice where the seals were most numerous. Yet Iceland with a population not very much bigger and with many of the same problems survived into the 20th century.

For centuries European minds have been exercised by this riddle. Arnold Toynbee believes all the various factors operated and the effect was cumulative. Who knows? Who will ever know? Vanished—one entire people.

3
Paraguay

════════════════════════════════

PARADISE—OF A KIND

For many centuries Europeans have imagined Paradise as a green and pleasant land full of flowers, fruits, and birds, a smiling place of eternal Spring. Such a land exists—Paraguay east of the river that gives its name to the country.

Two-thirds of Paraguay, however, lies to the west of the river. The contrasts between these areas are dramatic. On one side you have a wooded, gently rolling plateau; on the other the dry bed of an ancient inland sea. Nowhere else in the world does a river divide two such entirely different regions. Eastern Paraguay is one of the most inviting and best-watered parts of the earth; most of western Paraguay, or the Chaco as it is known, lacks permanent streams. The east is hills, meadows, valleys, and forests; the west is all flat claypans and isolated palms, the unaccountably tall *caranda-ý* predominating.

These two disparate regions of the country are mirrored in the racial composition of the Paraguayan people—the joking, mischievous Guarani and the grave, arrogant Spaniard. The Guaranies belong to the widespread Tupi Guarani family, stretching from northern Argentina to the Caribs of the Caribbean, from whose name, incidentally, comes both "cannibal" and "Caliban" (*Caraí*, a form of Carib, is Guarani for "lord"). The Spaniards sailed up the great rivers—the Plate, the Parana, and the Paraguay—at the beginning of the 16th century. They set up trading posts and took concubines from among the Guaranies (the first administrator had six of them). So began the Paraguayan race, a homogeneous mestizo cross in which the Guarani element has predominated.

The very name Paraguay is itself a matter of dispute. Leon Cadogan, an Australian-Paraguayan, who was considered the foremost authority on the Guarani (he was the official *Curator de Indíos* in the Department of Guairá), told me he thought it came from *para* meaning "variety" and *guá*, the verb "to crown." Thus the Paraguay would be a river crowned with variety, and this is indeed so. In fact, the whole country could be said to be crowned with improbability.

I went there in 1968 with Alan Whicker, the well-known British television reporter, to film *The Last Dictator*—a portrait of General Alfredo Stroessner (who is still in power) and, by extension, a portrait of the country. Knowing a little of Paraguay's bizarre history, yet being unable to relate it to our own experience, we decided to go over the ground thoroughly and search for clues.

We started with the Jesuit *reducciónes* ("reductions" or missions). These were begun in the south of Paraguay shortly after the first settlement. By choosing the banks of the Parana River, the Jesuits effectively cut themselves off from the Conquistadors at Asunción on the Paraguay River. In the end this aroused the suspicion of the Spanish Crown, who believed they wanted to be independent, which was bad, and to conceal gold mines, which was worse.

By the time of their expulsion in 1767 there were thirty *reducciónes* with more than 100,000 Indian inhabitants. The Fathers had had extraordinary success at making converts. They had also shown remarkable business acumen. In the mid-18th century they were estimated to be worth $28 million and owned 800,000 cattle, 230,000 sheep, and 100,000 horses.

Each mission was laid out checkerboard style with a plaza in the middle. On the north side stood a church—usually the size of a cathedral and all that remains today in most cases. But there was also a school, a hospital, an asylum, storehouses, and workshops. The Indians lived in long, one-roomed, low-roofed, windowless adobe houses, much as Paraguayan peasants still do.

Two Jesuits were in charge of a *reducción*—an older and a younger. The remaining officials were all Indian. The *cacique* or chief acted as Governor. Each village was strongly fortified, protected by extensive moats and defended with cannon.

Theocratically ruled, well organised and armed, self-sufficient in almost everything, a *reducción* drew its wealth from the surrounding countryside—perhaps the most fertile in Paraguay. They exploited the *yerba maté* (Paraguayan tea) that grew native in the forests. They cultivated maize, sugar cane, cotton, tobacco, and oranges. They grazed their flocks. In this ecclesiastical empire the Indians lived contentedly, singing and dancing in the shade of orange trees. Even when they tilled the fields there was always a little band playing, usually seated on a tree platform. The Fathers had discovered that their converts worked better to music—the first Muzak?

The fame of the *reducciónes* spread to Europe. Montesquieu compared them to Plato's Republic. Voltaire sent Candide there in search of happiness. The English poet Robert Southey wrote:

> . . . where the happier sons of Paraguay
> By gentleness and pious art subdued,
> Bow'd their meek heads beneath the Jesuits' sway,
> And lived and died in filial servitude.

No one has recorded what the Indians thought, but the preservation of the language and their traditional folk music can definitely be attributed to the *reducciónes*. Guarani was the everyday speech of the missions and Latin the language of hymns and prayers. Spanish was not used. Nor were visitors allowed. Bishops, governors, ministers of state, and private persons were expressly forbidden entrance to the *reducciónes*.

Morals were a constant source of concern to the Jesuits. They made every attempt to keep the sexes apart, even to providing separate doors for them to enter the church. Yet one writer says:

> The Fathers were compelled to rouse their flocks somewhat before working hours and to insist on them not neglecting their duty to Venus and begetting more souls to be saved.

Whether the Jesuits were good or bad for the Indians is a moot point. But there is no denying that the *reducciónes* in other hands declined swiftly. Those who followed the Order of Jesus plundered everything of value. So ended the first Utopian experiment in Paraguay (there were others, including an Australian one at Nueva Australia in 1893). The Indians had been unwillingly cast out of their cocoons.

Meanwhile, things had been stirring in Europe and finally reached South America. In 1810 the citizens of Buenos Aires took some half measures towards independence from Spain. Six months later those of Asunción took a similar stand but repudiated the leadership of Buenos Aires. General Belgrano (after whom the battleship sunk in the Falklands War was named) was sent to teach them a lesson, but he was defeated by the Paraguayans. Paraguay won its independence not from Spain but from the Argentine.

The Congress in Asunción gave full dictatorial power over the new country to Dr. José Gaspar Rodriguez de Francia. In all the four centuries of Paraguayan history, no name has been held in greater fear. He was known as *El Supremo*, and he ruled absolutely for twenty-nine years.

A dictator—any dictator—is a complex being. Francia was honest, cold, vindictive, and cruel. He always wore black, had no friends, shunned women, and never married. Paraguay was closed off from the rest of the world. No one was allowed to leave. Anyone who entered did so at his own risk. Francia preached a policy of austerity and hard work. And, while its neighbours were rent with civil wars, Paraguay gained a more diversified economy, self-reliance, and internal harmony. Such are the benefits of dictatorship—or so dictators would have us believe.

El Supremo was followed by his nephew—an extremely ugly and extremely fat man, who wore his hat indoors as well as out. He opened the shutters of the hermit republic a chink—inviting foreign engineers, surgeons, and mechanics to settle in Paraguay. A few came, mainly British, and a British firm built the first railway there in South America. (Some of the original rolling stock is still in use. I've travelled on it and must admire our forebears' hardiness.)

The nephew preferred to be known as *El Ciudadano* (the Citizen) and, impressed by the British, sent his son Francisco Solano Lopez to England to meet Queen Victoria. The Queen refused to receive him, so Solano Lopez (as he usually is known) went to Paris, where Napoleon III put on a military display in his honour. He also became decidedly anti-British, which gave the French great satisfaction.

During his sojourn in Paris, Solano Lopez, out strolling one evening near the Gare St. Lazare, picked up a whore. She was Eliza Alicia Lynch and, when he returned to Paraguay, she accompanied him. Madame Lynch was Irish and formidable. She bore Marshal (he had promoted himself to this rank) Lopez five or six children and egged him on in his military adventures, for he was determined to modernise his country by building a large standing army in the European manner.

His opportunity to use it came when he inherited the dictatorship on the death of his father. Paraguay declared war on Uruguay, Argentina, and Brazil. A European parallel might be if Belgium took on the Netherlands, France, and Germany. Called the War of the Triple Alliance, it lasted from 1865 to 1870. The odds against Paraguay were enormous. But it was a compact and courageous nation fighting on its own soil. Its enemies were a mixed bag, suspicious of each other and torn by internal rivalries. The Brazilian troops were also slaves and had little stomach for fighting free men.

There is a strange, heroic—one might almost say quixotic—streak in the fibre of Paraguay. The whole nation threw itself into the war with incredible bravery. With cannons mounted on rafts, the Paraguayans challenged the Brazilian navy trying to force the Paraguay River and defeated it. At Curupaity they wiped out the flower of the Argentine army as they attacked across swampy ground. The Argentines lost 9,000 men against the loss of 50 Paraguayans. It was a stunning victory and effectually put Argentina out of the war.

At Humaitá, where the Paraguayans had built a fortress above the Paraguay River on high ground protected by a great horseshoe bend (British engineers again), they held off the Brazilians for three years. Humaitá became famous in Europe and America as the Gibraltar or Sebastopol of South America. The picturesque ruins of its church still dominate the river bank. Lineas Aéreas Paraguayas planes flying to Buenos Aires always make a detour so the passengers can see Humaitá and Curupaity. Aerolineas Argentinas, for obvious reasons, does not.

It was left to the Brazilian Empire finally to defeat the Paraguayans. At Pirebebuy, when the men had all been killed, women took their places in the trenches armed only with broken bottles and pieces of glass. You can still see the trenches. At Acosta Ñu, the last major action of the war, Brazilian troops found themselves fighting boys between ten and fourteen, many of whom wore false beards to inspire caution among their enemies.

The end came when Solano Lopez was killed by lancers at Cerro Corá near the Brazilian border in the northeast corner of Paraguay. When they asked him to give himself up he replied, *"Muero con mi patria"* ("I die with my country"). So they ran him through. Madame Lynch buried him with her own hands.

It is possible that Solano Lopez knew of other leaders who had promised to die with their country but had not—Czar Alexander I of Russia, Napoleon I. Even his friend Napoleon III vowed to do the same six months later at Sedan. They had all chickened out, but Solano Lopez made the great gesture. No Paraguayan has ever forgotten it. He is the national hero *par excellence*.

Madame Lynch escaped with part of the Paraguayan treasury and set herself up in London, eventually becoming the madam of a brothel in Paris. The full circle. She is, nonetheless, another hero of the war as far as Paraguayans are concerned, though not ranking quite as high as Solano Lopez.

Before the War of the Triple Alliance began, Paraguay's population was about 1 million. When it was over only 106,000 women, 86,000 children, and 28,000 men—most of them old or crippled—remained alive. The towns were destroyed, the factories in ruins, the livestock driven off, the fields uncultivated. Paraguay lost 140,000 square kilometres and faced an excessive reparations payment which was never made. The peace that came to Paraguay was the peace of the graveyard. It was one of the most savage wars ever fought.

The country fell back into silence. Little progress was made. Few immigrants arrived. Paraguay was desperate for people, and so they offered the followers of William Lane, the Australian Utopian Socialist, some of the richest land in the country. The whole history of this strange episode is well documented in Gavin Souter's book *A Peculiar People*. Perhaps 500 Australians settled at Nueva Australia, and they were later joined by some 100 to 150 immigrants from the United Kingdom.

One Australian-Paraguayan who achieved fame was Major Arturo Bray, who is described in the definitive history of the Chaco War by David Zook, an American, as "a scholarly and brilliant officer with exceptional command ability." Bray was instrumental in turning the first major clash of this war into the decisive victory of Boquerón. After Boquerón he was put in command of the Fourth Paraguayan Division. This division withstood the siege of Nanawa—another Paraguayan fort in the Chaco—which is also claimed as a Paraguayan victory.

The Chaco War (1932–35) was between Bolivia and Paraguay. Both claimed it and the borders had never been settled. Once again Paraguay took on enormous odds—the population of Bolivia was three times that of Paraguay. The quixotic streak. Conditions were horrendous—in the dry season the Chaco is cracked, scorched, and dusty with temperatures hovering around 113° F (45° C); in the wet season the area is covered with about 7.9 inches (20 cm) of water, and the humidity is almost unbearable. There are blood-sucking flies, poisonous snakes, vampire bats, a toad with teeth that bites, and piranhas. Small wonder it was called Green Hell. What the Paraguayans did was to return genuine maneuver to warfare. The terrain made it necessary. Cavalry had to fight on foot, tanks proved of little value, artillery was less useful than mortars.

Bray initiated this mobility, which eventually allowed the Paraguayans to win. It is said that there was a German observer with the Bolivians—Erwin Rommel—who learnt Bray's lesson well, but I do not know if this is true. It may be. The commander-in-chief of the Bolivian army was Hans Kundt, a Nazi and a colonel in the German army. Ernst Röhm had also been in Bolivia at this time—another Nazi, another colonel—but he returned to Germany to become Hitler's closest crony, until he was purged. If it is true that Rommel was in Paraguay, then it is one of history's ironies that tactics developed by an Australian in desert conditions were used against other Australians (and British, Indians, South Africans, Free French, Poles) during the Western Desert Campaign in World War II, eight years later and 12,000 kilometres away.

After the Chaco War, Paraguay had a number of dictators until General Stroessner took over in 1954. He governed under a permanent State of Siege that was renewed every sixty days until it was lifted outside Asunción in 1970 and within Asunción in 1987. The secret police—*pyragües* or "hairy feet" as the Paraguayans call them—are everywhere: in cafes, taxis, trams, on the streets, in the hotel corridors. They occupied all the lounge chairs in the foyer of the Hotel Guarani when we stayed in Asunción. The army rules. Those who disagree with this go abroad, usually to Argentina or Brazil. There are an estimated 600,000 Paraguayans abroad.

Of course there have been some rumoured incomers—Martin Bormann, Joseph Mengele, etc. When we were in Asunción we used to go to the Deutscher Sportklub and try to pick them out. The Deutscher Sportklub began—before World War II—as the Hitler Youth Organisation. Nazi ideas influenced Paraguay after the Chaco War. There was a fair substratum of German settlers in any case. Stroessner's father, a Bavarian brewery worker, was one. He came from a small anti-Semitic colony established at the beginning of the century. Nietzsche's sister helped choose its members.

By this time we had filmed all over Paraguay, from the Jesuit *reducciónes* to Cerro Corá, where Lopez died, from the Iguazu Falls to the borders of the Chaco. We had seen the battlefields of the War of the Triple Alliance as well as those of the Chaco War. We had shot footage of the wildlife—tapirs, rheas (South American ostriches), jaguars, capybaras (a sort of giant guinea pig), armadillos, deer, alligators, anacondas, and pigs. We had been in the three main towns—Asunción, Concepción, and Encarnación. We had spent a few days at Lake Ypacaraí, we had visited the colonial church of Yaguarón with painted wood-carvings done by the Indians. We had filmed *conjuntos* (groups playing guitars and Paraguayan harps, smaller than the concert harp and without pedals). We had filmed gauchos rounding up cattle. We had filmed the flowery, cobbled streets of Asunción. We had filmed the urn containing Lopez's ashes in the Pantheon of Heroes, and the one containing Madame Lynch's in the Ministry of Defence. But we had *not* filmed General Stroessner, and the film was meant to be about him.

We had, of course, put in the obligatory waiting time. We had sat for hours in anterooms at the Palacío de Gobierno, assured that we would eventually see the General: "*No hay problema.*" But when they tell you that in Paraguay, there *is* a problem. General Stroessner, it appeared, had three pet hates—journalists, foreign journalists, and English-speaking foreign journalists—in that order. We began to lose hope.

One such day we were told that the General would be opening a fiesta at a place called Itacurubi del Rosario the following morning. If we got to the airport at six, we could go in one of the Paraguayan Air Force planes. We were there and made the trip on an ancient DC-3 in about an hour.

The Fiesta del Trigo (Harvest Home) consisted of schoolgirls marching, gauchos solemnly riding past, and a few floats. After it was over the whole populace assembled in the plaza and Stroessner addressed them in Spanish. He was followed by the leading Guarani poet, who spoke in Guarani. Whereas Stroessner's speech had been greeted in silence, that of the poet was rapturously received. The gauchos threw their hats in the air, the schoolgirls clapped and shouted, the citizens of Itacurubi del Rosario were all smiles. Paraguayans love, hate, fight, and live their lives in Guarani. Leon Cadogan once said that it is a rich language in which a single word often combines both a noun and its adjective or a verb and its adverb and sometimes has two meanings—the subject and its quality. But it is also full of difficult initial consonantal clusters like *nd* and *mb*.

Alan Whicker and the camera crew prepared to go back to the airstrip and sit under the wings of our DC-3. Although it was not much after 9 A.M. it was already getting hot. Stroessner, we had been told, was going to open a school and a hospital. He opens everything in Paraguay—nothing is too small. Since my Spanish was best, I decided to confront Stroessner and try to arrange a meeting.

As he came out of the new school I planted myself firmly in front of him and began, "*Señor Presidente, con su permiso.*" He glared at me—he has blue eyes—and his bodyguards, their shoulder-holsters bulging under their lightweight suits, pushed me out of the way. Stroessner crossed the plaza and headed for the half-built hospital. I saw him go in the front, so I ducked around the back.

I came out onto a small yard. The bodyguards were ranged in a semicircle around the General and he was having a pee. My appearance caused some comment and Stroessner looked up. He caught my eye and followed my gaze down to his member.

I retreated and returned to the airstrip. Alan Whicker and I concluded we'd done the best we could. Yet, that afternoon, we were told the General would grant us an interview the following morning at seven. When we were finally shown into his presence he looked at me and, with a twinkle in his eye, said, "*Al que me conoce intimamente tendré que otorgar entrevista*" ("I must grant an interview to one who knows me intimately"). As interviews go it was useless. Stroessner insisted on having the questions in writing and then he wrote out answers. These he read. But we were able to film him and he emerged as rather diffident and mild, not your demagogue by any means, just your usual military tyrant.

Paraguay has no income tax, no drainage system, no traffic lights, and only three surfaced roads of about 400 kilometres. It is the South American centre for smuggling whisky and cigarettes. Officially it is the highest consumer of American cigarettes in the world, but they are merely goods in transit. When they leave for the Argentine or Brazil (on unmarked planes) they are contraband, a perk for the generals. They say visitors to Paraguay cry twice—once when arriving, once when leaving.

The world owes to Paraguay a number of plants—the pineapple, the coca leaf (from which comes cocaine), ipecacuanha, sarsparilla, and that incomparable tea, *yerba maté.*

But it owes it something more—the quality of improbability, a sort of enchantment, a cessation of belief. There is a Guarani word—*ca'avó*—which conveys some of this. It means on the one hand the effusion of foliage in the humid air and, on the other, a melancholy sadness. The subject and its quality.

Paraguay has often been compared to Arcadia. It is divided in two. Paraguay's ancient inhabitants worshipped the equivalents of Pan, Eros, and Diana—primitive nature gods. The difficulties of communication have meant little outside influence. Like Grecian Arcadia, Paraguay has lagged behind its neighbours.

Maybe this is the secret of its charm.

4

São Tomé and Príncipe

━━━━━━━━━━━━━━━━━━━━━━━

IN THE GULF OF GUINEA

A chaplet of islands extends 700 kilometres southwest into the Gulf of Guinea from the bend in Africa's elbow. They are Fernando Póo, Príncipe, São Tomé, and Annobon and were once a chain of volcanoes connected to Mt. Cameroon. These four islands were discovered by the Portuguese in the second half of the 15th century. All, except Fernando Póo, the nearest to the mainland, were uninhabited.

The Portuguese began a settlement, at first on São Tomé. It was seen as an *Estalagem do Equador*—an Inn on the Equator, a way station on the route to the East. In 1778 the northernmost and the southernmost islands—Fernando Póo and Annobon—were ceded to the Spanish in exchange for an island off the coast of Brazil. Today they are part of the Republic of Equatorial Guinea while São Tomé and Príncipe constitute an independent state of that name. But, when we were there, the colonial powers still ruled in a somewhat desultory fashion.

Everyone has heard of the voyages of Bartholomeu Dias and Vasco da Gama, but we tend to forget how wide-ranging the Portuguese really were. They were among the first to pull the veil away from the lands beyond Europe. Newfoundland was possibly named by them, so was Labrador (Portuguese

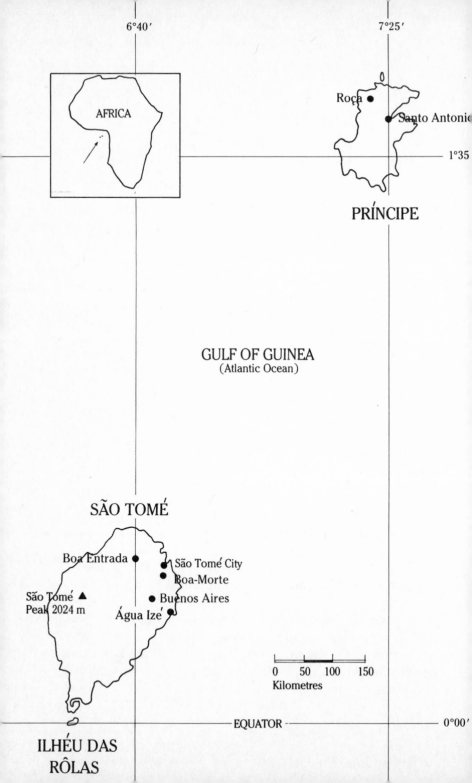

6°40'   7°25'

AFRICA

Roça ●

● Santo Antonio

1°35'

PRÍNCIPE

GULF OF GUINEA
(Atlantic Ocean)

SÃO TOMÉ

Boa Entrada ●

● São Tomé City

● Boa-Morte

São Tomé ▲
Peak 2024 m

● Buenos Aires

Água Izé ●

0   50   100   150
Kilometres

EQUATOR   0°00'

ILHÉU DAS
RÔLAS

for "yeoman"). They discovered Brazil ("red dyewood"), the Azores ("hawks"), and Madeira ("wood"). They christened the Cape of Good Hope, Bombay ("good bay"), and Formosa ("beautiful"). The map of Africa is dotted with the names they bestowed—Sierra Leone ("Lion Mountain"), Lagos ("Lakes"), Cameroon ("Shrimp"), Gabon ("Hood"), Natal ("Christmas Day"). So is the map of Indonesia—Flores is Flowers, Banda is Side, the Arafura Sea is the Sea of Free Men. They probably discovered Australia, though this is disputed; but they knew of its existence.

The Portuguese were restless voyagers. Their exploits are incomparable. They changed our perception of the world.

It is paradoxical that a country as small and as poor as Portugal should not only have founded an empire but a new concept of empire—one based on control of the sea-routes. They were the first conscious saltwater imperialists and began that process—the various European attempts to subjugate the rest of the world—which was to last for more than five hundred years.

It is also paradoxical that their empire—or the remnants of it—should have lasted almost the longest. Their influence still lingers on in many places. Portuguese fortresses can be seen from Dahomey (this fort, São João Baptista de Ajuda, and this fort alone was also a Portuguese colony until the 1960s) to Diu on the northwest coast of India, including superb examples at Mombasa and Muscat. Portuguese dishes, especially sweets, figure prominently in the cuisines of Sri Lanka, Malaysia, and the Cape. Japanese has borrowed many Portuguese words (one is *tempura* or deep-fried) as have Sinhalese and the South Indian languages. In the Arabic of the Persian Gulf most of the nautical terms are Portuguese. Portuguese Creole languages are spoken in parts of Sri Lanka, India, Malaysia, and the Guinea Coast. Portuguese folksongs are sung in one form or another from the Banda Islands in Indonesia to the Matto Grosso in Brazil.

The Portuguese are very proud of this astonishing achievement. Curiously enough, in the 15th century an impoverished and rural economy had its advantages in the matter of empire-building. The *fidalgos* ("sons of somebody"), their energies denied outlet in Europe, readily sought riches overseas; the sturdy peasantry, toughened by trying to cultivate barren or mountainous ground, supplied the manpower. Not everybody agreed with the official policy of looking towards horizons beyond the seas. Some, like King Canute in England, tried to stem the tide.

In Luís Vaz de Comões' (Camoens') epic poem *The Lusiads*, among those gathered by the banks of the Tagus to farewell Vasco da Gama was *"um velho de aspeito venerando"*—an old man of venerable appearance. He is known in Portuguese as the Old Man of Restelo, and he struck a note that surfaced constantly in Portuguese history until, in the 1970s, it prevailed and they gave up the idea of empire for good. What he said to da Gama was:

> You are enticed by the uncertain and the unknown,
> Flattered and exalted by the prospect of fame.
> Yet, for this, the ancient kingdom is depopulated,
> Weakened and brought to the brink of ruin.

We are not given da Gama's reply. He went on to fame, if not fortune, but the end result for Portugal was bittersweet. It was like an unrequited love affair. They strove mightily, but to what avail?

Towards the close of the Portuguese empire—though we were not to know then that it would end so suddenly—I made a film called *Portugal in Africa*. And followed, more or less, da Gama's path. First we went to Portuguese Guinea and the Cape Verde Islands. Later we were to go to Cabinda, Angola, and Mozambique but, for the moment, we were in São Tomé—and stepping into another age.

First impressions were of a very mountainous island (the highest peak is over 2,000 metres or 6,560 feet) about 50 kilometres long and covered in thick vegetation. The atmosphere was like a greenhouse. We put up at the Pousada

Miramar—the Sea-View Guest-House—which, while without air-conditioning, did have a swimming pool. We had arrived in the season known as *a gravana*—the dry season from June to mid-September. The rest of the year is called *as chuvas*— the rains. During the *gravana* there are constant winds, which keep the temperature in the mid-eighties (about 29° C). It is the best time of the year in São Tomé.

The Governor-General received us courteously. Never before (and I doubt since) had a film crew visited São Tomé. We became instant celebrities. He put a car and a driver at our disposal and offered us the use of his plane, an early De Havilland. He also introduced us to some interesting people.

These were exiles—intellectuals and others who had fallen foul of the PIDE, the Portuguese secret police. Because São Tomé (and other Portuguese colonies) were regarded as an integral part of Portugal—*o espaço português* or Portuguese space—exile to the island was considered internal exile. It was something Mussolini did, too. The exiles were not harassed in any way or under any restraints. The administration found jobs and accommodation for them if it could, but they were not allowed to return to Portugal—all in all a fairly civilised treatment. We found them a charming group. One was a mistress at the local high school, another an artist, a third a ballet master, and there were several journalists and writers. They called themselves *Os Nefastos*—the Sad Ones. When we left each gave us a little gift. Because of them we learnt much more about São Tomé than would otherwise have been possible.

The island has had a curious history. Soon after its discovery it was given by the Portuguese king to João de Paiva as a *donátaria*, which meant he held all rights, political as well as economic. João de Paiva sent out as colonists 2,000 Jewish children of about eight years of age, who had been forcibly separated from their parents and "converted" to Christianity. The Portuguese called them *novos cristãos*—New Christians—and gave them surnames, often after fruit trees like Pereira (pear tree), Oliveira (olive tree), Nogueira (walnut tree), Macieira (apple tree), and so on. These are among the commonest surnames in Portugal today. Secretly the *novos cristãos* continued to practise Jewish rites, while keeping one eye cocked at the Inquisition (*auto-da-fé* is a Portuguese word and was a Portuguese institution). The designation *novos cristãos* was only abolished with the Inquisition in 1750.

Other immigrants were recruited from Madeira (these brought sugar cane) and from Genoa (these brought the skills needed for cane farming and crushing). The king ordered that "native girls for breeding" be shipped from the Guinea Coast. So began the miscegenation that characterises Portuguese colonisation. They have a saying: "*Deus criou o preto e o branco. Os portuguêses criaran os mulatos.*" ("God made black and white. The Portuguese made the mulattos.")

Sugar cultivation, of course, needed slave labour. So slaves were increasingly imported. Fifty years after its introduction there were said to be sixty sugar mills on São Tomé and 2,000 assimilated slaves with 6,000 more in barracoons.

Big Houses were built, many of which still stand today, two-storied with verandahs all around, shuttered windows, Moorish-looking balconies. In front of the house across a patio stood the *senzala* or slave quarters—small huts in rows, a bell tower, whipping posts.

Each *roça* or plantation was a little community of its own. The master might have fourteen or more personal slaves. A Negress suckled his children, rocked their cradles, taught them their first words of Creole Portuguese. The little boys would have their first sexual experience with a slave girl, the little girls would pass the hours in lassitude, carried everywhere on a litter by slaves.

At night, after a good meal cooked by his Negro cook and served by his Negro servants, the master and his male guests would stroll across to the *senzala* and select a girl. The mistress knew about this but usually turned a blind eye, although there are stories of cruelty on the part of jealous mistresses. Teeth were pulled out, breasts cut off, ears cropped, faces burned. According to *Os Nefastos*, documented cases exist of attractive slave girls being put into the large bread ovens and baked. Any male Negro who made a sexual advance towards a white girl was castrated and buried alive. It was a sadistic society.

The other side of this coin, perhaps unsurprisingly, was the cult of virginity. Girls were married young, at twelve or thirteen, so the husband—often twenty, thirty, forty years older—could be sure he was getting a virgin. Infant mortality was high, which was attributed to Our Lord's insatiable quest for angels, and many a teenage mother died in childbirth.

São Tomé became one of the great sugar producers of the world, although the quality of its product was inferior to that of Madeira. Most of the sugar went to Flanders, where it was distributed to England and Germany. At the same time, the island was a giant warehouse for slaves en route to the newly developed plantations of Brazil. And this is what really killed the São Tomé sugar industry—the rise of Brazil. There were other factors: raids by the envious French and Dutch, slave revolts, and trouble with the *Angolares* or descendants of slaves from a ship that was wrecked on the coast. The *Angolares* settled in the mountains and established little republics of their own.

Planters emigrated to Brazil, the population fell, and those who were left behind took to dealing in slaves or growing vegetables to sell to passing ships. Again, the *estalagem do equador*. São Tomé became a backwater, and one hundred years of stagnation settled over the little community lost in the Gulf of Guinea.

Then, just as Brazil had been responsible for its decline, Brazil became responsible for São Tomé's regeneration. The coffee bush was introduced first and then the cacao tree from Brazil. Both thrived on the fertile volcanic soils and in the equatorial insular environment. The quality of the coffee and the cocoa was unsurpassed. In the coffee shops along the Rossio, the square at the heart of Lisbon, a premium is set on São Tomé coffee. Connoisseurs drink it mixed with a little wild coffee, gathered from the bush on the island of Ibo off the Mozambican coast. And the best Dutch and Swiss chocolate is made from Santomean beans.

The *roças* were cleared and replanted. As coffee and cacao will grow at higher altitudes than sugar cane, new *roças* were brought into production. By the turn of the century São Tomé and Príncipe were the world's largest producers of cocoa beans. Slavery had finally been abolished in 1876, so a system of indentured labour was introduced, the labourers coming from Angola and the overseers from the Cape Verde Islands.

In 1908, William Cadbury of Cadbury Bros. made a trip to São Tomé and Angola. The Cadburys are Quakers, and what William Cadbury saw horrified him. According to Cadbury, the indentured labourers were treated no better than slaves, and his campaign led to a boycott of São Tomé beans by all British cocoa and chocolate manufacturers. The Portuguese are a bit cynical about this. They point out that the cacao tree was introduced to the Gold Coast (now Ghana) shortly before Cadbury's fact-finding mission and that the Gold Coast was a British colony.

Be that as it may, the São Tomé cocoa industry went into a decline. Each year production got less. The trees (about the size of an apple tree) were ageing, the methods of working the plantations obsolete, the soil impoverished. Most of the *roças* were owned by absentee landlords or Portuguese corporations and managed by Europeans. Some of those absentee landlords were ennobled by the Portuguese crown before Portugal became a republic in 1910—the Barão de Agua-Izé (Baron Freshwater Shrimp) is one, the Barão de Boa Entrada (Baron Good Entry) another. After São Tomé and Príncipe became independent on July 12, 1975, the *roças* were nationalised.

When we were there we were told there were over one

hundred *roças* on São Tomé and Príncipe. Many were small, of course, but there were some large ones, a few quite large. We visited Buenos Aires, one of the largest and oldest, about 10 kilometres southwest of São Tomé City, the rather grandiose name for the only town on the island.

After we had filmed the various processes involved in the production of cocoa beans—harvesting the pods, breaking them open to extract the pulp, the fermentation and drying—we were invited to lunch. To our surprise the Governor-General was also a guest. We soon discovered why. We were going to be treated to a taste of the opulence from the days of *os grandes senhores*—the great owners.

The plates we dined off bore the coat of arms of the Casa da India, the royal monopoly formed in 1505 to market spices. Behind each guest stood four servants. Three were women and they served the meal. The fourth was a man and he served the wine. They were all dressed in white and barefoot. The women had small, short-sleeved bodices, a bare midriff, and long flounced skirts. They wore mobcaps. The men had on a long-sleeved shirt with no collar, a sash around the waist, and knee breeches. Rather 18th century, I felt.

The main course was *calulu*, the national dish. It is made by boiling okra and eggplant together, making a paste of them, seasoning this with two kinds of Guinea pepper, and adding shrimps, dried malaguetta (also called Grains of Paradise), and onions crushed with pepper corns. This is sprinkled with *dendê* oil (red oil from a palm), and to it is added a chicken, baked in an earthenware casserole with *piripiri* (small hot chili peppers). Altogether a spicy dish, a *very* spicy dish. To dampen down the flames it was accompanied by *angú* (bananas and salt mashed in a mortar with a pestle). The wine was *vinho verde* in stone bottles—from the north of Portugal.

As a dessert we were offered a mousse made of several tropical fruits. Then a cup of strong São Tomé coffee was followed by some good Portuguese port. After several ports each we almost felt like strolling across to the *senzala* to see what was available. (Fiery dishes are aphrodisiacs, or so the Portuguese claim—but they say this about lots of foods.)

Next we toured the Big House. It was full of heavy furniture, the windows covered with Venetian blinds, the walls of blue-glazed tiles or *azulêjos*, the floors parquet. Small tables were covered with pictures of the family's forebears in silver frames. There was a private chapel and an enormous kitchen. Right in the centre of the house was a room where the daughters slept. Over it all hung a cloying, slightly musty air.

The Governor-General had once again pressed his plane upon us, and the following day we took advantage of the offer. From the air it became obvious that São Tomé was oval-shaped and about two-thirds as wide as it was long. The north and northeast are fairly flat, but the south and west are a chaos of mountains, among them many volcanic needles and dikes. Rain forest clothed most of this terrain. The coast was a succession of rocky promontories alternating with sandy bays lined with coconut palms. In the north and east the *roças* presented an orderly pattern of cacao or coffee bushes interspersed with shade trees.

We flew over the equator. Actually it passes through an islet 2 kilometres south of São Tomé—the Ilhéu das Rôlas. The pilot told us there is a monument to mark the place.

That night *Os Nefastos* came round to the Pousada Miramar for a drink. There was something we ought to see, they said, and produced a handbill. I still have it.

PROGRAMA

Exibição da Tragédia
Marquês de Mântua
Pelo grupo Formiguinha
Nos dias 4 e 5 de Julho em
Boa-Morte

[PROGRAM: Exhibition of the Tragedy, Marquess of Mantua, by the Little Ant Group on the 4th and 5th days of July at Good Death.]

Os Nefastos explained. "The Marquess of Mantua" was an obscure 16th- or 17th-century Italian play brought to São Tomé, possibly by Genoese sugar boilers. It had been taken up by the Santomeans, who had made it their own by turning it into a medieval morality play. "The Marquess of Mantua" was the only play performed on São Tomé and, once a year, every village put it on. Príncipe had its own morality play, *Carlos Magano* ("Charlemagne").

There were twenty-one acts and the play took two days. But the acts weren't in sequence and, often, they were repeated. People came and went as they pleased. The audience in the morning was not the audience of the afternoon.

We went on the first day. An area about half the size of a tennis court had been roped off. At one end stood a roofed platform on high blocks, at the other end an open platform also on high blocks. Sitting on some portable steps was the *Tchiloli*, a small band that played a monotonous musical accompaniment on homemade guitars and drums. Every so often they moved from one side of the enclosure to the other.

The audience sat or stood along the ropes. The action took place sometimes on one of the platforms, sometimes on the other, sometimes in the area between the two. The players were dressed in elaborate costumes—Cavalier-style hats with feathers, capes, buckle-shoes, long hose. Those who were meant to be Europeans had their faces painted white, the others were their natural colour.

The Devil was dressed all in black with a red cap and horns and a long red tail that he carried over his arm. He was always being chased away from the scene by God, who wore wooden crucifixes over his back and front and carried a large crook with which He would prod the Devil whenever he took refuge under one of the platforms.

The play was in São Tomé Creole, of which I didn't understand a word but, because we were filming, bystanders took it upon themselves to give us a running commentary on the three acts we saw. There were the Emperor and the Empress of the West, who received the family of the Marquess of Mantua at their court. There were the ministers and advisers of the Emperor and the Great Men of the Court—Ganalão, Reinaldo de Montalvão, and Beltrão (these are some of the twelve paladins, the famous warriors of Charlemagne's court). Also there was Valdevinos, but he was dead and represented by a small white coffin. On the sidelines were the court jester (a white-faced dwarf) and the executioner, who carried a large axe and a rope. The Devil had a number of assistants, African fetish-men with monkey-skulls around their necks, who kept jumping up and down.

From time to time the whole cast would line up and dance a sort of rhumba with two singers directing them. This would cause uncontrollable giggles among the audience, and it appeared that the singers—Senhor and Senhora Gatela, which is what they were called (it means "star" in Creole)—were passing scurrilous comment on the citizens of Boa-Morte.

The day came when we were to go to the neighbouring island of Príncipe. It lies 150 kilometres north of São Tomé, but is about a quarter its size and is rectangular in shape though equally mountainous. There was a small grass airstrip on Príncipe, and we were met by some of the island officials. The population is small—about 5,000, a fraction of São Tomé's—and there are only 50 kilometres of road. But some of the *roças* are quite large—one is 80 square kilometres with an ocean frontage of 12 kilometres.

There really wasn't much we could add to the footage we had already shot—a few spectacular *roças* and the little town of Santo Antonio with its toy harbour. We had a long lunch at a *roça*, which had huge stables and its own hospital as well as a *senzala*. The Big House was built on the edge of a precipice to catch the breeze, and it overlooked the tops of palm trees stretching almost a kilometre to the sea.

In the afternoon we decided to go back to Santo Antonio, where I had seen a cafe, to have coffee and *bagaço*—a spirit made from the residues of grape-crushing (what the French call *marc* and the Italians *grappa*). We sat there, dawdling over our drinks and watching the goings-on in the minuscule port, until we heard the sound of an aircraft overhead and saw the De Havilland heading out to sea. A messenger soon arrived. The Governor-General urgently needed the plane. It would come back tomorrow. In the meantime accommodations had been arranged for us at the same *roça* where we had lunched.

The manager of the *roça* had six daughters but no sons. They were fairly typical Portuguese girls, dark-haired, dark-eyed, fresh-looking with wide smiles; they were between about twenty-four and sixteen years of age and included two sets of twins. We all sat in the *sala* or parlour, listened to music—mainly melancholy Portuguese *fados*—talked about Lisbon, discussed the war in Angola and the political situation in São Tomé and Príncipe. There were no political parties, the manager assured us, there was no political activity; all the people wanted to do was to remain dependent upon Portugal. Subsequently we found out that, generally, this was indeed the case; São Tomé and Príncipe were completely apolitical—but not for long.

Then we dined, but this time Portuguese-style. There was *caldo verde*, a soup made of finely minced cabbage and seasoned with olive oil, followed by *bacalhau à brás*, dried salted cod shredded and sauteed with onions, potatoes, olives, and hard-boiled eggs. The sweet was *pudim flan* or *crème caramel*.

Back to the *sala* and more *fados*. Eventually we were shown to our rooms. These were in a row and opened onto a verandah above the precipice. For a while we looked at the full moon on the sea, then we retired.

I was awakened by the cameraman.

"You'd better come," he said. "Those girls are here."

The sound-recordist was on the verandah and the girls were standing around him.

"*O que queren vocês*?" I asked. "What do you want?"

The reply was direct. "*Vocês, os tres. Um para duas de nos.*" "You three, one for two of us."

"Okay, if you split the twins up," the cameraman said.

During the night we learnt the reason for their invitation. They thought they would never see Portugal again. There were no unmarried Europeans on Príncipe. Their father had threatened to kill any native they had anything to do with. The servant girls talked about sex all the time. We were the only visitors the *roça* had ever had. We were young, we were European.

We left at mid-morning next day and within twenty-four hours were on our way to Luanda and Angola.

São Tomé and Príncipe is today an independent sovereign republic with a population of around 90,000 and an area of about 950 square kilometres. It is a member of the United Nations and ruled by the Movimento de Libertação de São Tomé e Príncipe—a one-party, Marxist state.

When it was announced after the 1974 coup that Portugal was going to foist freedom upon its colonies, whether they liked it or not, a transitional government was set up. The following year independence was granted, and 4,000 Portuguese left for home. So did most of the Capverdians, who had provided the lower echelons of management.

Initially the government was moderate but the collapse of the economy led to the left taking power. Since then the government has lived in constant fear of a coup, mounted from nearby rightwing Gabon. During 1978 unidentified ships and planes were frequently sighted off the islands. A thousand Angolan troops joined the Cuban soldiers and advisers already on São Tomé.

I wrote a letter to one of *Os Nefastos*—a man who now lives in Portugal—asking him if he had any news of the country. He replied: "You cannot go there now. Tourists are forbidden. The country is paranoid. If you walk along a beach at night smoking a cigarette you are arrested for signalling the enemy. There are Russians, East Germans, Cubans, and North Koreans everywhere. The *roças* have collapsed, though The Netherlands and Switzerland still buy some Santomean cocoa and Portugal a little coffee. You cannot get any imported goods—no cigarettes, no toilet paper, no soap—and as well there is no meat, no bread, no vegetables except manioc. My friend, we were there in the good days, the golden days. No one is even permitted to go to Príncipe now. And I know you have fond memories of Príncipe!''

So much for socialism in a Third World country. The people were probably happier with the colonialists.

Unfortunately for São Tomé and Príncipe they are no longer on the way to anywhere. They have no strategic bargaining power, no ports, no large airfields. Stagnation has set in again at the *Estalagem do Equador*.

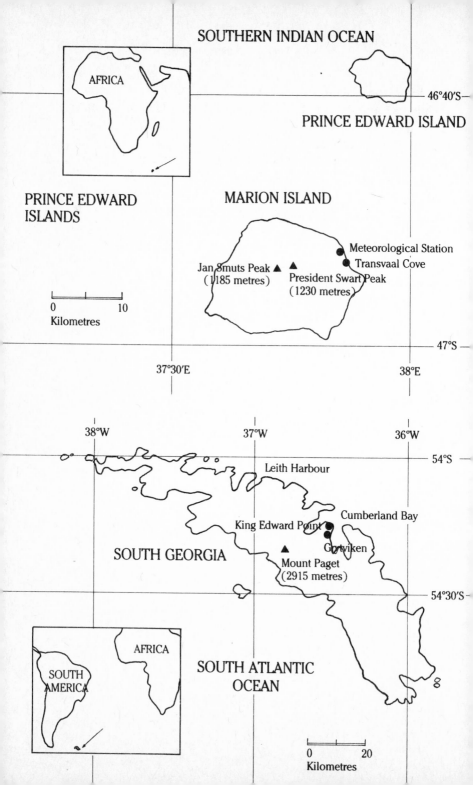

SOUTHERN INDIAN OCEAN

AFRICA

46°40'S

PRINCE EDWARD ISLAND

PRINCE EDWARD
ISLANDS

MARION ISLAND

Jan Smuts Peak ▲   ▲
(1185 metres)   President Swart Peak
                 (1230 metres)

● Meteorological Station
● Transvaal Cove

0   10
Kilometres

47°S

37°30'E   38°E

38°W   37°W   36°W

54°S

Leith Harbour

Cumberland Bay

King Edward Point ●
                  ● Grytviken

SOUTH GEORGIA
        ▲
Mount Paget
(2915 metres)

54°30'S

SOUTH AMERICA   AFRICA

SOUTH ATLANTIC
OCEAN

0   20
Kilometres

5

The Subantarctic Islands

========================

STORMY OUTPOSTS AT THE BOTTOM OF THE WORLD

The first time I saw a subantarctic island was from the bridge of a South African frigate. The island was Marion Island and from the sea it looked like an uninviting cloud-covered dome. The shore was lined with rocky cliffs at the base of which waves dashed constantly, while spray flew high into the air. Marion Island is in Latitude 47° South, 1,900 kilometres from Capetown. With neighbouring Prince Edward Island it makes up the Prince Edward Group. They are both peaks of the same submerged volcano—18 kilometres apart—and together their area is 388 square kilometres. (In December 1986 it was reported that South Africa was planning a $10 million runway on Marion Island, ostensibly to service the weather station there—maintained by South Africa since 1948—but possibly for military purposes.)

Why was I in this remote place? We had been in South Africa filming the battlefields, cemeteries, concentration camp sites (invented, incidentally, by the British), and museums of the Boer War. This exercise in military history was designed to illustrate the thesis that apartheid was an attempt by the Afrikaners to do to the non-Europeans what the British had done to them.

When we had finished, the South African Ministry of Defence suggested we might like to visit the Prince Edward Group. The annual relief boat, the S.A.S. *President Kruger*, was leaving Simonstown naval base with supplies and personnel for the weather station there. We could go and be back in not much over a week. So we decided to do it, arguing that any film footage we took might be useful one day (it is probably still languishing in a vault somewhere). In any case, the Prince Edward Group is South Africa's only overseas possession. This could turn out to be significant. And so on.

Marion Island was discovered in 1772 by Marion du Fresne, a French explorer. He went on to be killed, and eaten, by Maoris at the Bay of Islands, New Zealand. Four years later Captain James Cook, on his last voyage, rediscovered Marion and, in addition, found Prince Edward Island. He went on to be killed, but not eaten, by Hawaiians at Kealakekua Bay. Cook named the two islands the Prince Edward Group after the Duke of Kent, father of the future Queen Victoria.

Like most subantarctic islands the Prince Edward Group was, for many years, the haunt of sealers and whalers until their quarry vanished. I was shown caves on Marion in which they had lived. Some, it is said, were driven mad by the monotonous and harsh conditions. These, to use the expression current at the time, were "relieved of their miseries" by their companions to make life easier for the others. A brutish existence.

After the 1840s ships began to use the Great Circle Route from Britain to Australia, and this brought them close to the Prince Edward Group. Often too close in some cases—a number were wrecked there.

Because of the swell, the S.A.S. *President Kruger* anchored a kilometre off Transvaal Cove and the supplies were ferried ashore by motorboat. There is a small jetty suspended by cables from the cliff face, and a boat passage leading to it has been cut through the belts of kelp. We eventually made it to the jetty, but I half expected to see the camera and tape recorder—not to mention their intrepid operators—disappear into the depths at any moment.

Behind the cliffs a narrow coastal plain rises to the central mountain with two peaks—President Swart at 1,230 metres (4,034 feet) and Jan Smuts at 1,186 metres (3,890 feet). The plain is marshy and covered with moss and dwarf ferns. Perhaps the most unusual plant is the Kerguélen cabbage. It looks like an ordinary cabbage but the leaves contain a pale-yellow pungent oil that gives them a peculiar flavour. It also makes the cabbage extremely efficacious against scurvy. And who should have discovered the Kerguélen cabbage and its medicinal use but Captain Cook, who was always experimenting with anti-scorbutics (he is said to have been the first to introduce daily rations of lime juice on board vessels of the Royal Navy, the reason the British are known as "Limeys" in America). I later had some boiled and it was quite palatable. Not exactly savoy cabbage, but still . . .

South Africa took possession of the Prince Edward Group in 1948 after an agreement with Great Britain, the then owner, and proceeded to set up the meteorological station forthwith. The buildings are on the plain out of reach of the breakers and, because of the soggy ground, connected by wooden causeways. The twenty-five personnel stay twelve months. It is a lonely life and, in common with most of these isolated outposts, the staff are given to attacks of cabin fever. Some become aggressive, others morose. There were no non-Europeans among the group on Marion, which might be indicative of past strains.

We ran off limited footage, making sure we got the South African flag into as many shots as possible. There is a fair amount of wildlife. The seals and sea elephants have recently come back but not the sea leopards. And there are many birds—penguins, petrels, skuas, albatrosses, terns, and gulls.

But I was not sorry to leave the Prince Edward Group.

There was little to do, nothing to see, and the weather was vile. I vowed to keep away from these quarters of the globe in the future—and this of course turned out to be Famous Last Words.

There are three such quarters: the subantarctic islands in the far south of the Indian Ocean, those in the far south of the Atlantic Ocean, and those to the south of New Zealand. The Prince Edward Group belongs to the first of these. So does Kerguélen Island, which is French and about 2,400 kilometres east of Marion and slightly to the south. It is a large island, 130 kilometres long and the same across. Since 1950 there has been a scientific base there and some talk of an airstrip. But winds are a problem. According to a man I met, who had been there, they blow harder and more continuously on Kerguélen than anywhere else in the world. A comparatively windless day, he said, has winds of 50 to 60 kilometres an hour, and on a windy day they might go up to 200 kilometres an hour (in excess of hurricane force). In a latitude and with a climate similar to the Falkland Islands, Kerguélen has been considered for colonisation several times and once for a penal settlement. Australia even offered to buy Kerguélen from the French in 1901 but for which of these two purposes I do not know.

Last century there were, of course, the inevitable sealers. The explorer Sir James Clark Ross found the mummified corpse of one in a hut in 1840 with "a bottle in his hand, terror in his eyes and gigantic footprints leading up to him." A report in the *London Illustrated News* of the same year said that Ross had also seen mysterious hoof-prints in the snow although no animals except seals live on Kerguélen. This is the only mention of the supernatural I have ever found in literature about Antarctica—that is, if it is the supernatural, or just the calling card of the Devil.

France owns two other groups of subantarctic islands—St. Paul and Amsterdam, 1,500 kilometres northeast of Kerguélen, and the Crozets, midway between Kerguélen and the

Prince Edward Group. The Crozets are also extinct volcanoes. A base is maintained there as well.

But the nearest islands to Kerguélen are Heard and
McDonald Islands. They are Australian territories, 400 kilometres southeast of Kerguélen. They lie across the Antarctic
Convergence, that region where the north-flowing cold Antarctic water sinks under the warmer Subantarctic. This division is marked by a sudden change in the water temperature,
sometimes by as much as 9° F (or between 3° and 6° C).
Which means that, whereas Kerguélen has a small icecap and
the snow level is above 600 metres (1,968 feet), Heard is
almost completely ice-covered down to the sea.

Heard Island is really a huge volcanic cone rising 2,745
metres (9,004 feet), the highest peak in the Commonwealth of
Australia. I have never been there but, according to those I
know who have seen it, it is well worth the trip though it is a
bit out of the way (Western Australia is some 5,000 kilometres
to the northeast). Australia once maintained an ANARE
(Australian National Antarctic Research Expeditioners') station there.

Last century on Heard seals were completely exterminated.
Gangs of men would be landed on the island and expected to
kill as many seals as possible, mainly by clubbing them. Few
descriptions of these men exist, but those that do call them
"filthy dirty apes with matted beards and stinking of blubber" and talk of their clothes and hats made out of seal-skin
and their boots made of penguin skin. One member of a gang
put off from the *Offley* at Heard in 1858 had this to say:

> We were all ordered on shore on an island covered with ice
> and without shelter or covering for our bodies and amid the
> most intense and bitter cold with snow falling and no fuel to
> make a fire to warm our numbed and frost-bitten limbs. At
> length we succeeded in finding along the beach some old
> portions of a wreck which we managed to erect a place
> sufficiently large for us to crawl into. We were fully two days
> putting a few poles and a sail over this which was then our

home. We had to exist in this place six months, our fireplace was tussocks of grass and our fuel consisted of elephant blubber.

He went on to add that they filled four hundred casks of sea elephant oil by the time the *Offley* returned. For this they were paid less than the seamen on the vessel that had brought them there.

Most of the subantarctic islands in the far South Atlantic tend to be fairly near the coast of South America. One, however—Bouvet—is almost due south of South Africa. Although discovered by a Frenchman, Bouvet de Lozier in 1739, it was annexed to Norway in 1928 and used as a base by Norwegian whalers. The Norwegians changed the name to Bouvetøya, which just means Bouvet Island. It has the distinction of being the most isolated piece of land on the earth's surface. The northwest point of the island, which stands out prominently against the glacier behind it, is called Cape Circumcision, which is probably apt but unusual. (In fact, the island was discovered on the Festival of the Circumcision of Christ—January 1st.)

Seventy-five kilometres north-northeast of Bouvet lies Thompson Island. Or does it? Its position is one of the great sea mysteries. It was first sighted by Captain Norris of the *Sprightly*, who wrote in his log for December 13, 1825: "Island in Latd. 53.56 Long. 5.30." He not only made an entry, he drew a chart of the island and sketched it from half a dozen different aspects. It was lost for sixty-eight years until in 1893 an American sea captain, Joseph Fuller, saw it again in the same position. Since then many expeditions have searched in vain for Thompson Island. The British Admiralty decided that what Norris and Fuller had seen was a large iceberg, but there are those who disagree. (The location of Thompson Island has been the subject of a better-than-ordinary adventure novel by Geoffrey Jenkins called *Grue of Ice*.)

The other islands in the far South Atlantic are dependencies of the Falklands, technically subantarctic islands themselves. They are South Sandwich, South Shetland, South Orkney, and South Georgia. The last named was to be the next subantarctic island I saw.

In the summer of 1970 I was in Uruguay to meet the family of the girl I planned to marry. After a few weeks she returned to her job in London, and I prepared to go on to Australia to visit my parents. The quickest route was across the South Pacific on a weekly flight operated by LAN Chile, the Chilean airline. In those days they used DC-6s on the Santiago-Tahiti leg, and there was a compulsory twenty-four-hour stopover at Easter Island to allow the crew to rest after their eight-hour flight. Easter Island is a Chilean possession and was becoming popular as a tourist destination. So all the flights were booked up for a month.

It was at this juncture that the man who was later to become my brother-in-law proposed a trip to South Georgia. He was an engineer on R.R.S. *John Biscoe*, a ship belonging to the British Antarctic Survey. It serviced British bases in Antarctica, something that would have been easier done from the Argentine, but the Argentines claimed both the Falklands and its dependencies, so Montevideo was the *Biscoe*'s home port. The trip was an extra one. I would not have to pay.

We had a rough passage. Great grey-green billows swept continually past the ship as she toiled up and down the watery troughs. When I went on deck the wind was full of stinging droplets of rain, there was no sign of the sun, and the clouds seemed to be at masthead level. I was the only passenger and spent most of my time in my bunk reading thrillers and regretting my decision to come. The *Biscoe* rolled around a lot and, although I didn't get seasick, I was more than relieved to see Leith Harbour four days later. At King Edward Point, just inside the entrance to Cumberland Bay, is the headquarters of the British Antarctic Survey. About twenty men, some hardy wives, and a few equally hardy cats and dogs made up the entire population when I was there. They were a cheerful little community at the bottom of the world—Latitude 54° South. There was even a weekly dance and, on sunny Sundays, motorboat excursions to Leith Harbour complete with scones and afternoon tea.

To my surprise I enjoyed South Georgia. It reminded me of Greenland—green meadows, fjords and glaciers, and jagged snow-covered mountains. Discovered and charted by Captain Cook in 1775, it is really a mountain range 160 kilometres long rising 3,500 metres (11,480 feet) straight out of the sea. He named it after King George III. Since 1905 there has been a meteorological station on the island and, during the first decades of this century, South Georgia played a crucial role in Antarctic exploration.

Indeed, Sir Ernest Shackleton died there in 1922 on board the yacht *Quest* and is buried at Grytviken, some 40 kilometres from Leith Harbour. I visited his tomb. He lies in a little cemetery with a white painted fence around it. Sir Ernest's grave has a large granite headstone. Over everything hangs a silence, almost the silence of outer space.

Within a few years of Cook's discovery sealers were in South Georgia, and by the end of the 18th century they had virtually exterminated the fur seal. (Hunting the sea elephant continued until recently.) One hundred years later a Norwegian company opened a whaling factory at Grytviken (hence the Norwegian name of this harbour) and a whaling industry developed. Other factories were built, but in 1963 the company ceased operations. A Japanese company leased two of the factories for a further two years. They were then abandoned, which was how I saw them.

It was these abandoned whaling stations—there were eight —that provided the curtain raiser for the Falklands War. In 1979, Constantine Davidoff, a scrap metal dealer from Buenos Aires, applied to the British Government for permission to remove material from the whaling stations. On the surface this looked like any other business transaction, but British suspicions were aroused when, in mid-March, an Argentine naval vessel arrived with forty men on board. They landed without bothering to report to the leader of the British Antarctic Survey team—who is also the local magistrate, immigration officer, Customs official, etc.—and raised the Argentine flag. The Foreign Office protested to the Argentine Government, and two days later H.M.S. *Endurance* put a small party of marines ashore at King Edward Point.

On April 3, 1982, the day after the Argentine invasion of Port Stanley in the Falklands, two Argentine corvettes with helicopters appeared and about 150 troops launched an attack on the weather station. The battle lasted seven hours and, in the end, the Royal Marines surrendered. They had killed three Argentines, crippled one of the helicopters, and damaged a corvette. They suffered no casualties. War had come to a subantarctic island for the first time (though German raiders had used Kerguélen in the 1940s).

The Argentines were not to remain unchallenged for long. On April 25, helicopters from advance ships of the British Task Force sighted the Argentine submarine *Santa Fé* near Grytviken and attacked it. Badly hit, the submarine ran aground and about fifty soldiers clambered ashore. Thirty S.A.S. men were landed and rounded them up. The Argentine garrison at King Edward Point was given the opportunity to surrender. They said they would fight to the last man (as V. S. Naipaul pointed out, publicly that meant they were about to surrender) and next morning, when the S.A.S. attacked, they quickly gave in. One hundred and fifty-six Argentine soldiers and sailors were captured and thirty-eight civilians. The same evening on British television Mrs. Thatcher urged Britons to "Rejoice. Rejoice."

But these dramatic events were twelve years into the future. The long summer days at South Georgia were very pleasant. The British Antarctic Survey people seemed well

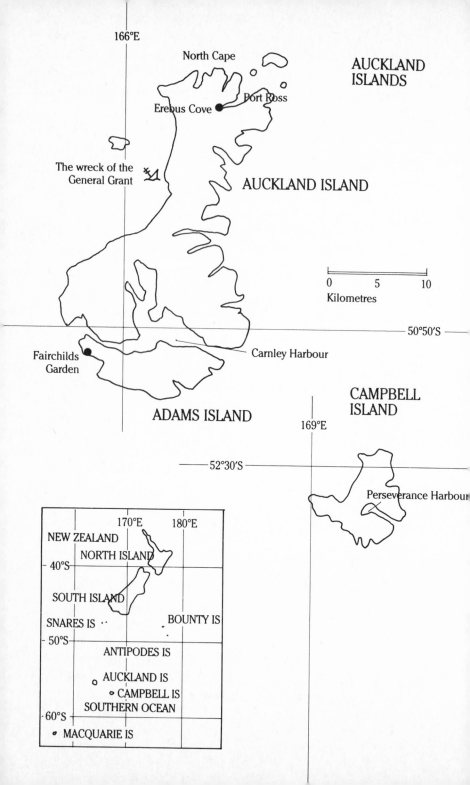

adjusted. No cabin fever here. Undoutedly they were selected partly because of their inner resources. The scenery is awe-inspiring—sharply pointed irregular mountains, deep blue fjords, glittering glaciers. And it is the major habitat in the world for the sea elephant—some 300,000 of them lying on the pebbly beaches like great black slugs or beanbags huddled together, from time to time trumpeting through their corrugated proboscides, which is why they are called sea elephants. Although the air was chill, I found walking across the grassy slopes and scrambling over the scree to be invigorating, and I began to like South Georgia. There were obviously subantarctic islands and subantarctic islands.

It was to be six more years before I visited another. By then I had moved to New Zealand and was the Executive Producer for South Pacific Television, the second New Zealand channel. One of a series of films that we made about castaways dealt with the wreck of the *General Grant* in the Auckland Islands in 1866 and the fate of the survivors. We needed to film the locations, though we did the dramatised sequences on Stewart Island because it was close to New Zealand, accessible by plane, and had accommodations.

Once again I found myself on a boat heading south, this time the R.V. *Acheron* from Dunedin. A string of islands stretches almost 1,000 kilometres from New Zealand towards Antarctica—the Snares, Bounty, Antipodes, Auckland, Campbell, and Macquarie Islands. The last named is a dependency of Australia and has an ANARE station on it; all the others belong to New Zealand.

None has had a more romantic history than the Auckland Islands. First discovered in 1806, the islands soon became bleak refuges for sealers and whalers and the occasional castaway. There was also a short-lived attempt at colonisation—the Enderby Settlement, which lasted from 1850 to 1852. When the Great Circle Route came into use between Australia and Britain, the Aucklands—like the Prince Edward Group—claimed their share of victims. Within a few years nine ships were wrecked on the iron-bound western coasts. Among them was the American square-rigger, the *General Grant*, in one of history's most bizarre shipwrecks.

The *General Grant* was off course when she ran into a gigantic cavern in the 450-metre-high cliffs (1,476 feet) that face the "Roaring Forties" latitudes. When the tide rose the masts were pushed through the bottom. There were eighty-three people aboard, of whom fifteen survived, including one young woman. Four later lost their lives trying to sail an open boat the 400 kilometres to New Zealand. One died of scurvy. The remaining ten were rescued after eighteen months of incredible hardships.

The ship had left Melbourne on May 1, 1866, with a cargo of wool, hides, and gold—70 kilograms according to the manifest, nine tons listed as zinc ingots, according to well-informed sources. This gold has never been recovered, although there have been twenty salvage expeditions, including one in 1986. If there are nine tons of gold at the bottom of a cave in the Auckland Islands, it is the largest known undiscovered treasure in the world.

It was a two-day voyage from Dunedin to the Aucklands, and on the way we passed the Snares. These are a pair of islands, the larger barely 2 kilometres long. In 1810 five men from the sealer *Adventure* were put ashore on one of the Snares "with a quart of rice, half a bushel of potatoes and an iron pot." The men planted the potatoes, which flourished in the peaty soil, and lived off seabirds and seals. Four of them survived for seven years until an American ship ended their dismal exile. The captain reported that "the men had built five houses, had 13,000 dried seal-skins and the sides of the island were covered with potatoes." I have quoted this story because I believe it is the most revealing one about sealing that I know. These grounds were opened up by Australian sealers out of Sydney and Hobart, many of whom made fortunes.

The Aucklands had a similar history of exploitation. They are considerably larger than the Snares and consist of one big island (Auckland Island) and five smaller ones. On their eastern coasts these islands are deeply indented, and the thickly wooded lower slopes of the inlets display a luxuriant flora (rare for a subantarctic island). On their western sides they present a forbidding and unbroken wall of cliffs 50 kilometres long.

We landed at Erebus Cove in Port Ross, one of the eastern inlets. This was where the Enderby Settlement had been situated. All that remains of it are a few tiles, bricks, and slates scattered among the ferns—and the graves of six people, some of them infants. Yet once over three hundred energetic colonists had lived there. They engaged in shore-based whaling, ship repair, and the provision of fresh meat and vegetables. It all collapsed. Most of the colonists went to Australia. The Aucklands were left in peace until, at the end of the last century, a sheep run was begun, but by the 1930s it, too, had failed. The islands were then designated a fauna and flora reserve. Now no one can go there without the written permission of the New Zealand Government.

One result of this has been the preservation of the birdlife. Altogether, fifty-two species of birds breed there, including four kinds of albatross. After we had filmed the site of the settlement we trudged 5 kilometres over peaty, boggy ground and through waist-high tussock grass to North Cape. This has the largest albatross rookery in the world. It is, quite literally, a city of birds—thousands upon thousands of them. The noise was deafening, a hoarse braying mixed with coarse grunts and clapperings. The scene was one of latent pandemonium. The albatross is the biggest seabird, but we could walk quite freely among them. They didn't move or object to our presence, and the cameraman, who was a wildlife specialist, was ecstatic. He had to be dragged away.

The following day we sailed down the east coast of Auckland Island. Flat-topped and conical hills, interspersed with rocky tors, stretched in a broken array as far as the eye could see. The land rose in tiers towards a western ridge, over which black clouds moved slowly. It was a savage, uplifted land-scape—Gothic, if you can apply that word to scenery.

The southernmost island—Adams—is separated from Auckland Island by a strait, which is called Carnley Harbour and is very sheltered. Here we stayed the night and next morning ran up the western side of Auckland Island to where the *General Grant* was supposed to have been wrecked.

There was a jumble of great frowning walls, knife-edged promontories, and savage black gashes. The tops of the cliffs were covered with mist which periodically cleared, unveiling strange knobs and gargoyle-like projections. One problem that has daunted the salvage hunters is the fact that these giant buttresses have as many caves as Gruyère cheese has holes. In addition, there are constant rock-falls and calving from the cliffs. It is possible that the cave the *General Grant* ran into doesn't exist any more.

Adams Island has a feature that is unique in all the subant-arctic islands—a natural garden called Fairchilds Garden. Flowers and herbs grow in profusion in an area of about 500 acres (200 hectares) as if laid out by a professional land-scaper. There is a sort of lily with long golden spikes, a flower that looks like a huge mauve aster, and another with pure white blooms the size of a big marigold. Others are blue, pink, and green. Botanists can give no satisfactory explana-tion for the garden. It gives one an eerie feeling to sit and watch these unfamiliar flowers bending and waving in the wind on a lonely island in the Southern Ocean.

On Adams I was chased, for the first and only time, by a sea lion. We were walking across the sandhills towards Fair-childs Garden when we heard a great bellow. A bull sea lion was advancing with some speed towards us. I grabbed a piece of driftwood and stood my ground. The others broke and ran. I had read somewhere that the most sensitive part of a sea lion's anatomy is his nose. The sea lion stopped about 3 metres from me and roared. His dirty yellow teeth were as long as my thumb. There were livid scars on his chest and his eyes were streaming. But what I was more conscious of than anything else was the creature's fetid breath. Abruptly he collapsed on his face in the sand and lay perfectly still. I walked away, still holding the piece of driftwood.

The film we made—"Castaways of the *General Grant*"— won a B.A.F.T.A. (British Academy of Film and Television Arts) Associate Award in 1979. I was so taken with the Auckland Islands that I set part of a novel there (*The Golden Spike*), which is loosely based on finding the elusive gold.

Four hundred kilometres southeast of the Auckland Islands lies Campbell Island. It has had a not dissimilar history to the Auckland Islands except that there was no settlement. But there is permanent occupation today—a weather station maintained by the New Zealanders, which includes New Zealand's southernmost post office.

The *Acheron* had to deliver some supplies to this station and collect the mail, so on our return trip we made a detour. Campbell is volcanic in origin and, from the sea, presents a harsh and forbidding appearance. There are sharp pointed peaks and bands of reddish scoria. Unlike the Aucklands there is no green vegetation and no trees. Like the Aucklands, however, are the deep indentations of the east coast. The weather station was on one of them, Perseverance Harbour.

I was not averse to seeing Campbell because of a very curious story attached to the island. A version of it can be found in Will Lawson's book *The Lady of the Heather*. The bare bones are as follows: Bonnie Prince Charlie had a daughter by his mistress Clementina Walkinshaw. She was brought up in France, legitimised as the Duchess of Albany, and became the focal point of Jacobite aspirations. She died, leaving in her turn a daughter, who took over her mother's role. When Victoria came to the throne in 1837, it was decided to wipe the slate clean of other claimants no matter how tenuous their links were. The luckless Duchess was kidnapped and, despite the fact that she was fifty or more, sent into exile "at the uttermost reaches of the earth." Campbell was the island chosen, and she was put ashore there with provisions for one year. A sod hut was built for her and furniture provided. The provisions were renewed annually from Dunedin until her body was discovered on the floor of the hut. Queen Victoria was duly informed and is said to have been suitably saddened.

There are other variations on this theme. One claims she was the granddaughter of Flora MacDonald, the Scottish Jacobite heroine; another that it was the Jacobites who exiled her because she was a Hanoverian spy. Yet another is that she was the granddaughter of Louis XVII but had a Scottish mother.

Whalers and sealers are said to have seen a woman roaming the bare hillsides of Campbell Island clad in Highland dress—a brocaded gown covered by a tartan plaid crossed at the breast. The tartan was Royal Stewart. On her head was a Glengarry bonnet with a silver clan badge. The hut was reported to have lace curtains and to be surrounded by white heather. A path of water-worn pebbles led down to the cove, where the woman patiently sat awaiting the arrival of a ship.

The hut and the path certainly existed. All that remains of the hut now is part of the fireplace. The path is badly overgrown. The heather also existed but, according to records of the weather-station, was wallowed out of that existence by sea elephants in 1953.

There is a depression near the hut, which I was told was the grave. Sir James Clark Ross (the same who was on Kerguélen) saw "the grave of a Frenchwoman" at Campbell in 1840. One hundred years later it was reputedly opened (there is no record of this) and the skeleton of a woman found. Her hands were folded across her chest and in them was a silver crucifix. On her finger was a ring with the Stewart crest (a pelican feeding its young) and motto—*Virescit vulnere virtus* ("Courage grows strong at a wound").

What is one to make of all this? The only feature common to these legends is the Franco-Scottish connection. The name of the island is Scottish. But what about the Frenchwoman? The only evidence for that is Sir James Clark Ross.

There are two other mentions of women being on Campbell Island. One is Elizabeth Parr, who was drowned in Perseverance Harbour and buried on the island in 1810. The other is a woman whom John Balleny, the explorer, took off Campbell in 1840. She had lived there for five years as the concubine of three men.

The story seems to have first appeared in a New Zealand newspaper in 1892. It took a while to surface, but this is not wholly unexpected if there is any substance to it. That substance, it must be admitted, is flimsy enough, but the tale does lend a certain flavour to Campbell Island.

6

Guinea

━━━━━━━━━━━━━━━━━━━━━━━━━━━

I SPEAK OF AFRICA AND GOLDEN JOYS

The first African country I set foot in was Guinea. And the first African leader I ever met was Sékou Touré. That was in Conakry in November 1958.

Later I was to meet many more African leaders: Kwame Nkrumah, Julius Nyerere, Agostinho Neto, Hastings Banda, Amilcar Cabral, Patrice Lumumba. Some became my friends. The closest probably was Abdul Rahman Mohammed, known as Babu, a postal clerk at Ealing, London, a correspondent for *Xinhua News*, a member of the Revolutionary Council of Zanzibar, a Minister for Commerce in Tanzania. He went on to be imprisoned without trial for years by Nyerere. Finally he was released and expelled from the country. "Babu the Zanzibarbarian," as he was wont to call himself.

In the old halcyon days Babu used to travel abroad carrying with him in his briefcase a copy of *Das Kapital* (which he had never read), a gun that Fidel Castro had given him, and $10,000 in used American money. "All a revolutionary needs," he said. But there were others like Tom Mboya, the intelligent and agile Kenyan minister, who was killed by an unknown assailant. Some say a jealous husband, others say terminal politics. One night Tom and I made a pitch for the same Ghanaian girl, but Tom's ability at dancing the Highlife (a sort of Ghanaian reggae) was better than mine and he won her. And there was Eduardo Mondlane, a large and gentle man, a former professor of anthropology at Syracuse University in New York and the founder of FRELIMO (*Frente Libertação de Moçambique*). He was blown to pieces by a parcel bomb delivered at his home.

They were all so full of enthusiasm, so full of hope, so sure of the future. But none impressed me more than Sékou Touré.

I was working in England for the *Manchester Guardian* at the time. Geoffrey Cox, the editor of Independent Television News, rang me and asked whether I could go to Guinea for them as a television reporter. After Guinea we would continue on to Sierra Leone, Liberia, and Ghana. The *Manchester Guardian* agreed, provided I send them pieces as well. So I got my yellow fever shots and, one rainy day, flew from Manchester to Paris and there boarded an Air France Constellation for Conakry.

In France the fortunes of the Algerian War had brought about the fall of the Fourth Republic, and General de Gaulle had assumed power. He decided to head off further Algerias by offering the French African colonies a form of self-government. It was to be put to a referendum in each territory. A "Yes" vote would give the colony local autonomy but leave France in control of foreign affairs, defence, and economic policy. A "No" vote would cut French ties forever. As de Gaulle put it: "What is inconceivable is an independent state that France continues to help."

Only in Guinea was the mood anti-France. Sékou Touré insisted on complete independence for the country: "We prefer poverty in freedom to riches in slavery." De Gaulle's reply to this was, "*Adieu, Guinée.*" As was expected, the vote was overwhelmingly "No" (95 percent).

Cut to the quick, de Gaulle decided to make an example of Guinea. He ordered all French army units, administrators, teachers, doctors, technicians, and citizens out of Guinea within two months. There was an exodus of over 3,000 Frenchmen, their wives and their families. They took with them any French Government property they could carry and destroyed what was left behind. All documents and plans were burnt, all telephones ripped out, all light bulbs and toilet bowls smashed, all windows broken, all uniforms cut up, all cables above ground severed. When Sékou Touré moved into the former Governor's house he found no furniture, no pictures, no cutlery, no linen. The kitchen was full of broken crockery and all the taps had been removed.

That was the situation when we arrived two months after the "No" vote. There were still a few French left—mostly *petits blancs* running garages or pastry shops, some unfortunate *interdits de séjour* (convicts forbidden to return to France), and a handful of left-wing volunteers from French-speaking countries like Belgium and Switzerland. But the Communists had moved fast. There was already a Bulgarian ambassador, and Czechoslovak Airlines planes were parked on the strip at Conakry airport. All was chaos. A visa was handwritten into my passport and signed (the rubber stamps had been burnt). Customs was nonexistent. Taxis were few and far between because of a fuel shortage. But the only real hotel, the Hotel de France, was still functioning and there we put up.

Conakry is on an island connected to the mainland by a causeway. Just off the city lie three other islands—Les Iles de Loos (formerly British). One of them had substantial deposits of bauxite that the Eastern Europeans were setting about developing. Another had the ruins of a British fort on it. When we visited this island—Roume—we were shown a description in *Treasure Island* of a fort that matched it uncannily. There was also a story of an English pirate who had operated in these waters and had buried a treasure somewhere thereabouts. Coincidence? Maybe, but it did make us wonder.

Guinea proper is the area south of the Sahara known to the

Berbers as *Akal n'Iguinawen* ("Land of the Blacks"), the same as in Arabic Sudan, in Greek Ethiopia, and in Persian Zanj, the first element in the name of the island off the East African coast, Zanzibar. The European nations each carved out a "Guinea" along this coast: Portuguese Guinea, French Guinea, Sierra Leone (which the French call English Guinea), and Spanish Guinea. These Guineas gave their name to New Guinea. "Guinea" was also attached to the guinea fowl, the guinea pepper, guinea grass, the guinea worm, the guinea palm, guinea grains, and guinea corn—all of which are native to West Africa. The odd man out is the guinea pig, which originated in South America. In 1663, during the reign of Charles II, a coin was struck "in the name and for the use of the Company of Royal Adventurers of England trading with Africa." These pieces were to bear for distinction the figure of a little elephant. They were made of gold from Guinea, and hence became known as "guineas."

The French took over their part of Guinea in the 1880s—the time of the Partition of Africa—and started banana plantations along the coast, a hot and steamy coast. From Conakry military expeditions marched inland up the mountains of the Futa Jallon (the only mountainous region in West Africa and the source of the Niger, Gambia, and Senegal rivers) to join other expeditions from Senegal on the broad savannah plateaus beyond. They then proceeded to annex what are now the countries of Mali, Burkina Faso, and the Ivory Coast. Before they could do this, though, they had to defeat Samori, a Mandingo warlord who controlled a vast area between the Volta and Niger rivers.

Samori was the product of a chance encounter between the Fulani emperor Ahmadu and a pagan concubine. He converted to Islam when he became an adult and took up slaving. From 1890 to 1898 he was preoccupied with defending his realm against the French. This he did with great vigour and no little skill but, in the end, he was captured and exiled to Gabon, where he died two years later. In Guinea, where the greatest number of Mandingos live, Samori is a national hero. French historians concede that he had an outstanding military record. But his character had its negative aspects. He walled up his son for advising surrender, and the contemporary scholar Amadou Bâ said he "roasted people like peanuts." Areas he conquered still use his name as a curse. He was Sékou Touré's great-grandfather.

The *Résidence* was on the Corniche opposite the Hotel de France. Getting to Sékou Touré was not difficult. He had never been interviewed on television before, and he was most anxious to spread his message to the English-speaking world. That message was an uncompromising pan-Africanism, a rejection of colonialism or neo-colonialism and the development of an indigenous Guinean society based on African models. He came across as a pragmatic, dedicated man. Time was to show that, like his great-grandfather, there was another side to him. Somewhere I still have a picture of myself sitting opposite Sékou Touré under a great tree in the garden of the *Résidence*. He is wearing a stylish black lightweight suit and looks like one of those French Africans you can see sitting at tables in the cafes along the Boulevard St. Michel.

Euphoria was in the air at the time in Conakry. Nkrumah had just proffered Guinea a £10 million loan and union with Ghana. Britain and the United States had accorded the new government recognition. The Eastern bloc was falling over itself to offer aid. Western mining groups were showing interest in Guinea's minerals (the country has huge deposits of bauxite and iron ore). In the heady world of anti-colonialism Sékou Touré was Top Banana and, for a brief period, he strutted the international stage.

Some of this rubbed off on us. We were all interviewed in the local press and on Radio Conakry, *"la voix de la révolution."* We were invited to a performance of the *Ballet Africain* and afterwards met the dancers. Guineans are the best dancers in West Africa, some say in the whole of Africa. A few years before this they had created a sensation in Europe, not the least because the female dancers were all topless. Most of them came from *griot* families, traditional per-formers in Guinean towns and villages. We also met Camara Laye, the Mandingo writer whose autobiography *L'Enfant Noir* (*The Dark Child*) had been hailed in France as a work of art and its author as "the first writer of genius to come out of Africa." And, at Sékou Touré's insistence, we were given a police car with ample petrol to see something of Guinea.

So off we went. Across the causeway, through the indus-trial zone that commences on the mainland, running on a tar-sealed road towards Kindia in the mountains of the Futa Jallon. Away from Conakry the Susus—the inhabitants of Lower Guinea—wear the absolute minimum of clothing. As we passed through the villages, naked children would run shouting and laughing out of the huts, calling "*Bonzurçava*" while their bare-breasted mothers waved from the doorways. The tourist brochure, printed in France naturally, made much of "*les femmes aux seins royaux*" and even had a picture of three posed on the Corniche outside the Hotel de France.

It wasn't until we were well up the escarpment that we saw fully dressed people. These were Fulanis, who are a cross between Tuareg or Saharan Berbers, North African Jews, and Negroes. Today they are mainly Muslims, but they were until fairly recently pagans with traces of Jewish rites and Christian symbolism in their religion. They are an extraor-dinarily virile and enterprising race who entered Guinea about a century before the French and have spread along the southern boundaries of the Sahel (the dry savannah lying between the Sahara desert and the rain forests of West Af-rica) as far as Nigeria. But the Futa Jallon is one of their primary dispersal points. Fulanis are very handsome, and the women wear their hair in a crest like a Roman helmut. Pas-toralists and traders, they are curious about the outside world. We were told a story about a Fulani who wanted to see a map of the globe. He studied it for some time, then turned it over. "Who lives on the other side?" he asked.

Well, on the other side of the Futa Jallon, in Upper Guinea, the Mandingos live. They are also Muslims but agriculturalists, living in compact villages with beehive huts and a central "palaver house." These three groups—Susu, Fulani, and Mandingo—are the main tribes in Guinea though, of course, there are others. Radio Conakry broadcast in eight languages, including French.

We pressed on. Guinea is bigger than Britain and we were traveling on dirt roads—red dirt roads. We got as far as Kankan on the Niger. It is the second most important town in Guinea, with a population of about 40,000 (Conakry has 200,000, and Guinea altogether has about 4.5 million), but it is really no more than a cluster of Mandingo villages around a central trading area. Kankan is the end of the railway line from Conakry. This line was built in the early years of the century in the face of formidable difficulties, and much of the track is like a Swiss mountain railway. The same tourist brochure calls the Futa Jallon "*la Suisse soudanaise*."

On the savannah we saw the only big game in Guinea—elephants—though the River Niger was full of hippopotamuses and crocodiles. We had been away a week, so it was back to Conakry. On the way we made a detour of about 300 kilometres from the village of Mamou to see the Labé Falls, which plummets down in two dramatic drops of about 100 metres each (328 feet). Later the Soviets were to build a tomato cannery at Mamou—the only problem being that no tomatoes would grow in the district, which was too dry.

A few days after our return a man called on me who said he was Her Majesty's Consular Agent (Acting). There was no British Embassy. He was a swarthy man of about forty or more and had one of those surnames that sounds Anglo-Saxon but is obviously made up—like Pecksniff or Chuzzlewit. I thought he might be Maltese or Cypriot. But from the way he was dressed—two-toned tan shoes, a light-weight hacking jacket, and a knotted scarf at the neck—I concluded he was a Levantine, not unlike the character Peter Ustinov played so well in *Topkapi* (1964).

84

HM's Consular Agent (Acting) had seen the reports in the local press of our presence and was anxious to put us in the picture. He was married, he said, "into the country." He was some sort of importer. I met him several times, once at his place of business. On one occasion, he asked me to do him a favour. He collected stamps and specialised in the British Commonwealth and Empire (as it then was). He wondered whether I could get him some of the unofficial stamps issued by Lundy Island in the Bristol Channel and Herm in the Channel Islands. I said I would go down to Stanley Gibbons' shop on the Strand in London and buy some. In return he offered to send me a First Day Cover when Guinea issued its own stamps (they were still using French West African ones). The First Day Cover duly arrived in Manchester. All they had done was overprint the French West African stamps with "*République de Guinée.*"

Over the years I kept a sort of mental scrapbook about Guinea. After all, I had been in on its birth as it were. Any mention of the country interested me. This was how I learnt about the tomato cannery. But there were other fiascos. The Czechs built a shoe factory that had a capacity twice that of Guinea's population, and despite the fact that only 5 percent of the people ever wore shoes. Then in 1961 the Russians sent a shipment of snowploughs to Conakry. One warehouse on the wharf contained 6 tons of Chinese-made quill pens, another cisterns for toilets but no bowls. The Soviets built a new radio station over a vein of iron ore and it never worked. They also built a million-dollar outdoor theatre which was never used. And so on. All these came under well-publicised barter agreements and had to be paid for, so the bulk of Guinea's bananas from the coastal regions and coffee from the Futa Jallon went to Eastern Europe.

Sékou Touré's opportunity to get out of this bearhug came when the Soviet Ambassador was discovered to be involved in an attempted coup. He was expelled, and Guinea cautiously tried to mend its fences with the West.

France still held back. One of the effects of Guinea's

"No" vote had been that the other French territories had readjusted their positions. By November 1960 all the French West and Equatorial African colonies had become independent—at least in name. French aid propped up their budgets, French troops their regimes. But Guinea was a *bête noire* to de Gaulle. He viewed Sékou Touré as a communist, with some reason. Sékou Touré had been a communist in his youth and was a delegate to the Communist Trades Union Conference in France in 1946. But in 1956 he had led a breakaway movement and set up the Federation of African Trades Unions, which, while Left-leaning, was not affiliated with the Communist Party.

What Sékou Touré had inherited from his Communist days, however, was a paranoia about plots equal to that of Stalin. Touré spoke frequently about "a permanent plot" to overthrow his regime, a supposedly vast conspiracy organised by "enemies of the Guinean revolution." Like his great-grandfather Samori, the dark side of his nature took over.

During the 1960s Guinea lived in a constant atmosphere of purges. Sékou Touré used the excuse of these real or imagined plots as a means of eliminating his opponents. Few of his close associates escaped. More than fifty ministers were shot or hanged. About a fifth of Guinea's population emigrated to Portuguese Guinea and Sierra Leone. Through it all Sékou Touré kept on, according to one historian, "like a bare-knuckle eighteenth-century prize fighter blinded by his own blood." The dynamic popular figure I had known and admired became "The Terror of International Imperialism, Colonialism and Neo-Colonialism" (to use one of his own self-imposed titles). I determined to see for myself what had happened in Guinea.

The chance came in 1970. We had been filming throughout Portuguese Africa and were on our way back to Lisbon. I stopped off at Bissau in Portuguese Guinea and took a plane the 400-odd kilometres to Conakry. The crew went on to Portugal.

No more handwritten visas. Everything had the trappings of a police state, and foreign journalists were now decidedly unwelcome. The Hotel de France had become the Hotel de la Révolution, but Sékou Touré still lived opposite it. It took an interminable number of telephone calls to get through to his secretary. A day went by before he replied. Yes, the secretary said, the President remembered me. He would see me the following morning. Did I have television cameras with me again this time?

In the meantime I looked up HM's Consular Agent (Acting). Only he wasn't the agent (Acting or otherwise) any more. There was now a British Embassy. He was still a businessman, though, but older and more worried-looking. I asked him how things were in Guinea and he rolled his eyes towards heaven. When I repeated the question he made the same gesture again. Then he asked me, did I collect stamps? I explained that I saved them and put them into a large box. With that he opened a drawer and produced an envelope full of Guinean stamps that he gave me.

Conakry itself had not changed much. A few new buildings, a larger shantytown, more giant posters of Sékou Touré. The first time I had been in Guinea I picked up hepatitis, so I was cautious about eating at street stalls or drinking anything except bottled drinks. I just wandered around and then retired to the hotel swimming pool.

Sékou Touré looked puffier about the face. Gone was the elegant suit. He was dressed in a Guinean *boubou* (a sort of ankle-length robe), a Muslim cap, and sandals. The interview—I was hoping to get a newspaper or magazine piece out of it—was a disaster. I was treated to a catalogue of plots by French nationals, plots by teachers, plots by traders, plots by the army, plots by trade unionists, and so forth.

"We have developed a strong sense of national identity," he told me, "and mobilised the people towards socialist goals. This is what the plotters strive to undo. But I am *Le Guide Suprême de la Révolution*. I know everything that

happens in Guinea and can nip these plots in the bud.'' I
asked him about the economy. "Good," he said. "Good. The
Western mining companies run our bauxite and alumina industries and market the product. This provides us with all our
revenue.'' Odd words for a confirmed socialist.

There was no reason for me to stay any longer in Guinea. I
rang HM's former Consular Agent (Acting) and said good-
bye. When he learnt I was going back to Bissau the following
day, he invited me to dine at his home that evening. The meal
was a spicy stew, a grass-cutter (a sort of vegetarian rodent) in
pepper pot. It was delicious.

After dinner my host asked me would I do something for
him in Bissau. There was a message he wanted given to a
businessman there. He wrote out his name and address. The
name I will never forget because it was so long: Domingos
Alberto dos Santos Monteiro Neves Fiadeiro. The message
was: *Expect delivery of the parcel of Portuguese stamps I
ordered on the tenth of next month*. It wasn't hard to find
Senhor Fiadeiro in Bissau. He said nothing about the message
but bought me a drink.

A few weeks later back in London I read reports in the
press of an invasion of Conakry from the sea by a force of
Portuguese troops and Guinean exiles. It was the tenth day of
the following month. The aim of the assault was to destroy
the headquarters of Amilcar Cabral's *Partido da Indepênden-
cia da Guiné e Cabo Verde* (PAIGC), which was one of the
most effective nationalist movements ever founded in black
Africa, and to overthrow Sékou Touré. This they nearly succeeded in doing and, in fact, were only stopped in the grounds
of the *Résidence* itself. Cabral escaped also, but he was
assassinated some three years later by PAIGC dissidents.

Sékou Touré carried out a massive purge. Hundreds of
people, including ministers, party leaders, and businessmen
were arrested and put on trial before "the supreme revolutionary court." They were denied lawyers and the opportunity to defend themselves. In truth they were not even

present all the time at their trial. Fifty-eight of them were hanged in public. I often wonder whether HM's former Consular Agent (Acting) was among them.

The plots thickened. In 1972 there was a doctors' plot, in 1973 a counter-revolutionary plot (actually a cholera epidemic), in 1976 a football plot (Guinea had been defeated in the African soccer finals), and later the same year the Minister of Justice, Diallo Telli, a former Guinean diplomat who had been first secretary-general of the Organisation of African Unity, was jailed, tortured, and finally executed by *"la diète noire"*—starved to death.

The economy foundered. An author sympathetic to Guinea, Claude Rivière, wrote: "To set up a textile factory with no cotton, a cigarette factory with no tobacco and to develop a forest region with no roads and trucks were gambles taken by ignoramuses." In 1977 Sékou Touré closed all except state-owned markets. When the market women in Conakry marched on the Presidential Palace, troops were ordered to fire on them. This was reported by the government as "an historic struggle between revolution and counter-revolution." The following year, however, the policy was reversed and the "economic police" who controlled it disbanded.

Then in 1982 Sékou Touré went to New York to appeal to Wall Street for investment. As well he visited Paris for the first time since the 1950s. Had he finally come face to face with facts? Who knows, for he was dead two years later. He had gone to Cleveland, Ohio, for heart surgery and died on the operating table. The following week the regime in Conakry was toppled by a bloodless coup led by Colonel Lansana Conté. The colonel immediately liberalised the country, abolished controls, reestablished normal relations with France, and brought the leaders of the former government to trial.

Perhaps Guinea has a chance at last. As one of its godfathers, so to speak, I wish the country well.

7

Burma

■□■□■□■□■□■□■□■□■□■□■□■□■■

THE ROAD TO MANDALAY

Not to put too fine a point on it, I first set out on the road to
Mandalay when I met Professor Rhodes at Sydney University
during World War II. He had been professor of English at
Rangoon and was evacuated to Australia when the Japanese
invaded Burma in 1941.

Kipling's poem I knew. It was a great favourite as a song in
my youth with its exotic couplets.

> For the wind is in the palm-trees an' the temple-bells they say,
> Come you back, you British soldier, come you back to Man-
>   dalay!

and:

> By the old Moulmein Pagoda, lookin' lazy at the sea,
> There's a Burma girl a settin', and I know she thinks o' me.

But Kipling's letters from there (in *From Sea to Sea*) I did
not know. Rhodes introduced me to them. "This is Burma,"
Kipling says, "and it will be quite unlike any land you know
about." Rhodes also introduced me to Maurice Collis' *Trials
in Burma* and to Shway Yoe (Sir J. G. Scott), who wrote the
two-volume reminiscences of a 19th-century colonial official
that is the great classic of Burmese life during British times.

About George Orwell's *Burmese Days* though, Rhodes was quite scathing. He had met people, who knew Orwell when he was a police officer in Upper Burma, and they had told him Orwell liked neither the country nor its inhabitants. "An upper-class intellectual trying to parade his social conscience" was Rhodes' view.

Years passed.

A cameraman I sometimes worked with in London was an Anglo-Burman, who had left the country when it became independent in 1948. He took me to a Burmese restaurant run by a middle-aged lady he called "Auntie." In Burmese, *"Daw"* or "Aunt" is the respectful form of address for an adult woman; *"U"* or "Uncle" is the same for an adult male. "Auntie" claimed to have the only Burmese restaurant outside Burma. Unfortunately, in the 1960s it was demolished—along with the whole block—to make way for a gigantic office complex. There is, however, a Burmese restaurant in Sydney, run by another Anglo-Burman, that now claims to be *the* only Burmese restaurant outside Burma.

Be that as it may, Burmese cuisine is not one of the world's greats, but it does have some interesting dishes. As might be expected from its geographic location, it is somewhere between Chinese and Indian—they have both noodles and curries. At "Auntie's" I first tasted two quite delicious soups—*hingyo*, a clear soup, and *mohinga*, a fish soup with rice noodles—as well as *kaukswè*, chicken and noodles cooked in a coconut sauce spiced with chilis, garlic, and ginger. Everything is served with *ngapi*—a fermented shrimp or fish paste. Kipling called it "fish pickled when it ought to have been buried long ago," while Shway Yoe noted that "there is nothing in nature more than *ngapi* that hath an ancient and fish-like smell." He was right. They both were.

More years passed. Harold Wilson came to power in 1964, and one of the few things he did was to offer to return the Mandalay Regalia to Burma. This was a gesture of goodwill after General Ne Win, who had engineered a coup in 1962, made a state visit to England two years later. Also it was symbolic. Wilson's government was the first Labour Government after Clement Attlee's, and Attlee had granted Burma independence and allowed it to leave the British Commonwealth, the first of very few countries to do so. The Mandalay Regalia consisted of gem-studded arms, swords, jewelry, and dishes. They had been taken when the British conquered Mandalay in the Third Anglo-Burmese War (1885–86) and sent King Thibaw and his queen, Supayalat (known to the Tommies as "Soup Plate"), into exile near Bombay. Some of the Mandalay Regalia had been stored in the Indian Museum, including Thibaw's throne, but the bulk had gone to the Victoria and Albert Museum in London. It was to be put on display before being sent back to Rangoon.

We judged the moment propitious to apply for a visa to film in Burma. But more of that anon. First, a little background—"a situationer," as Reuters calls it.

Burma is about the same size as Texas and Oklahoma combined. This makes it the largest country on the Asian mainland after China and India but a thinly populated one— only 39 million people. A river, the Irrawaddy, flows the entire length of the country.

There have been three major historical migrations into this area. First came the Mons, who are the same people as the Khmers of Kampuchea (Cambodia) and may have come originally from southwest China. Then came the Burmans, who migrated from eastern Tibet. They pushed the Mons further south and adopted Buddhism and an alphabet from them (it is originally a South Indian alphabet). The third group were the Shans, related to the Thais, who came from southern China. The Shans also gave their name to Siam and Assam where they settled as well. Other groups in the country are the Arakanese, who appear to be a cross between Burmans and Indians; the Kachins; the Karens, who probably came from the Gobi Desert; the Chinese; the Anglo-Burmans; and the Indians.

So Burma is a heterogeneous society and one in which the

constituent parts have often been at loggerheads with each other. At times the government's writ has hardly run further than the outskirts of Rangoon. Since independence the Kachins, Mons, and Shans have periodically been in revolt against the central (Burman) government, and the Karens (who, because of active proselytising by American missionaries, are today predominately English-speaking Baptists) continuously since 1949.

The British first became involved with Burma when the Burmese overran Arakan and Assam and arrived at the borders of Bengal. In 1824 the Burmese invaded India, but they underestimated the strength of the British and were badly beaten. This was the first Anglo-Burman War. As a result of it Britain annexed Arakan, Assam, and Tenasserim (the southern strip that runs along Thailand's western boundary).

In 1852 border incidents flared again and the Burmese sought to pressure the British by arresting two English ships' captains on false charges of murder. The result was the Second Anglo-Burman War, which saw the Burmese routed again and Lower Burma added to Britain's possessions. The Third Anglo-Burman War arose from a dispute about the activities of the Bombay Burmah Trading Company, which the Burmese had fined $4.5 million, and when it was over, Upper Burma had joined Lower Burma, Arakan, Assam, and Tenasserim in a new province of the Raj known as "Further India."

Burma prospered under the British. It became the great rice-bowl of Asia; teak was exploited and oil discovered. Rangoon became the second-busiest port on the Indian subcontinent. But the Burmese themselves were not so enthusiastic. To begin with, they didn't really care for the modern world. (In fact, after they became independent they more or less shut it out.) In addition, the British imported large numbers of Indians, who took over the commerce of the country (most of these were expelled on independence).

During World War II Burma was fought over savagely.

Tens of thousands of Allied soldiers were killed as well as hundreds of thousands of Burmese. Hand-to-hand combat was more common than pitched battles. General Joseph ("Vinegar Joe") Stilwell, Chennault and his Flying Tigers, Wingate and his Chindits, Merrill and his Marauders, General Slim—many will remember these famous names from the time. But the war devastated the country.

After the war the British wanted an interim period of direct rule before independence, but the Burmese demanded it immediately and the Labour Party acceded to their request. So in 1948 the Union of Burma was born with a constitution drawn up by the British to safeguard the rights of the minorities. (This was scrapped by Ne Win when he assumed control.) In economic terms independence was a disaster, and the Burmese Road to Socialism has meant decline and stagnation (and with a per capita annual income of about $190). In 1987 Burma asked the United Nations to classify it among the world's least developed countries.

Getting a visa proved to be a problem. At that time the maximum period foreigners were allowed in Burma was twenty-four hours (it has since been extended to seven days). If your plane was late in leaving (a common occurrence with the Union of Burma Airways) or didn't leave at all (an even commoner occurrence) and you overstayed even by a matter of minutes, you were arrested. To ask for a three weeks' visa, as we had done, was unheard of—and this was when we came up against *ana-dè*, the essence of Burmese courtesy. It means never saying the word No. All sorts of excuses were made for the delay—"We have to contact no less than three different ministries in Rangoon"; "The official responsible has not been on his chair for two weeks"; and so on—but we were never actually told they would not grant us a visa. It was no use explaining that we needed the film in time to coincide with the exhibition at the Victoria and Albert Museum. It was no good explaining that about all we could shoot in twenty-four hours would be a few views of Rangoon. We encountered a wall of polite surprise and regret.

Sterner measures were obviously called for. A mutual friend promised to make an approach to Ted Willis (the mastermind behind Labour's successful election campaign and, later, to be elevated to the peerage by Wilson; Willis was also the writer for *Dixon of Dock Green*, in the 1950s one of the longest-running television series in the United Kingdom). We were given to understand that Willis would apply direct to Wilson on our behalf, and—since the Mandalay Regalia *was* Harold's baby—I tend on balance to think this ploy made the difference, though the Burmese Embassy had another story: "The official responsible is back on his chair."

We flew to Delhi and on to Calcutta where we boarded the twice-weekly Union of Burma Airways flight to Rangoon. The plane was a shabby DC-4 that looked as if it could do with some proper maintenance. The cameraman pointed out the bare patches on the tires as we walked across the tarmac.

When we arrived at Mingaladon Airport, we found that the "official responsible" had failed to notify Immigration of our three weeks' visa. The officer crossed out "three weeks" and substituted "twenty-four hours." I finally persuaded the Chief of Immigration to ring the Burmese Foreign Ministry. It took more than an hour to sort that one out. But this was only the beginning. Although we had an International Carnet listing all our equipment duly stamped by H.M. Customs at London Airport, the Burmese Customs refused to accept it. They wanted us to post a bond equal to the value of the cameras and tape recorders. This was to be done in US dollars and represented considerably more money than we had between us. Once again I suggested a call to the Foreign Ministry. Two hours later someone arrived and signed the Carnet. Then we were escorted to the People's Bank counter and asked to change most of our money into *kyats* at the official rate, a third the black market one.

Finally out into the street. There stood a collection of ramshackle museum pieces—Rangoon's taxis.

"Thakin, Thakin," the drivers shouted, vying for our attention and jostling competitors out of the way, "Sahib,

Sahib!'' ''Very modern automobile,'' some cried out, proudly motioning towards a late forties Austin or Ford, ''first-class wheeling accommodation!''

We at last chose one a little less dilapidated than the rest. The driver even had a business card. His name was U Saw Percy Pe. Percy commandeered another taxi for our luggage, and as soon as we were safely aboard his he asked us—as is the custom of cab drivers in socialist countries—whether we had any whisky, cigarettes, or clothing for sale and would we like to change our dollars at the black market rate.

We arrived at the Strand Hotel—mildewing façade, peeling white paint, colonnaded front—the best hotel in Rangoon. Once mentioned in the same breath with Raffles in Singapore or the Taj Mahal in Bombay, it has sadly slipped. But there are still the little touches—a ''lost and found'' cabinet in the reception area with thimbles, hat-pins, and fans behind the glass; brown Windsor Soup on the menu; the musty smell; the slowly-revolving ceiling fans; the occasional scampering rat. From my room on the second floor I looked out across a broad road at a little park and beyond it the yellow-coloured Rangoon River.

''I pick you up tomorrow and drive you airport, Thakin,'' Percy said when he was being paid. He was quite taken aback when he learnt we would be there for three weeks. But he rallied immediately. ''I hiring you,'' he said. ''And I get girls. Some nieces, very young. You must go into the country—only five miles—police too active in the city.''

We were obviously in experienced hands so we agreed to employ him on a daily basis.

Rangoon was more or less laid out by the British. The tree-lined streets are wide—and pot-holed. There are no tall buildings and very little traffic. It is hard to believe that 3 million people live there. Much of Rangoon is run-down, dirty, decayed. Over everything hangs an air of neglect.

Percy took us for a drive around the city, pointing out many florid colonial buildings—the High Court, a Victorian-

Mogul edifice of red and yellow brick; the National Museum, which used to be the Bank of India and where the Mandalay Regalia was bound; the City Hall, a massive structure; and the Anglican Cathedral. ("Closed now, Thakin. All the Anglo-Burmans go. To Australia, I think.") The grid-style streets were still called by their English names—Godwin Road, Dalhousie Street, Phayre Street—though doubtless they had other, Burmese ones.

Right in the centre stands the Sule Pagoda. It is the highest building in the city (48 metres, or 157 feet) and sits in the middle of a traffic island. As with all pagodas, visitors should walk around it in a clockwise direction. There are eight sides dedicated to the eight days of the week, the eight cardinal points, the eight animals, and the eight planets. (In Burmese astrology the week has eight days—Wednesday being split in two—with each day represented by both a planet and an animal.) The Sule Pagoda is supposed to be 2,000 years old and to contain a hair of the Buddha. But the name Sule is the name of a *nat* or local nature spirit. It is the existence of these *nats* that makes Burmese Buddhism different from all others.

Theoretically, the Buddhism practised in Burma is the Theravada form (the doctrine of the elders), otherwise known as *Hinayana* ("small ferry boat"). This is the more rigorous form of Buddhism. To achieve *nirvana* a person must work at his own salvation. The other form of Buddhism—*Mahayana* ("great ferry boat")—is a bit less demanding. Belief alone is enough to ensure salvation and eventual *nirvana*. Theravada Buddhism is the form followed in Burma, Sri Lanka (Ceylon), Thailand, Laos, and Kampuchea. *Mahayana* Buddhism is found in Tibet, Bhutan, Sikkim, China, Korea, Mongolia, Japan, and Vietnam. Zen belongs to *Mahayana* Buddhism as do the various forms of Tantric Buddhism. Theravada is the more conservative of the two, but in Burma it has had to incorporate the *nats*.

There are thirty-seven *nats* who are the survivors of the

primitive spirits worshipped by the Burmese before they adopted Buddhism. Mostly they are malevolent. Burmese, they say, love Buddha but fear the *nats*. Theravedic Buddhists cannot invoke the Buddha (*Mahayana* Buddhists can), so when a Burmese needs help he calls on one of the *nats* and makes an offering to it of flowers, food, or money. *Nats* can also foretell the future, so soothsayers and astrologers frequent pagodas dedicated to *nats*. Which is why Sule Pagoda is the centre for Rangoon's fortune-tellers.

But the pagoda that dominates Rangoon stands 3 kilometres to the north—the great, gilded Shwedagon. Somerset Maugham described it in *The Gentleman in the Parlour*: "The Shwe Dagon rose superb, glistening with its gold, like a sudden hope in the dark night of the soul. . . ."

With its massive bell-like stupa soaring nearly 100 metres (328 feet) above the hilltop on which it is situated, the Shwedagon is said to have more gold on it than is in the Bank of England. Eight hairs of the Buddha are enshrined in the stupa. This rises from its platform in traditional pattern—first the inverted bell (Buddha's begging bowl), then the banana bud, and finally the *hti* or umbrella at the summit. The bell is covered with gold leaf but the lotus flower and the banana bud have 13,153 square gold plates. The seven-tiered *hti* is similarly gold-plated and the tip of the stupa is set with 5,448 diamonds and 2,317 rubies, sapphires, and topazes. (I didn't personally count these gems. The information came from a guidebook.) The topmost vane with its flag turns in the wind. This golden stupa is surrounded by more than one hundred other buildings—smaller stupas, pavilions, and administrative halls. To quote Maugham again: ". . . emerging from among them like a great ship surrounded by lighters, rose dim, severe and splendid, the Shwe Dagon."

The origins of the pagoda are encased in myths, but it certainly dates back at least 2,500 years though it has been rebuilt many times. Queen Shinsawbu (1453–72) gave it its present shape and ordered that her weight in gold be beaten into gold leaf and used to plate the stupa. This has become the accepted custom. I even bought a packet of gold leaf at a pagoda bazaar and made my modest contribution. The gold leaf doesn't last very long since Burma is in the tropics and has a heavy rainfall.

It was the lunar month of *Pyatho* (December/January), the month of temple festivals, and we filmed one of these at the village where Percy's so-called "nieces" lived. There were boat and pony races, magicians, astrologers, soothsayers, and boxing troupes. There were also *pwès*. This is Burmese theatre, popular street theatre. George Orwell described a *pwè* in *Burmese Days*. The one we saw and filmed was a *zat pwè*, a mixture of music, dance, and drama with clowns, dancers, acrobats, and epic figures out of the past—all clad in magnificent costumes. Burmese, like Chinese, is a mono-syllabic language and much of the humour rests on puns. But there is plenty of mime as well. People sit on the ground in front of a fenced-in area, hawkers weave in and out selling nuts and cheroots—the same "whickin' white cheroot" that Kipling's Burma girl was smoking. Burmese girls still smoke them, so do their grandmothers, holding a little brass basin to catch the ash and sparks. All Burmese smoke cheroots, even the children, though there is a saying that children are not allowed to smoke before they can walk. Being wreathed in smoke from a cheroot has one advantage, however. It insulates the smoker from the prevailing odour of excrement, urine, and decaying vegetation.

Despite my conditioning, so to speak, begun long ago with Professor Rhodes on Orwell and with the Anglo-Burman in London later to be reinforced by frustrating officialdom, I began to realise that Burma and the Burmese were special. There was an effortlessness, a timelessness about the land and the people. "When I die I will be a Burman," Kipling said. Physically, Burmese are very beautiful, a lithe and animated race. Their clothes are simple and the same for both sexes—the *longyi* or cotton sarong and the *aingyi* or transparent muslin shirt. They are friendly, always smiling, and they treat foreigners with great courtesy. But foreigners exist very much on the periphery of Burmese life. What little impact the West has had on Burma is more in the nature of a passing parade.

We had seen all we wanted to in Rangoon. It was time to move on. But we discovered that most of Burma was out of bounds to strangers, particularly strangers armed with cameras. In the end we were allowed to fly 620 kilometres north to Mandalay and, on the way back, to Pagan. We had wanted to visit Pegu, if only to see the club, reputedly the most splendid in the Raj after the West of India Club at Poona and the Ootie Club at Ootacamund. And we had also wanted to see Moulmein and go to the Inle Lakes, where the rowers use one leg to propel their fishing boats. But it was not to be.

Mandalay, the capital of Upper Burma, is a comparatively new city, a little more than a century old. It has none of the faded colonial charm of Rangoon, being instead a sprawling, dusty place. The city takes it name from Mandalay Hill, a 236-metre hill (774 feet) behind the site of the former Royal Palace. The city spreads south and east of the palace and the streets are arranged on the grid pattern again. Only this time they have numbers instead of names, a bit like New York. Roads run east-west, streets north-south.

We began with Mandalay Hill. It was not far from the Tun Hla Hotel, where we stayed, a Burmese-style hotel but quite comfortable albeit not exactly replete with modern conveniences. Mandalay Hill is a maze of covered stairways, which contain small temples on each landing. These have the usual signs in English: "No Umbrellaing," "No Footwearing," and I even saw "No Shorting," which I presume meant "Do not wear shorts." "No Spitting" was conspicuous by its absence, which was very odd as this sign really belonged there.

From the top of the hill we could see right across the Mandalay Plains and down onto the empty palace enclosure.

To the west was the Irrawaddy, to the east the Shan Plateau. The Japanese had a stronghold here during the war and in 1945, British and Indian troops suffered heavy casualties storming it. We returned to the base of the hill by the south-west stairway and took our shoes off again under the stony stare of the guardian *chinthe*—a sort of lion-griffin that guards sacred places. Wingate named his Chindit guerillas after the *chinthe*.

We then entered Kuthodaw Pagoda, known as "The World's Largest Book." This is because 729 marble slabs have been arranged around the central pagoda. On them is written the entire *Tripitaka* (the Buddhist canon). It was created by a team of 2,400 monks and it is estimated that a man, reading for eight hours a day, would require 450 days to read the complete book.

All that remains of the wooden Royal Palace is its walls and the moat. During the war it was completely destroyed by fire and is now the headquarters of the Burmese army.

The flight from Mandalay to Pagan took about half an hour. The plane followed the course of the "huge and ochreous" Irrawaddy and landed at the town of Nyaung-U, a few kilometres from Pagan. Pagan is in the same class as Angkor in Kampuchea or Polonnaruwa in Sri Lanka—one of the great ruined religious cities of the world. On the plain covering more than 40 square kilometres stand over 2,000 red-brick pagodas. In Shway Yoe's words:

> . . . the whole place is thickly studded with pagodas of all shapes and sizes and the very ground is so covered with crumbling remnants of vanished shrines, that according to the popular saying you cannot move foot or hand without touching a sacred thing.

It is an elephants' graveyard of pagodas. They were erected between the 11th and the 13th centuries. In fact, Kublai Khan overran Pagan in 1287 and put an end to the building of temples, but not before about 13,000 religious structures had been erected. Not only have many of them now dwindled to a pile of rubble, but the Irrawaddy has washed away as much as a third of the ancient city.

Pagan's greatest monuments are within easy reach of the village and, as the best way to get around is by *tonga* (horse-drawn cab), we hired two—one for the crew, one for the gear. By mid-afternoon we had filmed enough and returned to the hotel. Normally all the equipment would have been unloaded and carried into the hotel room but, as the cameraman wanted to get some shots of the ruins at dusk, we left it in the *tonga*. The driver assured us he would be there all the time, parked outside the hotel.

When the cameraman came out well before dusk, he found the driver asleep. He also found that all our unused film stock was missing—six 400-foot rolls of 16mm Eastman Colour Negative. Without film he could shoot nothing. We called the police who arrived, asked a few questions, and promptly arrested the driver. They released him soon afterwards for he came back to the hotel to get his money. "Some rascal took the box, Thakin," he said, "to sell the film on the black market in Mandalay."

We wondered who would buy ciné film. Burma does have a small film industry, mainly commercials for the cinema with the occasional feature based on legends of the past. But at that time it was all in black-and-white and, in any case, 35mm. For us, Burma was over. There was no point in trying to order fresh stock from England. We would miss getting a few shots, that was all.

We reckoned without the Burmese Customs. At the airport they accused us of selling the film and threatened to prosecute. They went so far as to call a policeman to arrest us. Once more I suggested phoning the Foreign Ministry. After all, an official from that ministry had signed the Carnet. Once more it took a long time to sort things out.

As it is forbidden to take Burmese money out of the

country, I spent the *kyats* I had left on lacquerware at the airport shop. Burmese lacquerware is particularly fine. The best has a horse-hair base underneath the resin. The supreme test is to bend the sides of the article together so that they touch without the lacquer cracking. I got a few pill boxes in the shape of the *shwe hintha*, the golden mythological duck. I also bought some *zi-gwe*, mythological owls. One is supposed to have two of them, and they must be placed facing the door so that they will protect the dwelling from evil spirits. If a real owl lands on the roof and hoots, however, the *zi-gwe* are powerless. Someone is going to die. My owls are sitting on my bookshelves facing in the right direction and, so far, evil spirits have kept away.

8

South-West Africa
(Namibia)

▭▭▭▭▭▭▭▭▭▭▭▭▭▭▭▭▭▭▭▭▭

AS I WAS GOING DOWN GOERINGSTRASSE

Germany was the last European power to acquire substantial overseas colonies. In 1878 it did not own any territory beyond its borders. Twenty years later it ruled over large tracts of Africa—in the south-west, in the centre, in the east. Germany also possessed a number of island groups in the Pacific and seemed set to inherit what was left of the Spanish and Portuguese empires.

Most of these acquisitions were the product of a single year—Cameroon and Togoland in July 1884; South-West Africa in August; New Guinea in December; German East Africa in May 1885. Thirty years passed and, in World War I, Germany lost all its colonies: Cameroon and Togoland to British and French troops, South-West Africa to South African, New Guinea to Australian, German East Africa to British and Belgian. The Australians took Nauru, the Japanese the Marshall and Caroline islands, the New Zealanders Samoa.

But the Germans are still sentimental about their brief colonial empire and are delighted to hear that there are German loan-words in New Guinea Pidgin or that they are remembered with grudging respect in Cameroon and part of former German East Africa (Tanzania). Above all, they are aware that German life and culture are alive and well in South-West Africa.

Since 1968, South-West Africa has been known as Namibia. That is, to all the members of the United Nations. To the South Africans it is still known as South-West Africa and considered a province of the republic. So it was to the South African Government that I had to apply for permission to film there. This I did in Pretoria. I had already filmed in South Africa, Lesotho, Botswana, and Swaziland. But this cut no ice. The head of the South African Information Services explained that foreign film crews or journalists were not allowed into South-West Africa. The issue of the future of the country was a running sore that needed no exacerbation. Even South African film crews had difficulty getting permission to go there.

Parliament was sitting so I flew down to Cape Town. The Minister for Foreign Affairs had been the South African Ambassador to the United Kingdom and I knew him personally. He received me and arranged an interview with the Minister of the Interior. I told him that we were not interested in taking sides in the labyrinthine dispute with the United Nations over the independence of Namibia. What we wanted to do was to present the country as it was and let the viewers make up their own minds.

This proposal was sent forward to the Prime Minister and quickly granted. South Africans are often impressive in their efficiency.

Back in Pretoria they refused to believe me until they had spoken to Cape Town. But, having confirmed that what I said was correct, they swung into action and the next day we left for Windhoek, the capital of South-West Africa. A man from the Provincial Administrator's office met us and was to accompany us everywhere we went.

South-West Africa was Germany's second largest colony

and the only one suited to white settlement. But there was no harbour on the inaccessible coast (Walvis Bay was at that time a British enclave), there was not enough water for agricultural development, and the minerals were difficult to extract. Settlers and capital had to be enticed from Germany.

Chartered companies were given concessions and expected to develop the country. Within a year the *Deutsche Kolonialgesellschaft* had lost a lot of money and failed to set up any lasting administration. Bismarck was forced to send an Imperial Commissioner, Dr. Heinrich Goering (the father of Reichsmarschall Hermann), to sort things out. There's a street called after him in Windhoek. The name—Goeringstrasse—is set into the pavement in brass letters.

Dr. Goering's first task was to persuade the African chiefs to accept German protection. Many were, understandably, reluctant. The Germans sent in troops. This led to two wars of pacification—the Nama (Hottentot) and the Herero War —between 1904 and 1907.

General von Trotha issued a *Vernichtungs Befehl* (Extermination Order) after the defeat of the Hereros. The British Government's *Atrocity Blue Book* for 1918 quotes the order as having required the killing of every Herero man, woman, and child. At the end of this period the Governor, Theodor Leutwein, reported:

> After having spent several hundred millions of marks and having deployed several thousand German soldiers we have, of the three assets of the Protectorate—mining, farming and native labour—destroyed the second entirely and two-thirds of the last.

In Germany these campaigns excited a great deal of interest. They were the German equivalent of General Gordon's exploits in the Sudan. Many books were written about them. One, an eye-witness account, is rather good, a sort of German *Red Badge of Courage*, called *Die Reise von Peter Moor nach Südwestafrika (The Voyage of Peter Moor to South-*

West Africa), and it was written by Gustav Frenssen, a Schleswig-Holsteiner. After one battle Peter Moor says to his comrades, "There is a large number of dead on the field but no wounded." And a Hussar replies: "Don't be stupid. We don't take any prisoners."

Later, when the Herero people break through the German lines and take to flight, Moor comments:

> The enemy had fled to the east with their whole enormous mass—women, children and herds. The next morning we pursued them. In the path of their flight lay blankets, skins, ostrich feathers, women's ornaments, cattle and men, dying or dead. All this life lay scattered there, both man and beast broken in the knees and spirit, helpless and in agony it looked as if it had all been thrown out of the air.

The war was over. Von Trotha boasted that his army had killed 65,000 Hereros. According to official German figures, only 15,000 starving tribesmen remained in South-West Africa. The victorious Von Trotha was recalled, and his successor, Governor von Lindequist, revoked the *Vernichtungs Befehl*. But, even then, the Hereros' troubles were not over. The survivors were put to work on railway and harbour construction, and many died from ill-treatment or disease. Herero women vowed never again to bear children while Germany occupied their country. They kept this pledge until South African troops entered South-West Africa eight years later.

The Nama and Herero Wars were the last wars Germany won this century. Despite his comments on the destruction they had caused, Governor Leutwein firmly believed that the native must be kept in his place. He also wrote a book about his experiences during this time. It is called *Elf Jahre Gouverneur in Deutsch Südwestafrika (Eleven Years Governor of German South-West Africa)*. In it are two photographs—both posed. One shows a group of German officers sitting and eating at a table. The napery is snow-white, the cutlery gleaming, the behaviour obviously correct. They are waited on by smiling Herero servants. The other photograph is a reverse of this scene though the people in it are the same. This time drunken Hereros, eating with their hands, throwing bones on the floor, etc., loll in the chairs while shocked German officers act as waiters. The message is blatantly pointed, and its flavour hangs, rather more subtly, in the South-West African air to this day.

Which brings us, as Joyce said, "by a commodius vicus of recirculation" back to apartheid. The League of Nations granted South Africa a "C" class Mandate—the only one granted—over South-West Africa. Which meant that the territory, being adjacent to South Africa, was to be administered as an integral part of the mandatory power. South African laws applied to South-West Africa. South-West Africans became South African citizens. Afrikaners from Angola (the Thirstland Trekkers) were resettled in South-West Africa, others migrated from South Africa as did English speakers. In 1966 the United Nations terminated South Africa's mandate. In 1971 the International Court of Justice ruled that South Africa's presence in the country was illegal. South Africa took the view that it had conquered the territory in 1915 and that this conquest had been recognised by the League of Nations in its sole "C" class mandate. Now that the League of Nations no longer existed, South Africa was entitled to full possession of South-West Africa. And indeed, until 1966, South Africa had complied with the conditions of the mandate despite the fact that the League of Nations shut up shop in 1946. No other mandate of World War I had been revoked and the affected country turned into an independent territory, which is, in effect, what the United Nations was trying to do. And there the matter rests, unresolved.

The argument behind the theory of apartheid is that each group—racial or religious—in a multiracial, multicultural society has the right to preserve its own identity. In South-West Africa's case this means the Hereros, Namas, Berg-Damaras,

Bushmen, Germans, Afrikaners, English, and mixed bloods (Basters and Coloureds) should all be kept separate from each other. It smacks a little of feudal fiefdoms—and it is patently unworkable.

I have heard representatives from these groups support this policy, often at the "I-don't-want-my-daughter-(son)-to-marry-a-man-(woman)-from-another-race-or-tribe" level. I have heard other representatives from the same groups deplore it, pointing to the iniquities of the system. Many Africans have told me that what they really want is simply to enter modern life and the middle class with a franchise based on income and education. Others—notably supporters of SWAPO (South-West African Peoples' Organization)—say that what they want is the "glorious misery" of independence: one man–one vote and a bloody struggle.

History has found solutions to similar seemingly intractable racial problems in the past. The commonest is hybridisation, which generally takes centuries or even millennia. South Africa's solution may well result in a bloodbath, if the world clamours for a quick result. In my opinion, it is more likely to come about through market and economic forces. But even that takes time.

I have also noticed a dichotomy of perception in Southern Africa. Most Africans see the white man as an interloper who not only has the Africans' cake but eats it too. For his part the white man just doesn't see the African. Physically he sees him, of course, but mentally he does not. And, in many cases, the African is put out of the way, in a township or on a Bantustan (tribal homeland). Since at present whites and Africans interact almost exclusively in an authoritarian/menial relationship that gives whites all the political and economic power, each race must walk parallel streets that cannot meet.

A similar situation exists in South America. The Andean Indians know that mestizos and whites live in their countries, but they don't really acknowledge them. Filming once in

Ecuador I was astounded to find that one could poke a camera almost into an Indian's face—only to be ignored. We were told, "For them you are not there."

Whites in Southern Africa are afflicted by a form of this blindness. Africans are there, but they are not part of the real world, or at least not of the world that matters to whites, the world of the cake.

The cake that constitutes South-West Africa is almost as big as France. The country has two large areas of desert—the Namib, which runs along the entire western Atlantic coast, and the Kalahari in the east towards neighbouring Botswana—with an area of fertile central highlands between them. And South-West Africa is a nearly empty country, with less than two people per square kilometre, half of them living in the relatively small tribal area of Ovamboland in the north on the border with Angola, the rest occupying the remaining four-fifths of the land.

It is also a thirsty country. The northern border is the Cunene River, the southern the Orange. Yet between these two rivers—1,400 kilometres apart—there are no other permanent rivers, only their dry beds.

Windhoek, the exact geographical centre of South-West Africa, lies at 1,800 metres (5,904 feet) in the middle of the Khomas Hochland, the richest, best-watered, most temperate part of the province. Here live the majority of South-West Africa's 25,000 Germans. And Windhoek is a very Teutonic place.

Strategically placed on a central hill is the *Alte Feste*, a fort straight out of *Beau Geste*. Not far away is the *Christuskirche*, the Lutheran cathedral. And in the same area are three Rhenish castles—*Schloss Schwerinburg, Schloss Heinitzburg*, and *Schloss Sanderburg*. They were built by a German architect named Willi Sander. He built *Schloss Sanderburg* for himself, the other two for Graf Schwerin, a German count who lived in one and installed his mistress in the other. It is said that every afternoon, before visiting her, Herr Schwerin would send his butler across to *Schloss Heinitz* with his calling card. If it was returned with the corner folded down he was not welcome.

All three castles are small buildings (as castles go) with thick stone walls, round towers, crenellated keeps, and big sash windows. The same architect built the former Administration Building—the *Tintenpalast* or Ink Palace—a long, two-storied, arcaded structure overlooking gardens full of palm trees and bougainvilleas and streets full of Mercedes Benzes and Porsches.

Behind the city are Moltkeblick and Bismarckhöhe, the highest peaks of the Auas Range, and along the Kaiserstrasse one hears mainly German spoken. Even the Hereros speak it to each other, the women in brilliantly coloured Victorian dresses with bustles and leg-o'-mutton sleeves, a legacy of German missionaries.

At the hotel where we stayed, the *Thüringer Hof*, the Muzak was Strauss waltzes, the menu had *Kraftbrühe mit Ei* on it and lots of dishes with sauerkraut, the furniture was Biedermeier (heavy Victorian German), the receptionist wore a dirndl and had plaits. The atmosphere was *echt Deutsch*.

It was decided that we should first go south along the spine of the central highlands to the karakul district of Mariental. Later we would cross the Namib Desert to Walvis Bay and Swakopmund and then travel north to the Etosha Pan.

Karakul sheep (the name means "Black Rose" in Uzbek) were introduced into South-West Africa by the Germans in the early years of this century. This breed came from Central Asia, and the pelt of the newborn lambs is called astrakhan or Persian lamb. It looks like watered silk and is highly valued by furriers. South Africa is the world's largest producer of karakul skins—both black and grey. The biggest buyer is the Hudson's Bay Company followed by Germany. Every German woman wants a *Persianer* coat.

On the way back from Mariental we made a detour to Rehoboth. This is a very curious place. It is the capital of the "Republic of Bastards." Most of the inhabitants are half-castes whose ancestors came originally from the Cape of

Good Hope. Known as Basters in Afrikaans, they trekked into South-West Africa long before the German occupation and established the *Baster Republiek*, 8,000 square kilometres of the finest karakul and cattle country in all South-West Africa.

They have their own *Volksraad* or Assembly and are, to a certain degree, self-governing. To get permission to enter the *Baster Gebied* (the Bastard Reserve), as it is now known, we had to apply to the *Kaptein*, who was also the magistrate. There are about 29,000 Basters, many of them wealthy sheep and cattle ranchers. They speak an old-fashioned Afrikaans dialect and wear wide-brimmed felt hats like Voortrekkers. Many of them have Scots surnames—McNab, Campbell, etc.—and they vary in skin colour from brown to a light tan.

Indeed, the Basters are supposedly eager to "whiten" themselves up—so much so that they encourage white men to marry into their community by offering a farm as a dowry. We heard stories of their paying a fee to any young white man who would sleep with a succession of Baster girls. They even kidnapped two German sailors who had jumped ship and held them for this purpose. "Going on a stud week," as it was called, is apparently one way of making money in Windhoek and enjoying it.

Under the laws of the *Gebied*, however, there is no civil imprisonment, a litigant cannot employ a lawyer unless the other side consents, all fines go into the community chest, and a Baster can sell his farm or ranch only to another Baster.

There did seem to be one problem in the *Gebied—dop* or cheap Cape brandy, made from the grape skins left over after wine production. Heavy fines are imposed on whites who sell or even give the Basters *dop*, but public drunkenness was widely evident in Rehoboth when we were there.

In Windhoek we had to submit the rest of our itinerary to the police—not because they thought we might try to contact political dissidents, but because where we were going was such dry country that there was always the danger of death from thirst if our vehicle broke down. The Diamond Police were also interested since illegal diamond dealing, poaching, and smuggling are all too common in the territory. South-West Africa in fact produces most of the gemstones that come onto the world market.

These can be found in the *Sperrgebiet* (Prohibited Area) on the Diamond Coast between Lüderitz and the mouth of the Orange River. Establishment of this forbidden region dates back to German times, hence the German name. We did not go there. No vehicle can enter the *Sperrgebiet*, no vehicle can leave it. Rumours are spread of electrified fences, watchtowers, armed guards who shoot on sight, and so on. The diamonds are found in windswept valleys parallel to the sea. They have come, geologists say, from ancient marine gravel beds formed during very high sea levels 70 million years ago. The scouring winds concentrated the gems on the valley floors, while removing most of the sand overburden. And there are the usual tales, such as the one of a visiting school-teacher who went for a short walk along the beach. When she returned she shook the sand from her shoes, and a diamond fell out. Such is the stuff of folklore. But as a result everyone in South-West Africa has diamond fever.

The Namib is one of the oldest deserts in the world, and its dunes, which invariably run northwest-southeast, are the highest. In Nama the word *namib* means "where there is nothing." This is not entirely true. The Namib is a cool desert, made so by the icy Benguela current that flows north along the South-West African coast. A clammy sea mist rolls over the Namib one day in five, protecting it from the sun and bestowing the moisture that allows a unique flora and fauna to flourish. The fauna is mainly beetles, scorpions, termites, and spiders, the flora largely succulents. The most remarkable plant is certainly the *Welwitschia Mirabilis*—Marvellous Welwitschia. Resembling a monstrous sea anemone, it squats on the sand—a metre in height with a trunk that may measure up to nearly 2 metres (about 6 feet) in circumference. Each century two leaves like wide straps grow from a woody central core. Around each plant is a tangle of dried-up leaf tissue, shredded by centuries of winds. Carbon datings have shown that the *Welwitschia* can survive up to 2,000 years. No wonder that the naturalist Friedrich Welwitsch, who discovered it in 1859, exclaimed, "I am convinced that it is the most majestic creation that Southern Africa can offer."

We crossed the Namib—it is about 160 kilometres wide, though 1,900 kilometres long—and arrived at Walvis Bay (Whale Fish Bay), the place where whales are said to come when they intend to make love. This is the only deep-water anchorage between Luanda in Angola and Cape Town in South Africa.

It is a waterfront—quays, cranes, fish canneries and fish reduction plants, warehouses and storage depots—but little else. Away from the port, nothing but wooden houses and tin shanties. And sandstorms. Walvis Bay has to battle against constant sandstorms. *Soo-oop-wa*, the Nama call these winds that perpetually moan, sough, and sigh amid the yellow-grey dunes.

Bartholomeu Dias discovered Walvis Bay in 1487 but, apart from the Dutch, nobody visited it except the British, who took possession in the late 18th century. After the American War of Independence put a stop to the transportation of convicts to Virginia and the Carolinas, the British Government looked for alternative sites. Indeed, before finally founding a penal settlement at Botany Bay in Australia, they seriously considered Walvis Bay. Today it is the centre of South-West Africa's pilchard industry—in the 1960s the largest in the world (the cold Benguela current again). But it can't be considered a pleasant place to live in.

Just 40 kilometres north of Walvis Bay, however, *is* a pleasant place—Swakopmund. Here the winds do not blow as insistently and the dunes never encroach on the town. It is South-West Africa's seaside resort and has a charm all its own. Partly this is due to the architecture—wherever one looks there are Gothic turrets, cupolas, and half-timbering—and partly because Swakopmund is a healthy place. In German times it was the port of entry, though a difficult one. There was no harbour and ships had to lie offshore. Cargoes were unloaded into lighters which carried them through the surf to a jetty. Soon German princes were being entertained in the mansions of the Hamburg merchants, who settled there, and it became the summer residence of the governor. (Bismarck sent his illegitimate son to Swakopmund.) There were tales of wild goings-on. The town had flair.

In Swakopmund I met a friendly resident who invited me into his mock Tyrolean home for a *Swakopmunder Bier* (light bitter) and presented me with a calendar carrying the picture of Sam Nujoma, the leader of SWAPO. (Our host was European!) He also gave me a large chunk of amethyst, that I still have. In the dried-up rocky bed of the Swakop River all sorts of semiprecious stones can be found, as indeed they can all over South-West Africa—aquamarines, agates, amethysts, beryls, chrysoprases, garnets, tourmalines, and topazes.

An hour's drive north of Swakopmund lies Cape Cross, known for its sealing, rock salt, and guano. It is a desolate place and is as far as one can go along the coast. Beyond Cape Cross the traveler is "outside the Police Zone," to use the official phrase. Here begins the Skeleton Coast, a treacherous area of shifting sandbars with no water and no vegetation that contains not only the skeletons of men, whales, and seals, but of the countless ships that have been wrecked on its ever-changing shore.

Cape Cross has the greatest colony of fur seals to be found anywhere in the world. They inhabit 10 kilometres of slippery rocks and, during the mating season, the bulls will attack a man. They will seize him by the arm, attempting to throw him off balance, then roll over him, crushing him to death. There's a special cemetery at Cape Cross for the men who have been killed by seals over the years.

From Cape Cross we headed northeast to Brandberg across the southern Kaokoveld. The sand of the inner Namib is brick red and the grassy plains between the dunes support large numbers of gemsbok and springbok. It was here that we came upon a small group of Bushmen. Our guide was at pains to discover where they had come from. He thought probably from the northern Kaokoveld. But, as they could not speak Afrikaans, English, or German, and as he could not speak their language, we never found out. They managed to get some cigarettes from us, despite the linguistic barrier.

While they were lighting up, I took the opportunity to examine them closely, having read all about Bushmen in Laurens Van der Post's books. I also knew that Hottentots were similar, though taller. Bushmen are a little people, barely five feet tall (152 cm), with delicate hands and feet and apricot-coloured skin. That skin becomes very wrinkled and loose when they get old. They have peppercorn hair, pointy chins, prominent cheekbones, and a pronounced epicanthic fold to the eye like Mongols. Altogether I was reminded of pixies.

But it is their buttocks that are the strangest feature. They protrude at right angles to their bodies and seem to sit in midair. The women's are swollen out of all proportion, a condition called steatopygia and one, I gather, much desired by the males.

They have other peculiarities. The man's penis is permanently semierect. The women possess the so-called "Hottentot Apron"—labia minora four inches (10 cm) long like wattles. This, apparently, turns other Africans on, not to mention whites. As our guide told us, "Once you have a Bushman you are spoilt for all other women."

We made signs that we would like to film them. They didn't seem to object and went on chattering among themselves. Bushmen speak the world's most complex languages phonetically. The distinctive feature of these languages is the click sounds. There are between five and seven of these sounds, dependent on the language, but each click has a number of consonantal accompaniments, which yield up to eighty different click segments.

When the click sounds are written down it looks like the

sort of language used in comic strips for extraterrestrials. There is the dental click (/), which sounds like "tsk, tsk"; the palatal click (!), a loud popping sound like pulling your finger out of your mouth; the alveolar click (‡), a snapping sound, like a twig breaking; the lateral click (//), the sound we use for urging a horse on; and the bilabial click (⊙), which sounds like a kiss.

The Bushmen are a race apart and were the first inhabitants of Southern Africa. They were followed by the Hottentots and, much later, by the Bantu and Europeans, who entered the country at about the same time from opposite ends. It is odd that the later comers all borrowed click sounds from the Bushmen. The Hottentots (a Dutch word meaning "stammerer") have the most (four), but some Bantu languages have three (dental, palatal, and lateral). The South African singer Miriam Makeba recorded a song about them in Xhosa (the *Xh* is the aspirated lateral click) called "The Click Song" that became well known around the world. Even Afrikaans (a language native to Southern Africa, after all) has a click, the dental one, spelled *tjie*, which serves as a diminutive.

Today there are about 34,000 Bushmen in South-West Africa. A few still live as their ancestors did, as primitive hunters and gatherers. Most now work for farmers, usually Afrikaner farmers, as goat and cattle herders.

Brandberg we saw from almost 100 kilometres away. It is like a giant version of the famous Ayers Rock in Australia, rearing up 2,600 metres (8,530 feet) out of the flat veld. We had come to Brandberg to see The White Lady, a rock painting that has aroused great controversy. First, though, we had to get to the cave shelter. This meant an arduous climb up the Tsisab Valley, a ravine strewn with granite boulders. The site is by a freshwater spring, and The White Lady is the central figure in a frieze that covers the wall of the main cave. I have seen Stone Age cave paintings at Lascaux in France and Altamira in Spain and I have seen Aboriginal cave paintings in the Northern Territory and on Cape York Peninsula in Australia, but I have never seen anything quite like The White Lady.

She is graceful, a lithe ballet dancer caught in mid-movement. She is decorated with anklets, necklets, and bracelets and has a girdle around her waist. Her feet are shod and she carries a cup in her hand. And, while she is white, her companions are black. They show, incidentally, steatopygia. What is such an unlikely figure doing in such an unexpected place? Some have thought she was Egyptian, others Cretan, others again Berber. No one knows. Perhaps she is, after all, simply Bushman. Beautiful, alluring, astonishing—The White Lady is all these with the added spice of mystery.

We pushed on, passing the mining complex of Tsumeb. Tsumeb is a mineral storehouse. It is the sixth largest copper producer in the world, has the second largest silver-lead mine in the Southern Hemisphere (after Mt. Isa in Australia), and produces zinc, cadmium, vanadium, with, most valuable of all, germanium.

At last we reached Etosha Pan. Etosha can be translated from Ovambo several ways but the most apt is "the place of dry water." The Pan is a vast inland sea of clay some 6,000 square kilometres in extent set in a national park the size of Switzerland. This is the world's largest game reserve and nowhere else is it possible to see such enormous herds of wild animals, even at Serengeti in Tanzania. Once the Pan was fed from the Cunene River and was a proper inland sea. Nowadays the Omurumba Ovambo, a watercourse which flows after heavy rains, is the main feeder, though there is another one with the resounding name of Etaka Nepoko Ekuma Oshana. When the rains come the Pan is briefly filled, and all around great seasonal migrations of game move across the landscape.

What struck us first was the number of zebra. This is one of the zebra's principal habitats, and there were literally thousands upon thousands. Alongside them were their grazing companions, the blue wildebeest (gnu), a large, clumsy-looking animal. But there were others: the three big antelope, the gemsbok, eland, and kudu; the giraffes; springbok, with occasional dik-diks (antelope no bigger than a hare). And the predators and scavengers: the lions, cheetahs, hyenas, leopards, vultures, jackals. Not to mention the elephants and ostriches.

We spent two days filming this abundance of wildlife, staying in the old German fort of Namutoni, which has been refurbished as a tourist rest house. It is a national monument, the most northerly of the German strongholds. If you close your eyes you can imagine the Foreign Legion emerging from its arched gateway. Namutoni was built to some medieval plan. Towers at each corner of a large rectangle provided the officers and men with comfortable quarters. High white walls enclosed the courtyard. To while away the time the officers would play cards, using a naked Herero girl's stomach as their card-table. Here, in 1904, seven German soldiers defended the fort against five hundred Ovambo and killed one hundred and fifty of them.

On the morning of the third day the cameraman decided to get some shots of the sunrise and climbed the walls of the fort. He was finishing filming when he missed his step and fell 6 metres (about 20 feet) to the ground. He was a heavy man and the camera was underneath him. Its turret was badly damaged, the lens knocked out of alignment. The cameraman was also badly damaged. Later we learnt that he had two broken ribs and a fractured pelvis. A plane was hastily summoned from Windhoek and we returned without our guide. He had to drive back. South-West Africa was over.

What does the future hold for this country? What the future holds for South Africa presumably. Or does it? In 1978 the United Nations formulated an independence plan for Namibia and recognised SWAPO as "the sole and authentic representatives of the Namibian people." Despite this the South Africans installed an interim government and, as of July 1987, a sixteen-member Constitutional Council was drafting a constitution that does not discriminate on the basis of race. The Europeans number about 100,000—65,000 shrewd and stubborn Afrikaners, 25,000 enterprising and industrious Germans, 10,000 commercially minded English. The Africans number about 1 million, of which the Ovambo are 590,000 and their near neighbours in the north, the Okavango, 111,000. In addition there are 89,000 Berg-Damaras, 89,000 Hereros, 57,000 Namas, and 34,000 Bushmen. The mixed bloods—Basters and Coloured—number 78,000. But maybe there are more Africans than these figures suggest. SWAPO has recently claimed that well over a million people live in South-West Africa.

Yet the Europeans are compartmentalised. They are involved in different areas and in different occupations. They rarely intermarry. The only place their genes mingle is in the veins of the Basters. But the Africans are also divided. The Hereros (Bantu) and the Namas (Hottentot) have waged bloody war against each other. Both despise the Berg-Damaras (non-Bantu of unknown origin), whom the Namas enslaved and the Hereros call "Baboons." Both fear the Ovambo (Bantu) because of their numbers and because of SWAPO, which is essentially an Ovambo organisation. Both fancy Bushman women, but they have driven them into the deserts. As for the mixed bloods, they are in between as usual. The template of apartheid. There is no easy solution.

9

Socotra

▭ ▭ ▭ ▭ ▭ ▭ ▭ ▭ ▭ ▭ ▭ ▭ ▭ ▭ ▭ ▭ ▭ ▭

SINDBAD'S ISLAND

The Federation of South Arabia—1964. Sweltering among the hot, barren rocks of Aden, an unattractive town if ever there was one. That year the easy-going torpor of colonial life came to an end for British officials as well as for Indian clerks and merchants, Somali and Yemeni labourers, and Gulf Arabs working in the oil refinery. A hand grenade had been rolled into the Oasis Bar in the docks area of Ma'alla, killing two British servicemen and wounding fourteen others.

That was followed by snipers on rooftops, soldiers searching cars at roadblocks, coils of barbed wire around government buildings, and a rapid buildup of troops. The British called their opponents extremists. They called themselves Freedom Fighters. They were mindless thugs, cast in the familiar Middle Eastern mold. So began three years of a particularly dirty little war until the United Kingdom pulled out and the People's Democratic Republic of Yemen was born—a Marxist state that left the British Commonwealth and immediately embraced the Soviets. Since then, a harbour which once handled more shipping than London or New York has become practically deserted, and the refinery that made it one of the greatest oil bunkering ports in the world has closed down. Politically, the People's Democratic Republic of

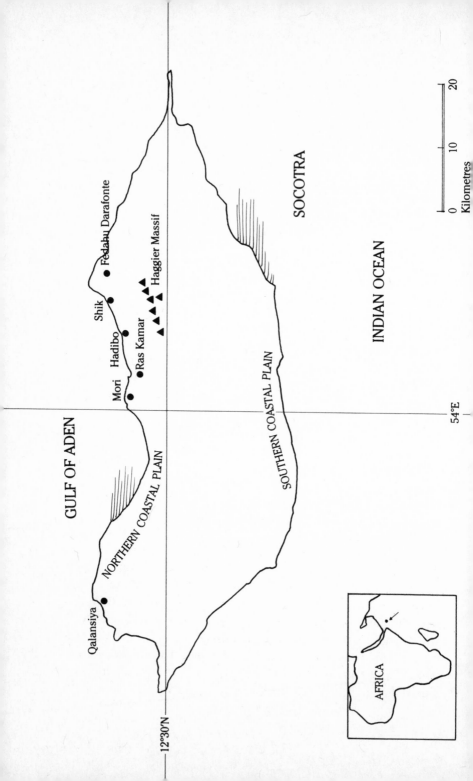

Yemen has followed a similar line to Libya's by giving refuge to terrorists and attempting to destabilise neighbouring states. It has launched an invasion of Oman to the east and has had a number of border clashes with Yemen to the north. January 1986 saw twelve days of pitched battle, using tanks, artillery, planes and naval vessels, between rival Marxist factions of the ruling party in which 4,000-odd were killed, not to mention those civilians who got in the way.

We were staying at the Crescent, a fairly clean hotel, and were about to return to London with a story on how the residents had been coping with the emergency when there was a cable from the office. It read: PROCEED SOONEST SOCOTRA STOP GERMAN EXPEDITION DISCOVERED ROCK STOP.

Thinking it was a joke, I cabled back: HARD ROCK BRIGHTON ROCK ROCK OF AGES QUERY. The answer was short and sweet: SINDBADS ROC REPEAT ROC STOP.

This took me back to my childhood, when I had read about the seven voyages of Sindbad the Sailor in Andrew Lang's *Arabian Nights Entertainments*. I borrowed a copy from the Union Club and refreshed my memory. As recounted in this version, Sindbad (usually spelled Sinbad) on his second voyage lands on a desert island having a wild aspect and thickly covered with strange trees. He wanders away from his companions, eats a meal, drinks some wine, then falls asleep by a little stream. When he awakes his companions have gone and so has the ship that brought them. Sindbad climbs a tree and sees, far off, something white that attracts his attention. When he gets closer he realises it is a gigantic white ball "with a circumference of about fifty paces."

The sun is setting and suddenly it becomes quite dark. A bird of most extraordinary size—"like a large cloud"—is approaching. Sindbad rightly deduces that the bird is a roc and that the white ball must be its egg. He positions himself alongside the egg and, when the bird sits on it, Sindbad sees in front of him "a leg as big as the trunk of a tree." Our resourceful hero takes off his turban and binds himself to this leg so that, when the bird flies away next morning, it will carry him with it and deposit him on another, hopefully inhabited, island. This it does and Sindbad finds himself in the Valley of Diamonds where he has further adventures.

Later, on his fifth voyage, Sindbad sees a second roc's egg on a different island. This time his companions break it open to extract the chick, which they roast and eat. They have hardly finished their meal when "two immense clouds" appear some distance away. They hurriedly reembark and put to sea but it is too late. The rocs quickly size up the situation and bomb the vessel with huge stones which sink it. Sindbad manages to float clear by hanging on to a piece of wood.

Marco Polo also mentions the roc. He says it lived on some islands off the east coast of Africa. Kublai Khan was brought what was claimed to be a roc's feather which was as big as the frond of a palm tree (this is what it may well have been). At the Forestry Exhibition in Edinburgh in 1884, roc's quills were supposedly shown. These were, in fact, the midribs of a *rofia* palm which had been stripped of its leaves and cooked to resemble a bird's quill. The roc features in Persian and Arab legendary tales as a bird so enormous it could carry off an elephant in its talons and whose eggs were sometimes as large as small temples.

One hardly knows what to make of these stories. Was the roc actually some sort of great eagle? Perhaps elements of the Mauritian dodo went into its description. Or was it purely mythical like the *garuda*, the Indian bird on which Lord Vishnu was supposed to have ridden? In any case, what on earth had the German expedition found? Surely not a live roc. Maybe a fragment of bone?

Aden Airways had no service to Socotra. There was nothing there, the girl explained. No hotel, no vehicles, no roads, no electricity apart from the generator that supplied the radio station, no visitors, nothing. The only way to get to Socotra was by dhow from Mukalla in the Hadhramaut. That

Socotra

didn't sound too promising but, still, the Germans had made it across somehow.

"Go and see the Royal Air Force," said the public relations man at The Secretariat on Steamer Point (the seat of the British colonial administration). "They run routine training flights there. Maybe they'll put you on the next one."

And they did. They also provided us with camp beds, sleeping bags, and folding chairs, and advised us what to take in the way of provisions—tins of bully beef, soda biscuits, raisins. They were doing a series of flights in transport aircraft at weekly intervals, so we could come back whenever we wanted. A week would be enough, we said. More than enough by the sound of the place.

So, bright and early one morning we took off from Khormaksar. The first leg of the trip was 500 kilometres due east over the Hadhramaut, which means "Death is Present" in Arabic. It is an apt name for a jagged, bare landscape with occasional fertile patches between dry, windswept mountain ranges. After putting down at Mukalla, we headed southeast across the Arabian Sea towards Socotra. Another two hours of flight brought us over the airstrip at Ras Kamar and, because of the southwest monsoon, we had a rather bumpy landing.

Ras Kamar was an old RAF base and during World War II had quite an important anti-submarine function since Socotra sits astride the sea route between Suez and India. Ruined huts lay all around.

By the time we had our gear and provisions unloaded, some men had appeared with camels. They came from the village of Mori, which was close to the airstrip. One had a smattering of English. I spoke no Arabic except for some common barrack-room expressions, *shufti, bint, imshi*, and *mafish* ("look," "girl," "go," and "finished"), but I was soon to learn another essential word—*kam* ("how much?").

Kam shillings for the camels? They held up their hands, closed their fists and opened them twice. Twenty shillings for

125

a camel. We needed five—one for each of us and two for the gear. Socotra was not going to be cheap in the area of transport. They wanted half in advance, half when we got to Hadibo, the capital, 12 kilometres away. Otherwise they would not budge. So we had to agree.

Socotra lies in the Arabian Sea about 550 kilometres south of the Hadhramaut and some 250 kilometres east of the Horn of Africa. The island is roughly 130 kilometres long and 40 kilometres wide (its area is 3,600 square kilometres), and the population when we were there was somewhere around 10,000. Half the people live on the coastal plains, where they graze small black sheep, cultivate tobacco and dates, and trade in both. They are the result of centuries of mixing between Arabs, Indians, and Africans with a few European elements—mainly Greek and Portuguese. The other half, who live in the mountainous interior—the Haggier—have cattle the size of calves and grow a sort of millet. They are the aboriginal inhabitants, known as the Sokotri.

The latter are fascinating, not the least because they are one of the most unknown peoples in the world. Small, light-skinned, curly haired, round-headed, they belong to the general group of Veddoids—a category into which Australian aborigines are sometimes put. Veddas exist in Sri Lanka (Ceylon) while the Andaman Islanders and certain groups in India display similar characteristics. They were the ancient inhabitants of the Arabian Peninsula until driven into remote fastnesses by long-headed, straight-haired Semites.

No European has ever learnt Sokotri, which seems to be a daughter tongue of the ancient language of South Arabia—Sabaean, the language of Balqis, the Queen of Sheba. A Sabaean inscription has been found on a rock near the only port—one that is partly silted-up—Qalansiya. And some of the brands on the camels appeared to be letters of the Sabaean alphabet. Europeans have, of course, heard Sokotri. We heard it ourselves, and it was a stimulating experience to listen to sounds that perhaps the Queen of Sheba herself might have uttered—somewhat jerky, sibilant sounds, a bit like Welsh. As Mabel Bent, the wife of an archaeologist, wrote in her book *Southern Arabia*: "In subtlety of sound Sokotri is painfully rich."

The ancient Egyptians knew of Socotra. In fact there is some suggestion that it is the "Land of Punt" though there are two other contenders—Somalia and Dhofar, the westernmost province of Oman. There is an Egyptian story about a nobleman shipwrecked on the Island of Pa-anch, a strange, rugged, wooded place. He meets a huge serpent, its coils covered with gold. The serpent tells him that it is the ruler of the country, and the nobleman promises to give it riches from Egypt in return for helping him get back to his homeland. The serpent replies, "You are not rich in myrrh but I have myrrh all of my own."

The interesting thing about this fable is that Socotra is the only island that produces myrrh. Socotra also has aloes, frankincense, and dragon's blood. They were used with myrrh for medicinal purposes and embalming—but not only for those, as this verse (an invitation to love-making) from the Book of Proverbs shows: "I have perfumed my bed with myrrh, aloes and cinnamon."

The Egyptians also called Socotra "The Terraces of Incense," and there exist to this day in the mountains a number of man-made terraces the significance of which is unknown. The name of the island in Sanskrit was *Dvipa Sukhadura*, from which Socotra is derived (and also the Greek name for the island—Dioscorides). It means "Isle of Bliss," but this demi-paradise of the ancient world is today a poor, barren, backward, forlorn place.

And so we came to Hadibo, the ramshackle capital of Socotra and the seat of the Sultan's government (the Sultan, who was also Sultan of Mahra in the Hadhramaut, was deposed in 1967, when the People's Democratic Republic of Yemen came into existence), a small town with narrow streets of one-storey houses, a mosque, and about five hundred people. Our self-appointed cameleer cum guide deposited us in front of a house occupied by a small detachment of the Hadhrami Bedouin Legion, which guarded the government radio, the only link between Socotra and the outside world. The wireless operator, who was in charge, spoke English of a sort—radio English, I suppose one might call it. At the end of every sentence he said, "Over and out."

We explained why we were there, but he had already had a message from the British Adviser and Resident at Mukalla. First he would have to find a house and some women to clean and cook for us. Then we would have to pay our respects to the Sultan. He wasn't in Socotra at the time, but his Prime Minister was.

The house was right next door—really only four mud walls, a courtyard, a cooking place, and a flat roof where we slept for coolness. Two women were hired to sweep out the house and courtyard and to prepare the meals. They were young and African in appearance. Indeed most of the people we saw in the streets of Hadibo would have been at home in Zanzibar or Malindi. The women were prepared to provide us other services as well. Whenever we went to the communal toilet on the palm-fringed beach, they would follow us, lift their skirts, make discreet but obvious gestures, and say *"Kam?"*

The Prime Minister was a scrofulous-looking, one-eyed individual whose main concern was whether we had any cigarettes of not. We gave him a couple of packs and a Bic lighter, which pleased him no end. In his turn he offered us camels at a cheaper rate.

The Germans, we discovered, had been there for more than a month and had their own radio. They were camped in the *jebel*—the Haggier—a day's journey away and were excavating old grave sites. No one knew what they had discovered, if anything, so we decided to delay our trip into the mountains and film a little background material in Hadibo and the other nearby towns.

There was really only one—Shik, the former capital, a decayed little village on a silted-up freshwater lagoon lined with date palms. Yet this was the port where the Egyptians, Indians, Greeks, and Romans had arrived. It is first mentioned in a shipping manual called *Periplus of the Erythrean Sea,* written by an unknown Greek mariner in the first century A.D. According to him many of the inhabitants of the northern coastal plain were Greek. Alexander the Great had reportedly stopped off in Socotra after attempting to conquer India, and some of his soldiers had stayed behind when he sailed away.

St. Thomas was supposed to have been wrecked here on his way to India and to have converted the Sokotri to Christianity. The Alexandrian traveler Cosmas reports that, in the 6th century, the people were Greek-speaking Nestorian Christians under a bishop appointed by the Metropolitan of Persia. Marco Polo, some eight hundred years later, says much the same. Certainly the Sokotri were Christian for a long time but well out of the orthodox stream.

A Carmelite friar, Padre Vincenzo, saw the last vestiges of the religion in the 16th century. People carried crosses before them in processions, assembled three times a day in small stone churches where they prayed before an altar with candles on it, burned incense, frequently used the word "hallelujah," were monogamous, and buried their dead in caves "walled up to the roof with stones."

All this disappeared when the Wahabis (a puritanical Muslim sect to which the ruling house of Saudi Arabia belongs) attacked Shik in 1800, destroyed the towns on the northern plain as well as the churches and graveyards, and converted those left alive to Islam. Most of the Sokotri fled inland, where their descendants still are, but Arabs with their African slaves gradually resettled the northern area.

Before this happened, however, the Portuguese briefly occupied Socotra. One of their navigators, Captain Fernandes Pereira, discovered the island in 1503 and, noting the nominal

Christianity of the inhabitants, thought he had found an obscure part of the kingdom of Prester John, the legendary medieval Christian priest and king. Three years later Admiral Tristão da Cunha arrived at Shik to conquer the island and protect the Christians "against the Moors," who already had a fort and a mosque there.

It was to be a bloody fight. There is a painting of the siege in the Military Museum in Lisbon done by an eyewitness, Jorge Colaço. The Portuguese lost heavily but, in the end, overran the position. They converted the mosque into a church and christened it "Our Lady of Victory." Four years later they left. Socotra was not worth the trouble. The road-stead was unsafe during the monsoon, the lagoon only suitable for ships with a shallow draft. The Portuguese became established at Mombasa and Hormuz, but all that remains of their presence in Socotra is a hill to the east of Shik called *Fedahu Darafonte* (Delafonte Hill) and oranges (the Sokotri word for orange is *tanija*, the Portuguese *laranja*). Arabs from Mahra moved back and mixed with the Sokotri.

When William Finck, the first Englishman to visit Socotra, called at Hadibo in 1609 for his vessel to take on fresh water, he found the son of the Mahri Sultan of Qishn installed there. Finck had this to say about Sokotri women: "Some of them are reasonable white, much like to a sunburned country maiden in England, very dainty yet scarcely honest." Sir Thomas Roe, the Elizabethan ambassador to the Great Mogul at Delhi, dropped anchor there in 1615 and said that the Mahri Arabs had assumed control of the island by a recent conquest. He added: "The old inhabitants dwell in the mountains and are very numerous." In 1834 the British Government occupied the island with Indian troops and tried to purchase it. When they gained possession of Aden in 1839 they moved out, Aden being a much better place for a coaling station. Then in the 1880s the sultanate of Mahra along with the rest of the Hadhramaut came under British protection and Socotra was British for the next eighty-seven years—eighty-seven virtually undisturbed years. It was one of the Empire's more stagnant backwaters.

At dawn on the third day we repaired to the Sultan's camelry and chose five beasts for our venture into the interior. The women wanted to come with us, suggesting by gesture that liaisons would be easier in the Haggier. Their price had come down too, but we firmly resisted the temptation. Later we learnt that to be taken *in flagrante delicto* meant instant exile by the next dhow for any Socotran woman. As Mukalla was the usual destination, where absolutely no work was to be had, the town's only brothel was full of such women.

Our goods were put in coconut-frond panniers, but first a number of rugs were placed on each camel's hump. The load was then forced into a high ridge along the animal's back by ropes around its belly. The purpose of this was to raise the rider and whatever is carried above the height of the scrub that grows everywhere and prevent their being brushed off.

Perched precariously on these elevated humps, we followed a wooded valley in a southeasterly direction. After about an hour some frankincense bushes were pointed out to us. Apparently they were few and far between in this part of Socotra but in abundance near Qalansiya on the northwest tip. It looks like something rotten and is middling high with a blotchy trunk, many straggly branches, and spiky leaves. The bark is thick and bluish, and the woody fibre of the trunk, distended with sap, reminded me of a bloated fish. A clear yellow resin oozes out. The Sokotri make a dozen oblique slashes in the trunk of a bush, digging the lower end out into a little hole. In this the resin collects and hardens. This resin, known as olibanum, is burnt nowadays (at first it emits a thick, black smoke that soon turns to curling, white wisps with a fragrant, slightly antiseptic smell), though in former times it was also used as a medicine (it was recommended to

Pliny as an antidote against the hemlock). For thousands of years it was one of Socotra's most valuable exports, but today very little is harvested.

It is the same with myrrh. The myrrh tree grows at a slightly higher altitude and is like a low, spreading cedar. It also exudes an aromatic gum that is used in perfumes and incense but it is ruddy brown (the painkiller given to Jesus at his crucifixion was probably myrrh and wine). Socotra is full of strange trees—Sindbad the Sailor was right. The highest parts of the Haggier Massif are among the oldest land surfaces in the world. They have never been submerged by the sea and support forms of plant and animal life not found anywhere else.

As we climbed higher up a wadi we became conscious of this. Above us, great craggy peaks soared 1,500 metres (4,920 feet) into the clouds. All around was a moonscape dotted with alarming shapes. Adenium trees were like naked torsos stuck upside down in the ground. From one base, two or three pulpy trunks would spring, each crowned with a garland of stiff leaves. Or cucumber trees, their grey trunks so distended they seem to have elephantiasis, with a fruit like a cucumber hanging from each trunk. And everywhere aloes. Socotra aloes was once the most highly prized of all. A purgative—bitter aloes—was made from it, and the trade flourished until well into last century. But modern laxatives have replaced it. About the only use for bitter aloes these days is to prevent children from biting their nails.

Above 600 metres we came upon groves of dragon's blood trees. They resemble nothing so much as an inside-out umbrella. Dragon's blood is a sort of palm and a thin, watery deep-red resin flows from the fruit at the end of the short branches. It also used to be in demand as a purgative. In this barbaric and distant place the silence was absolute, and there were insects as well as plants and trees that I had never seen before. It was like entering a primeval world, the *Urwald*, and my soul shivered.

At midday we were in some sort of pass, the wadi far below us. Looking back we could see the coastal plain and the sea beyond. Once through the pass there were meadows with tinkling streams. Low stone huts stood in little groups. *Bombe*—small-grained millet—was cultivated in gardens, and grazing on the meadows were the tiny, short-horned Sabaean cattle. These are unlike the usual African or Asian cattle. They have no hump, possess a deep dewlap, and make excellent milkers. Ghee or clarified butter is the principal product of Socotra. It is renowned along the shores of the Arabian Sea and even as far afield as the East African coast.

This was the country of the Sokotri and soon we saw them, though we felt sure they had been watching us for some time. Slight little people with European-looking features and close-cropped hair, the men wore *futa* or Yemeni kilts, the women a sort of shift. Both garments were brown. Some of the young women were very beautiful with fine, large eyes and flashing smiles. Their simple diet—milk, dates, and millet—was apparently healthy.

Our guide, who spoke Sokotri—as did all the coast Arabs—asked where the Germans were. Five kilometres further on, we were informed, at the head of another wadi. Their camp was on one of the ancient Terraces of Incense.

The archaeologists had just returned from their dig when we arrived. A group of students who said they were from Tübingen University on the edge of the Black Forest, they had been inspired by an expedition from Oxford some years before that had removed a large number of skeletal remains and made some interesting discoveries. Socotra, they said, was virgin territory, and to prove it they showed us what they alleged (tongue in cheek) was a piece of a roc's eggshell. Well it was something anyhow. We had to wait until morning to film it. What we saw in the cold light of day was a slightly curved, yellow-white, pitted bit of material about half an inch thick and the size of a small bathroom tile. In fact, it looked suspiciously like a bathroom tile that had buckled under heat. But it wasn't ceramic and they assured us the composition was definitely calcium. By measuring the curvature, they had estimated the so-called egg was the size of a beach ball. Not exactly Sindbad's "fifty paces" but still, bigger than a dodo's egg and much larger than an ostrich's.

What was it? They really didn't know. The roc's egg story was in the nature of a publicity stunt and they certainly hadn't expected a British television team to show up. A bit of a flurry at Tübingen was all they had counted on. At first someone in the group had suggested a phoenix's egg. That mythical South Arabian bird is also associated with Socotra. The phoenix that arose from the ashes, according to Pliny, took the nest of its predecessor to the City of the Sun in Paanch and there deposited it on an altar. But then it was remembered that the phoenix sprang from the fire that had destroyed it as a worm before it turned into a bird—hence, no egg. The roc was a far better peg on which to hang the mysterious discovery. Besides, everybody knew about Sindbad the Sailor. So what was probably meant to be a harmless undergraduate prank ended up costing us both time and money.

My own opinion is that what they had found was a shard of some unknown pottery-like substance. In ancient Socotra there was supposed to have been a sort of glassware made of lime fused with dragon's blood resin. Of course, dragon's blood resin is deep red. Frankincense resin is yellow, though.

We filmed the caves the Germans were excavating. Piles of bones dating from about 1000 A.D., a few baked clay beads, some still coloured, nothing more. There have been reports of rock paintings from Socotra but we saw none. We also filmed the Sokotri and their everyday life. Some of them lived in caves similar to the burial caves. They had almost nothing in the way of possessions but seemed happy. Happy and hospitable. We were always offered some milk and dates. Just before our camelcade left, a little Sokotri girl shyly gave me a bunch of flowers. They were a bit like geraniums. I kissed her, which astonished her, and saved one of the flowers, pressing it in my diary. I had it for some years but, unfortunately, mislaid it.

Our cooks/housemaids were reluctant to see us depart from Hadibo. As a last concerted effort they lowered their price to what might be considered the bargain-basement level but to no avail. I tried to make it up to them by giving each an extra five shillings in addition to her wages. They could scarcely believe their good luck on getting such an amount, but I thought they really *had* tried their damnedest.

The RAF transport was on time and on a direct flight. Three hours later Aden came up under the port wing, looking just as Kipling describes it in "Barrack Room Ballads":

> . . . 'umped above the sea appears
> Old Aden like a barrack stove,
> That no one's lit for years and years.

I sent a cable to London: STORY A BEAT-UP STOP. Then I went down to Aden Airways to book our passage home.

The Russians have a base in Socotra today, presumably the old RAF station at Ras Kamar. It has also been reported that they have some submarines there. If this is true it can only mean they have dredged out the lagoon at Shik and made it into a port again. I wonder whether the women at Hadibo now ask, "*Kam* rubles?"

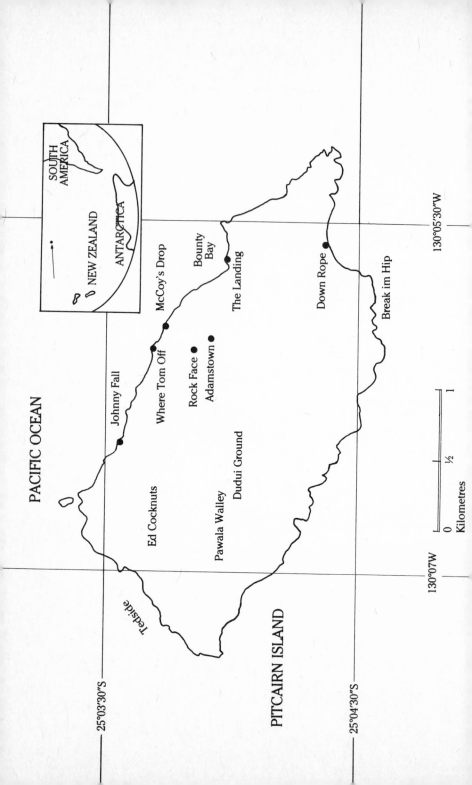

10

Pitcairn Island / The Cook Islands

THE BOUNTY MUTINEERS

The mutiny on the *Bounty* is one of the South Sea's most enduring legendary tales. Almost everyone knows, in one form or another, the story of Captain Bligh and Mr. Christian, of the seductive maidens of Tahiti, and finally the mutineers' search for a safe haven far from the reach of the British Royal Navy. But comparatively unknown is the fate of Fletcher Christian's party—the nine Britons, twelve Polynesian women, and six Polynesian men—which landed on Pitcairn Island and became castaways after they set the *Bounty* afire.

The setting might seem ideal for a variation on Adam and Eve (and the apple) in a South Pacific Eden, or for the man-and-woman-on-a-desert-isle fantasy that is the staple of many of those who have written about the South Seas. But the *Bounty* mutineers did not find Paradise and they did not live happily ever after.

There is a Polynesian proverb— *"He wahine he whenua i ngaro ai te tangata"* ("By women and land men are destroyed"). And on Pitcairn Island it proved all too true. This unique multiracial, multicultural experiment failed. The mutineers held the racist and sexist attitudes that were common to their time (and not uncommon in our own); they quarrelled over the land and fought over the women; factions formed and reformed within the little community—and finally they fell upon one another with murderous intent. In the end, only one man, John Adams, was left alive along with the women and children who had survived. Then, perhaps surprisingly, he turned in remorse to the Bible for solace, and Pitcairn became an oasis of piety, sobriety, and gentleness—at least during the reign of Queen Victoria, who was greatly impressed.

In 1977 we decided to make a dramatised documentary on the *Bounty* mutineers and the lesser-known events that made up the formative years of their Pitcairn Island colony—from the burning of the ship in 1790 to the island's rediscovery by an American sealing captain in 1808. I was an executive with New Zealand's second television channel, and this was to be one of a series of such films set in the South Pacific. Since New Zealand had a small community of Pitcairners and the Office of the Commissioner for Pitcairn Islands was in Auckland, it seemed natural for us to attempt this project.

Research, however, proved a daunting task. The *Bounty* story is not just a story—it is an industry. The mutiny on the *Bounty* has been the basis of more books than all the other maritime mutinies put together. Captain William Bligh was himself the first off the mark. In 1790 he published his account of the mutiny and the subsequent incredible journey in an open boat from Tofua in Tonga (where the mutiny took place) to Timor. He followed this two years later with another book that focussed on the voyage of the *Bounty*. After 1808 more books appeared. Sea captains and visitors to Pitcairn Island found an interview with John Adams to be mandatory, while those who went to Tahiti sought out Te Ehu-te-atua-o-noa (Jenny), one of the Tahitian women who had returned to her homeland on a whaler in 1817. There were several poems, including one by Byron ("The Island," not one of his

138

best efforts), and novels (the first purported to be by Fletcher Christian himself but is an obvious forgery). One of the more accurate earlier books was Louis Becke's *The Mutineer*; but Becke, an Australian, had actually set foot in Pitcairn in the 1870s and had spoken with many of the first-generation Pitcairners. The most popular fictional account (based on fact) was the trilogy written by the Americans Charles Nordhoff and James Norman Hall—*Mutiny on the Bounty* (1932) and its sequels, *Men Against the Sea* (1934) and *Pitcairn's Island* (1934). In addition, there has been at least one stage version—"A Romantick Operatick Spectacle," performed at the Theatre Royal in Drury Lane in 1816—and four films. The first was an Australian production with Errol Flynn as Mr. Christian (1933), but the other three have been American. In the most famous, with Charles Laughton and Clark Gable (1935), and in the remake with Trevor Howard and Marlon Brando (1962), Hollywood gives us the stereotyped image of Bligh the villain, Christian the hero/victim. The most recent version, *The Bounty* (1984), with Anthony Hopkins and Mel Gibson, takes a revisionist stance that is more sympathetic to Captain Bligh. (Nevertheless, we discovered that the Laughton/Gable film is the favourite viewing material on Pitcairn Island and is regarded as revealed truth.)

For our film we were not, technically speaking, concerned with the voyage of the *Bounty* or with the mutiny and its immediate aftermath (the subsequent sojourn of the mutineers on Tahiti and Tubuai or their months-long crisscrossing of the South Pacific to find an uninhabited, unvisited, harbourless island), but it all provided useful background. I read as much of this material as I could find in the Auckland Institute and in the Mitchell Library in Sydney, which was about as much as existed anywhere. Gradually, from the confused and often contradictory accounts of life on the island during the first period, a pattern began to emerge.

I believe a convincing case can be made against Midship-

139

man Edward Young as the instigator of both the mutiny and the later massacres on the island. This has been suggested before. Young was a half-caste West Indian who had, according to Bligh's description of him, a "dark complexion and rather a bad look." He was a womaniser and the most fecund of the mutineers, leaving seven children. He was also devious and Machiavellian. Errol Flynn was one of his descendants through his mother, whom he claimed had inherited these traits.

Something that has not, to my knowledge, been suggested before is that John Adams was Young's righthand man and fellow conspirator. This goes against the standard picture of him in the Pitcairn literature—that is, as a completely reformed sinner and patriarchal father figure. I feel this view is too facile. When the first ships called at Pitcairn, Adams monopolised the visiting captains and told them what they expected or wanted to hear. I think it unlikely that a man in his authoritarian position would have been contradicted by the other Pitcairners, yet Adams himself gave five different versions of Christian's death and several varying accounts of his own participation in the mutiny. It is my belief that he was covering up the true story. Naive he might have been, but innocent he definitely was not.

Among Louis Becke's papers in the Mitchell Library is a letter to an unknown correspondent dated June 17, 1898 (he had just published *The Mutineer*). In the letter Becke states that he had been told "over and over again by the old natives" that Christian had died of a gunshot wound accidentally received from John Adams. I think "accidentally" is a euphemism. Christian (the only mutineer, incidentally, whose grave has never been located) was shot in his garden during that fateful week in 1793 when nine men were killed. There is little doubt in my mind that John Adams was the one who pulled the trigger.

Consider the allocation of the spoils after the killings were over. There were four white men left and no Tahitian men (two of them had been killed previous to the massacre). One Tahitian woman had died. The remaining eleven women were divided as follows: Young, four; Adams, three; Quintal and McCoy (the other two men), two each. Quintal and McCoy were soon disposed of and their women shared between Young and Adams. Then Young died of asthma—the only man to die a natural death on Pitcairn (although it has crossed my mind that Adams had perhaps helped him along). Adams wound up with nine women (two more had died in the meantime). He gathered them into a kind of harem and reputedly sired several children by them, though these children took their surnames from the mother's dead husband. In more sense than one, John Adams was indeed the father of Pitcairn.

Adams had been born in Hackney, a borough of London, and brought up in the poorhouse. In his own words he was "a poore Orfing." Now, for the first time in his life, he suddenly found himself in the position of being the leader of a group. There was no Fletcher Christian to turn to, no Edward Young. So he turned to God. And evidently got feelings of guilt, which he then transferred to his charges. All the early visitors remark on the remorse that Pitcairners felt for their bloody history.

The other area where we broke new ground in our research was trying to discover the status in Tahitian society of the women who accompanied the mutineers. H. E. Maude, of the Australian National University, says, for instance: "Of the women, there is reason to believe that Christian's wife, Mauatua, and Young's wife, Teraura, were at least of *raatira* stock—the landed gentry. The remaining women were non-descripts of the Polynesian lower classes, who alone were normally permitted to consort with crews of visiting ships." Judge Jock McClelland, an expert on the Polynesians and a fluent speaker of Tahitian and Cook Islands Maori, disagrees. According to him, "The chance of being a *taiake* or close companion of a European would have been the prerogative of the upper class." Going on to analyse the women's names, he suggests that at least six of the twelve women belonged in this category, two possibly even being of chiefly rank. He further quotes a Tahitian saying: "The types of men are three. Take a breadfruit. When it is cooked, take off the skin—that is for the people. The meat is eaten by the nobles. The core is given to the slaves." A glimpse of the way they lived in the "New Cythera," as Tahiti was called by the French navigator Bougainville.

The question for us now was, where to shoot our dramatised documentary? Pitcairn itself was out. It was too difficult to get to, and once there we would find no accommodations for cast and crew. Indeed, we needed Tahitians and Europeans for extras, hotels to stay in, and an airstrip to land on. Our first thought was of Tahiti, but there were problems. It was expensive, only a few of the people spoke English, and even in those days before the *Rainbow Warrior* affair New Zealanders were not very popular with the French (as one of the Windward group of the Society Islands, Tahiti belongs to France).

The obvious place was Rarotonga in the Cook Islands. It was an associated state of New Zealand, the currency was the New Zealand dollar, the people were closely related to the Tahitians, Cook Islands Maori was almost the same as Tahitian, and they all spoke English as well.

We *would* need some background shots of Pitcairn, however. Not much, but we wanted to get Pitcairn from the sea, Christian's cave where he was wont to retreat, the dramatic cliffs, the Polynesian rock carvings at Down Rope, and so on. We didn't want to film any of modern-day Pitcairn with its one small village and fifty-eight inhabitants. There was some stock library footage available, but none of it suited our purposes. So we set about investigating whether we could get a cameraman, a director, and me to Pitcairn.

The Office of the Commissioner for the Pitcairn Islands puts out some "Notes for Visitors," and from these we learnt: "Access to Pitcairn is possible only by sea through an irregular and infrequent service provided by cargo vessels that ply between the United Kingdom and New Zealand via the Panama Canal. Such vessels are scheduled to call at approximately three monthly intervals in each direction. There are some unscheduled calls at the option of masters of passing ships but these cannot be relied upon." That didn't sound too promising. Through enquiries with the New Zealand Shipowners' Committee in Wellington, we discovered that the only reliable calls at Pitcairn were made by southbound ships. Northbound ships would occasionally call if they were carrying Pitcairners returning from New Zealand, or to bring the replacement schoolteacher every two years, or to deliver supplies urgently needed on the island, or for other such relatively rare events.

We considered the fact that New Zealand imports most of its bananas from Ecuador and the banana boats go within reach of Pitcairn. But here again we drew a blank. As one representative put it: "Do you know how much it would cost to go off course for twenty-four hours and maybe have to hang around another twelve hours because of bad weather? Plenty." This was in the days of high oil prices. We got the same answer from the agents for Scandinavian refrigerated ships carrying sheep-meat to Europe.

Then we hit another snag. "Under the Landing and Residence Ordinance all persons who are not natives or residents of the Island require a licence from this office issued by the Governor after approval of the visit has been given by the Pitcairn Island Council to land and reside there." The "Notes for Visitors" went on to say: "The only houses are owned by island families and there are no hotels or guest houses. Accommodation for visitors with one of the island families may be arranged by application to the Island Magistrate." A Catch-22 situation loomed: No licence—no arrangement for lodging; no ship would take us. No ship—no licence; no accommodation. We explained our plight to the staff in the Office of the Commissioner and found them sympathetic. They were in touch with Pitcairn Island by radio, and the matter of the licence and accommodation was soon cleared up. But the matter of transport was not.

The only solution seemed to be to charter a private yacht, so we rang Papeete in Tahiti. Yes, there were private yachts available. But when they heard we wanted to go to Pitcairn, we met with a pause. Since there was no harbour there, the yacht would have to deliver us off-shore to a Pitcairn long-boat and return later to pick us up. The best spot to charter a yacht was Mangareva, about 500 kilometres from Pitcairn. We could fly from New Zealand to Tahiti, and from Tahiti to Mangareva in a small aircraft (there were no scheduled flights at that time). If we intended to take cameras we would have to get clearance from the French military authorities because the *Centre d'Expérimentations du Pacifique* (which is how the French refer to their nuclear testing site at Mururoa) was uncomfortably close. Despite the difficulties then between New Zealand and France, they did not foresee any problems in getting this clearance, only delays. This complicated plan seemed possible, but when we asked for a figure on the cost of the charter it suddenly became impossible—they wanted $6,000!

Someone next suggested chartering a yacht from New Zealand. We found one in Auckland, and the owner asked only for a third the previously quoted amount. The distance from Auckland to Pitcairn was 5,310 kilometres, and the skipper estimated it would take about three weeks to get there. His boat was 12 metres long, he had an ocean-going certificate, and he was enthusiastic about the project. His plan, if he couldn't anchor or heave-to off the island, was to keep sailing around Pitcairn until we were finished and ready to return. But as Pitcairn is only about 2 by 3 kilometres, the thought of his yacht endlessly circling the island for several days was somehow grotesque. Still, we put it in the possible basket— but when the Director-General of the television channel heard the idea he immediately vetoed it. Among other things the insurance premiums would have been too high.

Finally, sitting in my office one morning going over the shipping colums in the newspapers (something I did regularly at the time), I noticed that a Soviet ship was in Lyttleton (the port of Christchurch) to take on a cargo of wool. I rapidly checked the list provided by the London-based New Zealand Tonnage Committee for any southbound call at Pitcairn by another ship in the near future. There was one scheduled for ten days ahead.

As I had already had some dealings with the Soviet Embassy in Wellington, I rang the First Secretary. Could they help? They were delighted to be of use. The ship was sailing at 6 P.M. We would have to get our crew to Christchurch that day. The Russians had come to the rescue. No talk about the problems associated with going out of their way or about using too much oil. No talk about money (though, ultimately, we were charged a nominal amount). The interval on Pitcairn would be five days—ample for our purposes. We were set.

Pitcairn from the sea is not unlike a rather scaled-down Rock of Gibraltar. There is no reef, so waves break ceaselessly at the foot of cliffs—some as high as 150 metres (nearly 500 feet)—that rise straight out of the sea. A lonely place in the middle of a lonely ocean, it appeared remote and out of time.

"It is so high we saw it at a distance of more than fifteen leagues," wrote Captain Philip Carteret, the island's discoverer, in his log for July 1767, "and it having been discovered by a young gentleman, son to Major Pitcairn of the marines, we called it PITCAIRN'S ISLAND." (Major Pitcairn was killed at the Battle of Bunker Hill in the American War of Independence.)

Pitcairn Island had, of course, been discovered before—and occupied—by Polynesians. Mangareva traditions speak of a high island with a difficult landing place called Makiterangi. It was a fertile spot, and they grew bananas, breadfruit, coconuts, paper mulberry, yams, and taro on it. When the *Bounty* mutineers arrived, they found these in abundance as well as evidence indicating previous human occupation, such as *maraes* (sacred enclosures) with stone statues. The mutineers rolled the helpless gods over the cliffs into the sea. Later they were to find rock carvings and stone adzes, but the people who had made them had vanished into the wide South Pacific as mysteriously as the mutineers themselves had.

On board the *Bounty* had been seeds and plants as well as goats, pigs, and chickens. These augmented the native foods, and the mutineers seemed to possess everything necessary to establish that illusory South Seas paradise so avidly sought by Georgian England. But they had also brought with them avarice, lust, and intolerance.

Today's Pitcairners represent six or seven generations of interbreeding. The men—with their lined faces, hazel eyes, light-brown hair—look remarkably like English labourers. The women tend to be more Polynesian in appearance— black-eyed, black-haired, and prone to run to fat (which lends credence to the theory that hereditary characteristics are sex-linked and appear in the same sex as their progenitor). An initial impression of their living conditions suggested lower-class poverty: they wear secondhand clothing, their houses are shanties, their furniture is makeshift and often consists of just boxes for chairs and beds made from driftwood. The island's only settlement, Adamstown, situated on a small plateau high above the sea, bears little resemblance to the picture painted by the early travelers—that of neatly thatched cottages around a village green. It has become a jumble of rickety unpainted houses roofed with galvanised iron and surrounded by litter—empty oil drums, bottles and cans, scraps of timber, rusted bits of machinery, broken toys and furniture.

There was a small community library, open for thirty minutes a week, but it apparently attracted few borrowers.

The Bible seemed to constitute the main reading. Nor did the Pitcairners appear very interested in the outside world. There was little to stimulate the intellect and simple pleasures were in short supply. The inhabitants have been Seventh Day Adventists since 1887, and dancing and frivolity are banned. So are tea, coffee, and liquor. How do the islanders amuse themselves? Well, there's always sex. About 30 to 40 percent of all births are illegitimate. There are no contraceptives. Girls have an active sex life from about fourteen on, but fertility seems to be low. Hybridisation—at least in the plant world—usually produces sturdy stock for a few generations then subsides. Perhaps this has happened on Pitcairn. Visitors are welcomed because they may add to the gene pool, a pool that already has some exalted members among it. According to Anthony Wagner of the Heralds' College, London: "It is doubtful whether any British community contains so large a proportion of descendants of our early kings." This is because Fletcher Christian was descended from Edward I through his elder daughter Joan of Acre (afterwards Countess of Gloucester), and every Pitcairner shares some Christian ancestry.

Among themselves Pitcairners speak a language called Pitcairnese, though they are more or less fluent in standard Australasian English. Essentially, Pitcairnese is a mixture of English and Tahitian. Norfolk, spoken on Norfolk Island, is similar. In 1856 the entire population of Pitcairn (one hundred and ninety-four in number) was evacuated to Norfolk Island (most of the present inhabitants of Norfolk Island derive from them). In 1859 two families of Pitcairners (sixteen individuals) returned to Pitcairn, to be followed five years later by a further four families (twenty-seven individuals). From them, in the main, come the present Pitcairners.

What do they do and how do they live? On average, a man will spend one day a week in his garden tending the taro, yam, and kumara plants; one day fishing either in a canoe or off the rocks; one day getting fruit (bananas, pineapples, grapefruit, guavas, Tahitian limes); one day on compulsory public works; one day (the Sabbath) at church or resting; and two days making souvenirs for sale. These souvenirs are carved out of *miro* wood (a tree once common on the island but now scarce) and are usually in the shapes of sharks, flying fish, turtles, birds, and walking sticks or models of the *Bounty* and Pitcairn's unique low-slung wheelbarrow. The women weave hats, fans, and baskets out of pandanus leaves and collect shells. These souvenirs are sold to passing ships or by mail order, mainly to the United States. Basically the economy of the island is one of subsistence agriculture, and there is little real cash in circulation. The current rate for wages is 37 cents an hour. But then there *is* no income tax. Public revenue comes almost exclusively from the sale of Pitcairn's postage stamps, which are known to collectors all over the world.

We kept out of the way of all this, mainly because we were only interested in getting second-unit footage (material we could cut away to when we needed to establish that the action in the film was indeed taking place on 18th-century Pitcairn). Unfortunately, the natural forest that met the *Bounty* mutineers has been destroyed, and the island is now covered with secondary bush or grassland. Most of the shots were taken on Tedside ("T'other side"), the westerly tip of the island, in places with names like Ed Cocknuts, Pawala Walley ("Small yam valley"), Dudui Ground ("candle-nut tree ground"), and so on. We concentrated on cliffs called, rather dramatically, Where Tom Off, Johnny Fall, McCoy's Drop, and Break im Hip. An essential location was Christian's cave into which he often retreated to brood. It is about halfway up Rock Face, the grey pinnacle that looms over Adamstown. And of course Bounty Bay—though it is hardly a bay, and the landing has a small jetty and boat sheds, which we had to avoid. Pitcairn is really not a very inviting island after all, and the sturdy, self-reliant, pious Pitcairners who once so delighted Queen Victoria have disappeared. Most of their descendants are today on Norfolk Island or in Australia and New Zealand.

Rarotonga in the Cook Islands was an altogether different place, though here too there has been a steady hemorrhage to Auckland. At Rarotonga we had to deal with Sir Albert Henry, the Premier. Sir Albert later had his title revoked and was dismissed for electoral fraud, but at that time he ruled Rarotonga like a robber baron and without him we could have done nothing. It was he who put the Cook Island National Arts Theatre at our disposal. This accomplished dance organisation usually wins the annual Bastille Day *tamure* (dances imitating love-making) competitions in Papeete. From the company we chose eighteen dancers to play the twelve Polynesian women and six Polynesian men in our film. Also, it was Sir Albert who waived the strict immigration rules on visiting yachts, which permitted us to employ some of their crew members as extras. We had brought actors from New Zealand, but only for the principal roles of Christian, Young, Quintal, McCoy, and Adams.

But the most important thing Sir Albert did was to allow us to burn the *Yankee*, an iron-hulled, two-masted barque that had been driven ashore at Avarua in 1967. He called in the Receiver of Wrecks and got him to issue a document that gave us limited salvage rights in the vessel.

"At least you'll shift the rust off it," Sir Albert said. "Spruce it up a bit."

We had two masts made with rigging and sails, which we erected on the ship. Then we filled the hull with dry coconut fronds soaked in diesel oil. The side of the *Yankee* facing land was covered in mats of similar material. Finally ready to shoot the scene, at dusk we set fire to the *Yankee* and, as the flames leapt along the yardarms and engulfed the hull, we filmed the mutineers and their Polynesian companions as they waded through the lagoon towards the shore, carrying their possessions and what had been of value on board the

"*Bounty*." (The noted director David Lean later saw the finished film in New Zealand and thought this particular sequence very effective.)

Another major problem in making the film was to find a suitable place to build a replica of the original Adamstown. We needed a spot with a high plateau overlooking the sea but yet screened from it by trees. All the various sites we inspected had some disadvantage—they were not high enough; they overlooked not the sea but the lagoon, and one could see the reef; there were no trees or too few trees or too many trees; the land was not flat enough, or it was within sight of other houses. And so on. In the end, however, we found the ideal location.

"Get something in writing from the owner," Sir Albert warned. "Every coconut on this island belongs to someone. I know these Cook Islanders. If you so much as try to put your arms around a tree without their permission, they'll sue you. They're litigation-happy."

The owner turned out to be an elderly lady. She gave us written authority to use the land, put buildings on it and film there provided that the buildings would later be removed, no trees would be cut down or lopped, and no excavations would take place. We agreed, promising her a suitable remuneration when we had finished. No figure was put on this, but shortly before we left Rarotonga we received a bill for $25,000 (this seemed to be a magic amount for the Cook Islanders). We had used her land for only three weeks. Lawyers eventually settled the matter for $1,000.

Sir Albert had an obsession with guns, which were forbidden in the Cook Islands. He was forever imagining political plots against himself involving guns, so we had great difficulty in persuading him to let us bring into the country some 18th-century flintlocks we had obtained from England.

"They must not be fired," he said. "On any account."

It so happened that none of us had the slightest idea how to fire them or how much gunpowder to use, and no one was prepared to experiment. Yet fired they had to be, because this was how the mutineers had killed each other. But, as is often the case, an expert was at hand—and of course it would be none other than the Leader of the Opposition, Dr. Tom Davis (later Sir Tom Davis and a Prime Minister of the Cook Islands). It turned out he had always been interested in antique guns and knew exactly what to do.

Knowing that the Leader of the Opposition was teaching us how to fire the guns was just the sort of thing that would have thrown Sir Albert into a paroxysm of paranoia. We had to proceed very discreetly. The lessons took place in a secluded valley in the interior of the island. Our cast and crew were sworn to secrecy but, towards the end of our stay, someone informed on us and Sir Albert found out, becoming very irate. Luckily, it was too late for him to do anything. Filming was almost completed.

The firing lessons were not without some excitement of their own, however. Two of the Polynesian actors using the flintlocks managed to singe their eyebrows, and one of the European extras burned his beard so badly that we had to re-trim it and re-shoot all his scenes. But that, as they say, is show business.

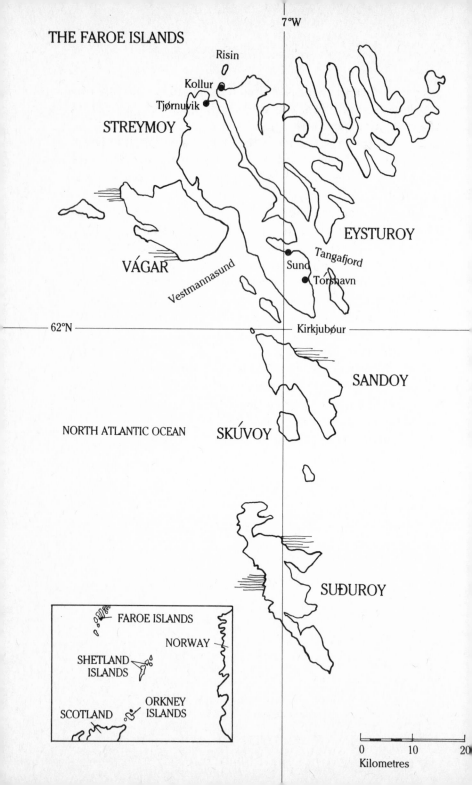

THE FAROE ISLANDS

7°W

Risin

Kollur

Tjørnuvik

STREYMOY

EYSTUROY

VÁGAR

Sund

Tangafjord

Tórshavn

Vestmannasund

62°N

Kirkjubøur

SANDOY

NORTH ATLANTIC OCEAN

SKÚVOY

SUÐUROY

FAROE ISLANDS

NORWAY

SHETLAND
ISLANDS

SCOTLAND

ORKNEY
ISLANDS

0   10   20
Kilometres

11

The Faroes

THE SLAUGHTER OF THE WHALES

In the early 1950s in Sydney I was introduced to a novel published by Penguin Books called *Barbara*. It had been written in Danish by Jørgen-Frantz Jacobsen and translated into English not long before. The setting was the Faroe Islands in the 18th century. As I recall, it was a love story of great sensitivity.

I think this was the first time I had ever heard of the Faroes, and I went to my atlas to find them. They lie northwest of Britain, halfway between Norway and Iceland— twenty poor, naked, craggy islands and stacks. Years later I was to get to know them fairly well.

The person who had recommended *Barbara* to me was Danish, a big, angular girl not unexpectedly known to all and sundry as The Great Dane. She worked as a radiologist at Sydney Hospital and was the girlfriend of a friend. What she didn't tell me was that *Barbara* is one of the few books written by a Faroese, but perhaps she didn't know.

Faroese is not a dialect of Danish. It is a language in its own right, related to Icelandic. But unlike Icelandic, which had a rich literary life during the Middle Ages, Faroese had none. The islands were ruled by Denmark, and Danes had a monopoly of all trade. This kept the Faroes in isolation.

Danish was the official language, the only one allowed in the churches and schools and law-courts. So it is small wonder that Jørgen-Frantz Jacobsen wrote in Danish. What Faroese does have, though, are hundreds of songs in which magic and sorcery play a leading role, and he drew on this oral tradition. To a degree a similar oral tradition exists in the Shetland and Orkney Islands. Until the late 18th century a language called Norn—the closest relative of Faroese—was spoken there, and it survives in dialect words, a few proverbs, place-names, etc. But we didn't go to the Faroes on a linguistic quest. We went there to film the *grindadráp*—the slaughter of the whales. This takes place during the summer months when schools of caaing or pilot whales appear quite frequently in the fjords and sounds of the Faroes. These schools, or *grind* as they are known in Faroese, may number anywhere from fifty to a thousand whales. The caaing whale, a docile animal, varies in size from 4 to 8 metres (13 to 26 feet).

The *grindadráp* must be one of the cruellest forms of hunting that exists. Yet in the Faroes it is the only way in which these whales can be killed successfully—add to which it is dangerous and exciting—and no opportunity for a *grindadráp* is missed there. The slaughter of the whales has had a long history in these islands. The laws governing a *grindadráp* are hallowed by tradition and custom as is the division of the spoils. For the whale is the main source of meat in this region. The Faroes are desolate specks in the great ocean. Winters are stormy. Summer must be devoted to securing a good stock of dried and salted meat. Thus the *grindadráp*.

As a result of our film there was an outcry from environmentalist groups, and enormous controversy over the practice persists to this day. There has even been some suggestion that the Danish Government might move to prevent future *grindadráp*. But so far nothing has come of it, probably because the ritual killing is so deeply ingrained in Faroese life.

Getting to the Faroes would seem to present no problems.

Icelandair flew regular scheduled flights from London to Reykjavik via Glasgow and Vágar, one of the western islands. But we reckoned without the Faroese fog. The Faroes group is one of the foggiest places on earth during summer and one of the wettest the year round. We were held up for three days in Glasgow. It was this fog that delayed the discovery of the Faroe Islands. The Shetlands and Orkneys only 400 kilometres south have a history stretching back three to four thousand years. But the Faroes, shrouded in perpetual mist, remained unknown until about the middle of the 8th century.

About seventy-five years later, in 825, a learned Irish monk called Dicuil compiled a geography book, which he called *Liber de Mensura Orbis Terrae (Book of the Measure of the World)*. In it he described every land then known.

"There are many other islands in the ocean to the north of Britain," Dicuil wrote, continuing:

> which can be reached from the northern islands of Britain in a direct voyage of two days and two nights with sails filled with an undropping wind. There is a set of small islands, nearly all separated by narrow stretches of water; in these for nearly a hundred years hermits sailing from our country, Ireland, have lived. And, just as they were deserted at the beginning of the world, so they are now. Because of Northmen sea-rovers they are emptied of anchorites and filled with countless sheep, and very many diverse kinds of sea-birds.

This description fits the Faroes to a tee. The fjords between the islands are indeed narrow stretches of water. A small boat with good following winds can sail from the Shetlands in two to three days. The Faroes are known for the wealth and variety of their bird population. And the sheep are still there. In fact the name Faroes in Old Norse means "Islands of Sheep." These sheep are a type of Soay or Hebridean sheep and were obviously brought by the religious recluses for practical as well as Christian reasons.

That Irish Culdees had been in the Faroes for quite some

time is also borne out by the *Navigatio Sancti Brendani Abbatis (The Voyage of St. Brendan the Abbot)*, that fabled early traveller, who may or may not have crossed the Atlantic in a boat made of oxhides. The *Navigatio* recounts how St. Brendan and his monks landed on an island with many large streams of fish. It was called the Island of Sheep because flocks of energetic sheep ran wild all the year round. Here the voyagers stayed from Maundy Thursday to Holy Saturday. An islander brought them bread and gave them directions to the Paradise of Birds, a neighbouring island to the west.

At Kirkjubøur in South Streymoy there is conclusive archaeological evidence of Celtic occupation and a Celtic place-name, Brandansvik, the creek of St. Brendan. Of the life of these *papar*, to use the Old Norse term for them, we know nothing. Nor do we know how this thin and fragile Christian occupation ended. Was their flight sudden and empty-handed in the same curraghs (small oxhide boats) that had brought them from Ireland? Or did they stay and try to convert the Vikings?

According to the *Faereyinga Saga* the most important of early Norse settlers was Grim Kamban. After his death his fellow settlers are said to have worshipped him and offered sacrifices. (His first name must have had some significance!) The earliest document describing life in the Faroes is part of the famous *Flateyjarbók*, an extensive codex written in Iceland in the 14th century. It describes the lifelong feud between a Christian, Sigmund Bretisson of Skúvoy (one of the southern islands), and a heathen, Tróndur í Gøtu. Sigmund is finally murdered at Sandvik in Suduroy when lying exhausted on the beach after swimming from Skúvoy (15 kilometres) to escape Tróndur. This scene is couched in the unvarnished realism typical of Icelandic sagas and concludes: "And it is not told that any other great things happened in the Faroes in the days of Sigmund's descendants."

Thus began the Dark Ages of the Faroes. They were incorporated with Norway in 1035 both as a tributary and an ecclesiastical province. This was continued under the union of Norway and Denmark but, in 1814, when Norway was ceded to Sweden (and Heligoland to Britain), the Faroes remained with Denmark. Up till the middle of last century the Faroes were a closed country, a strange relic of the Middle Ages preserved intact into the age of steam. It was a patriarchal society of poor farmers and fishers turned in on itself. Yet this isolation did preserve the language and the folklore of one of Europe's frontier peoples on the very edge of the grey Atlantic.

Today the Faroes are a self-governing part of the Danish Kingdom like Greenland. They have their own stamps, their own bank notes (the coins are Danish), their own flag, and their own passports (though their nationality is given as Faroese/Danish). Faroese is the official language of the country, but Danish is also taught in schools. And they have their own parliament, the *Løgting*, which can legislate on all matters except foreign affairs. All this has happened since World War II when the islands were occupied by Britain and the Faroese learnt to be self-reliant.

The Faroe Islands, with a combined area of about 900 square kilometres, resemble an inverted triangle. Very little of this is cultivable. Many of the eighteen islands are ringed with cliffs. The seventeen inhabited ones usually have a fringe of tilled land below the knees of cloud-capped mountains. There are no trees and bushes are rare. Apart from seaweed along the shoreline, the vegetation consists entirely of grasses where the land is drained and marsh plants where it is not. The Faroes leave a lasting impression of riven islands, dark-green grass, blue water smashing against the cliffs, and a constant flicker of seabirds. About 50,000 people live there, more than a fifth of them in the capital, Tórshavn. Here we duly arrived after landing in Vágar, crossing Vestmannasund between Vágar and Streymoy, the main island immediately to the east, and driving 20-odd kilometres over some high hills.

We found accommodation at the Hotel Hafnia, a rather

gloomy but not uncomfortable place. It was 1967—some sixteen years since I had read *Barbara* and the Faroes had first swum into my ken. I mentioned as much to the manager of the hotel and he was delighted. Jørgen-Frantz Jacobsen, in his view, was so far the pinnacle of Faroese literary achievement. Thereafter, whenever the manager introduced me to someone, he always made a little aside in Faroese, which included the words "*Barbara*" and "Jørgen-Frantz Jacobsen." That I was an Australian equally amazed him. He said we were the first of that nation he had ever known to visit the Faroes. But the Faroes are hardly a tourist destination, and they are, in any case, practically teetotal—which would preclude most of us Australians! (The only drink available, beer, is virtually nonalcoholic, and it is against the law to consume it in a public place.)

What were the chances of a *grindadráp*? we asked. Very likely, was the reply. How soon? we wanted to know. The whales didn't issue timetables, we were told. We would have to wait. The *huldúfolk* knew in advance, of course, but they wouldn't pass this information on to humans. In Faroese folklore the *huldúfolk* were large grey creatures somewhat resembling people and who lived underground. So wait it was. Wait for the *grindabod*—the message that a *grind* had been located.

Most of the *grind* are first seen by small boats fishing outside the fjords. Some garment—a shirt, jacket, jumper, whatever—is hoisted on an oar as a sign to other boats. Only the boat that first sights the *grind* hoists a garment, and the rest at once haul in their lines and go to join the one that made the discovery, which by now would be following the *grind*. This attracts the attention of workers in the fields and the cry "*Grindabod!*" goes up, being shouted from one to the other. Soon whole districts are aroused.

Grindabod has priority over all other calls on the telephone. The directory carries a long and carefully worded instruction to subscribers as to the correct procedure.

It is a public duty to pass along the *grindabod*. Like Melbourne Cup Day in Australia, everything stops. Children are sent home from school, banks and shops shut their doors, farming ceases, courts adjourn. Everyone heads for the sea or the inlet where the killing will take place. We held ourselves in readiness, knowing that it would be impossible to miss the *grindabod*.

In the meantime we did a little filming around Tórshavn. The centre of the town is the harbour. Here are black-slatted, two-storied buildings alongside turf-roofed houses and warehouses. Nearby is Tinganes, a small peninsula where the *Thing* or Assembly once met. This is the oldest part of Tórshavn. Fishermen were going about their work, many of them wearing the distinctive Faroese headgear—a worsted stocking cap of striped red and black gathered in a rosette on one side. For some reason I later bought one in a shop.

The hotel manager had produced some pretty Faroese girls in their national costume, which consists of a long dress with a laced bodice, a striped apron, and a cape caught at the throat with a silver clasp. The Faroese are a handsome race, mainly fair but there are some brunettes and the occasional striking redhead with hair the colour of henna.

Fishing is the national industry and a very efficient one at that. They have a fleet of several hundred modern vessels ranging the North Atlantic from Labrador to the White Sea. Approximately half of all deaths among males recorded in the Faroese parish registers are deaths at sea. At one time the main export used to be salt cod and *klipfisk*—cod split and dried in the sun. Nowadays it is frozen fish and fish fillets. The markets are the countries of the European Community (formerly the European Common Market).

Away from the harbour Tórshavn is narrow hilly streets with houses standing singly, each one a different shape or size but all constructed of wood and galvanised iron. The wood is usually tarred, the galvanised iron gaily painted. And the sod roofs sprout long grass, which makes the whole a part of the landscape. So much so that I saw hens wandering about on them and buttercups blooming in the green turf. Inside the houses are scrupulously clean. Each one has a basement where fishing, farming, whaling, and bird-fowling gear are stored. It is also the place where dried and salted provisions are kept.

The Faroese depend to a large extent on such food. Dried strips of mutton called *skerpikjøt* are a great delicacy. It is very chewy—a bit like South African biltong or Canadian pemmican. Most meals consist of dried or salted meat (mutton, whale, seabirds), salt fish, potatoes (with rhubarb), and curds. As well, various sausages are prepared from sheep's intestines and black puddings from sheep's blood. Not exactly an inviting cuisine but a healthy one.

The hilly streets we walked were named after famous sons of the Faroes. One such, who deserves to be better known, is Niels Finsen, the discoverer last century of the curative properties of ultraviolet rays. If one considers for a moment that a sunny day is a rare occurrence in the Faroes, this discovery in such an out-of-the-way place was a quantum leap forward.

Came the day of the *grindabod*. We were filming around the harbour again and suddenly noticed that everyone had stopped working and made off. No one had let us know, but all we did was load up the car and follow the throng. They headed north on the main road out of Tórshavn along the sound separating Streymoy from Eysturoy, the second largest island, lying to the east. The road ran along the crest of the hills, and we could see the crescent of boats slowly moving northwards up the Tangafjord. As we got closer we stopped and took some long shots.

Driving the whales (*grindarakstur* as it is called) to the place of slaughter was, we were informed, the most skillful part of the hunt. First the *grindapláss* (the place of slaughter) is chosen, and then it is the responsibility of the captain of the hunt to get the whales there. He has to take into consideration the set of the tide, the strength and direction of the wind, the time of day, and so on. The *grind* cannot be driven against the tide and it prefers to swim against the wind. The whales behave like a flock of sheep and, as long as they are not alarmed, will cruise in front of the boats.

They are guided rather than forced in the desired direction. White stones attached to short lines are used for this purpose. They are thrown into the water and quickly retrieved. The whales nearest the disturbance shun the white stone and turn away. These white stones are part of the statutory equipment of all boats.

The *grindapláss* this time was the village of Sund, about 8 kilometres from Tórshavn. It is a small village of maybe ten houses with a well-cultivated area close by—the in-field. Cars lined the side of the fjord, and people packed the gently shelving shore. The object of the exercise was to strand the whales and then kill them.

As the whales approached the little bay the spectators raised a cheer. The men in the boats responded by shouting and making as loud a noise as possible to urge the *grind* forward. The whales came on unswerving, though they were already in shoaling water. Then the captain of the hunt chose his first victim. This is a crucial moment, for as soon as the whale is struck by a lance, it thrashes about in pain and stampedes the whole *grind*. The trick is to wound it in the rear part of its body so that it bounds forward to its destruction, taking the rest of the school with it.

This is exactly what happened. In water too shallow for swimming, the whales tossed and turned out of control. Now the men stood up in the boats and unsheathed their lances. Some of the bystanders lining the shore jumped into the water with similar weapons. An orgy of killing followed. The water was churned to a lather of white foam streaked with blood. More men waded into the bay slashing and lunging at the stricken whales. Some had sharp iron hooks attached to ropes that they made fast in the animals' heads. Others, on shore, heaved at the ropes, dragging the luckless whales high onto the beach, where their spinal cords were cut.

The naturally reserved Faroese seemed to be consumed by blood lust. The atmosphere was that of a carnival. It brought to life an old description I had read of the Viking as a berserker, a frenzied killer. We filmed nonstop. Some of the images that still remain with me are: blood spouting 30 cm into the air from a wounded whale; sand piling up in front of the nose of a whale as it was dragged up the beach like snow before a snow-plough; children hitting dying whales with clubs and stones; waves coloured crimson gently breaking on the shore; the muted squeals of agony that came from the unfortunate creatures; the strong smell of death that lingered long after the *grindadráp* was over.

When all the whales are lined up on the shore (it is the obligation of every citizen to help in this), they are counted and measured by the *metingarmenn*, traditional officials who estimate the total value of the catch and oversee its proper allocation. The largest whale is the property of the boat that first sighted the *grind*, and the head goes to the member of the crew who raised the alarm (the *grindabod*). Next, meat is given to all the houses in the village where the slaughter takes place. A quantity is set aside to compensate the owners of damaged boats or whaling gear. Guards, who watch over the whales to prevent pilfering, are also paid in kind as are the *metingarmenn* and the captain of the hunt.

The total of these payments is subtracted from the whole and the remainder distributed to the inhabitants of the whaling district in which the *grindadráp* occurred. The names are on a *grind* register and there are nine such whaling districts in the Faroes. Each has a whaling bay, to which the *grind* is normally directed. The whaling bay for South Streymoy is Tórshavn, and it was only the tide and the wind direction that forced the captain of the hunt to decide on Sund as an alternative.

All night long there was a stream of people coming to the bay to receive their portion of the catch. The guards would give them the number of their whale and tell them how much they could take. By law this must be done within twenty-four hours.

We waited a while and then went back to Tórshavn. There was dancing on the quay and in the dance-halls of the town— dancing that went on far into the small hours. In the Faroes a *grindadráp* is an event to be celebrated. Many of the dancers were in national costume and dancing Faroese ring-dances. In these they link hands and provide their own music by singing ballads to which the dance steps are a choreographic comple- ment. The ballads sound monotonous and tuneless. The whole scene resembles something out of the Middle Ages.

Over the next few days we filmed in various parts of the islands, mainly on Streymoy. We had met an Englishman at the hotel who asked could he accompany us. He was an Oxford don and interested in the archaeology of the Faroes. Not that there was much, as he explained. A few sites existed, such as Kirkjubøur and Tjørnuvik. They had yielded evi- dence of Celtic occupation, but very little from Viking times had been discovered, which was curious.

First we went to Kirkjubøur. *Kirk* means "church" and *bøur* means the "in-field" or "home-paddock." Kirkjubøur is probably the most fertile part of the Faroes. It was the seat of thirty or so bishops before the Reformation. There are the ruins of the unfinished Magnus cathedral (late 13th century), the remains of the medieval bishop's palace, and a little white-washed church by the sea dedicated to St. Olaf. The farmhouse is the oldest in the islands and has been occupied by the same family for eighteen generations—that is, for more than five hundred years.

Tjørnuvik lay at the other end of Streymoy, at the northern tip. It was about 40 kilometres from Tórshavn. There was a cluster of little houses, all painted red or green, a rich *bøur* given over to meadow grass with a little stream winding through it, and a semicircular bay. The view was superb. The bay looked straight at the mountainous sugarloaf that was Kollur on nearby Eysturoy, with the stacks of Risin and Kellingin standing apart in the sea. We spent some time there. The don wanted to look at a Viking burial mound and wandered off. I walked towards one of the heads of the bay. At first there was a path but it soon gave out and I found myself scrambling over scree. Eventually I could go no farther and found a convenient rock to sit on. The day was reasonably fine and the sun was visible. Even on the longest day of the year it is often hidden by the lowering mountains, and I admired the view. Taking my handkerchief out of my pocket, I inadvertently pulled the car keys out with it and they fell into a cleft in some boulders below me. There was nothing for it but to try and retrieve them.

I cautiously climbed down until I was almost at the water's edge. The keys were wedged in a crack and my fingers couldn't reach far enough to get them. I looked in vain for a stick and then remembered that the Faroes have no trees and only a few bushes. As I was about to go back to the crew to see if anyone had anything like a screwdriver or a nail file that could be used, I took one last look around and something caught my eye. It was also stuck in a cleft, but when I got it out I then realised that it was the head of a spear, though badly corroded. But with it I was able to pry the keys loose.

Yes, the Oxford don told me when he examined the spearhead, definitely Viking. He would see to it that my name was attached to this find. I don't know if he ever did, but he took the spearhead with him when he left for Iceland.

Later, much later, in New Zealand I met a Faroese woman. She believed she was the first Faroese ever to go to New Zealand and thought the authorities should allow her to extend her visa because of that. (They didn't.) She did tell me, though, that since my visit to the Faroes there had been many more Viking remains found—spindle whorls, loom weights, and ring-headed pins. She also told me a charming Faroese story. Seals are said to have human eyes because they are people who have committed suicide by drowning. They are forced to lead a ceaseless ghostly life in the cold waters of the North Atlantic, but once a year, on Twelfth Night, they are allowed to throw off their animal skins, after which they go inland and dance on flat rocks. She claimed to have seen them and wondered did this also happen elsewhere? Alas, I was unable to help her.

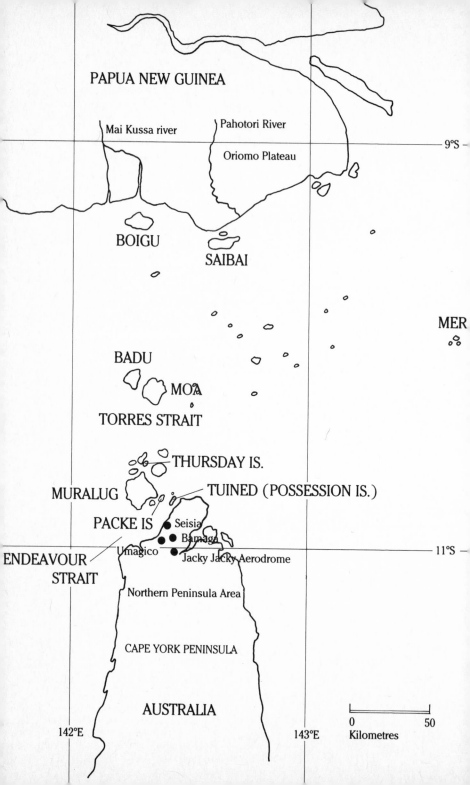

PAPUA NEW GUINEA

Mai Kussa river   Pahotori River

Oriomo Plateau

9°S

BOIGU

SAIBAI

MER

BADU

MOA

TORRES STRAIT

THURSDAY IS.

MURALUG   TUINED (POSSESSION IS.)

PACKE IS   Seisia

Bamaga

ENDEAVOUR   Umagico

STRAIT   Jacky Jacky Aerodrome   11°S

Northern Peninsula Area

CAPE YORK PENINSULA

AUSTRALIA

0   50
Kilometres

142°E   143°E

12

Torres Strait

▬ ▭ ▭ ▭ ▭ ▭ ▭ ▭ ▭ ▭ ▭ ▭ ▭ ▭ ▬

AUSTRALIA'S DEEP NORTH

In 1849 a boat party from H.M.S. *Rattlesnake*, surveying the islands in Torres Strait between Australia and New Guinea, came upon a white woman living among the natives on the island of Muralug. She was Barbara Thompson, a 21-year-old Scots girl, who had been shipwrecked there with her husband four years before. Barbara said that, when the boat struck the reef, her husband and the crew members drowned while trying to swim to shore. The next morning she was discovered by two men out fishing for turtle, adopted into their tribe and later married to one of them.

On board the *Rattlesnake* were some distinguished scientists, including Thomas Huxley, the friend of Charles Darwin and the grandfather of the writer Aldous Huxley. Barbara Thompson was closely questioned by them about the peoples, languages, and customs of the strait. She had spent more time there than any other returned European, and although she was illiterate she was able to supply a wealth of information.

She also told them the story of an escaped convict who in the 1830s had established himself as "king" of two islands in the middle of the strait. He was a white man, but wild and given to killing and head-hunting. When the news about Barbara Thompson reached him, he twice tried to abduct her from her island sanctuary. She felt she had much more to fear from this white savage than from the black natives and for this reason had given herself up to the *Rattlesnake*'s party.

This story, a version of which I had first read as a boy in Ion L. Idriess' two novels *The Wild White Man of Badu* and *Isles of Despair*, seemed suitable material for a dramatised documentary, and in 1977 I began to do research on it.

The distance between Cape York Peninsula, the northernmost tip of Australia, and New Guinea is 150 kilometres. On both sides of Torres Strait the fauna and flora are virtually the same—tree kangaroos (kangaroos that live in trees), wallabies, echidnas (primitive spiny anteaters that lay eggs), cassowaries (large flightless birds like ostriches), sulphur-crested cockatoos, goannas (a monitor lizard that can grow up to 6 feet—about 2 metres—in length; "goanna" is really a borrowed version of "iguana" but the lizard is not the same species and goanna has become the official and scientific term); eucalyptus and ti trees. This similarity is not surprising when one considers that the two countries were once joined and only became separated when the sea rose 8,000 years ago. Yet the peoples on either side of the strait are markedly dissimilar. Australia has its nomadic Aboriginal hunter-gatherers, while in New Guinea there are settled Papuan horticulturists. The former use the spear and woomera, the latter the bow and unfletched arrow. They come face to face in Torres Strait.

There are three roughly parallel groups of islands between the two land masses: the high islands of the western chain, representing the Great Dividing Range and stretching practically right across the strait to the Oriomo Plateau in New Guinea; the coral cays of the central islands, which are spread over the middle of the waterway; and the volcanic eastern islands closer to New Guinea.

Progressively from south to north the peoples merge from Aboriginal to Papuan, so that the inhabitants of those islands nearest Australia are what might be called Papuanised Aboriginals while on those islands nearest New Guinea they are Aboriginalised Papuans. Mabuiag, an Aboriginal language with Papuan modifications, is spoken in the western and central chains, while in the eastern chain there is a purely Papuan language, Meriam. But despite these differences, the way of life of all the various Islanders is remarkably uniform. It is neither strictly Aboriginal nor strictly Papuan. In some respects it combines elements of both with the added ingredient of a sea-based culture. There were well-defined trading networks across the strait and a dominant religion—the Malu or Deepwater cult with its headquarters on Mer in the eastern chain. There the priests were called *zogo le* and practised sorcery or *pouri-pouri*, ritual cannibalism, and, surprisingly, telepathy. Malu probably originated on the southwest coast of New Guinea in what is now the Indonesian province of Irian Jaya. Head-hunting assumed enormous importance in the cult. The sacred words taught to all initiates were: "Jawbones His Food. Heads His Food."

But the Aborigines also contributed culture heroes. A Jupungati legend from the tribe living on the western side of Cape York Peninsula tells of a sorcerer who left them to travel northwards in a canoe. He married an Islander woman from Mabuiag and his son was Kuiam, the subject of many myths and the greatest warrior of them all. Once when Kuiam was attacked by three canoe loads of his enemies he turned himself into a swallow and flew away. The place is still pointed out also where he rested for a while before returning to human form.

It was information like this that Barbara Thompson gave to the naturalist John McGillivray, the doctor Thomas Huxley, the captain Owen Stanley, and the artist Oswald (later Sir Oswald) Brierly. They took copious notes and, by the time I had come to the story, all except Brierly's work had been published (this was done in 1979). His journals and manuscripts—sixteen bundles of them—are in the Mitchell Library in Sydney (Mitchell Library holds the greatest repository of books about the Pacific that exists). In addition, I was able to consult the six volumes of the *Reports of the Cambridge Anthropological Expedition to Torres Straits*, surely the most comprehensive expedition ever mounted to Australia in the 19th century (it was in 1898 in fact). That I did so was later to prove invaluable. And, through an article about Barbara Thompson in the Sydney *Sunday Telegraph*, I was able to track down her grand-niece and tap into family history.

In 1606 a Spanish ship under the command of Luís Vaz de Torres sailed through the strait between Cape York Peninsula and New Guinea. It took them four weeks. During that time Torres' men shot two Islanders and kidnapped three young women who were taken back to Spain. The first the outside world heard of this discovery was when a British fleet occupied Manila in 1762 and found an old copy of the chart.

Eight years later Captain James Cook on the *Endeavour* entered Torres Strait. He noted in the log that he had seen his first "Indian with a bow and a bundle of arrows" instead of the "lances" he had seen previously. He also saw some women with "not a rag of clothing on them collecting shellfish." Cook landed on Tuined Island and formally took possession of New South Wales (Eastern Australia) in the name of King George III. He then gave Tuined its English name, Possession Island.

In the years after 1606 a number of Spanish ships appear to have come to grief in the Strait. On Mer tradition insists that a village called Las on the south side of the island was settled by shipwrecked sailors. Certainly the people of Las were fairer than the other natives of Mer. In the early days of European occupation (from 1870 on) Spanish coins, swords, and guns were often found by pearlers and bêche-de-mer fishermen. There is even a story about some skeletons dressed in rusty armour in a cave. And there is the legend of Fire Eye, a giant ruby that the Islanders found in a box belonging to a woman castaway. Fire Eye adorned the idol of the *zogo* or god until the arrival of the missionaries (in 1871) forced the *zogo le* to bury the idol in a secret place.

The time had come to see the locations. I wrote from New Zealand to Joh Bjelke-Petersen, the Queensland Premier, explaining what I intended to do. He replied that he had passed my letter on to P. J. Killoran, the Director of the Department of Aboriginal and Islander Advancement (D.A.I.A.) for action. So I flew to Brisbane. Killoran received me cordially and promised the cooperation of his department. Indeed he had already sent a telex to the Administrator at Thursday Island, the only government centre in Torres Strait.

Thursday Island was a run-down derelict sort of place, a motley of houses on high blocks, tin shanties, western-type pubs, and colonial-style buildings dating from the time when it was the northern gateway to Australia. It didn't resemble much the description in the song "Old T.I. My Beautiful Home" (known, incidentally, as the Torres Strait National Anthem). Nor was there much sign of the industry that once brought prosperity to the island—pearling. By the mid-1880s it had the largest pearling fleet in the world and the first part of the 20th century saw the founding of great pearling dynasties. But plastic buttons and cultured pearls put an end to that by the 1950s.

People descended from Europeans, Japanese, Malays, Timorese, Chinese, Filipinos, Torres Strait Islanders, and Aboriginals lived there—and mixed promiscuously. So much so that gonorrhea was endemic (the "T.I. Handshake," it was called locally). Another oddity on the island was the number of taxis—at least twenty for a population that totalled only around 2,000. Some families spent up to 20 percent of their weekly income on taxi rides, which were considered a form of entertainment on Thursday Island. People would take a tape player, hire a taxi and load it with cases of beer, then proceed slowly around the island, often stopping here and there to greet friends. Sometimes a ride would go on from night till dawn.

All the other islands in Torres Strait are reserves, and permission must be obtained from the D.A.I.A. before outsiders can set foot on them. So, after receiving permission, I first visited Muralug, where Barbara Thompson had been. Only about a kilometre from Thursday Island, it is by far the biggest island in the group (about 20 by 13 kilometres). Muralug means "Everybody's Place" in Mabuiag, and since the original inhabitants—the Kauralgals—disappeared long ago, it has indeed become everybody's place. Mixed-race families have moved in, and their houses are scattered around the coast. Inland are rocky ridges intersected by grassy valleys.

At the southeast point of Muralug lies Packe Island (reputedly named after Piaqui, Barbara Thompson's adopted father), and opposite it is the place where the Kauralgals camped. It was here that she gave herself up to the *Rattlesnake*'s boat party. She was naked except for a girdle of possum tails and burnt black by the sun. When she threw herself at the feet of one of the officers, he thought she was a native until she said, in halting English, "I am a Christian. I am ashamed," and covered her breasts with her hands.

The closest point on the Australian mainland is only 16 kilometres from Muralug, and there was constant intercourse between the Kauralgals and the Aboriginals. Not always friendly, however. Barbara Thompson told of frequent head-hunting expeditions to the mainland. The Kauralgals held a key position in the trading network across Torres Strait. They were the go-between with the Aboriginals who traded turtle oil, red ochre, and spears for sago, bird of paradise plumes, and the hulls of sailing canoes from New Guinea. Over thousands of years the Kauralgals intermarried with the Aboriginals and came to have the same appearance. As a result the Islanders further north called them Island Aboriginals. But they had more in common with the other Torres Strait communities than they had with the Aboriginals, and they spoke Mabuiag. One universal belief was that white people were *markai* or ghosts from the spirit world, and the proper way to treat them was to send them straight back by killing them. Barbara Thompson was saved only by the intervention of Piaqui, who recognised in her his recently deceased daughter, Gi'om.

Badu, a rather hilly, round island about 12 kilometres in diameter, lies some 50 kilometres north of Thursday Island. It has a little over five hundred people living on it, a grass strip, but no accommodations. This was where Wini, the wild white man of Badu, reigned, and what we know of him comes mainly from Thompson's account: ". . . that he first came to the island in a small boat. When he landed he told the Blacks he had killed the men who were in the boat with him."

She went on to describe him as a tall elderly man with light hair and pock-marked complexion burnt very dark from his long exposure to the sun. Later, when he tried to abduct her, she says she talked with him in Mabuiag because he could not speak English. He was dressed in the headdress and ornaments of a war chief and had many wives. The man who ordered him shot on sight in the 1860s, Frank Jardine, the Resident Magistrate for Cape York Peninsula, called him an escaped convict. This seems more than likely. But from which penal settlement? The 1830s were too late for Moreton Bay (in Queensland where Brisbane now stands) and too early for the French *bagne* (or prison) on New Caledonia. There can be only one possibility, Norfolk Island, and the records show that an Irish-speaking convict called Sweeny did escape from there with four companions in a boat at about the right time. And the name Sweeny would have emerged as Wini on the lips of the Islanders. Although there are sibilants in Mabuiag, combinations like *sw* or *st* are impossible for native speakers to pronounce and, when present in borrowed words, are invariably turned into *w* or *t* sounds.

The logistics of trying to shoot the film on the islands

where the story had happened posed insurmountable difficulties. I needed people, both Aboriginals and Torres Strait
Islanders, for the extras; accommodations for the actors and
crew; and a setup for regular communications. Back on
Thursday Island I put the problem to the Administrator. He
asked me had I heard of Bamaga. I had not.

Bamaga is a township in the Northern Peninsula Area, a
reserve of over a million acres (about half a million hectares)
almost right at the tip of Cape York Peninsula. It lay just
across narrow Endeavour Strait from Muralug and consisted
of five communities—two Islander and three Aboriginal (one
with the delightful name of Umagico)—with a combined
population of about 1,500. There was a motel, a shopping
complex, a picture theatre, a high school, and a few canteens
where liquor was served. Twice a week a scheduled airline
called at Jacky Jacky airfield. I chartered a small plane and
flew there to look the place over. It seemed to fit our requirements—there were beaches, islands on the horizon, palm
trees, dugongs, crocodiles, sharks, bush, and billabongs. I
went on to Brisbane, and once again Mr. Killoran proved
obliging. He would arrange for the motel to be available for
the period we needed it as well as for additional accommodations (the motel had only five units). All we had to agree to
do was to work through the community councils.

This turned out to be a stumbling block. When we eventually got to Bamaga, we found that the council chairmen
really had no authority to help us obtain either vehicles or
people. Those decisions rested with the manager of the
Northern Peninsula Area, who of course had been instructed
that we were to work through the councils. We also discovered that none of the Islanders had any idea how to build
the sort of huts in which their ancestors had lived. (It was at
this point that the drawings and descriptions in the *Reports of
the Cambridge Anthropological Expedition to Torres Straits*
came in handy.) Nor did the Islander women know how to

weave the *zazi* or grass skirt. We had a similar problem with weapons—bows and *kimus* or cassowary claw–tipped arrows; *upis* or bamboo beheading knives; *gabba gabbals* or circular stone-headed clubs. Fortunately in Bamaga there was a woodworking shop which turned out souvenirs (mainly carved fish and model boats), and we were able to persuade the staff to direct their skills towards these more traditional objects. The Aboriginals were no better at being able to reconstruct their past, and I ended up having to rent the spears and woomeras we needed from a shop in Cairns (the nearest big town, 400 kilometres to the south).

One of the local schoolteachers produced a *dari* or Islander headdress made of white reef-heron feathers, a *dibidibi* or pearl shell chest ornament, and some armbands. But mainly we were forced to rely on our own efforts. I phoned New Zealand and told the wardrobe mistress to buy up all the raffia she could before flying to Bamaga. She then showed some schoolgirls how to make a *zazi*. We managed to hire a truck, and all of us went out to cut reeds for building the huts.

As background we were planning to use two villages—one makeshift and Aboriginal, the other permanent and Islander. But we had no warriors to populate them. We did what we could. There were also a number of scenes involving our actors and local women and children as extras, and here we ran up against another unexpected problem. The Aboriginal women, especially the older ones, did not object to appearing topless (as historical accuracy dictated), but nothing would induce the Islanders to do likewise—the long arm of the London Missionary Society. Filming ground to a shuddering halt.

Almost at the same time a notice appeared on the announcement board at one of the canteens saying that Joh Bjelke-Petersen would soon be visiting Bamaga for a day. An election was imminent in Queensland, and the Premier was touring the marginal seats. I went out to Jacky Jacky to meet him. He got off the plane followed by Killoran. I stepped forward.

"Mr. Premier," I said. "I am the film producer who wrote to you from New Zealand. I want to thank you for your help."

"How's it all going?" he asked. "Well, I hope."

Grabbing my chance, I explained our difficulties. He listened intently and, when I had finished, turned to Killoran.

"Pat, help these people."

Killoran beckoned the manager over and said two words: "Fix it."

The chain of command.

Next day we had all the vehicles, all the bodies we wanted. A cast of thousands. Well, not really, but at least enough to stage a convincing battle between two groups of Islanders and enough Aboriginal extras to serve as the Kauralgals. We discovered that nearly everybody in Bamaga wanted to be in the film. The Aboriginals were natural actors, not really surprising perhaps when one considers that, in a way, their life was very theatrical—corroborees, the dreamtime, and even their body posture. Islanders were less so. They were more like Europeans—self-conscious. We became more genuinely friendly with the Aboriginals than with the Islanders. On the day we left many Aboriginals wept openly.

One, in particular, had taken a liking to me. His name was Roy Stephens. Dear boss, he called me. During the filming Roy insisted on buying me a drink. We met in the Umagico canteen and he ordered two beers. After a while he shyly produced a tobacco tin with some war medals in it—a Pacific Star, a General Service Medal, a Victory Medal. They had been awarded to him when he was with the Australian army in World War II. He told me he had been a cook in the New Guinea campaign.

"Ever see action?" I asked, truly interested in his experiences.

"My word yes, dear boss. That was the worst part. When the unit moved up into a forward area, they flew me in with the camp kitchen and together we parachuted down, sometimes into the middle of a battle."

"What do you mean by 'together'?"

"I was tied to the stove. They always did that. Often I was knocked unconscious by its weight when we hit the ground. And I couldn't get free. I had to wait for one of the soldiers to untie me. My word, dear boss, I was always black and blue after parachuting."

I still have a picture I took of Roy with his greying hair, white stubble, fleshy nose, and I wonder whether this gentle, kindly man is alive today.

For one sequence in the film we needed some shots of outrigger sailing canoes in the middle distance. These had long since gone from Torres Strait, but occasionally a *lakatoi* (traditional Papuan outrigger canoe with a crab-claw sail) would pay a visit to one of the islands in the deltas of the Mai Kussa and Pahoturi rivers, a stone's throw from the New Guinea mainland. There were two of them, Saibai and Boigu. We let the Administrator on Thursday Island know that should any *lakatoi* be sighted we wanted to get some shots of them.

One day news arrived that three *lakatoi* were at Saibai. Taking the assistant cameraman I flew there, to be truculently received by the chairman of the Island Council. Who were we? What did we want? Where were our permits? And so on. He ordered us to remain at the radio station while he contacted Thursday Island. What the chairman had neglected to do until then was switch on the two-way radio. Thursday Island had been trying to get in touch with him most of the day. We were able to stay at the nurses' quarters since they were away on leave, and the next morning we got the film we wanted from the air.

Saibai is either swamps or mudflats. The twenty or so houses are built on a very narrow strip of land between the two. At low tide you can almost walk to New Guinea. Since there is nothing to do, absolutely no work available of any kind, there is not even a subsistence economy. People must exist on government pensions. Girls have illegitimate babies just to qualify for the government's supporting parent's benefit. Arguments and fights are frequent and, when they happen, the island policeman, who wears a khaki uniform and a slouch hat, can never be found. There were suggestions that he usually took off in his official motorboat and headed for the other side of the island.

Not long after World War II, Saibai was flooded by extremely high tides. Most of the population saved themselves by climbing trees to avoid being swept away. After it was over, the then leader Bamaga Ginau asked the D.A.I.A. to transfer his people to another site. So it was that in 1948 those who wanted to move went to the newly proclaimed Northern Peninsula Area and resettled at Bamaga.

On my return there, I discovered that two of the crew had left for Cairns on the morning plane. I learnt that the night I was away there had been a ruckus. The actor playing the role of Wini was himself a rather wild Irishman, and he had overheard the two crew members make disparaging remarks about his acting ability. Inflamed by alcohol, he had found an axe and chased them. When they took refuge in their motel rooms, he had split open the doors with the axe. His explanation was that he had only been showing them how well he could act. So now we were without a make-up man and a script-girl. Thankfully we were almost finished—and it turned out the Irishman had studied make-up at a drama school in London. We got by but everybody's nerves were frayed. Bamaga was that sort of place. It didn't exactly bring out the best in people.

The whites living there were mainly employees of the D.A.I.A., and most seem to have come from small country towns in Queensland. One or two were married to Aboriginals, but the views of the majority had a decidedly racist flavour. They would openly declare that the answer to Bamaga's problems was to march the inhabitants at gunpoint off Seisia jetty (a notorious place for sharks because of the adjacent abattoir). There were frequent quarrels between the whites and the Islanders, and one night we woke to the sound of shots—the result of one such dispute. On the other hand, we heard boasts from the male Islanders about the number of white women they had slept with and how these women preferred them to their husbands. Also, between the Aboriginals and the Islanders themselves, relations were never easy. The Islanders treated the Aboriginals with contempt, calling them drunken, lazy lay-abouts (good-for-nothings), while the Aboriginals retorted by referring to the Islanders as *pouri pouri* men and claiming they smelled like "rotten snake." With such sentiments having common currency the white police sergeant had his work cut out for him, and the jail was always full.

The last night we were there the unit manager and I were invited to the home of one of the more bigoted whites. He was an Australian German who had been a great help to us. He made his own home-brew that he kept in the community cold store, which he controlled. We had settled down for a civil evening, but the grog soon ran out and we had to go to the cold store for some more.

"Now that you're here I'll get you to give me a hand," our host said. He unexpectedly pulled back a tarpaulin and rather grandly showed us a corpse—an Islander built like an ox. It was one of our extras, and I remembered we hadn't seen him for the past few days.

"Found poisoned," the German announced. "Dead in bed. At least the natives think it was poison. There's a lot of witchcraft around here. If you believe them, no one in this place dies a natural death."

What he wanted was for us to help him get the dead man into a coffin which had been made that afternoon in the woodworking shop. So, ever accommodating, we strained and struggled, but it was impossible. Rigor mortis had set in and the corpse's arms were stiffly akimbo.

"Only one thing to do," the German said. "I'll get a chainsaw and cut them off. Then he'll fit."

A postscript on Barbara Thompson: She married again—twice—the first time shortly after her return to Sydney, the second some twenty years later. When she died in Sydney in 1916, she was 88 years old. Her sojourn among the Kauralgals had left her permanently disabled. She had lost the sight in one eye from an infection, and she had walked with a limp because her foot had been badly burnt when she rolled into a fire one night while asleep. But, according to her great-niece, she remembered the natives she had lived among with real affection. She is supposed to have said: "If I had only had a child by the Kauralgal man who was my husband, I would never have left them."

She died childless.

13

Armenia

━━━━━━━━━━━━━━━━━━━━━━━━━━━

IN AND AROUND THE CAUCASUS

In April 1965 I was at Gallipoli, filming the return to that peninsula of surviving Australian, New Zealand, British, French, Newfoundland, and Turkish veterans fifty years after the Dardanelles Campaign. Those who saw Peter Weir's film *Gallipoli* (1981) might have gained the impression that Australians were on their own there. Not so. Under British command were Indian and Gurkha brigades; under French, Moroccan and Senegalese detachments. Cypriots and Maltese served in the British forces and there were some German staff officers among the Turks.

Ours was the only film crew there, apart from several Turkish units, and we came to the attention of Emin Hekimgil, the Turkish Minister for Tourism and Information. Would we consider discussing a film about his country? It had to be a documentary suitable for television and shot in colour (colour was just coming into television then). We agreed to call on him in Ankara and, in the end, spent almost five months in the country, travelling from one end to the other.

Not only did we make a film for the Turks which, incidentally, won an award at Brussels some time later, but we also shot one for National Educational Television (now the Public

Broadcasting Service) in the United States on the American Peace Corps in Turkey. And, as well, we did several shorter items for various television news magazine programs in the United Kingdom.

One of these items, I recall, was about the *Kârhane*—walled brothel quarters, which exist in all Turkish cities, complete with restaurants, coffeehouses, and shops selling women for hire. These women, some naked, others half-clothed, lolled around on divans, occasionally getting up to answer staggered rings from a battery of telephones attached to the wall. The telephones were fake, but the sight of a naked woman speaking into the mouthpiece of what they considered the ultimate in sophisticated modern instruments sent the peasants, who crowded around the barred shop fronts, into instant lust.

Another brief bit was about the apotheosis of the muezzin. The more rustic, attached to small one-roomed mosques without minarets, clambered onto the backs of their assistants or into nearby trees and summoned the faithful to their duty. Those in larger villages would diligently mount the minaret and use lung-power. Some had megaphones, but the muezzins in cities would often just sit in a little room at the base of the minaret and flip a switch. An amplified call on tape would then float out from the *serefe* or minaret gallery.

We booked into a hotel on one of Ankara's seven hills (overlooking the *Kârhane*, we later discovered) and arranged an appointment with Emin Bey. It was to be the first of many meetings, not only with the Ministry of Tourism and Information but with the Ministry of Finance. The sticking point, as one might expect, was money. How much and in what currency? They wanted to pay us Turkish rates and in Turkish *lira*. At that time Turkish currency was almost worthless outside Turkey. I decided to ask the British Embassy for advice. They produced Mr. Wotherspoon, a Levantine in two-toned shoes, a hacking jacket with a vent that almost reached his shoulder-blades, and an old Etonian tie, who would attend the meetings, watch out for our interests, and even interpret for us when needed.

It didn't take Mr. Wotherspoon long to put his finger on the problem. "You need a hunchback," he said.

"A hunchback?"

"Yes, essential for financial matters. The best possible omen."

I explained that I didn't know any hunchbacks.

"We can hire one."

The next day Mr. Wotherspoon turned up with a small, neatly dressed man. He had a fine face, a rather large head, and a hump on his back. Throughout the proceedings he sat quietly and did not utter a word. But the deal went through— exactly as Mr. Wotherspoon had predicted. It was a compromise. We were to be paid British rates but in Turkish currency by the Ministry of Tourism and Information. The Finance Ministry guaranteed that, within six months, permission would be granted to convert the *lira* into pounds sterling, and they kept their word.

We shot a great deal of footage in the various different regions of Turkey and, towards the end, found ourselves filming in the eastern *vilayets* (the Armenian uplands). Only there wasn't an Armenian face to be seen, just Turks and Kurds—or Mountain Turks as the Turks insist on calling them, though they are an Indo-European people quite different from the Turks.

The Armenians had occupied this plateau since time immemorial, but in 1915 the Turks committed the first modern genocide against them. Adolf Hitler later studied the Armenian massacres with a great deal of interest and incorporated some Turkish practices into his infamous Final Solution. Like the Nazis, the Young Turks, the Junta ruling Turkey during World War I, fell on an unsuspecting, commercially minded, quiescent, and mainly loyal population. Like the Germans the basis for their attack was racial. In all perhaps a million people were deported or slaughtered—about half the total number of Armenians living in Eastern Turkey. When I was a boy, Franz Werfel's novel *Forty Days at Musa Dagh*, about an incident in this campaign of mass murder, enjoyed great popularity. It has been claimed that it was never made into a Hollywood film because of Turkish objections at an official level, but this is hard to prove.

Twenty years earlier (1895) widespread killings had occurred during the time of Sultan 'Abdul Hamid. More than 300,000 Armenians were slain, often by Muslim Kurds. The Armenian Question was much debated in the chancelleries of Europe. Gladstone, the British statesman and Prime Minister, toured England preaching a crusade against "the unspeakable Turk." Pressure was finally brought to bear on Sultan 'Abdul Hamid and he desisted. In the end he lost his throne.

The Armenian massacres were the result of a long historical process which really began with the collapse of Turkish power in the Balkans. The Turks, as befits nomadic pastoralists from Central Asia, regarded subject races as *raiye* (flocks). The non-Muslim *raiye* were organised into a *millet* or national community. For example, all Greek Orthodox members of the Ottoman empire were placed under the Greek patriarch and all Armenians belonging to the Gregorian church under the Armenian patriarch. The patriarch had considerable power. Like the ambassador of a foreign state he ranked with a Turkish pasha. Not only was he responsible for the spiritual well-being of his people but also for their education and civil administration. He collected taxes from them both for himself and for the sultan. To help him do this he had his own police force and his own jails.

For centuries the system worked. Christian and Jewish subjects of the Ottoman sultan lived in peace and security, although they were strictly segregated from Muslim society and kept outside the mainstream of Turkish life.

Two events damaged it severely. The first was the Greek

War of Independence during the 1820s (Byron died of fever at Missolonghi in 1824, five years before the final liberation), and the other was the conquest of Eastern or Persian Armenia by the Russian general, Count Paskevich, in 1827 (from 1500 to 1700 constant wars between the Ottomans and the Persians had divided ancient Armenia into two unequal parts). Paskevich then advanced into Turkish Armenia, and thousands of the Armenian *millet*—the *sadik millet* or the faithful *millet* as the Turks called them—accompanied the Russian troops to Eastern Armenia, now a Czarist province.

Thereafter every Christian *millet* was regarded with suspicion. The Russian Czar claimed to be the protector of Christians within the Ottoman empire, something that led directly to the Crimean War, from which Romania emerged as a free nation, soon followed by Serbia and Bulgaria. Turkey became known as "The Sick Man of Europe."

In the long run the Armenians suffered all the pent-up fury, humiliation, and frustration of these past events. The Turks took it out on them in a particularly horrible manner, and it is this genocide that Armenian terrorists are avenging today, with the victims now mainly Turkish diplomats and their families. There have been more than thirty assassinations, the last (at this writing) occurring in Vienna in 1985. The justification in militant Armenian quarters is that these actions serve to draw world attention to the wrongs suffered by the Armenian people. But to some extent the world seems to agree with Hitler, who, according to documents produced at the Nuremberg trials, in a discussion with Goering once asked, "Who still talks nowadays of the extermination of the Armenians?" Who indeed apart from the Armenians?

Today they are, like the Jews, a people in Diaspora. The largest number, about 600,000, live in North America. But there are Armenians in almost every country in the Middle East, Europe, South America, and North Africa. They are to be found in India, Bangladesh, Burma, and Singapore. Australia has some 25,000. Altogether worldwide there are probably between 7 and 8 million Armenians, half of whom live in Soviet Armenia, a quarter of the ancient homeland.

What manner of people are they? Well, the Armenoid physical type is well known to anthropologists. It is one of the three brunette groups in the brachycephalic branch of the white (or Caucasian) race. The hair is brown or black, the eyes the same colour, the nose has the shape usually called "Semitic," the skull is flattened at the back. The complexion is swarthy or sultry with heavy features. They have a reputation for business acumen and, some allege, sharp dealings. How far the animosity extends is shown by a Turkish proverb that says: "Trust a snake before a Jew. Trust a Jew before a Greek. But never trust an Armenian."

Yet Armenians have given the world some interesting people·--Charles Aznavour (Aznourian), for instance, and William Saroyan, the American writer. Another writer is Michael Arlen, the *nom de plume* of Dikran Kouyoumdjian. His best-known work is *The Green Hat*, a novel about scandalous goings-on among English flappers in the 1920s. It hardly has the power to shock nowadays, but Stalin credited the suicide of his second wife to its influence.

There are other well-known Armenians—Avram Khatchaturian, the composer; Rouben Mamoulian, the film director; Karsh of Ottawa, the noted photographer; Herbert von Karajan, the conductor; and Manoug Parikian, the British violinist. And we ought not to forget Artyom Mikoyan, younger brother of the former veteran Soviet statesman Anastas Mikoyan, who invented the MIG jet fighter.

Most Armenian names end in "ian" or "yan" which means roughly "belonging to the clan of." Armenians often call themselves Hayq and their country Hayastan. Urartu (Ararat) was an ancient kingdom centred on Lake Van in what is now Eastern Turkey. Around 600 B.C. it was invaded by a people known as the Hayasa, who came from central Anatolia and were perhaps related to the Hittites. They are generally considered the ancestors of the modern Armenians. The language is Indo-European and lies somewhere between Greek and Persian. It has its own alphabet, invented by St. Mesrop at the beginning of the 5th century A.D. St. Mesrop went on to invent an alphabet for the Georgian language as well. Both Armenia and Georgia were early converts to Christianity—Armenia in 301 A.D., making it the oldest Christian nation in the world. An alphabet was needed to translate the gospels and, as both Armenian and Georgian have consonantal groupings that do not exist in Greek, Hebrew, or Aramaic (the languages of the Bible), a new alphabet had to be invented from scratch.

Bitlis, Erzurum, Diyarbakir, Malatya, Trabzon, Elazig, Van—we filmed in these towns that once had large Armenian populations living in harmony with their Turkish and Kurdish neighbours. Now there is no sign of them. The towns look like any other Turkish towns: peasants with flat caps and four-days' growth of beard; a man and a dancing bear; *döner kebap* turning slowly on the spit; vendors of drinks, with the different-flavoured cannisters on their backs—*ayran* or yoghurt and water, *visne* or sour cherry, *kizilcik* or cornel berry; the hanging sheets of dried apricots or strings of tiny dried okra for use in cooking.

There were sweetshops selling not only the familiar baklava, dripping with syrup, but other tempting and delectable morsels like *dilber dudagi* ("charming lips") and *kadin gobegi* ("ladies' navels"). Among the more favoured stalls were those dispensing *imam bayildi* ("the imam fainted"), a sort of eggplant stew with olive oil, and *iskembe corbasi* (tripe soup), not your usual bleached tripe but with all the pristine juices still in it. The Turkish kitchen is one of the three greatest in the world (the others being the French and the Chinese). As the French, the Turks have refined dishes that belong to other peoples like the Arabs, the Persians—and the Armenians.

We saw the battlements and cathedral of Ani, the citadel of

Van, the castle of Hosap, the ruins of Kars—all testaments to the glories of Ancient Armenia. They were stark symbols in a stark landscape and I was minded of the words of the 11th-century Armenian historian, Aristakes of Lastivert: "Now if all this has befallen us because of our wickedness, then tell heaven and all that abide in it, tell the mountains and the hills, the trees of the dense woodlands, that they too may weep over our destruction." We gazed on Mt. Ararat, rising alone out of the plateau to a height of 5,185 metres (17,000 feet). It has two peaks about 12 kilometres apart—Great Ararat, a dome-like mass, and Little Ararat, a sharp-pointed cone. The mountain is just inside the Turkish border and we climbed part of the way up its bare flanks. There was no sign of Noah's Ark but, in any case, that was supposed to have come to rest in the col above a small tarn and we didn't get that far.

And we filmed Van cats, a rare breed much in demand by cat fanciers. When the kittens are born, they are placed in a bucket of water—not to kill them but to see how well they swim. For Van cats are swimming cats. They like swimming and they have swimming races in Lake Van. The sight of several little cats' heads bobbing in the bay as their owners and trainers urge them on is unforgettable. I might add that Lake Van has a very high saline content, so it is really impossible to sink, or at least not to float. It also has cobalt-blue dragon flies and only one species of fish.

But the place that impressed us most in the former Armenian heartland was Aghtamar. This is a small island in the southeastern corner of Lake Van where, in the 10th century, King Gagik Ardsruni, founder of the royal house of Vaspurakan, built his palace and church. The ruins can be seen today. The exterior of the church is carved with friezes illustrating a variety of Biblical scenes as well as bas-reliefs of contemporary life. It is recognised as one of the earliest and finest examples of Romanesque architecture. The church has the traditional square central chamber roofed by a dome and flanked by four apses.

It has been argued that the Greeks who built Hagia Sophia in Constantinople and the Italians at St. Peter's in Rome only elaborated on an idea which the Armenians had developed. And that idea was to place a dome over a square as with the church at Aghtamar. The Romans had placed domes over circles, but the great architectural achievements of the Middle Ages came from the dome being placed over a square.

Thomas Ardsruni, a member of the royal house, described King Gagik's palace as having walls decorated with paintings

> of gilt thrones, on which are seated, in gracious majesty, the king surrounded by young pages with resplendent faces, groups of magicians and marvellous maidens. There are also companies of men with bared swords; wrestlers fighting with one another; lions and other fierce animals; birds with varied plumage.

Back in London I put the Armenian material, as I called it, to one side, since we hadn't used it in our Turkish film. But later, through the actor Stanley Meadows, I met a prominent Armenian businessman and, through him, Archbishop Bessak Toumayan, the Primate of Armenians in England. I asked the Archbishop for help in getting permission to film in Soviet Armenia. He promised to contact the office of His Holiness Vazken I, the Supreme Catholicos of All the Armenians, at Echmiadzin near Erevan, the capital.

My original intention was to film the Armenian homeland, about part of which I already had the earlier footage, and to cover both the genocide and recent history of the Armenians. I soon discovered, however, that no archival film existed of the genocide nor had any film ever re-created it. There was some stills material (photographs and so on) in the Hulton Picture Library in London—not much, but some.

Then I met Nubar Gulbenkian. This was arranged through

the Turkish Embassy as Gulbenkian was a Turkish Honorary Consul (he had previously been an Iranian Honorary Consul but had had some falling out with the Iranians). Nubar was a well-known eccentric and often featured in the gossip columns of the British press. He was the son of Calouste Gulbenkian—Mr. Five Per Cent—who had obtained drilling concessions for the Iraq Petroleum Company (nationalised by Iraq in 1972) from the Ottoman government. His fee was 5 percent of every barrel of oil, and he rapidly became a multimillionaire.

The meeting took place in the Ritz Hotel, the place where Nubar lived. We were to have afternoon tea together. Nubar was larger than life. He wore an orchid *boutonnière* and sported a monocle. His Bismarck whiskers, streaked with grey, were carefully brushed back. He listened intently but was not too pleased with my proposal, pointing out that his role as Honorary Turkish Consul would preclude his being involved in anything that mentioned the genocide. He suggested another tack. By all means film in Soviet Armenia, he urged, and combine that with what I had already shot in Turkish Armenia. But then look at the Armenians in Diaspora. He could contact Charles Aznavour on my behalf and get the cooperation of the French Armenian community (about 400,000). He could contact Kirk Kerkorian in the United States, at that time one of the owners of Western Airlines and the MGM motion picture company. And so on. When the time to leave came, Nubar Gulbenkian passed the bill across to me. "I'm like Royalty," he said. "I carry no money."

He walked out of the hotel with me and we stood for a while on the pavement as traffic streamed past in Piccadilly. Nubar was waiting for his chauffeur to bring the London taxi he used as a car. The reason he gave for this choice of vehicle was that it had the tightest turning circle of any car—on a sixpence it was said, whereupon Nubar Gulbenkian is reported to have asked, "What is a sixpence?" (The American expression is that a car can "turn on a dime.") Just as the taxi drew up I seized the bull by the horns.

"Would you assist financially, Mr. Gulbenkian?" I asked. "The Armenian story has never been told on film before."

"I do believe I would," he said, getting into his taxi. "Provided I like what I see about Soviet Armenia. I can't help you there. Turkey's a member of NATO. I have my position to consider." And he was off with a wave of the hand.

Not long afterwards permission was granted to film in Soviet Armenia. There were a few restrictions, and I had to use a cameraman from Armenian television. This was to prevent any "military objectives" being filmed, which, in the Soviet Union, includes bridges, railway stations, highways, etc.

The problem still was who was going to pay for it? The Armenian businessman came to the rescue. He contacted the Armenian community in Iran (then numbering perhaps 200,000), and they expressed interest. A trip was arranged on Arayana (the Iranian airlines), and I went briefly to Teheran to meet my sponsors. The sum of money involved was not really large. I had to provide film stock and pay the Armenian cameraman. There were my fares and expenses, and as I was going to do the sound-recording myself, it was all rather on the cheap.

So I came to Erevan, getting a good view of Lake Sevan, the Ararat Plain, and the mountains beyond as the Aeroflot Ilyushin prepared to land. The city, which has about 800,000 people, is comparatively modern and full of Soviet-style apartment blocks stretching endlessly along broad avenues. Most of them were of light-red stone. Trolly buses linked the suburbs and Lenin Square, in the centre of the city and where both the hotel I was staying in and, naturally, a statue of the revered man were located. Here I met my guide, who introduced the cameraman. There was a moment of confusion when I indicated the box of film stock. It was 16mm and the cameraman had a 35mm camera with him. But he went off and returned with a 16mm one, rather heavy and bulky by Western standards.

We drew up a schedule. First a visit to Echmiadzin, the seat of the Holy See. This, the spiritual centre of all Armenians, lies about 15 kilometres from Erevan, almost beneath Mt. Ararat. The official ideology (theology) of the Soviet Union is of course Marxism-Leninism, but in Armenia special privileges have been granted to the Holy See. I did not meet His Holiness Vazken I because he was away at the time, but I was given a conducted tour through the Theological Seminary.

Not far from Echmiadzin were the ruins of Zvartnotz Cathedral, and I was shown other ruins at Dvin. In general, Soviet Armenia is not as studded with remnants of Armenian history as Eastern Turkey but, after all, Eastern Turkey does represent about 75 percent of the ancient kingdom.

It was very hot. The olive-drab hills surrounding Erevan seemed to concentrate the sun's rays on the dusty city below. I went for a walk. As everywhere in the Soviet Union in summer there were ice-cream stands. Soviet ice cream is quite good, arguably the best in the world. Meandering along I stumbled onto a market. Here were piles of tomatoes, pomegranates, peaches, and apricots. There were also figs and small black cherries that had a very sweet taste (I found out afterwards that the English name for them is mazzards). These all came from the Ararat Plain—from private plots. The best quality fruit and vegetables, I was told, went to Moscow, taken by the individual growers. I was assured by my guide that it is a fact that some Armenians have become ruble millionaires by taking their produce on a plane to Moscow's free market. Armenia *does* have the highest number of cars per capita in the Soviet Union.

One day we went to Leninakan, an industrial city, another day to Kirovakan, a similar place. We saw chemical, textile, precision instrument, and nonferrous metal plants. We visited vineyards and the State Cognac Factory. We were taken to the Byurakan Astrophysical Observatory, the Erevan Opera House, and the Erevan Film Studios. In other words, we did all the safe things. We never once went into an Armenian house or sampled an Armenian meal. When the time came to leave, the cameraman asked whether he could buy some of my shirts. The ones with button-down collars took his fancy. They were very popular in the Soviet Union then and were called *botonop*. I gave him two Arrow shirts I had once bought in the States, and he gave me in return a bottle of Armenian brandy, which is also very good.

As I was so close, I decided to take a brief look at Georgia before returning to London. I wanted to see two things—Stalin's birthplace and Pirosmani's paintings in the Tbilisi Museum of Arts, which is housed, incidentally, in the old Theological Seminary where Stalin studied. Pirosmani, a sort of Georgian Henri Rousseau (le Douanier), a primitive or naive painter, eked out a life of poverty and died in squalor at the time of the revolution. I had seen reproductions of some of his work—much of it done on panels in inns to pay for meals—and was keen to inspect the originals. Some years later in 1971 a film was made about Pirosmani (or Pirosmanashvili, as his name really was).

Like the Armenians, Georgian names have distinctive endings—*shvili* (Stalin's name was Jughashvili) and *idze* or *adze* are the commonest (they are also forms of patronymics). On my return to Britain I met David Marshall Lang, professor of Caucasian studies at the School of Oriental and African Languages, University of London. Discovering my interest in the Caucasus, he kindly invited me to join his class in Caucasian studies and, for a year, when I could spare the time, I studied the language and history of Georgia. In class we read, with some difficulty (there were only three of us), Shota Rustaveli's great romantic epic *Vepkhistqaosani (The Lord of the Panther-Skin)*. The title of this work gives some idea of the Georgian language's "exuberant clusters of consonants," as Professor Lang called them.

Tbilisi, the capital of Georgia, dates from the 6th century. The old city lies either side of the Kura River, where it enters a ravine. After the Russian annexation in 1801, a European quarter was built with elegant boulevards and Germanic-looking public buildings. Today the population is about the same as Erevan, but the city is long and narrow, entwined for almost 25 kilometres around the river. Overlooking it is the holy mountain of Saint David. A rocky spur above the old city has the ruins of a citadel with an ancient church.

Gori, where Ioseb Jughashvili (Stalin) was born, is not far from Tbilisi—about 30 kilometres or maybe a little more. The road goes through the ancient capital of Mtskheta (some more of those exuberant consonants) and crosses the Inner Kartlian plain (the Georgians call themselves *Kartveli* and their homeland *Sakartvelo*; they are not Indo-Europeans but belong to the Ibero-Caucasian race). Beyond the plain at the confluence of the Liakhvi and Kura rivers stands Gori with an old fortress perched on a rocky hill.

The Georgians are quite proud of Stalin (they are not proud of his security police chief Beria) and have built a museum to him at Gori. The two-roomed cottage in which he was born has also been preserved. The museum is not a very large building but has an imposing tower that looks faintly like a campanile. Amongst all the memorabilia and pictures of Stalin (including some with Churchill and Roosevelt), I was not able to identify a copy of Khrushchev's famous speech in 1956 to the 20th Congress of the Communist Party of the Soviet Union in which he criticized Stalin and the excesses of his reign of terror.

The people of Tbilisi seemed more in the habit of eating out than those of Erevan, and so on the main street, called appropriately Rustaveli Avenue, I found a number of restaurants serving Georgian food. There I sampled two famous

Georgian dishes—*shashlik*, grilled marinated lamb with dried barberries and pomegranate juice, and chicken *tabak*, fried chicken with walnut sauce—washed down by a surprisingly good Georgian red wine.

In London I lost no time in calling Nubar Gulbenkian. "I'm sorry to have to tell you this," he said on the phone, "but I do not wish to be associated with anything that Archbishop Toumayan is involved in. That man is an anathema to me." And he hung up.

While I had been away in Soviet Armenia, a row had developed between Nubar Gulbenkian and Archbishop Toumayan. St. Sarkis Church, the Armenian church in Kensington, a London borough, had been built by Calouste Gulbenkian in memory of his father, Sarkis. Nubar Gulbenkian was one of the trustees. He had argued with Toumayan over some obscure matter and, because he owned the land on which the church was built, refused to allow the Primate to set foot in the church—in fact, he actually locked and bolted the doors against him! It all sounded very Comic Opera, but it effectively killed the Armenian Project. I was unable to sell the footage I had to anyone except a film library for use as stock shots.

Of course, in the end Nubar Gulbenkian and Archbishop Toumayan made up their quarrel. And both are, sadly, now dead. But the idea is still alive, though not all that well.

14

The Guianas

━━━━━━━━━━━━━━━━━━━━━━━━━

STEP-CHILDREN OF FADED EMPIRES

The Guianas, like Gaul, are usually divided into three parts. They used to be called British, Dutch, and French Guiana, but nowadays two of these three little countries on the shoulder of South America are independent states—Guyana and Suriname. French Guiana is still French Guiana. To the three Guianas purists would add two more—Venezuelan (disputed with Britain but eventually divided in two by an arbitrator) and Brazilian (originally claimed by France but awarded to Brazil in another such decision)—so that the Guianas might properly be considered to stretch from the delta of the Orinoco to the mouths of the Amazon. In any case, this was the historical connotation of the term, the one that Raleigh and other English and Dutch captains used when they explored these coasts in their quest for El Dorado, the legendary king of a legendary empire of gold.

Guiana comes from a Carib word meaning "the watery land." It is aptly named, for the region receives a heavy rainfall and is full of great sluggish rivers that flow through low-lying land to the mudbanks of the coast. There are no golden beaches to be found here. No blue water either. The sea is brown, full of silt carried down the Amazon and Orinoco rivers from the far-off Andes.

For 1,500 kilometres from west to east the coast of this

region is flat, swampy and lined with mangroves. The first hills do not appear until Cayenne Island in French Guiana is reached. The highest, Montabo, is 87 metres (285 feet), and about 60 metres up the hill stands the only modern hotel in Cayenne, the Hotel du Montabo, where we stayed. The hotel sticker, which was immediately affixed to our luggage, shows a galleon at anchor off a peak that looks a bit like an ice-cream cone turned upside down. At the base was a date—1598—the first French voyage of discovery. The French have been around Guiana for a long time.

Cayenne is the only real town in French Guiana. It has 30,000 inhabitants, about half the population of the country. Cayenne is called an island because of the canalisation of some creeks between the Cayenne and Mahury rivers. The town has a few interesting buildings. The residence of the *Préfet* was once a Jesuit monastery, and Fort Diamant, at the mouth of the Mahury River, dates from 1652 and is a good example of a late medieval fortification. But perhaps the best word to describe Cayenne is *ratatiné* ("decrepit" or "shrivelled up"). I have been in some other towns that merit this description—Lomé, the capital of Togo in West Africa, Bata in Equatorial Guinea (formerly the Spanish colony of Rio Muni), even Cooktown in Queensland in my own country of Australia—but none suits it better than Cayenne, the forlorn and shabby capital of a country no one ever goes to for pleasure. It is a lost place full of lost people living on the edge of the jungle.

Driving in from the airport at Rochambeau (13 kilometres from Cayenne), we saw two jaguars lying on the road. "Don't get out and try to photograph them," the driver said as he stopped. "A Chinese did that and was killed." The beasts slowly stirred themselves and slunk away. "You should photograph jaguars in the zoo." He said this as if it was self-evident. He was right about the zoo, though. Later we visited it and were quite charmed. It is one of the most exotic small zoos I have ever seen.

Life in Cayenne revolves around the *Place des Palmistes*, a central park with a row of the giant double palms native to French Guiana. It is said a priest planted them. Opposite the *Place* is the *Bar Palmiste*, where *le tout Cayenne* seems to spend most of the day sipping coffee and aperitifs. And among them were the street girls, sitting slightly apart, chattering gaily and keeping a weather eye open for customers (there are French troops in Guiana). Most of them were Creole—mixed bloods—but some were Indians. They call them Amerindians in the Guianas to distinguish them from immigrant Indians, who are known as East Indians. To add to the confusion there are also West Indians in French Guiana. They come from the British island of St. Lucia and are mostly fishermen.

My camera crew and I had come to the Guianas because they were the step-children of three faded European empires, because they were remote, because of their interlocking history, because of El Dorado—in short, because of anything that would make an interesting television documentary. And the most interesting—and once-notorious—thing about French Guiana is *le bagne*, the penal settlement.

The main object of our visit was the Iles du Salut—the Islands of Recovery. These are a group of three small islands 40 kilometres northwest of Cayenne. The two largest are Royale and Saint-Joseph. The smallest is Devil's Island, which was, of course, the name popularly given to the whole infamous penal colony. (Still, these are, rather surprisingly, healthy islands since the dangerous anopheles mosquito can't make it from the mangrove swamps of the coast 15 kilometres away.)

But there were penitentiaries and prison camps at other places in Guiana—Kourou, Saint-Laurent du Maroni, Oyapoc, and one, 6 kilometres from Cayenne, at Montjoly. The French first investigated the possibilities of the country as a repository for unwanted criminals during the Revolution. In 1798 a group of political prisoners and "refractory" priests were sent there. Within two years more than half of them were dead and the rest returned to Europe. During the Second Empire the idea was revived, and 17,000 prisoners were transported to French Guiana between 1852 and 1867. Of this number more than 7,000 perished, and this heavy death rate—from yellow fever, malaria, and typhus among other things—gave pause to the French authorities, who then temporarily shifted their attention to New Caledonia in the Coral Sea. But in 1886 it was decided New Caledonia was *trop douce*—"too soft," the words actually used in the official report—and the French turned once more to Guiana. The transportation of prisoners to the penal colony finally ceased in 1937, and it was closed in 1947. The 800 remaining prisoners were offered the choice of staying in Guiana or being repatriated. Most chose the latter, but a few of these ex-cons (who were known as *bagnards*) stayed. In all, over 80,000 prisoners passed through *le bagne*, and less than a quarter of them saw France again. It was not for nothing that the Guianese penal settlement was known as "the Dry Guillotine."

There were various categories of convicts: the *transportés* (usually murderers), the *relégués* (habitual criminals), the *déportés* (political prisoners not supposed to be put to work), and the *libérés* (those who had been released but forced to stay in Guiana for an additional period equal to their original sentence). Most of them were employed on public works, such as road building, draining the marshes, and getting timber, but some were hired out to private individuals while others were used as domestic servants by the prison service. The celebrated French journalist Albert Londres visited *le bagne* in 1925 and reported (I translate):

> The prison colony was shameful for Guiana and there were many injustices. Many convicts endured hunger and the threat of illness. It is understandable that, in such a situation, the dream of every old lag was escape—the beautiful thing—and at certain times escapes were very frequent, and the scandal of bands of criminals from Guiana located in Latin America (Caracas, Buenos Aires) rebounded against France.

There were still a handful of *bagnards* left in French Guiana when we were there. In the *Place des Palmistes* two were pointed out to us sitting on a bench; they were barefoot, emaciated and vulpine-looking old men, clad in dirty white duck trousers with loose white blouses in the French style, and wearing cardboard topees. We found out that they lived in a shack made of pieces of wood, iron, and palm fronds on the outskirts of Cayenne. The Salvation Army helped them out with some food but could not persuade them to move into its home.

"*Pour nous c'est pas la liberté,*" they are supposed to have said ("For us it ain't liberty"), but cynics pointed out that the Salvation Army didn't allow alcohol on the premises, and the *bagnards* usually passed the time drinking tafia, a kind of cheap rum.

I asked them about the best-selling author Henri Charrière (more widely known by his nickname, Papillon), and they were highly critical—a *blagueur* ("bullshit artist"), a *homme orchestre* ("one-man band," though this term in argot has sexual overtones), and so on. We heard much the same from the other citizens of Cayenne. Papillon, it seemed, had drawn on a common fund of experience to embellish his own famous account of *le bagne*. Well, if true, I don't hold that against him. And if memory serves me correctly, Papillon wound up owning a bar in Caracas.

Another elderly *bagnard* owned what was probably the best restaurant in French Guiana. It was on the seafront at Montjoly about ten minutes from town and called *Le Cric-Crac*, after his nickname. This was because of the *crime passionel* that had sent him to *le bagne* in the first place (he had reputedly killed his mistress by snapping her neck). Around the walls of the restaurant were a series of paintings done by the *patron* himself, and all were scenes from *le bagne*. We tried to film them, but he stopped us and offered instead a set of postcards of the paintings. The price was one hundred dollars.

"*Ces peintures sont incomparables*" ("These pictures are incomparable"), he explained. I suppose he had a point, so I bought a set.

The food at *Le Cric-Crac* was mainly French but there were some special creole plates since the *bagnard* had a young Martinican wife. This was the only time in French Guiana I tasted Cayenne pepper in a dish. It is not a native of the country nor does it grow there, so how the name Cayenne became attached to the chilli is something of a mystery (a possible explanation is that the Tupi word for the plant became confused with Cayenne, a form of Guiana).

At dawn we left on a fishing ketch for the Iles du Salut. The trip took four hours and the crew were St. Lucians who had come to French Guiana because of overcrowding at home and because they could speak a French Creole patois. We arrived first at Royale, the largest island, about 1.5 kilometres long. Dark green hills rose to a little plateau on top. The pier was made up of granite blocks, with a couple of dilapidated warehouses nearby, and from it a road ran up into the hills. A toothless *bagnard* greeted us. He looked after the lighthouse and, for a few francs, acted as unofficial guide. He showed us around the buildings on the plateau, most of which had fallen into decay—the penitentiary, the hospital, the church, the governor's residence, the warders' quarters. He was particularly eager to point out where *la Veuve*—the Widow, or the Guillotine—had stood. It was brought out of a shed and assembled on five white stones arranged in two rows, four in front and one behind.

Only those prisoners who had committed a further crime in *le bagne* were sent over to the Iles du Salut. In the penal settlement's heyday, there were usually as many as 1,200 men located on these three islands. On Royale they were kept in long stone sheds, where two continuous wood platforms served as beds. These were tilted slightly since there were neither pillows nor mattresses. Fifty men were locked into each shed and allowed half an hour's exercise in the morning and afternoon but otherwise nothing. Pederasty flourished, and there were constant fights. Our guide told us that when he was there in the war years, a corpse was dragged out of the sheds almost every morning. He pointed out a hole on some of the platforms which was called *un matelas perforé* ("a perforated mattress"), where prisoners dying of dysentery were laid.

Saint-Joseph, about half the size of Royale, was the island of *reclusion* ("solitary confinement"), a cruel punishment that could last anywhere from five to ten years. From the pier a winding road led past the quarters for the insane—often the end result of *reclusion*—to a low stone building. Here the cells were individual (3 by 2 metres, or roughly 10 feet by 6) with an iron grille ceiling only 4 metres high (about 13 feet). Separating the grille from the roof was an open space, and in the roof above each cell was a hole about 7 cm wide (2.75 inches)—the only source of light and air.

Down the centre of the building between the cell blocks, and on a level with the top of the walls, ran a narrow platform perhaps a metre wide along which a warder would patrol to make sure the major rule of *reclusion*—absolute silence—was kept at all times. I walked the length of it, peering at the cells below. In each of them was a tilted bed of boards, at its foot the *fer* or iron horseshoe which clamped the prisoner by one ankle to his bunk. The prisoners were never allowed out, and their only company was vampire bats, which could easily enter the cells.

Around the three islands of the Iles du Salut runs a rapid current that is at its strongest between Royale and Devil's Island, and it took us quite some time to cross the hundred-odd metres separating them. In the days of *le bagne* a flying fox (a two-stranded cableway that allowed packages to be drawn by hand from one side to the other) between the two islands was used to get provisions across to Devil's Island.

Devil's Island is very small. You can in fact walk around it in the time it takes to smoke a cigarette. There's a path lined by two little rows of stone cottages which used to have gardens, a proper lavatory at the back, and chicken coops. The prisoners were locked in their cottages at night, but otherwise they had free run of the island. Books were provided, and chess sets.

Devil's Island was used for political prisoners only. We saw Dreyfus' cottage—it had two bedrooms and a dining room—and we were told that he always had wine with his meals. At any given time there were never more than twelve prisoners on Devil's Island plus a few guards and trustees.

Because they were deliberately fed by guards, sharks used to swarm in the waters around the Iles du Salut; similarly, sharks got the bodies of those convicts who had died or were executed. Yet, in spite of these hazards, some convicts did manage to escape—usually trustees, who made rafts from the husks of coconuts. But countless other prisoners perished in the attempt.

The 1985 edition of *The South American Handbook* says: "There is a twenty-bed hotel (ex-mess hall for warders, with good food) on Ile Royale." So obviously times have changed since I was there.

Another place we wanted to cover in French Guiana was Kourou, which is on the mainland opposite the Iles du Salut. We drove there along the only highway in the country. It parallels the sea, but all one is aware of is mangrove swamp. Kourou, once a lazy little backwater with no more than 600 inhabitants, grew to an instant town of 6,000 when it became the site of the French Space Centre, which opened in 1966. The Space Centre occupies an area about 4 kilometres deep along some 30 kilometres of coast and is less than 5° north of the equator. Thus, the rotating speed of the earth here is much faster than at Cape Canaveral, which means, in effect, that the same propulsion will lift 24 percent more weight—a clear advantage when it comes to satellite payloads and launches.

Kourou has also been the site of some other French ventures. Between 1763 and 1765 there was an attempt to establish a colony there. More than 15,000 settlers from France—including a company of professional musicians—arrived with their various goods and chattels, among which was a large quantity of ice skates (but no ploughs or agricultural tools)! The first building to be erected was an opera house. Within two years some 14,000 had died in *l'Enfer Vert*—"the Green Hell," as French Guiana has also come to be called. Still, as recently as 1976, the French Government announced plans to settle 30,000 colonists in this *département* (French Guiana is regarded as an integral part of France, not as a colony) in order to develop its resources—important deposits of bauxite, hydro-electric potential, forestry, and so on (the scheme collapsed within two years).

In Suriname this approach has already been tried, but it doesn't appear to have helped much. When we were there the country was called Surinam and was an equal partner with the Netherlands in a sort of Dutch Commonwealth. In 1975, however, it became independent (adding a final "e" to become Suriname), with the result that a third of the population left for the Netherlands. The first military coup was in 1980, and since then there have so far been two more. After the coup in 1982, parliament was dismissed (its fifteen opposition members were publicly executed), the Constitution suspended, media censorship introduced, a People's Militia formed, democratic rights abolished, Cuban aid sought, and a military agreement signed with Libya—a familiar pattern (even up to the attempted right-wing coup in July 1986, which led to a crippling guerrilla war).

Suriname is twice the size of French Guiana but has six times the population, half of the inhabitants living in Paramaribo, the capital. The rest, as in all the Guianas, live along the coastal strip, much of which is empoldered behind dikes. The country has a very diverse population. The largest group is the East Indians, followed by Creoles (mulattos of Afro-

European origin), Javanese, Bush Negroes (descendants of runaway slaves), Amerindians, Chinese, Portuguese Jews, and Europeans. There is very little intermarriage, but some miscegenation and racial tension exists between the East Indians and Creoles.

Although Dutch is the official language, the lingua franca is Sranan Tongo (Suriname Tongue), otherwise known as Talkie-Talkie, an English Creole or Pidgin that dates back to the days when Suriname was a British colony. Here's an example from a poem about Suriname by the Creole poet R. Dobru:

Wan bon	One boom [tree],
Someni wiwiri	So many leaves,
Wan bon	One boom.

There is a more Africanised version of this language spoken by the Bush Negroes called Sramaccan Tongo or Deep Talkie-Talkie (the Saramacca is a river that runs parallel to the Suriname River). Sramaccan is also used by two tribes of Bush Negroes in French Guiana, who have crossed over from Suriname.

Paramaribo lies on the left bank of the Suriname, 12 kilometres from the sea. Zanderij Airport, where we landed, is 50 kilometres away. The capital is a rather provincial and slightly rundown place. Most of the older houses are wooden, with stilted balconies and heavily shuttered windows, but they are brightly painted and the streets are lined with beautiful trees—tamarind, mahogany, and flamboyant (royal poinciana). There is a 17th-century fort, Fort Zeelandia (formerly Fort Willoughby), and some mellow 18th-century Dutch brick buildings situated around a little square called, at that time, Oranjeplein. The 19th-century cathedral is said to be the largest wooden structure in the Northern Hemisphere, and there are also a mosque, some Hindu temples, and a synagogue. The hotel where we stayed, the Torarica, had a swimming pool, casino, tropical gardens, and a restaurant that served Indonesian and Creole dishes (the latter included the national one—*pastei*, a sort of vegetarian turnover not baked in a dish, similar to what they call in England a Cornish pasty).

In the market Creole women were dressed in the *Kota Missie* (Misses' coat) costume, which is a long full skirt with a bustle and a wide starched collar. This is topped by a matching kerchief knotted over the head in a variety of ways to indicate the present mood of the wearer—joyful, sad, looking for a sexual adventure, not looking for one, and so on. The market was very colourful with its Javanese women in sarongs and *kebayas* and East Indians in saris.

On the opposite bank of the wide Suriname River is Joden-savanne ("Jews' Savannah"). Here the first Jews settled, from the Netherlands, and the Berachah ve Salom synagogue is the oldest in the Americas. Closer to the sea a tributary called the Commewijne joins the Suriname and along it are plantation mansions dating from English times and bearing some resemblance to those found in Virginia. They distill their own rum (a light rum like Demerara) but otherwise seem fairly moribund.

The English first arrived in 1630—sixty settlers, who planted tobacco. These were followed by others, and in 1651 Lord Willoughby of Parham, Governor of Barbados, sent an expedition of royalists to establish a colony. Soon there were five hundred sugar plantations with some 1,000 whites and 2,000 African slaves. In time Jews from Holland and Italy, as well as those who had originally emigrated to Brazil, joined them. In 1665 the Jews received a special grant from Lord Willoughby, the first of its kind made by an English government to Jews.

The first novel written by a woman in English—Mrs. Aphra Behn's *Oronooko or the Royal Slave* (published 1678)—was set in Suriname. She had spent some years in the colony before marrying and returning to England. The story contrasts the nobility of the supposedly savage Oronooko and

the baseness of the supposedly civilised English settlers. It
stirred up the same kind of outrage that *Uncle Tom's Cabin*
did 173 years later. Today Mrs. Behn is something of a cult
figure in the feminist movement. During the Second Anglo-
Dutch War, Suriname was conquered by the Dutch and, at
the Treaty of Breda, in 1667 ceded to them in exchange for
New Amsterdam (now New York). Aphra Behn wrote:

> Certainly had his late Majesty [Charles II] but seen and
> known what a vast and charming world he had been master of
> in that continent he would never have parted so easily with it
> to the Dutch.

She also wrote of plantation life and for her readers included
such exotica as eating electric eels, which she described as
"most delicate meat."

In the 18th century there was a series of slave revolts
against the Dutch that were put down with great cruelty.
Then, during the Napoleonic wars, the colony was occupied
by Britain. It was finally restored to the Netherlands in 1814
but without the three westermost provinces of Berbice, Demerara, and Essequibo, which became British Guiana (and
later Guyana).

Suriname is the third largest producer of bauxite in the
world (led by Australia) and also has an alumina refinery and
an aluminium smelter. The power for these comes from a
giant hydro-electric complex completed in Dutch times. The
Suriname River was dammed, creating a large lake called
Brokopondo ("Broken Lake"). We had a look at it and also
at the town of Moengo, 160 kilometres up the Commewijne
and Cottica rivers from Paramaribo, where the Suriname
Aluminium Company has its mines. Not far from Moengo is
the village of Albina on the Marrowijne River—the boundary
with French Guiana.

We stayed there a few days, mainly to film some Bush
Negro villages along the river. These were above the rapids
and often in places that were difficult to reach. Here runaway

slaves had tried to reproduce their West African way of life, hunting and fishing predominantly with spears (not bows and arrows like the Amerindians), and cultivating yams, okra, chick peas, and bananas. Except for small girdles, they go mainly naked. Great importance is placed on their drums or *tam-tams*, which women are never allowed to touch. The head of each tribe is known as the *Granman* and under him are several *Bassias* ("bosses"). Dances, accompanied by rhythmic drumming, are called *dansie-dansie*. But, aside from such words, I couldn't make head nor tail of Deep Talkie-Talkie.

The only other trip we made in Suriname was to Nieuw Nickerie on the border with Guyana. This took us the breadth of the country along a flat coast, through rice fields intersected by straight canals. To us, Nieuw Nickerie's main distinction was the number and voracity of its mosquito population. But the citizens are fanatics about cricket—because most of them are East Indians—and we watched a game during which all the players were constantly slapping themselves, even when bowling.

On the way back we called at Coronie. The people there are Creoles, and the area is given over to coconut plantations. Indeed Coronie itself is but a single long avenue lined with palm trees. The original plantations were held by Scots settlers, and their names—Inverness, Hamilton, Hope, and so on—still remain, as do their graves in the local cemetery (plenty of Morrisons, Blacks, Douglases, Grants). There are still plenty of Morrisons, Blacks, etc. around, but they are now Creoles—Creoles who are proud of their reputation as *de luiste negers in de wereld* ("the laziest niggers in the world"). "Nigger" isn't a pejorative in Suriname, and in fact an up-market or classier term for Talkie-Talkie is *negerengels* ("nigger English"). As explained to me by one of the Blacks ("Black by name, black by nature"), the people of Coronie believe in the Law of Least Effort: "Why work, man? Coconuts fall off a palm tree. Chickens find their own food.

Yams grow wild. Fish give themselves up in the river. We don't need anything, so why work?''

Against such logic, why, indeed?

Two days later we were in Georgetown, Guyana, and the first order of business was to find a doctor. The crew all had gonorrhea, contracted from the street girls of Cayenne. The doctor was of Portuguese extraction, and one of the bits of advice he gave us was to be careful of anti-white feeling.

"Don't wear shorts," he said. "They regard it as colonialist. Don't get involved in an argument with anyone." And to the crew: "Stay away from prostitutes. They will offer you drugged sweets and rob you."

Georgetown was even then getting an unsavoury reputation. Yet the town itself is probably the best-preserved early Victorian one in existence, though mainly built of wood. The houses are white with green shutters and stand on high blocks. The streets are laid out in a grid pattern, and during Dutch times narrow canals ran down the middle of them; these have now been filled in and replaced by footpaths under shady trees, which lend a certain elegance. The town lies below sea level and is protected by a series of dikes and sluices. Much of Georgetown's life revolves round the Stabroek Market, a large iron structure with an elaborate clock tower, where you can buy almost anything. (I got an Amerindian hammock there.)

Just as Suriname is twice the size of French Guiana, Guyana is twice the size of Suriname. The population is nearly 800,000, of which about a quarter lives in Georgetown, and 61 percent are East Indians, 32 percent Creoles, and the other 7 percent Amerindians, Chinese, and Europeans. Most of the Europeans are Portuguese from Madeira or the Azores.

The country was first settled between 1616 and 1621 by the Dutch, who built a fort in the Essequibo District, called Kykover-Al ("Look over All"), the ruins of which can still be seen. Some years later a colony was founded on the Berbice River. Britain gained possession in 1814, and in 1899 a commission arbitrating a boundary dispute between Britain and Venezuela awarded over half the present territory of Guyana to Britain. Venezuela still lays claim to this, but many have called it "the dispute of two bald men over a comb."

Guyana was granted independence in 1966 with a Governor-General appointed by the Queen. This was the situation when we were there. In 1970, however, Guyana became a Cooperative Republic. The bauxite and sugar industries were nationalised. The Executive President was Forbes Burnham, a Creole, and some elections have been marked by allegations of fraud because the East Indian party, led by Dr. Cheddi Jagan, gained only a quarter of the seats although East Indians represent two-thirds of the population. In the meantime the economy has collapsed, unemployment runs at about 40 percent, the country has sunk into chronic poverty, and Guyana has failed to meet its foreign-debt payments, including compensation for the bauxite and sugar industries, and so on. (Burnham died in 1985.)

What has come to be known as "the Jonestown massacre" also occurred in Guyana. On November 18, 1978, at a jungle settlement near the Essequibo River more than 900 Americans, members of the People's Temple Cult, committed suicide either by drinking or being forced to drink a mixture of soft drink and cyanide. Some hours previously a United States Congressman and four others (including an American reporter, photographer, and cameraman) had been killed in an ambush by armed cult members as they were about to board a plane and leave the settlement. The sect had been led to Guyana by the Rev. Jim Jones on the promise of creating a "socialized utopia" where all races would mix in peace. It has been alleged Jones bribed Forbes Burnham into granting land for the colony.

Georgetown lies on the Demerara River. We crossed this by ferry and visited one of the Booker Bros. plantations, called

Uitvlugt ("Out Flight"—and pronounced locally as "I Flucked"). The Bookers were, at that time, comparatively enlightened proprietors. (They did, after all, institute the Booker Prize, Britain's most prestigious literary award.) But the problems of cane-farming in Guyana were enormous. To begin with, it was carried out on empoldered land, which meant maintaining expensive drainage canals. Mechanical harvesters could not be used, so a large labour force was needed. Originally, of course, this had been provided by slaves and, after them, Portuguese and Chinese immigrants, then finally by indentured East Indians. It was a classic situation of latifundia, and the evils of that system—slavery and indenture—have helped create a distorted picture of the Guyanese character as one of resentment, suspicion, and tension. Other West Indians call them "the lying Guyanese." Yet these "lying Guyanese" have produced some fine writers, among them Edgar Mittelholzer (with his well-known Kaywana series based on the first settlement near Kyk-over-Al), Jan Crew, Wilson Harris, and the poet A. J. Seymour, who writes of "the dream of perished Dutch plantations." There are many more.

We also filmed the other Guyanese industry—bauxite. Guyana has the world's largest deposits, but as a producer it was then fifth in the world. These deposits are at Linden, which is made up of three towns on opposite banks of the Demerara River in dense jungle. There is a calcining kiln and an alumina plant. Most of the staff were Canadians since before nationalisation the Demerara Bauxite Company was a subsidiary of Alcan.

What we had shot in Suriname and Guyana was so far very similar. We had not gone any great distance from the coast in Suriname for a number of reasons. The country is mostly impenetrable jungle and though there are a few airstrips, flights are irregular and heavy rains often make it impossible to land. It was the same in French Guiana with the additional hurdle of having to obtain permission to film from the *Pré-*

fecture. In Guyana, on the other hand, there was an airline operating on a fairly regular schedule to remote parts of the territory.

Some of these we wanted to see if possible—the Kaieteur Falls on the Potaro River, certainly one of the highest in the world; Mt. Roraima, the inspiration for Conan Doyle's *The Lost World*, in the Pakaraima Mountains (where W. H. Hudson set his novel *Green Mansions*); Lake Amuku, said to be the site of Manoa, the city of El Dorado, the Gilded Man; and the Rupununi, a vast savannah along the Brazilian border, where they still go in for open range ranching much as it was done in the American Old West.

We didn't get to them all, but we did make the Kaieteur Falls, landing in a small Grumman amphibian above the falls and walking back to them. The gorge has narrow straight sides, and there is a perpendicular drop of nearly 250 metres (820 feet). A rainbow always forms over Kaieteur, and when we were there it was a completely circular one, something that I have seen only once since. The pilot had some stores to deliver to Kamarang, 50 kilometres north of Mt. Roraima, and after he had done so he flew around the mountain for us. It is a great plateau some 3,000 metres high (9,842 feet), the highest in the Pakaraimas and surrounded by cliffs plunging 600 metres (1,968 feet).

We unfortunately missed out on Lake Amuku, in the northern Rupununi. But we did get to Lethem, on the Brazilian frontier and the administrative centre for the Rupununi. We flew there on Guyana Airways. Lethem consists of a military post, telegraph office, police headquarters, an abattoir, and three bars, one of which will allow you to sleep on the tables free of charge. Lethem has changed but little since Evelyn Waugh came this way in the 1930s. We stayed at the Manari Ranch, owned by one of the Melville family, in a two-storey building about 10 kilometres from the airport.

There are two great ranching families in the Rupununi—the Melvilles and the Harts. The original Melville, a Scot, came there at the end of the 19th century, took two Amerindian wives, and began cattle-ranching. Hart, an American, arrived soon after and did much the same. Our host showed us around, and we filmed a number of Amerindians, including an attractive young girl with light skin, green eyes, straight brown hair cut in a fringe, and a full figure. "You see where the stories about white Indians come from," he said.

This particular Melville supplemented his ranching and guest-house activities by catching animals for the London Zoo. These included tapir, armadillo, and agouti (a sort of large rodent), which he kept in hutches. To give our film a little excitement, he agreed to catch an anaconda. Behind the ranch-house was a creek with numerous big waterholes. His Amerindian cowboys drove an anaconda into this creek, and he dived in after it. There was a flurry of water as snake and man seemed interminably intertwined in the ensuing struggle. Finally he managed to stuff the snake into a sack he had with him and climbed out nonchalantly.

"Got to get them in the water," he explained. "Then they can't get a purchase on anything. They're a type of boa constrictor and crush their prey." This specimen was about 4 metres long (13 feet) and as thick as a man's leg!

We spent New Year's Eve 1969 at Manari and prepared to fly back to Georgetown on January 2nd. The plane was due after lunch, but during the morning a group of ranchers and cowboys attacked the Lethem police station and nine people were killed in the affair. It was supposedly led by members of the Melville and Hart families. The ranchers had allegedly plotted with Venezuelan authorities to secede from Guyana and establish a separate state. They were said to have been given training in Venezuela and armed with automatic weapons and bazookas—the old border dispute brought up to date and given a new twist!

Our problem was to convince the Guyanese security forces that we just happened to be there by chance. This seemed to be too much of a coincidence for them and so we were taken into custody. In vain did we protest that we had been 10 kilometres from the scene of the action. They decided to send us back to Georgetown on a military aircraft and to inform the British High Commission that we were *"personae non gratae."*

After all that I was not sorry to leave the Rupununi. Besides, the area has a little biting fly—the kaboura—which does not carry disease but whose bites itch for days. Only the sound recordist was a bit reluctant to go. "I'd like to see more of those white Indian girls," he said.

So back we went to the Park Hotel, a Somerset Maugham-type establishment with a huge cupola'd verandah and colonial-style (wooden with cane backs) lazy-boy chairs—until we were rather unceremoniously put on a plane and sent out of the country.

15

Juan Fernández

▭▭▭▭▭▭▭▭▭▭▭▭▭▭▭▭

ROBINSON CRUSOE'S ISLAND

On February 1, 1709, the crew of an English ship lying off the island of Juan Fernández, 670 kilometres west of Chile in the South Pacific, saw a light ashore. It was the signal fire of a marooned sailor, Alexander Selkirk, who had spent four years and four months there completely alone. The next morning he was brought on board, clad in goat skins and looking "wilder than the first owners of them."

This is our first glimpse of a man destined to become the archetype of the castaway. Selkirk's enforced stay on Juan Fernández was the chief inspiration for one of the seminal myths of English literature, Daniel Defoe's *Robinson Crusoe*, a marvellous adventure story about a man's struggle against Nature while attaining mastery over himself in the process.

The captain of the English ship was Woodes Rogers, a privateer (or licensed pirate), and he wrote a verbatim account of Selkirk's experience in the ship's log. Rogers' expedition had been financed by the Corporation of Bristol and was in the South Pacific to prey on Spanish shipping, which it did very successfully. When Woodes Rogers returned to London, his journal was published and Selkirk found himself lionised by fashionable society. Sir Richard Steele, the essayist, wrote a piece about him that described Selkirk as "a self-absorbed dreamer, full of quiet confidence and strength."

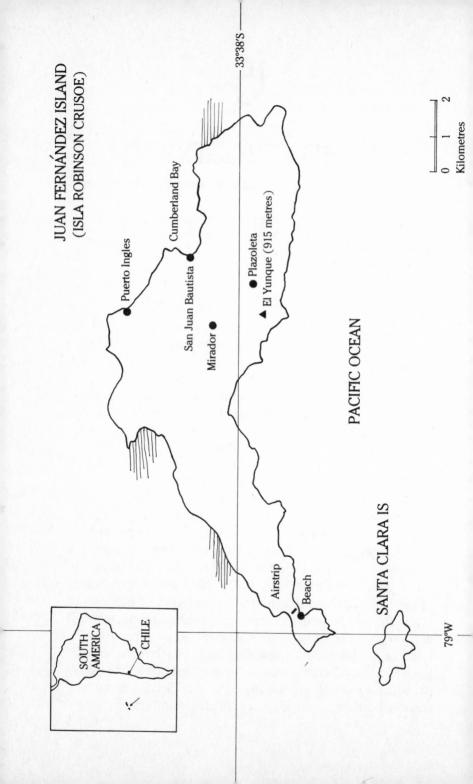

JUAN FERNÁNDEZ ISLAND
(ISLA ROBINSON CRUSOE)

Puerto Ingles

Cumberland Bay

San Juan Bautista

Mirador

Plazoleta
▲ El Yunque (915 metres)

PACIFIC OCEAN

Airstrip

Beach

SANTA CLARA IS

SOUTH
AMERICA

CHILE

33°38'S

79°W

0 1 2
Kilometres

Selkirk was much in demand in the salons of Bristol and London and is even supposed to have asked Defoe at one time to put his papers in order. They are said to have met in 1713—the date and place are in dispute, and indeed the fact of their meeting always will be. For some reason or other, Defoe could never bring himself to identify Selkirk definitely as the man who had inspired the portrait of Robinson Crusoe. All he would say was: "There is a man alive and well-known too, whose life is my just subject and to whom all or most part of the story directly alludes." And that is as far as he would go.

We know that many of the details of *Robinson Crusoe* came from other sources but, in its essentials, the story is Selkirk's. Defoe got the name "Crusoe" from a school friend but "Robinson" seems to point to Juan Fernández. Some twenty years before Selkirk's arrival there, William Dampier, the English buccaneer, on a voyage around the world, rescued a Mosquito Indian who had been accidentally marooned on that island. His name was Will, and the first man to leap ashore to greet him on his return happened to be another Mosquito Indian called Robin. Prints of their reunion were almost as popular in England as prints of Selkirk dancing with his goats eventually became—though both were subsequently eclipsed by prints showing Robinson Crusoe and Man Friday. Robin is almost certainly the origin of Robinson Crusoe's first name and suggests he is the "son of Robin." (Though Willson Crusoe would have been more accurate, it somehow doesn't have quite the same ring to it.) Possibly Defoe himself wasn't sure which was Robin and which was Will. The only caption I have seen on a print of them reads simply: AFFECTING INTERVIEW OF TWO MOSKITO MEN.

Alexander Selkirk had in many respects a far more interesting story to tell than his fictional counterpart, and in 1976 we decided to tell it in a film documentary. In the end this brought me to what is now officially known as Isla Robinson Crusoe, but which used to be known as Más a Tierra

("Closer to the Land," i.e., mainland South America) and, more popularly, as Juan Fernández. The other islands in the group are Isla Alejandro Selkirk (formerly Más Afuera or "Further Out"), lying 150 kilometres west, and Santa Clara, only 1.5 kilometres south of Juan Fernández.

These three small, extremely mountainous islands are of volcanic origin and were discovered by the Spanish priest and navigator Juan Fernández in 1572. Today they belong to Chile and support a combined population of about 650 individuals, most of whom live in the only village, San Juan Bautista, on the shores of Cumberland Bay. The chief industry is lobster fishing, but there is also a fish processing plant. The German raider, the *Dresden*, was sunk in Cumberland Bay by British warships during World War I, by the way.

Originally Juan Fernández tried to settle natives from the South American continent on the island but, failing to obtain a government charter, he and they abandoned it, leaving behind a few goats whose descendants feature so prominently in Selkirk's (and Crusoe's) accounts of the island. During the 17th and 18th centuries the island was a victualling place of English, French, and Dutch buccaneers, mainly because it was well away from the Spaniards and they could take on fresh water and fresh meat largely unmolested. But not only buccaneers called there. Almost every explorer who entered the Pacific through the Straits of Magellan put in to Juan Fernández. Captain John Davis, Commodore George Anson, Commodore John Byron all left descriptions of the island, its light airs and delights. So did Captain George Shelvocke, who also was wrecked there and provided another literary link. Before this disaster his ship had endured bad storms in the waters around Cape Horn; it is Shelvocke's account of this and the shooting of "the black albatross" which accompanied the vessel for days that is the source of Coleridge's poem "The Rime of the Ancient Mariner."

Inevitably, troublesome mariners found themselves marooned there by their ships' captains, thus Selkirk had a number of predecessors apart from Will. And, at times, the Spanish authorities in Peru used the island as a penal colony. During the Chilean War of Independence in 1817 many of the patriots were imprisoned there by the Spaniards, and for a while the Chileans continued the practice.

But all this was ephemeral. It was not until the middle of the 19th century that a serious attempt at colonisation was made. The prime mover was Alfred de Rodt, a Swiss baron, motivated by romantic Robinsonian notions. He was succeeded by others, including a Scot called Green, who had always been determined to follow in Selkirk's footsteps. Some were themselves shipwrecked on the island—a Frenchman called Charpentier and a German called Schiller. And some—like Recabarren, González, López, and Araya—came in sealing gangs from the district of Maule in the central south of Chile. So the population of Juan Fernández today has a decidedly mixed origin with these same surnames well represented (they are in fact a virtual roll call).

Yet, despite this, the island is still much as it was in Selkirk's time. The vegetation is hardly changed except for the introduction of eucalyptus trees, seals continue to bask on the rocks, goats roam the craggy peaks, and crayfish are there for the taking. Out of sight of San Juan Bautista one might even be moved to say, as Cowper did of Selkirk:

> "I am the monarch of all I survey
> My right there is none to dispute,
> From the centre all round to the sea,
> I am the lord of the fowl and the brute."

We had begun our film on Selkirk (a dramatised documentary to be called *The Real Robinson Crusoe*) in Largo, Fife. The County of Fife is cut off from the rest of Scotland, and its inhabitants consider themselves a race apart. Other Scots look on them as rather odd, and Selkirk was surely one of the oddest Fifers ever. He was the seventh son of a seventh son— fey or gifted with second sight according to Scots folklore.

"Unruly, brawling, strongwilled and fractious" say contemporary accounts. These abrasive character traits got him castaway in the end, and now we needed to get to the island where that had happened.

In Santiago, Chile, we found out that over the past few years a small airline called Taxpa had been flying to Juan Fernández on a more or less regular basis. It was run by a man named Carlos Griffiths. I called on him, and he was quite sympathetic to our needs but, unfortunately, unable to help us. Taxpa had only two aircraft that could land on the small airfield at Juan Fernández, an airfield that Taxpa itself had built. However, it happened that just then one plane was undergoing an engine refit while the other had damaged its undercarriage when it hit a dog on an airstrip in the north of Chile. He was sorry.

Then we heard of a Commandante Paragues, who airfreighted crayfish from Juan Fernández, so we rang him in Valparaíso. Alas, it was not the crayfish season and his Catalina flying-boat was down for maintenance. If we could wait a month perhaps . . .

Then the production assistant we had hired in Santiago came up with the idea of the Chilean Air Force. Her name was Maura Brescia, and she later wrote the definitive history of Juan Fernández called *Mares de Leyenda (Legendary Seas)* in which our filmic expedition gets an honourable mention. At that time the Commander-in-Chief of the Chilean Air Force was General Gustavo Leigh, a member of the ruling Junta. With Maura's help I contacted him. He listened and said he would see what he could do. The Chilean Air Force, it appeared, had some Catalinas. He got back to us a few days later. Unfortunately, the mooring buoys at Juan Fernández had been carried away in a storm and he couldn't risk losing a Catalina. "What about a land plane," I asked, "a twin-engined Cessna or Piper? Does the Chilean Air Force have them?"

Yes, they did.

"There is a strip there," I said. "One that will take a light plane."

"I know," General Leigh replied. "But none of my pilots would think of trying to land on it. Only Taxpa pilots are that *loco*."

It looked as if we were not going to get to Juan Fernández by air, so we investigated the boat situation. Every six months a supply boat made the round trip—Valparaíso, Easter Island, Juan Fernández, Valparaíso. It had just come back. At irregular intervals small *goletas* (fishing schooners) made the three-day voyage to the island but, of course, none were then contemplating it. We got the same response from private yachts. We had come full circle and still had only half the story in the can. What were we to do? I sat morosely at the rooftop bar of the Carrera Hilton, ordered a double pisco sour, and looked down on the Moneda Palace opposite. It was still pitted with bullet holes from the Allende Affair.

"Something will happen," Maura said. "Give it a few more days. The *mañana* principle."

Three days later something *did* happen. Carlos Griffiths, all smiles, came to see us. "I have a plane," he announced.

General Leigh had found one and asked the owner to hire it to Taxpa "as a personal favour" to him. When a member of the Junta put it that way, it was considered prudent not to refuse. I later told this story to the First Secretary at the British Embassy. "Good man, Leigh," he said. "One of ours that got away, you know. None of that *mañana* nonsense about him."

We were finally to be on our way. Two trips would be necessary—one with the actor and crew, the other with our film gear including Selkirk's props and wardrobe. Among the props was a replica of his sea chest. The original is in the National Museum of Antiquities of Scotland at Edinburgh. Ours had been made by BBC Scotland. When we left Juan Fernández I gave it to the *Carabineros* as we no longer had any use for it. Now, I am reliably informed, it is proudly shown to visitors to Juan Fernández as "the authentic sea-chest of Alexander Selkirk that he left on the island when he was rescued." Such is the stuff of history.

The flight took over three hours. The island is shaped like an axe-head, the blade being about 12 by 4 kilometres, the haft 7 by 1 kilometres. The blade part runs NNW to SSE and the haft NE to SW. All the haft and the southern side of the blade are barren and without vegetation. The northern part of the blade is covered with dense and luxuriant vegetation down to sea level. The highest peak on the island is El Yunque, rearing 915 metres (3,001 feet), but in reality Juan Fernández is a mass of mountains—it is mostly all vertical. There are only two relatively flat places—a thin strip along Cumberland Bay where San Juan Bautista stands and a little plateau under El Yunque called the Plazoleta, really no bigger than a bowling green.

The airfield was on what was virtually the narrowest part of the haft near its end. We came in over a 300-metre-high cliff (1,074 feet) with boisterous updrafts and put down on a small dirt strip that literally ran uphill to the edge of another 400-metre-high cliff (1,314 feet). I realised why the Chilean Air Force was so reluctant to land there.

Once on the ground we had to walk for half an hour down a winding road to a cliff-bound bay where fishing boats waited to take us another 20 kilometres round the island to San Juan Bautista. Our baggage rode in the only vehicle on the island, an ancient jeep that had recently replaced pack mules.

The fishing boats were like whale-boats—open and pointed at both ends. In the centre was a little hearth where the crew could cook lobster when they were hungry. Lobster is often eaten three times a day on Juan Fernández.

Once aboard we still had to traverse a sandbar before we could get out of the bay. Apparently tourists have been tossed into the sea at this point, and we heard that one man, returning to Santiago, had lost his camera and all the film he had shot.

Outside, the waves were mountainous, but the scenery, it must be admitted, was very impressive. Herman Melville called Juan Fernández "high, wild and cloven—an island of immemorial solitudes." And: "Its great overhanging height and rugged contour gives it much the air of a vast ice-berg drifting in tremendous poise. Its sides are split with dark, cavernous recesses, as an old cathedral with its gloomy lateral chapels. Drawing nigh one of these gorges from the sea and beholding some tatterdemalion outlaw, staff in hand, descending its steep rocks, conveys a very queer emotion to a lover of the picturesque."

The boat trip took two and a half hours, and it was nearly nightfall by the time we reached San Juan Bautista. A place of unspoilt charm and idyllic beauty, it has a wharf, a plaza, a dozen or so streets, two churches, a small cemetery, and one bar. We put up at the Aldea Daniel Defoe, a hostelry on the outskirts of the village, which consisted of a number of cabins among the trees. On the menu that night was lobster, which was on the menu almost every night. In Selkirk's time he was able to catch lobsters along the shore, but now the fishermen go farther afield, as far as Isla Alejandro Selkirk, even as far as San Félix and San Ambrosio, two uninhabited islands nearly 800 kilometres to the north. The demand for *la langosta chilena* far exceeds the supply.

We wanted to start filming straightaway, but first we needed a beach, something I had not seen on the north coast during the boat trip from the airport. There was only one, it turned out, a bay almost under the strip but on the south side of the island. Selkirk said he was landed on a beach so we figured this had to be the right place. (He was a sailing master on the *Cinque Ports* when he was put ashore by William Dampier.) To quote from the account he gave Woodes Rogers:

I had with me my clothes and bedding, a fire-lock, some
powder, bullets and tobacco, a hatchet, a knife, a kettle, a
Bible, some practical pieces and my mathematical instruments and books. . . . The island was a place of rendez-vous
and relief to all such as cruise on the Spaniards in those parts,
being in reality a very convenient and good one. I thought
some English ship would anchor in the bay within one month
and I would be taken off. The days passed slowly and I had
much ado to bear up against melancholy and the terror of
being left alone in such a desolate place. At first I never ate
anything till hunger constrained me, partly from grief and
partly from want of bread and salt. Nor did I go to bed till I
could watch no longer. Nor did I sleep once there. And the
lighting of the dawn only roused me to a sharper sense of my
forlorn and miserable state. The island had become my
prison, for God had chosen to punish me in that wherein I
most delighted. The restlessness of body and mind that had
ever been my commanding sin had led me to this sorry state. I
was scarce able to refrain from doing myself violence.

How does one show this on film? To make a film about a
man alone is an extraordinarily difficult thing to do. Many
film directors have tried, few have succeeded. One who has
managed it, in my opinion, is the Spanish director Luis
Buñuel in his film *Robinson Crusoe* (1952). His *isolato* carries a torch at night and lets it drop into the dark sea as a
symbol of his despair. He takes delight in simple things like
rain and the sound of birdcalls. He shouts at God to help
him—only to get back the echo of his own voice from the
cliffs around him.

We also tried to use symbols as a way to show the intensity
of insight that enables the solitary personality to perceive
itself and to discover the vast interconnectedness of the uni-
verse. Our Selkirk built sand castles—quite elaborate ones—
then destroyed them. For long periods of time he watched
small crabs and waving fronds of seaweed. He would dash
into the waves and imperiously order them to cease their

movement. He would stare into the horizon as if to see infinity.

What eventually drove the real Selkirk off the beach and to a discovery of himself was seals. To quote again from the Rogers account:

> Seals swam about that island as if they had no other place in the world to live. In November they come ashore to whelp and engender, when the beach is so full of them for a stone's throw that it is impossible to pass them and they are so surly that they'll not move out of the way, but like an angry dog run at a man: so that at their whelping season 'tis dangerous to come near them and they lined the shore very thick for above half a mile of ground all around the bay.
>
> I was forced to leave the beach and go among the rocks, but the seals gave me no quiet. They kept up continual voice day and night, some bleating like lambs, some howling like dogs or wolves, others making hideous noises of various sorts.

Selkirk found a cave (still shown to visitors at Puerto Ingles). He barricaded the entrance and made a ladder:

> It was close to the place where I got crawfish, which are as large as our lobsters and very good and lie under the rocks. They are easy to be catched. These I sometimes broiled and at other times boiled. I might have had fish enough, but could not eat 'em for want of salt because they occasioned looseness or flux.

Some eighteen months after his arrival Selkirk turned his attention away from the sea:

> I built two huts with pimiento trees and covered them with the leaves of the umbrella tree and lined them with the skins of goats. In the lesser hut I dressed my vittles and in the larger I slept. They were situate in a glade near a good run of water and away from the shore.

We decided to shoot this section of Selkirk's life in the Plazoleta, and there I became conscious of the richness of the plant life. It is said that over forty-five varieties of ferns and palms are not to be found anywhere else in the world. In one case a whole plant family, the *Lactoridaceas*, is unique to the island. The pangue (or umbrella tree, as Selkirk called it) grows to enormous proportions on Juan Fernández; so large are the leaves that the locals often use them as parasols. Since 1935 the island group has been a national park, and all species of fauna and flora are protected. Apart from seabirds the only birds are hummingbirds—red and green and white, no bigger than a bee. All the fauna was introduced to the islands; nothing is native except the seals.

It is often the case when a film crew arrives in an unusual location that someone attaches himself to them as a guide, helper, and general gofer. Ours this time was a giant of a man called Ernesto. He had come from the mainland and was himself a bit of an outcast. There was some story of his having married an island girl, who proved unfaithful. Whatever the truth, he devoted himself to us and asked no recompense.

One of the places we wanted to film was Selkirk's *Mirador* ("Look-Out"), a saddle 550 metres (1,804 feet) high with a view 50 kilometres out to sea in all directions. Here Selkirk watched and waited for the ship that would deliver him. In 1868 Commodore Powell and the officers of H.M.S. *Topaze* erected a bronze tablet there in memory of Selkirk. There are one or two errors on it (notably the date of Selkirk's death), but we needed some shots from the *Mirador* and of the tablet.

The ascent was at first gentle but became increasingly steep and rocky. Finally, about 200 metres short of the saddle, the mules refused to go any farther. The driver pushed them, pulled them, beat them, but they would not budge. Whereupon Ernesto, to our astonishment, carried the gear on his back up to the Look-Out.

All in all we spent two weeks at Juan Fernández and covered most of it by boat or mule. Twice a week we saw far overhead a LAN Chile plane *en route* to Easter Island and

Tahiti, but otherwise nothing disturbed the calm and restful atmosphere. There are no newspapers, no television, no telephones, no cars. Contact with the outside world is maintained by radio. There was a small school and two nurses but no doctor or dentist. Although the land is very fertile and will grow almost anything, there is no cultivation. All food is imported from Chile. "We are fishers, not farmers," the inhabitants told us. Remarkably little has actually changed there since Selkirk's day.

The last weekend we were on Juan Fernández there was a dance in the local hall, which we attended. Most of the population was there, including the belle of the island, one of the de Rodt family. She was without doubt a very pretty girl, green-eyed and black-haired with an animated expression and lively manner. Although only nineteen she already had three children, each reputedly by a different father (a common occurrence, we were told).

Two tuns of rather sour Chilean white wine were resting on rough cradles with large wooden faucets in their bungs. A wind-up gramophone provided the music. Families sat together at the tables, children ran in and out the door. Outside, the more macho males drank from bottles of pisco and smoked homegrown marijuana.

Our departure was a repetition of our arrival in reverse, and I held my breath when we surfed across the sandbar to the airport bay. I held it again when our plane trundled downhill and shot over the cliff's edge to be immediately buffeted by a strong updraft.

As for Selkirk, for a while he led a heady life around the taverns of London and Bristol. But in the end he tired of it. "The town has quite altered his face," Steele reported after a second meeting with him.

Selkirk decided to return to Largo, like a prodigal son, with money in his pocket, gold-lace on his coat, and stories to tell of his adventures. But his joy was short-lived. He soon became moody and took refuge in solitary walks. He tried to build a replica of his Juan Fernández hut on the hillside behind Largo, where he often sat, staring out to sea and, according to contemporary accounts, "bemoaning the fact that he had lost an earthly paradise." As Selkirk himself said about Juan Fernández; "There can scarcely be found a more happy seat for flights of fancy or the pleasures of the imagination than this island. Oh my beloved island. How much would I have given never to have left you. Never was I so happy as when I lived there."

Suddenly one day he disappeared with a local milkmaid, leaving his few possessions behind. He married once, maybe twice. Then he joined the Royal Navy and went to the Gulf of Guinea, where he caught yellow fever. He died in 1721 and was buried at sea.

To this day descendants of his brothers live in Largo. His legacy was not only Defoe's *Robinson Crusoe* but a whole genre of literature called Robinsonnade about desert island castaways. There are to date more than three hundred titles in various languages, with characters—men, women, even animals—of all nationalities. And many films have been made from these. Including ours—which is why we went to Juan Fernández, the first and only film crew to have made that pilgrimage.

16

The British Main

TO THE MOSQUITO COAST

When people think of Central America they usually think of it as wholly Hispanic—Spanish-speaking, mestizo, Catholic, unstable regimes, and violent politics. Yet scattered along the islands and shores of the Western Caribbean from the southern border of Yucatán (Mexico) to the Panama Canal are English-speaking, Protestant, Creole communities. Among them is a member of the British Commonwealth (Belize), a former British colony (the Bay Islands), and a former British protectorate (the Mosquito Coast).

During the 1960s I had seen the Union Jack pulled down all over Africa and a new, often garish, flag hoisted in its place. It was the decade of de-colonisation. But in London there were rumours that the Central American communities Britain had handed over to their neighbouring states a hundred years ago ardently wanted the colonialists back. It was a story certain to pluck British heartstrings, and we decided to make a film about it.

The Empire was never very grand in the Western Caribbean, nor was Britain in the habit of giving away anything of value. It was tenacious, though, in the face of overpowering odds, and it left a legacy of Anglo-Hispanic rivalry that has continued unabated for almost four hundred years. To this

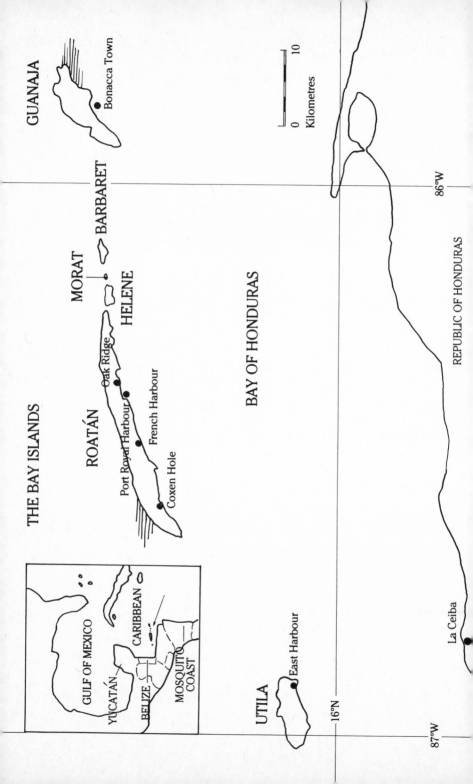

THE BAY ISLANDS

GUANAJA

Bonacca Town

BARBARET

MORAT

HELENE

ROATÁN

Oak Ridge
Port Royal Harbour
French Harbour
Coxen Hole

BAY OF HONDURAS

REPUBLIC OF HONDURAS

La Ceiba

86°W

UTILA

East Harbour

16°N

87°W

0   10
Kilometres

GULF OF MEXICO

YUCATÁN

BELIZE

CARIBBEAN

MOSQUITO COAST

day Belize fears Guatemala, the Bay Islands cling stubbornly to their English ways, and the inhabitants of the Mosquito Coast refer to their Nicaraguan compatriots as "them Spanish fellers in the interior."

It all began when the Earl of Warwick floated an emigration scheme in 1629 called the Providence Company. The object was "to settle colonists in such parts of the West Indies as are not occupied by Spain for the advancement of the Protestant religion." The company's ship, the *Seaflower*, left England ten years after the *Mayflower* with much the same hopes and much the same type of passenger. Keeping well clear of Spanish possessions—most of the West Indies in those days—they headed for the coast of Central America. About 250 kilometres from it they came upon a group of small islands, where they found some Dutch buccaneers.

They were warmly greeted as brother Protestants by the leader, Captain Willem Blauwveldt, who suggested they settle there as he and his men had no intention of staying permanently. This they did, renaming the island they were on Providence Island. It now belongs to Colombia but is English-speaking.

Blauwveldt advised them that it would be necessary to fortify the island against the Spaniards and offered not only the help of the Dutch "Brethren of the Coast," but also that of his allies on the mainland of Nicaragua—the Mosquito Indians. Their name (sometimes spelled Miskito) has nothing to do with the insect, though the low swampy shore is indeed the breeding place for a particularly savage variety. The Mosquito Indians were more warlike—and more numerous—than any other tribe on the Main, and they had never been conquered by the Spaniards. They hated them and still hate their descendants, or perhaps it is vice versa. For two hundred years they were to remain faithful allies of the British in a determined and touching way.

Providence Island is not very large and soon some of the colonists took to buccaneering. They proved such a thorn in the side of the Spaniards that several attempts were made to dislodge them. Eventually, in 1641, the island was sacked, but offshoots from it had already taken root on the mainland. One was at the mouth of the Belize River, where Peter Wallace, a Scot, accompanied by eighty buccaneers and their women, had settled the year before.

One theory derives Belize from Wallace through Valys, Bullys, and Bellise, but a more likely contender is the Mayan word *beliz* ("muddy water"). The country, about twice the size of Puerto Rico, is a strip of not-very-fertile Caribbean coast that is frequently right in the path of hurricanes. It has some slow-moving rivers and large tracts of tropical forest, which have been plundered rather than harvested. There are a few archaeological remains that show the original people were once a peripheral part of the great Mayan civilisation. Apart from that, history has virtually passed Belize by. There were no gold and silver, no plantations, no Indian wars, no slaves to speak of. It was the country of buccaneers and logwood cutters—desperate and forgotten men. They mixed and mingled with the Indians and those Negroes who had found their way there from Jamaica. Black Caribs (Afro-Indians) were later transported to the Bay of Honduras from the West Indian island of St. Vincent, mestizo refugees fled from wars in Yucatán, and Mennonites, a North American (or rather German) sect, came seeking land for their closed communities. From time to time the occasional American drifter or British remittance man arrived, while a small number of Chinese and Lebanese came to open shops. The result has been a cocktail of peoples, but a thin, watery one (there are only about 150,000 of them in the country), and one not properly shaken, to boot. Still, the first Prime Minister, the Honourable George Cadle Price, was of Mayan, European, and African extraction. He was also celibate, had studied for the priesthood, and attended mass every morning at 5:30—which might explain the somewhat austere character of Belizean government.

Belize gets into the newspapers, however, mainly because

of the Guatemalan claim to it. This is one of the world's longest-running international disputes—even longer-running than the Falklands one. Guatemala argues that as heir to Spanish suzerainty in the area, Belize is part of its department of Petén. The problem dates back to the beginning of settlement. The buccaneers and logwood cutters were only allowed in Belize on sufferance. Spain claimed the territory and, every so often, an expedition from Yucatán would try to drive the interlopers out. But they clung on and increased their tiny toehold. In all the various treaties Britain signed with Spain, Belize (or British Honduras, as it became more widely known) was always referred to as a settlement, never a colony. In fact it was not proclaimed a colony until 1862 after the borders had been sorted out with Mexico and Guatemala.

Despite several attempts by Britain to take the matter to arbitration, Guatemalans remain obdurate. And, at times, they have gone through the motions of trying to invade Belize, though in a rather haphazard fashion. In the 1960s the then President, Ydigoras Fuentes, said, "What we can't have by right, we'll take by might." Field Marshal Bernard Montgomery, who was on a visit to Central America at that time, politely enquired of the President how many battles he had won. Ydigoras Fuentes had to admit he had never been in battle. "Well, I have," Monty is alleged to have replied. "And idle boasts don't win them."

Because of the constant rumblings from Guatemala, a detachment of British troops and an RAF squadron (with Harrier Jump Jets) were stationed in Belize. They remained after independence was finally forced onto the reluctant Belizeans on September 21, 1982. As a result, Guatemala broke off diplomatic relations with the UK and petitioned the United Nations not to admit Belize as a member. It was admitted on September 25. (During the Falklands War, Guatemala offered to send troops to support the Argentines, but they never arrived. There is nothing new in this. It has been the same for a hundred years.)

Guatemala *does* have a grievance, though. In 1856 Great

Britain and the United States signed a treaty that effectively doubled the area of British Honduras at the expense of Guatemala. In return, Britain pulled out of the Bay Islands and the Mosquito Coast a few years later. Guatemala, weak and without friends, agreed to this carve-up in 1859, but it continues to rankle.

So there we were in Belize City, having flown from Jamaica to stay at the Fort George Hotel. Belize City is a ramshackle huddle of wooden buildings on high blocks and a few more substantial concrete ones, hugging the rim of a wet and soggy land. Indeed, to be buried in a dry hole is considered a desirable aim in life by most Belizeans. Canals intersect the city, serving as arteries of transport, drains, and sewers. The people seem proof against the odours and miasmas that arise from these. The population is predominantly Creole and credited in Central America with being impervious to disease ("Belize it or not," the government public relations officer said, but his wan smile and tired tone suggested he had made this groaner on many similar occasions).

The real charm of the country, however, lies in the coral reef that runs 300 kilometres along its coast. After the Great Barrier Reef of Australia, it is the longest in the world. The Governor lent us his launch so that we could visit the reef and its cays—some no more than a few hectares in area.

Here in 1798 took place the Battle of St. George's Cay during the Napoleonic Wars. The Governor-General of Yucatán, Arturo O'Neil, set out with a fleet of thirty-two ships carring 2,000 soldiers to put an end to the settlement for once and for all. Against him the Belizeans could muster two sloops, two schooners, and seven gun-flats of logwood rafts. Some of them had the improbable names of *Towser, Tickler, Teaser, Mermaid*, and *Swinger*. Later a British man-o'-war turned up fortuitously. When the battle was joined, amid treacherous coral reefs, the logwood cutters, no doubt remembering their buccaneer blood, hurried to the scene in

234

canoes, dories and pitpans with impetuosity to join their companions and share their danger. Negroes, armed only for the most part with Poke-'em'-Mo palm spears of fire-hardened wood, proved themselves particularly loyal.

The Spaniards were unable to manoeuvre among the reefs and, in the end, broke off the fight. The smallest force ever to be engaged in a sea battle had won against incredible odds.

For the rest we travelled over the greater part of Belize from Corozal Town in the north, where the people are mestizos, to Stann Creek Town in the middle, where they are Black Caribs, and to Punta Gorda in the south, where they are Maya. We saw the sugar fields of Corozal Town, the timber industry of Orange Walk Town, the citrus orchards of Stann Creek Town. We visited the Mayan ruins of Xunantunich near El Cayo. The Maya were obsessed with time (their religion, some say) and able to work out elaborate mathematical calculations with only three symbols—a dot for one, a bar for five, and a shell for zero. Instead of writing these from right to left, they wrote them from the bottom to the top of a column and such columns exist at Xunantunich. The Maya (who regarded crossed eyes as a mark of beauty) also discovered the manufacture of rubber out of which they made balls, sandals, and other articles. They were the first to cultivate the cacao, the papaya, and the avocado. And they invented chewing gum. *Chicleros* still work the same forests in Belize, bleeding the sap of the sapodilla tree just like rubber trees are bled. When the sap is cooked it becomes chicle, the main ingredient of chewing gum.

We filmed the new capital of Belmopan, built after Hurricane Hattie had almost destroyed Belize City in 1961. Belmopan must surely be the smallest capital in the world. I felt I had stumbled onto a dolls' village. We went to the Guatemalan border at Benque Viejo and looked across the shallow creek at the Guatemalan border post. Upon one occasion some Guatemalan soldiers invaded Belize but got lost. In the end policemen had to escort them back to Benque Viejo. Such is the flavour of Belize.

It was time to go to the Bay Islands in the Bay of Honduras. The route was roundabout. We flew from Belize to San Pedro Sula in the north of Honduras, where we chartered a small plane for La Ceiba on the Caribbean coast (William Sydney Porter, otherwise known as O. Henry, lived on this coast from 1897 to 1904 and used it as the setting for many of his stories). As there was then no airport in the Bay Islands (one has since been built), we were forced to take a boat the remaining 75 kilometres to Roatán. There we put up at the only hotel in the islands, the Welcome Hotel. Today I believe there are some fifteen to twenty hotels and guest-houses. The Honduran Government is trying to encourage tourism to the Bay Islands. Later, in the capital, Tegucigalpa, I happened to open the telephone directory. In the front part were a series of pictures of the various departments of Honduras. The words accompanying the rather smudged view of Guanaja in the Bay Islands read (I translate):

> The information that we have been able to obtain indicates that the islanders do not consider themselves Hondurans; an intensive campaign by the Ministry of Public Education is called for in order to awaken patriotic sentiment and pride in citizenship among these Hondurans so that they are not ashamed of being different.

There are eight Bay Islands and sixty-five cays. The most important island is Roatán with the towns of Coxen Hole, French Harbour, and Oak Ridge, but settlements also exist on Utila and Guanaja—a most unusual one in the case of Guanaja.

The Bay Islands were discovered by Columbus in 1502 on his fourth voyage. He sent his brother ashore who reported that the inhabitants were "very robust people who adore idols." The locals know the sites of these temples and dig up artefacts for sale. They call these *Yaba Ding Dings* (perhaps: "things that talk"?) and I bought one—a small ceramic ocarina decorated on its surface with a stylised interlocking pattern. By far the most intriguing episode of Columbus' stay was the capture of a large canoe with a Mayan merchant and his cargo. This has often been cited as the first European contact with a representative of the higher civilisations of the Americas. Strange to say, Columbus made nothing of it, but he did note that they used cocoa beans for currency and snatched up any "as though it was their own eyes that had fallen to the canoe bottom."

For 136 years the Indians were left alone, until the British established a colony on Roatán. Four years later in 1642 the outbreak of the English Civil War left the colony at the mercy of the Spaniards, who soon overran it. For good measure they removed all the Indians to Cuba as slaves.

The islands became a nest of buccaneers for another hundred years until the British returned with 1,000 soldiers and reoccupied them. This time the Spaniards lacked the power to drive them out. But, under the terms of the Treaty of Aix-la-Chapelle (1748), which ended the War of Jenkins' Ear, they agreed to evacuate their fort called, naturally, Fort St. George. Its rampart still remains at Port Royal Harbour (not to be confused with Port Royal in Jamaica).

There was a second military occupation in 1779 which the Spaniards managed to dislodge, but in 1797 there was a permanent settlement which survives to this day. In 1852 the Bay Islands were proclaimed a British colony. The United States argued that this infringed the Monroe Doctrine, so a deal was struck and in 1859 the Bay Islands were handed over to Honduras, where they have remained ever since. This made no difference to the inner convictions of the islanders, however. They consider themselves British subjects, and bitter feelings exist between them and the coastal Hondurans. Though Britain gave up the Bay Islands, the Bay Islanders did not give up Britain—and they still try to live in the middle of the 19th century as if expecting that the next boat will bring news of yet another resounding Redcoat victory over the Fuzzy-wuzzies. They have retained the English language, English customs, and the Protestant religion. There has been some muttering about independence, though that is all it is.

Who are these 10,000-or-so people? As in Belize there are different elements—Black Caribs, Negroes, and even some Honduran mestizos, but unlike Belize there is a sizeable group of whites. They are the descendants of Cayman Islanders.

By 1830 the slave population of the Cayman Islands outnumbered the whites five to one. Knowing that (when abolition came) they would lose political power, many of the whites left for the Bay Islands. There they quickly established a reputation as seamen and boat-builders. They were energetic and prospered, being the first people to ship bananas to the United States and to organise the fruit trade (in fact, through their efforts, Honduras became the original banana republic). They also intermarried rather more closely than the Book of Common Prayer allows. Today there are villages in which every person has the same surname and is related. One on Roatán is called Jonesville where all the people are Joneses.

At the end of the British Colony some thirty whites moved to two small cays 500 metres off the island of Guanaja. The cays are in a lagoon with a depth of about 3 metres. After the cays were covered with houses, they began building on the bed of the lagoon by putting their dwellings on piles and connecting them with elevated boardwalks. They ran a pipeline under the sea from a spring on a nearby hill— Guanaja is very hilly—so they have a constant water supply. Today Bonacca Town, as it is known, has 1,500 people and covers about 42 hectares (104 acres). It is a picturesque and crowded maze of walkways and higgledy-piggledy wooden buildings. The people are entirely self-sufficient and have hardly intermarried with any of the other groups in the islands. Indeed they will not mix with the Black Caribs or Hondurans. They fish, they go to sea as seamen on American vessels, they tend their gardens on Guanaja. But there is another reason, apart from wanting to be exclusive, for the existence of Bonacca Town—*No-see-ums* or sandflies. They make life unbearable on the island. Not to mention ticks and mosquitoes.

There were, however, compensations. Roatán is a quite beautiful island with undulating hills and little beaches. And the people of Coxen Hole (named after a buccaneer) were very friendly as soon as they knew we had come from Britain. They even tried to enlist our support for the burning local issue—resistance to the efforts of the Honduran authorities to create a Spanish-type *plaza* in the town. We left with mixed feelings.

Back to La Ceiba by boat, then a plane to Tegucigalpa. From here we flew to Managua, the capital of Nicaragua. And from Managua across the country to Bluefields, the English version of the name of that old Dutch pirate Blauwveldt. Bluefields is a poor but clean place with weatherboard houses all painted white. They are mainly two storeys high and have dormer windows with red roofs. Each stands in a small garden enclosed by a paling fence. There is a port and a little light industry.

I was unpacking in the Hollywood Hotel when the proprietress informed me there was a delegation waiting for me on the verandah. Word apparently had gotten around quickly among the 25,000 inhabitants of Bluefields.

Three elderly people were sitting on a swing-bed. They introduced themselves—Princess May, granddaughter of the last King of Mosquitia; a Mr. Lampson, who represented the Creole community; and a Mr. Taylor, who simply said, "I'm English." When I asked him where he came from, he answered, "Devon," then added, as an afterthought, "in 1749." They all carried umbrellas and sat back, looking well satisfied with themselves.

I waited and, after a little while, said, "How can I be of assistance to you?"

"You can tell us," Princess May replied, "when the British are coming back."

I tried to explain as gently as possible that I did not think the British were considering any such action.

"Why are you here?" Princess May wanted to know, and I did my best to tell them the reason. They digested this information, then decided to try another tack. Mr. Taylor asked whether I was a friend of the Queen or not. I said I had seen her, that was all. He persisted: "Does she have a secretary?" I replied that I thought she had a number of them. "That would account for it," he said.

I was at a loss to know what he meant.

"We have written to the Queen many times, asking her to come back, and we have never received a reply," he told me. "Also we have asked her for some pictures of the Royal Family and some Union Jacks. We only have pictures of Queen Victoria and no flags."

The conversation continued for some time along these lines, and they left not entirely happy about the result. This didn't stop a procession of citizens from calling on us that evening. Somehow our appearance in Bluefields armed with cameras and sound gear had made them think a British warship with Her Majesty on board was just over the horizon.

The Mosquito Indians have always been like that. When Britain stood alone against Napoleon, King George of Mosquitia (most of the Mosquito kings had good Hanoverian names like George, Frederick, Augustus, etc.) sent a message offering immediate help and begging for a Union Jack "as we mean to fight under English colours."

The Mosquito Coast comprises the whole Caribbean shore of Nicaragua and part of Honduras and Costa Rica. English names are common—from the Black River and Nasty Creek, Turtle Lagoon and Brewer's Lagoon in Honduras to Sandy Bay, Bragman's Bluff, Pearl Lagoon (the centre of the Mosquito kingdom), Bluff, Corn Island, Square Point, Sandeye, Monkey Point, and Greytown in Nicaragua.

The Mosquitos placed themselves under the protection of the British in 1687, who promptly designated one of their chiefs as king. He was invited to send his son to London to be educated, which he did, and to recognise Charles II as his liege lord, which he also did. When his father died he was crowned king. The symbol at the ceremony was an old hat. Two later Mosquito kings were educated in England but the coronations now took place in Jamaica and the old hat had been replaced by a gilt crown. Then, from the beginning of the 19th century, the kings were crowned in Belize cathedral, the only cathedral in the British Empire (apart from Westminister and Nuku'alofa in Tonga) so used.

The protectorate (which had officially been declared in 1720) came to an end in 1856. Behind the treaty that Great Britain signed with the United States (the Dallas-Clarendon Treaty, never ratified by the USA) lay Commodore Vanderbilt and the Trans-Isthmian Canal. Gold had been discovered in California in 1849, and the quickest and safest way to get from the east coast of America to the west coast was by one of the Commodore's steam packets to Greytown (now known as San Juan del Norte), up the San Juan River into Lake Nicaragua and across it to the western side. A short coach ride of 25 kilometres brought the traveller to San Juan del Sur on the Pacific coast where he boarded another of the Commodore's packets for San Francisco. Plans were floated in New York to build a canal across the isthmus between Lake Nicaragua and San Juan del Sur but faltered when the promoters discovered that the Atlantic end of the route was a British protectorate (the Pacific end had been part of the Republic of Nicaragua since 1838).

So perhaps 50,000 Mosquito Indians were handed over to

their traditional enemies (the figures are guesswork as there was no census). They still refer to this treaty as "The Great Betrayal." There was a proviso in the treaty and in the subsequent Managua Treaty (1860) between Great Britain and Nicaragua that any Mosquitos who wished could emigrate to Belize and a guarantee that the king be allowed to retain his territory as a semiautonomous English-speaking, cricket-playing enclave within Nicaragua. But these promises were never kept by Nicaragua despite the fact that the matter was referred to the Austro-Hungarian emperor, Franz Josef, for arbitration in 1878, when he found in favor of the Mosquitos. In 1895 the British occupied the port of Corinto (where the CIA had Central American mercenaries plant mines in the harbour in 1984) because of the treatment of their consul at Bluefields, and as late as the beginning of this century the Mosquitos were asking Britain for help against Nicaraguan persecution. Nicaragua incorporated the Mosquito Coast as a province in 1896 and, when they finally abolished the kingdom in 1905, a British gunboat rescued the last king, Robert Henry Clarence, and took him to Jamaica where the government gave him a pension.

Next morning we went for a walk through the town. It is quite West Indian in appearance with numerous Moravian churches, tree-lined streets, and high-buttocked women market-vendors. On all sides we were greeted. A man attached himself to us and beckoned that we should follow. At one end of the town was a grassy slope down to the water with a few dilapidated jetties. Here were six men, dressed only in ragged shorts. They were Rama Indians and had rowed from their island during the night to see us. Once again the same question: Did this mean the British were returning? Other Indians, we were told, were on their way from Marshall Point, Brown Bank, and Haulover (there are Ramas and Sumos as well as Mosquitos on the Mosquito Coast, but the last are the most numerous).

The sound recordist felt so sorry for the Rama Indians that

he went to a store and bought each of them a shirt. They asked us for English coins "with the Queen's head on them." And so it went on. During the day more arrived.

They looked as William Dampier, the buccaneer and navigator, who knew this coast well, had described them three centuries before—"tall, well made, raw-boned, lusty, strong and nimble of foot, long-visaged with lank black hair, look stern, hard favoured and of dark coffee-coloured complexion." In fact, Dampier had a Mosquito with him when he became the first Englishman to set foot on the coast of northwest Australia in 1688.

As it was May Day, the month-long annual festival, we were invited to film the national dance of the Mosquito Coast—the Maypole. Instead of a pole a tree was used. It was decorated with festoon lights and coloured streamers. And instead of nymphs and shepherds there was a lively, boisterous crowd of Mosquitos and Creoles. Teeth flashed, eyes rolled, feet stamped all to the accompaniment of drums.

After a few days during which it rained we went down the Bluefields Lagoon to Bluff mainly to see the turtles, which come ashore from April to July to lay their eggs. The reason they migrate at this time of the year is because there are millions of tiny blubber fish on the surface of the sea. The fishermen call them "thimbles" and the turtles eat them. They also eat a type of seaweed that grows in the shallower waters.

Another day we took a plane to Corn Island, almost 100 kilometres off the coast. This is a cay about 12 kilometres long and 2 kilometres wide. It is completely covered with coconut trees, and no wheeled vehicles are allowed. About 1,500 English-speaking Creoles live there. The sole entertainment is going to church, not just on Sunday but practically every evening. There are four churches to cater for this preference.

When we returned to the Hollywood Hotel we found some soldiers waiting for us.

"*Los vamos a llevar al cuartel por incitar actos de trai-ción*," one said. "We are going to take you to the military quarters for inciting acts of treason."

Now in Hispanic countries the *cuartel* is a dangerous place. It is outside the jurisdiction of the legal system. Anything can, and frequently does, happen to someone who is thrown into the *cuartel*'s prison. And that's where we were put. A small, windowless room with no bunks, a dirt floor, a bucket in the corner—and all cockroach-enlivened. We were not given any food or water. That night we squatted with our heads on our knees, almost driven crazy by the plagues of nameless insects. Early in the morning the guards gave us some tortillas and beans as well as a mug of water each. At midday we were taken back to the hotel. No apologies, no explanations.

The proprietress, it appeared, had rung the British Embassy in Managua and told them of our arrest.

"Them *Pañas* ['Spaniards': from *España* or Spain] from Nicaragua," she said scornfully. "No brains, not like us British." She spoke of Nicaragua as if it were a foreign country. "Norton Cuthbert Clarence is no use either. Doesn't go in much for king stuff."

This was the first we had heard of Norton Cuthbert Clarence. A cousin of Princess May, he was the heir to the Mosquito throne and a grocer at Pearl Lagoon. Later we were told that he sometimes flew the Mosquito flag, when no *Pañas* were around. This had the Union Jack in the corner and twelve blue and white stripes, a bit like the Hawaiian flag. Otherwise, all Norton Cuthbert Clarence did was sell certificates of nobility. If you care to write to him and enclose a suitable fee, you can become a Duke, an Earl, or a Prince of Mosquitia.

In Managua we learned what had happened. The sound recordist had some postcards in his luggage, postcards he had bought in Carnaby Street, postcards that were the Union Jack. He had given them to the three old people who had waited on us the first day—Princess May, Mr. Lampson, and Mr. Taylor. They had pinned them to their front doors. The British ambassador was understanding. "I went straight to President Somoza," he said. "Those people in Bluefields are something of an embarrassment. Forever writing to the Queen, signing themselves 'Your most faithful subjects'. I have to intercept their letters."

Somoza has, of course, gone. The Sandinistas now control Nicaragua. One of the first things they did was to forcibly relocate a large number of Mosquito Indians in camps away from the coast. This, they said, was for military reasons connected with the activities of the counter-revolutionaries (the contras). But one wonders whether there wasn't some of the old animus involved as well.

Later the Sandinistas realised they had made a serious error in the eyes of world opinion and, in an attempt to rectify it, they put forward the idea of autonomy for the Mosquito Coast—the very idea the British had sought to enshrine in the Managua Treaty. But the Nicaraguans had not changed their spots. The Mosquitos are no nearer real autonomy than before.

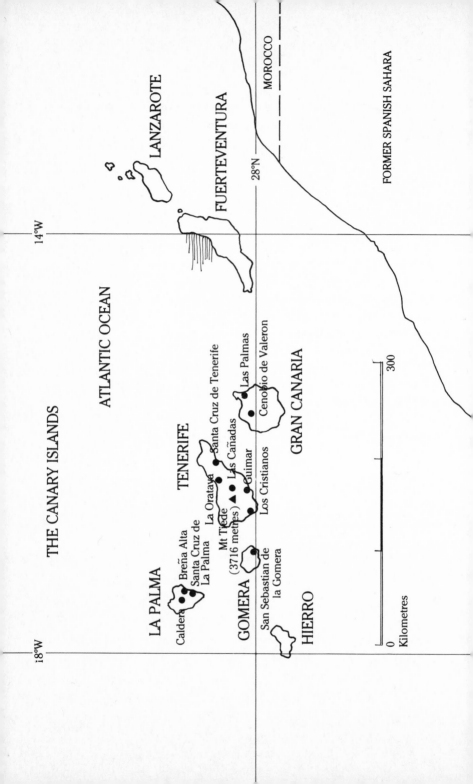

THE CANARY ISLANDS

ATLANTIC OCEAN

18°W

14°W

LA PALMA

Caldera
Breña Alta
Santa Cruz de
La Palma

TENERIFE

La Orotava
Mt Teide
(3716 metres)
Las Cañadas
Santa Cruz de Tenerife

GOMERA

San Sebastian de
la Gomera

HIERRO

Los Cristianos
Guimar

LANZAROTE

FUERTEVENTURA

28°N

MOROCCO

Las Palmas
Cenobio de Valeron

GRAN CANARIA

FORMER SPANISH SAHARA

0   300
Kilometres

17

The Canary Islands

■━■━■━■━■━■━■━■━■━■━■━■━■━■━

IN SEARCH OF THE MYSTERIOUS GUANCHES

The Canaries consist of seven islands off the west coast of Africa, the most easterly island lying about 100 kilometres from the African mainland. That mainland is a desolate place, formerly known as Spanish Sahara and now disputed between Morocco, Mauritania, and a group of guerillas called *Polisarios* because it is believed to have immense mineral resources. The seven Canaries—Lanzarote, Fuerteventura, Gran Canaria, Tenerife, Gomera, La Palma, and Hierro—stretch from east to west for over 600 kilometres. They all show signs of volcanic activity and range from barren sand or lava deserts (those islands nearest Africa) to lush, subtropical islands with high mountains (Mt. Teide on Tenerife is 3,716 metres high, or about 12,200 feet).

It was October 1961, and we were in Las Palmas, Gran Canaria, to film the arrival of the evacuees from Tristan da Cunha on the *Stirling Castle*. The volcano on Tristan da Cunha in the South Atlantic had erupted, endangering the settlement there, and the British Government had arranged for the removal of all 264 people who were living in this solitary island. The ship had travelled first to Cape Town and was destined for Southampton in England, but Las Palmas was to be the evacuees' next contact with the outside world

247

after South Africa. I remember the bewilderment on their faces. The men and boys were dressed in homespun; the girls had bonnets and long white stockings rolled above the knees, while the women wore ankle-length dresses. We couldn't get much out of them about their ordeal. They were painfully shy and spoke their own brand of English.

It looked as if we would have to return to London with no story, but the office decided it wanted a documentary on the islands. Two of the Canaries—Gran Canaria and Tenerife—are well-known tourist resorts, and the idea of tourism-as-pollution crossed my mind. But it was a bit late in the year for the holiday-makers (mainly middle-class Scandinavians) and a bit early for those escaping winter (mainly upper-class English). There was, of course, the resident British community centred on Tenerife. They numbered perhaps five hundred (some families had been there as long as a century) and had their own club, tennis court, bowling green, croquet lawn, and a library that claimed to have the largest collection of books in English of any library outside an English-speaking country. However, since such expatriate communities are often sterile and inward-looking, almost as if they lived in a plastic bubble of their culture, I pigeon-holed this notion. If worse came to worse, I thought, we could always do a straight travelogue. I wanted to have a look at some more of the islands, so I flew to Fuerteventura and Lanzarote (the most easterly) with my cameraman, leaving the others behind in Las Palmas.

Fuerteventura is a long narrow island with great dried lava plains, brown sand wastes, and nothing much else. Half the island is *malpaís* ("badlands"), and camels are the usual means of transport. Lanzarote is similar. From 1730 to 1736 there was a series of violent volcanic eruptions that destroyed most of it and left behind more than three hundred craters and cones. This has resulted in a special sort of cultivation. A low circular wall of lava stones is built and a fig tree or a vine planted in the middle of the volcanic soil. Ash is sprinkled over the ground which traps the heavy night dew and provides enough moisture for the plant to grow. The wines produced by this method are called "volcanic" wines and are very strong (with a 20 to 30 percent alcohol content). One wine, Malvasia, has always been associated with the Canaries. In England it was known as Malmsey or Canary Sack and tasted a bit like sweet sherry. Shakespeare knew it well (Mistress Quickly in *Henry IV* admonishes one of her clients for drinking too much of it). In fact the 16th and 17th centuries were steeped in Canary Sack, but in the 19th century phylloxera (or vine-pest, a plant-louse that attacks European vines) ended much of the trade. The women who tend these vineyards wear a white wimple over the head and a broad-brimmed straw hat; their dress is black and they have long white gloves up to their elbows. As they weave their way through the lava fields, mounted on donkeys, the effect is quite medieval. One can often find them sitting by their vines playing one of the melancholy Canarian songs on a *timple* or small mandolin— helping the plant to bear the sorrows of this world, they say. So Lanzarote was not without local colour.

I returned to Las Palmas feeling that there was a film in the Canaries if only I could find a thematic peg to hang it on or some thread to link the various sequences. Carlos Diaz O'Shanahan, the *Jefe de Protocolo* of the *Cabildo Insular* turned my thoughts in another direction. He asked me had I been to the *Museo Canario* and seen the display of Guanche relics. It was the first time I had even heard about the aboriginal inhabitants of the Canaries.

The Canary Islands have been known off and on to Europeans for perhaps 2,500 years, but they did not enter modern history until the 15th century. Homeric legends refer to them as the Elysian Fields lying beyond the Pillars of Hercules (Gibraltar). This was where the souls of dead heroes went. Herodotus calls them the Gardens of Hesperides and talks of golden apples guarded by dragons breathing fire (fumaroles?) and of Atlas, kneeling on his cone-shaped mountain (Mt. Teide?) and supporting the heavens on his shoulders. Pliny reports that the king of Mauritania (not the present-day state but a Roman satellite kingdom that included modern Morocco) sent an expedition to two of the islands, probably Fuerteventura and Lanzarote. They found no people, only packs of large, ferocious dogs, so they called the islands after them—*canis* is Latin for "dog." (Thus, the bird was named after the islands, not the islands after the bird. Canaries *are* everywhere, but not the more familiar canary we know. The wild bird is grey or brown with only a few greenish-yellow feathers.) There is still a breed of savage native dog surviving in Fuerteventura called *Bardino*. They have white feet and are said to be good watchdogs.

In the early Middle Ages the islands were rediscovered. An Italian, Lancellato Marocello, settled there in 1270—probably on Lanzarote, which was named after him—but it was not until the arrival from Normandy in 1402 of Jean de Béthencourt that a serious attempt to occupy the whole group was made. De Béthencourt called himself "King of the Canary Islands" and set about exploring his newfound realm. In the more westerly islands he discovered Guanches in possession and they resisted him stoutly. Spain and Portugal, in the meantime, also showed signs of interest in de Béthencourt's kingdom, and it finally fell to Spain in 1486. The Spaniards promptly baptised the Guanches after defeating them and enslaving the men. The women they took as wives or concubines. So they could be baptised they had to be given names, and a single surname would often be bestowed on a whole tribe, which accounts for the paucity of Canarian family names. One, de Béthencourt (usually in the form Betancur), is held by at least 5 percent of the inhabitants. The Canary Islands were Spain's first colony, and what they did there set the pattern for the rest of their empire. The empire has long since gone, and today the islands and their million or so residents are not regarded as a colony but as an integral part of the mother country.

Who, then, were the Guanches? Most scholars believe they

were Berbers. The evidence for this is fairly sound: the languages show similarities (though there are only about eight or nine extant sentences in Guanche, plus a few word lists); both peoples practised mummification of the dead; both preferred living in caves, which they adorned with primitive drawings and strange spiral whorls that can also be seen in North Africa. And both races were fair—contemporaries described them as tall with fair or reddish hair, blue or grey eyes, and an olive skin. The women, apparently, were especially attractive (this would apply equally to many of the Kabyles who are Berbers in Algeria today). As well, most everybody commented on their large hands—"larger than among our poorer classes" was how one conquistador put it.

Another theory is that they were Cro-Magnons. Cro-Magnon is a village in southwest France where the first skeletal material that identified this intelligent, large-brained race was found. The Iberians, who gave their name to the peninsula shared by Spain and Portugal, were Cro-Magnons. They are possibly represented today by the Basques. Berbers, too, show Cro-Magnon characteristics as do many Canarians. On some islands, the percentage of people with these traits is as high as half the population.

Fray Alonso de Espinosa, writing in 1594 about the Guanches, says:

> This people had very good and perfect features and well-shaped bodies. They were of tall stature with proportionate limbs. There were giants among them of incredible size and, that it will not appear fabulous, I will not repeat what is said on the subject. Of one, however, it is generally said as verified and ascertained fact that he was fourteen feet high and had eighty teeth in his mouth.

And Don Antonio de Viana in 1604 described them as "virtuous, honest and brave with the finest qualities of humanity, to wit magnanimity, attentive powers, strength of soul and body, pride of character, nobleness of demeanour."

Guanche is really the name of one tribe only (a combination form of the words *guan*, meaning "man," and *chinech*, "of Tenerife"). When the first conquerors arrived, they found the Guanches living as though they were in the Neolithic Age—a basically pastoral existence with flocks of sheep, goats, and dogs, but they also practised some rudimentary agriculture, growing wheat and barley. The grain was toasted, then ground and kneaded into a stiff dough called *gofio*, which was a staple of their diet (it still is in these islands). Meat was eaten rare, and shellfish formed an important part of their meals, but apparently they did not eat fish. And not only did they not eat fish—they had no boats or knowledge of navigation, which is very strange. (After all, how did they then get to the Canary Islands?)

Their utensils were made of stone sharpened on basalt, and they used chipped obsidian to make *tabonas* or cutting instruments. Scrapers and polishers were usually porous lava. They also had grinding stones used to crush their grain, but they did not have the potter's wheel, even though they made a number of decorative bowls and containers out of baked clay.

Society was organised into three groups: the nobles, the yeomen, and the serfs. The chief was called the *mencey* and carried a staff of office. Although the tribe was patriarchal, women were treated as equals and it was forbidden for a man to approach a woman when she was alone or away from the village. The penalty for this was death—as it was for murder, robbery, and adultery—death by stoning or by being flung over a cliff. While not a warlike people, they had weapons made of wood (javelins, shields, lances, battle-axes, and clubs studded with pebbles) as well as polished basalt balls that they threw accurately over astonishing distances.

Clothing was made out of skins or rushes. Both men and women wore a kind of shift called a *tamarco* that fastened in front and at the sides with thorns while leaving the arms bare. Under the *tamarco* the women wore a skirt of rushes that went all the way to the ground (it was considered immodest to show the feet but not the breasts). For ornamentation they used objects of baked clay or perforated shell beads to make pendants and necklaces.

Corpses were not buried but were placed in caves on wooden platforms. The bodies were mummified by treating them with various plant and tree juices and exposing them to the sun and air. Alongside a corpse were placed its worldly possessions and vessels containing milk, butter, and *gofio*. By these the bodies of dogs have sometimes been found (perhaps as guides to the journey beyond the grave). All this suggests a belief in an afterlife, and it is known that the Guanches worshipped a single supreme diety.

Long after they became extinct, the Guanches were held up as Noble Savages to the Neo-Classicists of 18th-century Europe. The truth is they were a hospitable, chivalrous, and peaceful people whose women possessed a rare beauty. To quote the Archdeacon of Fuerteventura, writing soon after the conquest (my translation):

> All their contracts and sales consisted, as in the time of the Trojan Wars, in exchange and barter. Barley against sheep, cheese against honey, figs against skins. Their conversation was neither of gold nor of silver nor of jewels. It was rather of rains in due season, of fruitful sowings, of rich pasture, of happy breedings. Quiet sleep, sweet peace, the fertility of their wives, the strength of their arms, the blessings of heaven poured over their flocks and store-houses, all these were necessary possessions, simple and innocent, which our vanity cannot lessen in value.

This was all on display at the *Museo Canario*—skulls, bones, mummies with red hair on their heads, tools, arms, ceramics, and rectangular little objects called *pintaderas* used like signet rings for tattooing marks on the skin. In addition, Señor Diaz told us, there were any number of caves on Gran Canaria which had been inhabited by the Guanches. One of these sites, a cliff-face at Cenobio de Valeron, had more than three hundred cells and caves hollowed out of the soft rock and is thought to have been a religious centre where *harimaguadas* (the Guanche equivalent to vestal virgins) lived. Their only duties were to sit and grow fat. We visited it and also the Cueva Pintada not far away where there were some of the mysterious whorl-like inscriptions, a few in colour.

But museums and caves, artefacts and inanimate objects, are not enough to make a documentary interesting. A film must have motion, something animate, something alive. We explained this to Señor Diaz, and after a while he came up with three still-surviving aspects of the Guanche Age—*silbo*, or the whistling language; *astia*, or pole-vaulting as a means of locomotion; and *lucha canaria*, or Canary-style wrestling. This seemed more like it. We saw how we could combine these curious activities with film footage about the islands and even add a little touch of the feeling that here was a lost earthly paradise.

Lucha canaria we discovered we could film anywhere, but *astia* was practised only on the islands of Gomera and La Palma, and *silbo* (which was truly dying out) was restricted to Gomera. Because *silbo* sounded the most intriguing, we decided to go to Gomera. But first we shot some footage on Gran Canaria—golden beaches, stupendously deep ravines, sandy desert areas, and subtropical forests; vineyards, coffee plantations, date palms, sugar cane, and almond trees; small mountain villages, folk-dancing, Spanish colonial architecture, dragon's blood trees (the same as in Socotra), and some cave dwellings that are still in use but provided with carpeted floors, plastered walls, electricity, and many more of the comforts of home we take for granted.

Next we flew to Tenerife, the largest island, triangular in shape (Gran Canaria is more round) and quite striking scenically. The name comes from the Guanche words *tener* ("snow") and *ife* ("mountain"). The snow mountain is Mt. Teide, which dominates the island. According to Herodotus: "In the ocean there is a mountain, cone-shaped and of such a height that its summit cannot be seen."

We booked into the Mencey Hotel in Santa Cruz de Tenerife, enquired about flights to Gomera and learned that it was one of the only two islands in the group without an airport. We would have to drive to Los Cristianos in the south of Tenerife and from there take a boat to San Sebastian de la Gomera. The boat went once a week, on Fridays, and the crossing took about three hours and was usually rough. Since it was Monday we had three days to kill, so we arranged to film *lucha canaria*. The bout was organised by the tourist bureau, the *Dirección General del Turismo*, which also informed the local newspaper, *El Día*. The paper sent a reporter and a photographer to cover us filming the bout, and the next day a story appeared under the headline: LA TELEVISIÓN BRITÁNICA BUSCA RELIQUIAS GUANCHES (BRITISH TELEVISION SEEKS GUANCHE RELICS).

Lucha canaria is a sort of freestyle catch-as-catch-can wrestling. There are ten or twelve men on a team and they wrestle in pairs, one after the other. Each wrestler is clad in thick canvas shorts, the legs of which are rolled up, and open-necked short-sleeved shirts. The wrestlers are barefoot, and the object is to hurl your opponent to the ground. No blows are allowed, but tripping and butting are permitted. Most of the men seemed to concentrate on grabbing their adversary by the testicles and lifting him off his feet. Each bout lasted about a minute. If so much as an elbow or a buttock touched the ground, it was counted as a fall.

The next day we went to the summit of Mt. Teide, climbing through the beautiful Valley of Oratava to the dry, hot lava plains of Las Cañadas and taking a mule 3 kilometres to the top of the mountain.

And on Thursday we filmed the British Club. I took advantage of the library there to do some brief research on *silbo*. *Silbo* is not a system of whistled signals (like, for example, a series of wolf whistles or some birdcalls). It is Spanish whistled rather than spoken. Other whistling languages exist in Africa and Mexico, but Gomera's is unique because, according to Professor Classé of Glasgow University, it is "the only system based not on periodic notes but on purely articulated ones." In other words, it is a phonetically whistled Spanish in which vibrations in the pitch and tone of the whistle replace vibrations of the vocal cords. Of course, a language like Spanish in which consonantal clusters are rare and, with few exceptions, syllables are consonant/vowel groupings is better suited to this than a language like English. Even so, there are a number of Guanche words in *silbo* including, oddly enough, the word for yes (*eye-o*), though it is not difficult to whistle *sí*.

How to turn this information into interesting visual images presented a problem. Two things had to be established—first, that *silbo* wasn't merely a series of prearranged signals, and second that the whistling carried farther than the human voice (it was said that *silbo* was effective over 1 kilometre but that in Guanche times this had been more like a league). We gave the matter some thought and, helped by the *Dirección General del Turismo*, borrowed a megaphone from the police.

We were up early on Friday for the 100-kilometre drive to Los Cristianos. This took us south through the Valley of Guimar, a replica of the Valley of Oratava on the other side of Mt. Teide. As a local guidebook put it: "These valleys are the result of envious geography wishing to repeat itself." Los Cristianos lay on a sheltered bay with a small brown sand beach. The boat was waiting.

Gomera was ringed with cliffs. The mountainous centre rises to 1,500 metres (4,920 feet) and is split by jagged wide *barrancos* (ravines) that lead to the coastal cliffs like spokes in a wheel. The island is thickly wooded and the little town of San Sebastian is an attractive place with about 7,000 people.

It was Columbus' last port of call before he discovered America. You can still see the well in the courtyard of a house where he took on water and the church where he heard mass. There was another reason for Columbus' visit to Gomera—Beatriz de Bobadilla. She had been a maid of honour at the court of Ferdinand and Isabella and had attracted Ferdinand's attention. Isabella got rid of her by marrying her off to Hernán Peraza, the son of the Lord of Gomera, and shipping them both back there. Hernán, however, had a Guanche mistress called Iballa, whom he continued to see. This offended Iballa's father, who was a *mencey*, and he resolved to kill Peraza. They waylaid him in a cave when he was making love to Iballa. She heard the whistled signals from her father's men and shouted a warning: "*Ajel ibes jujaque saven tamarec*" ("Run, they are climbing by your path!"). It was too late, however, and Peraza was killed. Rebellion followed but the uprising was not successful. The Spaniards came to terms with the Guanches and the four major tribes regained their influence, so much so that Guanche blood predominates on Gomera today. And Iballa's warning is the only complete sentence that survives of the Guanche spoken on the island. Beatriz, the young and reputedly hot-blooded widow, soon found solace with Columbus (or so the story goes).

There was no hotel in San Sebastian and we put up at a pension. We let the patron know we were in the market for some *silbadores* or whistlers, and next day two labourers came to see us. They were middle-aged men who worked on a nearby banana plantation. I asked them how they had learnt *silbo* and they replied, from their parents. Had they taught their children? Yes. Did women also whistle? Sometimes, but they always understood. They told us that on the banana plantation the overseer habitually issued instructions in *silbo*, and the man in charge of the irrigation channels serving the farms behind San Sebastian whistled to his workers which channel to open and which to close. In the old days, they said, when the taxman's boat was sighted coming from Tenerife, the news would be whistled from farm to farm and the owners would vanish into the *barrancos*.

I asked for a demonstration, and one of the *silbadores* stepped out onto the pension's patio and whistled two notes. He repeated it and then said he had called José. The whistle was shrill and penetrating but I thought I caught the rhythm of "Jo" and "sé" in the sound. About five minutes later a man in the uniform of the fire-brigade appeared. He was José.

We decided to film. There was a small plaza in the centre of San Sebastian with a restaurant and open-air tables along one side. We set the camera up opposite this on a first-floor balcony. One *silbador* sat inside the restaurant. The other was in the street around the corner from the restaurant out of sight of the first but within camera range. I stood behind him and so did the sound recordist, but we were both hidden from the camera. The assistant cameraman was with the cameraman on the balcony. He had a ball-point and a notebook.

When we were set up, I stepped into the road and shouted to the cameraman to roll. Retreating quickly, I asked my *silbador* to tell his companion to come out of the restaurant and sit at one of the open-air tables. He joined his right forefinger and thumb into a circle, placed it in his mouth and whistled. Then I gave him a series of instructions to whistle to his companion: signal the waiter and order a cup of coffee; take off his hat and scratch his head; bend down and tie up his boot laces; drink the coffee; engage the attention of a passer-by; change his table then go back to the original one; and, finally, to pay his bill and leave a tip in the saucer.

The assistant cameraman had jotted all these actions down and they tallied with my notes. We then filmed the *silbador* close up and made him go through the instructions again. After that we changed camera angles and swapped the *silbadores*, getting them to perform a different series of actions. The second *silbador* used the first and second fingers of his left hand. There was no doubt that they could issue commands by *silbo*. But could they carry on a conversation in it?

To test this we went out into the country, driving along the northern coast. In amongst some laurel groves we placed the two *silbadores* out of sight of each other but within sight of the cameraman. This time I asked the *silbador* with whom I stood to question his friend about the different members of his family. When the other replied I asked him to translate what he had said into Spanish. Using the answer as a basis I then continued the conversation. It appeared that they could say anything they said verbally in Spanish in *silbo*. (Playing the tapes back to myself one day I thought the whistling language sounded rather like birdsong—a forceful trill. How did it originate I wondered. Perhaps in imitation of the canary, which is a notable songbird in full flight. But maybe this notion is too fanciful.)

There was one more matter to be cleared up—the distance over which *silbo* carried. We set one *silbador* on the side of a *barranco* at least a kilometre from the other but within sight of him. We took the megaphone and got our *silbador* to shout to the other to raise his right arm. Nothing happened, so we asked him to whistle "Jump up and down" and the other responded. This sort of thing we repeated several times. *Silbo* could be heard over a greater distance than the megaphone. No doubt the broken nature of Gomera's terrain has helped *silbo* to survive there. Men working their terraced plots on the sides of the *barrancos* could communicate with each other, even though it might take as long as half a day to get close enough to use speech. Sadly, however, the telephone has eroded the usefulness of *silbo*.

Driving back we were lucky enough to see a man using the *astia* as we crossed some heaths dotted with giant tree ferns. He ran with the pole—about 3 metres long (10 feet)—then vaulted, not very high but as far as he could, and did it again. Within a short space of time he was out of sight, but our *silbadores* whistled him back and he repeated the performance for our camera.

The two *silbadores* were delighted with their experiences and invited us to dine with them that evening. They insisted on taking us to the restaurant on the plaza where a *gomero* specialty had been prepared for the occasion—roast wild boar. And there was also entertainment, a sad slow dance called the *tajaraste*, accompanied by monotonous blows on a small catskin-covered drum. The drum and dance were also Guanche. There was a little dispute when we tried to pay the bill. They were poor labourers. We were wealthy television people. Yet such was *gomero* pride that they would not hear of our paying it.

The following day we left by boat for Hierro and La Palma. Hierro is the smallest and most westerly island. At one time it was thought that Hierro was the most westerly part of the world and the first meridian was drawn through it. From the sea it appeared to be surrounded by steep cliffs rising to wooded mountains. We did not stay there, but went on to La Palma and another Santa Cruz. This is an old town founded on the site of the Guanche capital with winding cobbled streets and typical Canarian architecture. We stayed at a hotel, the Mayantigo, and booked our return flight to Tenerife. Unfortunately, mist and low clouds closed the airport at Breña Alta (it is at an altitude of 500 metres, or 1,640 feet), and we had to wait a few days for it to clear. So in the meantime we took an excursion to the Caldera crater, about 6 kilometres across and 700 metres (2,296 feet) deep with some rock faces reaching as high as 2,500 metres (8,200 feet). The whole spine of La Palma is a chain of extinct volcanoes and the mountains are the highest (in relation to the size of the island) in the world. The mist lifted at last and we were soon back in Santa Cruz de Tenerife.

There were two messages, one from a Señor Betancur and the other from the British Club. The British Club was having a croquet tourney. "Not exactly the same as the one in *Alice in Wonderland*," the secretary commented, "but fun nonetheless." Señor Betancur said he had seen the article in *El Día*. He might have something we would be interested in, so I suggested he call at the hotel the following morning.

We filmed part of the croquet tourney. No one hit anyone over the head with a mallet, but it helped round out the picture of the British community with its protective life-support system. There was something else I wanted a shot of—El Tigre, the cannon that is supposed to have taken off Admiral Nelson's arm. El Tigre stands outside the Military Museum in Santa Cruz.

Various English sea captains had called at Santa Cruz over the years, some peacefully, some not so peacefully. Admiral Robert Blake had caught a fleet of sixteen Spanish treasure ships there in April 1657, defeated them without loss to himself, and sacked the town. Captain Cook put in at Tenerife on his voyage round the world in 1772. Fifteen years after him the First Fleet on its way from England to Australia did the same (one of the convicts bound for Botany Bay preferred Tenerife and escaped but he was later recaptured). Bent on taking the island, Nelson arrived in 1797 with four ships of the line, three frigates and a cutter. The attack was launched on the night of July 24, with Nelson personally leading a force of 1,000 men in a frontal assault on the fort. They were met by devastating cannon fire. Most of the long boats were sunk with heavy casualties, and Nelson's right arm was shattered by a cannon ball. The British retreated. It was a humiliating defeat, the only one in Nelson's career.

Señor Betancur called about five o'clock. He had a little suitcase with him. In it were various clay beads, a necklace, some obsidian cutting instruments, and a few mummified hands. These were all for sale. I bought a baked clay necklace. The mummified hands, rather large and appearing to have been varnished, looked a little too fat. Señor Betancur insisted they were genuine and came from caves known only to himself. It seemed a macabre souvenir but he alleged the Scandinavians in particular were keen on them.

"I can't get enough," he said.

Later in London I mentioned this to the press attaché at the Spanish Embassy when we met after the film had been transmitted.

"That man has been arrested!" he exclaimed. "He was caught robbing graves. It has shocked the citizens of Tenerife. A great scandal. A terrible thing in a Catholic country."

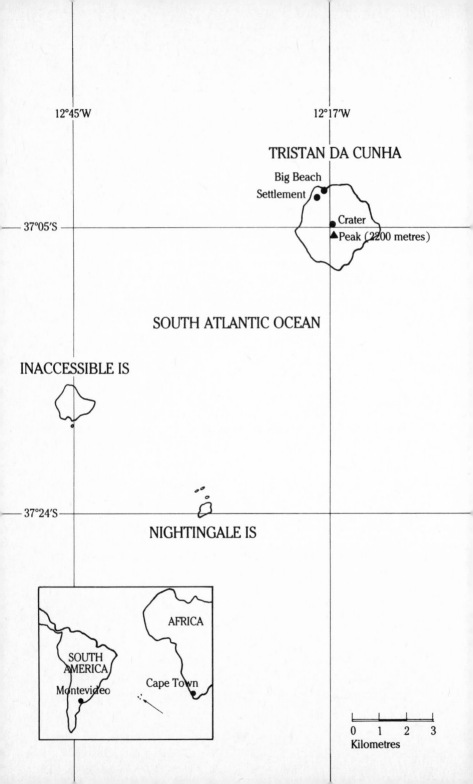

12°45'W   12°17'W

TRISTAN DA CUNHA

Big Beach

Settlement

37°05'S

Crater

▲ Peak (2200 metres)

SOUTH ATLANTIC OCEAN

INACCESSIBLE IS

37°24'S

NIGHTINGALE IS

AFRICA

SOUTH
AMERICA

Cape Town

Montevideo

0   1   2   3
Kilometres

18

Tristan da Cunha

▬▭▬▭▬▭▬▭▬▭▬▭▬▭▬▭▬▭▬▭▬▭▬▭▬

THE LONELIEST PLACE ON EARTH

While "Tristanians" is the name used in official publications for the citizens of the island of Tristan da Cunha, they call themselves "Trisstns" and the British press generally refers to them as "Tristan da Cunhans." But I feel that the bureaucrats, for once, got it right when they created such a poetic word to describe this unpoetic but singular people.

I first saw the Tristanians in Las Palmas, Canary Islands. They were lining the rail of the *Stirling Castle* on their way to Britain. It was towards the end of October 1961. For about three months there had been a succession of earthquakes on Tristan da Cunha and then, at the beginning of October, a new crater had opened on the slopes of the extinct volcano behind the township. The British Government decided to evacuate everybody on the island—all 264 inhabitants.

Later, when they were settled in the south of England, we filmed them at various times to see how they were adjusting to the 20th century. When their home island was pronounced clear of volcanic activity in 1962, the Tristanians voted overwhelmingly to go home. "Hengland's wery nice," they said, "but hain't nothing we want 'ere."

A few soon found out that this was not the case and returned to Britain. One, Gerald Repetto, claimed in press and television interviews that as many as 75 percent of the people really wanted to come back and that twenty-five men, women, and children were in fact preparing to leave the island for good the following year. At this point we decided to go to Tristan da Cunha to see if we could discover why the simple life that sounded so attractive to many Britishers palled for those who had experienced it at first hand.

The island lies in the South Atlantic almost midway between Cape Town and Montevideo. Its nearest inhabited neighbour is St. Helena, of which it is a dependency, 2,000 kilometres to the north. This makes Tristan da Cunha the most isolated place on earth with people living there. Looking from the sea like a three-tiered wedding cake, the island is in reality a volcano 2,148 metres high (7,045 feet) and roughly 80 square kilometres in area. Southwest of Tristan da Cunha are two small islets called Nightingale and Inaccessible, and the three together constitute a British Crown Colony.

The discoverer was the Portuguese navigator Tristão da Cunha, but it was the Dutch who first showed signs of interest in the island. They sent a couple of expeditions from Cape Town (then a Dutch possession) to see if a naval base could be established there but decided against it. However, the practice of keeping well out into the Atlantic until the "Roaring Forties" (latitudes 40° south where the winds blow continuously from the west) were picked up, as commonly followed by ships' captains bound from Europe to the East, soon made Tristan da Cunha a familiar landfall to sailors.

One who decided to take advantage of this was an American from Salem, Massachusetts, called Jonathon Lambert. He landed there in 1810 accompanied by an Italian, Tommaso Corri (who had anglicised his name to Thomas Currie), and proclaimed himself king of the islands "grounding my right and claim on the rational and sure principle of absolute occupancy." Lambert called his kingdom "The Islands of Refreshment" and designed a flag of blue and red diamonds on a white background. He sent copies of his proclamation to every government in Europe and offered to supply visiting ships with water, fresh meat, and vegetables. Lambert's rule didn't last very long, however. With two other Americans who had joined him, he went out fishing one day in 1812 and never came back. Thomas Currie was left alone.

Despite Dutch doubts about the usefulness of Tristan da Cunha, during the War of 1812 American privateers used it as a base to prey on British shipping in the South Atlantic. After the war the British decided to annex the island but nothing really practical was done about it until Napoleon had been exiled to St. Helena. Fearing that an attempt might be made from Tristan da Cunha to free him, a garrison of soldiers was sent from the Cape of Good Hope (now a British possession) in 1816. They found Thomas Currie in possession.

Currie was delighted to accept British protection. He was even more delighted when they opened a canteen. Here he became drunk daily, spending handfuls of gold from some hidden store. In his cups he boasted of the treasure he had buried. He alleged that Lambert had brought it ashore with them when they landed and hinted at its being the proceeds of piracy. Furthermore, he promised to show its hiding place to the British soldier who treated him the best. So the soldiers plied him with drink—and questions. One day he announced he was at last going to reveal where the gold was. As they all stood around waiting, Currie, in a dramatic gesture, lifted his arm to point in the right direction. And fell dead from a stroke. (The story of "Old Thomas' kettle," as the Tristanians called the hoard, lingers on. It is supposed to be hidden somewhere near the settlement between two waterfalls. No one has admitted to finding it, but many have searched.)

Fifteen months later the garrison was removed, leaving behind three men, one of whom, Corporal William Glass, has descendants on the island to this day. He was a native of Kelso in the Scottish border country. Before he left the Cape, Glass had married an Afrikaans-speaking Coloured woman—though there is some question about this. She may have been Cape Dutch. Her surname, Leenders, was certainly Dutch, but most of the Cape Coloureds have Dutch surnames and Afrikaans is their language. She married very young, at the age of thirteen, which was not at all common among the Calvinist burghers.

Whether Glass saw himself as the inheritor of Currie's island or whether he just didn't want to face the racial discrimination of Cape Town is not known. In any case, he and the other two men signed a rather remarkable document. In it they agreed to enter into a partnership "That, in order to ensure the harmony of the Firm, No member shall assume any superiority whatever, but all to be considered equal in every respect, each performing his proportion of labour, if not prevented by sickness—." The ideas embodied in this early constitution still inspire and motivate the Tristanians and this, more than anything else, makes them unique. The document itself, incidentally, is in the British Museum.

Over the next few years men came and went. Some were shipwrecked, some were deserters. All were invited to join the new society based on freedom and equality. But since there were no women and no liquor, most got tired of it after a while and took passage on ships that called for provisions. Then one of the original three settlers went to Cape Town with their small stock of sealskins and sea elephant oil and never came back (it was said he spent all the money on drink). So Tristan da Cunha went from one crisis to another, and at one point there were only four men and two women on the island. Yet William Glass and his five children stayed firm.

Soon there were new arrivals. One of them, whose name is still found on the island, was Thomas Swain. He claimed that as a lad he had served under Lord Nelson. He even alleged that he was the sailor who had caught Nelson in his arms as he fell dying to the deck of the *Victory* at Trafalgar. Though this is still believed on Tristan da Cunha it is not true. Swain spent most of the Napoleonic Wars in prison. He had, however, served under Nelson on the *Theseus*.

Swain joined the colony in 1826. He was fifty-two at the time and, since he had decided to settle there, desired a wife. So did the other four bachelors then on the island. They persuaded a Norwegian sea captain who visited the island regularly to find five brides for them on St. Helena. He was promised twenty bushels of potatoes a head.

The captain eventually kept his side of the bargain and a year later landed four mulattos and one Negress on Tristan da Cunha. The men drew lots. Two of the women had brought at least four children with them. But things worked out satisfactorily. A census conducted by William Glass in 1832 showed six couples on the island with twenty-two children among them (ten of these belonged to William Glass). The colony had started to take hold and, as it was not long before Tristan da Cunha had its own marriageable girls, other sailors settled there. "Please God," Tristanian girls used to pray, "send a good shipwreck so we get 'usbands."

Such were the beginnings of this small community. All the first-generation men were white, the women coloured. Thus, today's Tristanians are of mixed origin. They are not homogeneous, however. As a piece of island doggerel has it:

> Some iz white and some iz black
> And some the colour of chawed toback.

But they do have a similar look to them—a lean, wiry, tough, and rather weather-beaten look. And psychologically they are very similar. One gets the impression that meeting one is much the same as meeting another, since there seem to be no outstanding differences in their personalities. Despite the fact that many marriages are between cousins (there are only seven surnames on the island—Glass, Swain, Green, Rogers, Hagan, Repetto, and Lavarello), this does not appear to have had any undue effect. The Tristanians are remarkably healthy. If they don't die from an accident they die from old age. There are no diseases—no typhoid fever, no malaria, no smallpox, tuberculosis or diphtheria (mostly, of course, this is due to the near-complete isolation; the small population could be quite vulnerable to disease brought in from the outside). Their teeth are the most perfect in the world, free entirely from decay and scale. A Tristanian smile is the proverbial pearly-white one. Yet they don't use toothbrushes. They wipe their teeth with a cloth and they have a soft diet— fish and potatoes three times a day. Most dentists think it must be the water but apart from that offer no explanation. Another feature that marks Tristanians off from other small communities is their high birthrate. When they were evacuated to Britain in 1961 there were 264 of them, but in 1986 the population was 312 (despite the fact that there has been steady emigration).

As sail gave way to steam the raison d'être for Tristan da Cunha faded and ships called infrequently. Nevertheless, there were some distinguished visitors to the island during the 19th century. The Duke of Edinburgh (Queen Victoria's second son) called there in 1867. The Tristanians named their settlement after him, Edinburgh of the Seven Seas (the consort of Queen Elizabeth II visited it in 1957). And in the early 1880s, the chaplain there for a while was the Rev. E. H. Dodgson, the brother of Charles Dodgson (the author Lewis Carroll). Although a lifelong supporter of the islanders he proposed that they be moved, either to the Cape of Good Hope or Australia.

In the early years whaling provided employment for the younger men (Tristanians are superb seamen), but increasingly the inhabitants found themselves thrown onto their own resources. This meant a subsistence economy of fishing and farming, not unlike that in the Western Isles of Scotland. The Tristanians had sheep and cattle. Their only crop was potatoes, their only fruit apples. Wool was carded, spun, and knitted into garments—stockings, jumpers, caps, coats. The cattle were milked and butter was churned; from the hides they made moccasins. Seabirds augmented their diet, though they tended to depend on fish and fishing is sometimes chancy. Tristanians often went hungry but they never starved.

The Rev. J. G. Barrow said in a report to the Colonial Office in 1906:

> With all their privations they are much better off than many a working man at home. The scarcity of potatoes and milk intensified the privation which is always present but did not cause distress.

Then in 1916 a letter appeared in the London *Times* stating that there had been no mail to the island for ten years. A London solicitor stepped into the breach and set up the Tristan da Cunha Fund under the patronage of the Royal Geographical Society and the Royal Colonial Society (now the Royal Commonwealth Society). The main purpose of the Fund was to establish "regular periodic intercourse with the island and to mitigate the hardships of life by consignments of necessary food, clothing, tools, utensils and other goods." In short—hand-outs.

The British Government took the view that this should not continue and that the Tristanians ought to be moved elsewhere. The Tristanians refused to leave. "Hevery man on Tristan da Cunha can make 'is own living," they said. All they needed was regular communication with the outside world. The British Government bowed to their wishes.

World War II changed Tristan da Cunha's isolation forever. A naval garrison that included a surgeon, a chaplain, and a teacher was put on the island. For the first time Tristanians went to school. A radio station was built and a general store opened. After the war the South African Government decided to maintain a meteorological station on the island, which meant regular supply ships. And South African interests set up a fish-canning factory to exploit the enormous numbers of crayfish and pelagic fish in Tristanian waters. Another source of income was found in 1952 when the first stamps were issued. Today all Tristanian projects—including closed-circuit television, local broadcasting, and electric generators—are financed from stamp sales.

But these developments occurred long after the volcanic eruption and my first contact with the Tristanians that sunny morning in Las Palmas harbour. Even months later, when I got somewhat better acquainted with them at Calshot in Hampshire where they were settled (in the former married quarters of an old seaplane base), I felt I never really knew them. I don't think anyone did outside their closed circle.

So what manner of people were they and what can be said about them? In a way they were people from another time, as though they had stepped through a portal from the 19th century, from before the machine age. For 150 years everything on Tristan da Cunha had been done by hand. They had built stone cottages with thatched roofs, made furniture, knitted clothes, cooked over open fires, hauled water from a stream, lit their homes with oil lamps, used cesspits, dug their potato patches with primitive hoes. They lived with their backs to the mountain and their faces to the sea. The wind blew incessantly. Time meant nothing (a few owned clocks but never bothered to wind them). They had no real folklore or myths. No crime had ever been committed. There were no policemen, no jails. There had been a few illegitimate children and one case of incest, but aside from these lapses their pleasures were simple—visiting each other, sharing feasts, playing the accordion or mouth-organ (harmonica), picking apples or gathering crowberries, dancing, and courting.

Their English was Dickensian. *W* replaced *v*, an initial *h* was dropped but haphazardly inserted before other vowels, *family* was pronounced "fambly" and *chimney* "chimbly," and so on. They also had words of their own: "watron" for stream, "angcher" for head scarf, "pinnamin" for penguin, "willies" for windblown waves.

And they lived in an economy without money. True, a certain amount of cash existed on Tristan da Cunha, but it could hardly be said to circulate. Most of them lived quite comfortably on barter. Every man was the equal of his neighbour and did his equal share of the work for equal gain—as

Corporal Glass had set out in the founding charter. That bound them together.

When they arrived in Britain they had never seen a train, a car, an aeroplane, a horse, or even a real tree. The authorities acted on the assumption that the Tristanians would be absorbed into the general community and proceeded to conduct classes in the art of living 20th-century style. They were taught traffic safety, how to use electrical appliances, how to pull the chains in toilets, how to cook on gas stoves, what the value of money was, and how to shop. They were introduced to a whole new range of foods and drink.

They were also introduced to a whole new range of social problems. Muggings were something they were totally unprepared for and were horrified when one of their number was assaulted and robbed. Prostitution was another shock, especially when they discovered that some of the young men had spent their entire wages on whores. And disease took its toll. Along with venereal diseases, Tristanians found they were not immune to the common cold, to pneumonia, to bronchitis, to hepatitis. Within the first three months three people had died, with others to follow. "Hit wouldn've 'appened on Trisstn," was the verdict. At one point only one Tristanian was *not* sick.

Under these conditions it seemed a pointless exercise to ask if they were content. "Hengland's wery nice," they would always respond, "but . . ." and trail off. Still, they were together and that gave them some consolation. So when Tristan da Cunha was pronounced free of volcanic activity, nobody was really surprised that they voted 148 to 5 to return. As the *Daily Mirror*'s columnist Cassandra (William Connor, the favourite journalist of Winston Churchill, by the way) wrote: "It was the most eloquent and contemptuous rebuff that our smug and deviously contrived society could have received."

We filmed them shortly after this. Proudly they stood beside their packing crates labelled TRISTAN DA CUNHA

SOUTH ATLANTIC OCEAN. These were filled with curtains, carpets, clothing, kitchen utensils, transistor radios, tools, etc. that they had bought to take home with them. The Tristanians were happy now, happy and excited. They were going back to their island.

But the grass was not quite as green on Tristan da Cunha as they had fondly remembered. Although only one house had been destroyed by the eruption, the fish cannery was buried under 20 metres (65 feet) of lava and the landing beach obliterated. The settlement's dogs had gone wild and attacked the sheep (there is a theory too that a visiting ship's crew had shot them), while the unharvested potato crop had been trampled or eaten by the cattle. As a Tristanian summed it up: "When we came back to Trisstn we 'ad nothing; hall our sheep gone, hall our potatoes gone, no nothing." One family returned to Britain on the very ship that had brought them home.

What saw the others through the first two years were the savings they had been able to put aside in Calshot "for a rainy day." It was estimated that altogether they had around £18,000. Tristanians are thrifty people, but seeing these savings so quickly depleted only served to fuel the discontent that Gerald Repetto had voiced—the discontent that brought our film crew to the island.

The South African survey ship, the *R.S.A.* (which stands for Republic of South Africa) had been chartered by the British Government to make two trips a year to the island with stores and supplies, and it was not difficult for us to arrange passage on it. We flew to Cape Town where we embarked. There were a few other passengers, mainly South Africans attached to the radio stations. Less than a week later we saw on the horizon a broad-based cone ringed with clouds, the peak standing clear—Tristan da Cunha.

On the northwest point of the island is an irregular flat plain 30 metres (108 feet) above sea level. It is about 6 kilometres long and half a kilometre wide. At one end was the settlement—sixty small rectangular cottages looking like birds' nests hugging the ground. None of the famous and elegant longboats (one of which was presented to Queen Elizabeth when they had arrived in Britain in 1961) put out to welcome us. Instead a sort of landing barge appeared, took off the passengers, and was winched up a wooden ramp over the lava rocks.

The first thing that struck me on arrival was the pungent smell—a kind of strange salty odour that clung to everything. It had traces of rotting kelp in it and dead fish, but there was something else besides, something elemental—"the whispering, lapsing, unsoilable sea," as the Irish poet Oliver St. John Gogarty calls it.

Each house was surrounded by a low stone wall. There were no gardens, only a mass of hardy New Zealand flax plants almost as high as the eaves. These were used for thatching. By the front door, in most cases, stood a painted sentry box. At least, it looked like a sentry box but it was, in truth, the lavatory. (The lavatories had been installed just before the volcano erupted, and there was now running water to all the houses.)

There were other evidences of the modern world: women in short skirts shopping in the store, transistor radios tuned into the commercial station in Cape Town, a rubbish dump on the outskirts of the village. For ill or good, two years of living in an industrial society had changed the islanders and their attitudes. They wanted the good things of life but they also wanted their separateness. Unfortunately, the two are rarely compatible. It now proved even more difficult to talk with them. They seemed to have become defensive and surly and withdrawn. We were almost completely ignored. Apart from the settlement and the potato patches, there was not much to film. The mountain seemed always wreathed in clouds, there was only tussock grass and a type of stunted tree. It rained a lot. Flies were a pest. We spent much of our time at "the Station," a group of wooden houses a little distance from the settlement. Here were the Outsiders—the schoolteachers, the radio technicians, the meteorologists, the administrator and his staff. Their social life did not involve the Tristanians. It was a Them and Us situation.

On the voyage back to Cape Town I became friendly with one of the *R.S.A.*'s officers, and the night before we arrived he showed me some coins—rix-dollars, pieces of eight, etc. He was selling them on commission to a coin dealer. Every trip he brought a few. Where had they come from I wanted to know. From a couple of Tristanians, who had found them in a gulch that wasn't there before the eruption. (Perhaps "Old Thomas' kettle" has finally surfaced?)

Over the next few years Tristan da Cunha lost almost a quarter of its population to emigration, causing the London *Times* to comment:

> This return to what they pronounce 'the Houtside Warld' shatters the potent, sentimental myth about happy isles beyond the sunset, frugal life and the golden age of Calypso and Crusoe. Having tasted the fruit of the tree of affluence have they been corrupted so that they can never again enter into the simple life?

The answer appears to be no. Many of those who went back to Britain subsequently returned for good to Tristan da Cunha. Of course by then things had improved on the island. A harbour was built and a new cannery with a freezing plant and two modern fishing vessels. And they have, as I mentioned before, closed-circuit television. But perhaps the most compelling reason was their closed-circuit social structure. This they could not replace in Britain.

19

The Persian Gulf

THE MAN WHO READ THE CLASSICS

On the last day of May 1957 I left Karachi on board the S.S. *Gwalior*, an aging vessel of the British India Steam Navigation Company, bound for Basra, Iraq, at the head of the Persian Gulf. After many months in the Indo-Pakistani subcontinent, I was on my way to London (from Basra I was to travel overland by train).

The S.S. *Gwalior* sailed at midnight and, by ten o'clock the following morning, she lay off Gwadar on the Makran Coast of Baluchistan (in Pakistan). In those days Gwadar (not to be confused with Gwatar, in Iran) belonged to Oman, the last colony of an Arabian empire that had once stretched down the eastern coast of Africa as far as Zanzibar. (Sultan Said bin Taimur of Oman was to transfer Gwardar sovereignty to Pakistan the next year in return for financial compensation.)

The sea was steely grey and the barren headlands behind the town shimmered through the morning haze. Pulled up on the beach were some ungainly bugalows (a type of boat), and squatting beside them some rather wild-looking Baluchi sailors (for fishing and smuggling were the two principal occupations of Gwadar).

Among the flat-roofed, mud-walled houses stood one that was somewhat larger than the rest, and above it flew the flag of Oman—possibly the simplest in the world, a plain red rectangle (it is now red, white, and green). This was the Governor's residence and, as one might expect in such a desolate spot, the Governor was an Englishman. Lean and tanned, with horn-rimmed glasses and a straw hat, he had represented the Sultan of Oman for eight years—eight long years in which he had been deprived of the company of other Englishmen (there were no Europeans in Gwadar), of the chance to speak English there (Baluchi was the language of Gwadar), of the use of tobacco or alcohol (both strictly forbidden under Omani law), even of the conveniences of electricity and running water.

Nonetheless, Gwadar had had its share of interesting history, Martin Wynne (the Governor) told me. It had been sacked by the Portuguese in 1581, for instance, but that was in the days when it belonged to the Khan of Kalat. Also, in 1784 during a dynastic dispute, the son of the sultan of Oman had fled across the Gulf of Oman to Gwadar, which he occupied and from which he was able to reconquer his father's domains. Since that time Gwadar belonged to Oman, although the ruling Khan of Kalat had never ceased to lay claim to it (and on one occasion even the Persians had joined in). Yes, said Martin Wynne, there was a certain amount of history in the old place.

I moved a little in my chair, so that my shirt didn't stick to my back, and agreed. One thing, though, puzzled me. How did the Governor pass the time when he was not dispensing Omani law to the 20,000 inhabitants of Gwadar or patrolling its 80 square kilometres of territory?

"Why," he said, "I read the classics. Come and I'll show you."

There they were, piled on the floor of his bedroom—Latin in one heap, Greek in the other. I saw works by Plautus, Catullus, Horace, Cicero, Livy, Tacitus, Ovid, and Virgil separated in a haphazard manner from those of Homer,

Aeschylus, Herodotus, Sophocles, Plato, Hesiod, and Pindar. I opened one, a volume of Terence's plays, at random. Neatly pencilled on the title page was a date (*8/1/50*) and below it another (*7/2/52*). It was the same for all the books. He was evidently a student of Latin as well, for alongside *quippe qui* ("namely in that") on one page he had written "should take the subjunctive not indicative." (I later looked this up in a Latin grammar and learnt that the conjunction could take both moods.)

I was to spend the rest of that day with this self-reliant, studious man as he later came aboard and shared my cabin (I was the only European passenger) for the transit to Muscat. He had to go there to report to the Sultan of Oman, but from the expression on his face one might have thought he was going to Paris. Then again, he *hadn't* had a drink for a long while, and the S.S. *Gwalior* carried a well-stocked bar.

There is an Arab saying: "When a sinner goes to Muscat he gets a foretaste of what to expect in the afterlife." This is because Muscat and its twin city Mattrah are like furnaces most of the year. They lie side by side on neighbouring rocky coves ringed with barren, craggy mountains that almost seem to pulsate as they eagerly absorb the sun's scorching rays. At night waves of heat from these same peaks sweep down onto the towns. With air-conditioning the rigours of the climate are somewhat ameliorated, but between 1800 and 1810 the first four British Residents perished from heatstroke.

Despite the climate, the setting is wild and romantic. Sir Ronald Storrs once wrote of Muscat, "nothing could be more Byronically picturesque"—and he should have known about Byronic landscapes, since he had travelled extensively in the Balkans. Muscat sits at the head of a horseshoe-shaped cove. The waterfront, barely 200 metres wide, provides only enough room for about eight or nine buildings. Two rise above the others—the British Consul-General's house and the Sultan's Palace. Behind them other buildings crowd the small expanse of flat land and then begin to go up into the hills. The mouth of the cove is guarded by a fort on either side.

Both were extensively rebuilt by the Portuguese (the Portuguese ruled the coastal areas of Oman from 1507 to 1649), and the anchorage they protect is bounded by sheer rock walls on which it has long been the custom to write the names of visiting ships in white paint. The Sultan called this his "Visitors' Book," and among the signatories is H.M.S. *Seahorse*, said to have been painted there by Nelson himself when he was a midshipman on the warship and spent two months in Muscat during 1775.

Mattrah, at the head of a similar though more exposed inlet, is the commercial centre. From there camel caravans set off to the interior. The town has a dark *souk* or bazaar full of exotic aromas, and bales of produce are piled on the beach awaiting distribution. The beach itself is lined by old Indian-style houses with sagging balconies. When I was there Muscat and Mattrah boasted a few cars, a telephone system, a small British community (Martin Wynne's only connection with his compatriots), and a powerhouse to generate electricity. There were no cinemas (the Sultan specifically excluded these), schools and universities were regarded as hotbeds of political agitation, and it was forbidden to wear dark glasses. The currency was Indian rupees and Maria Theresa dollars. They used British stamps. Every night at eight a big gun went off from the battlements of Fort Murani to signal the closing of the Bab el-Kebir, the land-gate into Muscat. If you went out on your own in the city after that hour, you were compelled by law to carry an oil lamp for visibility.

Visitors were not encouraged. In addition to a visa, everyone landing in Muscat had to have a Non-Objection Certificate, a document personally signed by the Sultan. The purpose and goal of this policy was fairly simple: to insulate the country from Arab nationalism, Western liberalism, and American consumer products (kitchen gadgets, etc.). But these medieval ideas were soon to come to grief because of the smell of oil and the increasing demand for it in the world market. (War was to break out shortly after I had left Muscat, but talk of it was in the air when I was there.)

Since Martin Wynne had arranged a Non-Objection Certificate for me, I was allowed to go ashore while the S.S. *Gwalior* was in port. So I was able to meet the various administrative functionaries (all British and all former bureaucrats from India or the Sudan—the Acting Foreign Minister, the Commander-in-Chief of the Army, the Minister for Customs, the Chief of Police, and the representative of Iraq Petroleum). Although never a British protectorate, Oman could be said to be well and truly in the British pocket.

In those days the country was known as Muscat and Oman—Muscat was the capital, Oman the rest. Although the Sultan was technically head of the whole country, in fact the temporal and spiritual leader outside Muscat was the Imam of Oman. He had already begun to stir up the various dissident sheikhs, who were becoming dissatisfied over the oil drilling being done in their territories and who wanted any future royalties to be paid directly to them, not to the Sultan. As the representative of Iraq Petroleum pointed out to me, they were beginning to entertain visions of Cadillacs, ideas about trips to luxurious European gambling casinos, and fantasies over fresh faces in the harem. Even then I could see that this pot was brewing briskly.

Oman is about as big as Great Britain and occupies the lower southeast corner of the Arabian peninsula. To preserve order over this substantial area the Sultan had an army numbering only about two hundred men, so whenever trouble did erupt he was forced to call on the British for help. As it happened, trouble was soon to arise (in July that year), when the dissident sheikhs rebelled. Eventually, the British would succeed in putting down this revolt—the War of the Jebel Akhdar (or, Green Mountains), as it became known. Incidentally, one can see the Green Mountains from Muscat, the peaks reaching as high as 3,000 metres (9,840 feet).

That event was to be a harbinger of change, of course. In 1970 the Sultan's son Qaboos, whom his father had once imprisoned for four years, staged a coup and took over. Sultan Said bin Taimur was exiled to England and died two years later. Qaboos, who had been educated in England and was a graduate of Sandhurst, shortened the country's name to Oman and opened its doors to the world. The result was that he, too, soon had a war on his hands—this time against the People's Front for the Liberation of the Occupied Arab Gulf (PFLOAG), a communist organisation supported by Chairman Mao, the Soviet Union, and the People's Democratic Republic of Yemen. The fighting was done by *Jebali* or mountain dwellers, led for the most part by a hardcore group of Omanis who had been trained in Soviet bloc countries. These *Jebalis* were not Arabs, but remnants of the original population of South Arabia and related to the Sokotri. They speak Hymiaritic languages, similar to ancient Sabaean. British, Jordanian, and Iranian troops (this was in the days of the Shah) finally overcame the PFLOAG after an arduous campaign in Dhofar, the southwesterly province of Oman bordering the People's Democratic Republic of Yemen (this country actually invaded Oman in 1972, only to be stopped by the Royal Air Force).

Other memories from my brief stay in Muscat are of the black-robed women and white-robed men (they call this robe a *dishdasha*), who sported the traditional curved dagger or *khanjar* in its richly ornamented sheath. And I recall the handmade silver coffee pots fashioned out of melted-down Maria Theresa dollars (one was later presented to the United Nations by the government). The lid is hollow and filled with beans that rattle when the pot is used. This device was meant to frighten jinns away—but it also discouraged slaves from helping themselves to a cup of coffee. Mentioning slaves, I am reminded of a flagpole that stood outside the British Consulate-General. Any slave who made his way there and embraced it was given his freedom and a certificate of manumission to prove it. This practice continued up to the mid-1960s.

Soon the S.S. *Gwalior* was steaming north along Oman's Batinah Coast towards the Strait of Hormuz. The Batinah

Coast, flat and sandy, has a beach that stretches uninterruptedly for almost 300 kilometres. The Phoenicians are supposed to have originated here, at least Herodotus thought so. Halfway along the coast is the town of Sohar, the home of Sindbad the Sailor and described in former times as "one of the most splendid cities of the Islamic world."

Then on we went to the northernmost headland of Oman jutting out into the strait—the Musendam Peninsula, a great horn of towering rock and wild mountains completely cut off from the rest of the country by one of the states of the United Arab Emirates. The most eastern part is known as the Cape of the Graves of Indians, or so the captain informed me.

Once round that we entered the Persian Gulf and were on the Trucial Coast, low and barren merging inland with empty desert. Here are the seven sheikhdoms that make up the United Arab Emirates. Formerly they were called by a variety of names that included the Pirate Coast, the Trucial States, the Trucial Sheikhdoms, and Trucial Oman. The states comprising the federation are: Abu Dhabi, Dubai, Sharjah, Ajman, Umm al-Qaiwain, Ras al-Khaimah, and Fujairah (the one that separates the Musendam Peninsula from Oman).

Had it not been for the skill of their inhabitants as pirates, it is doubtful whether they would ever have attracted attention before the oil era. But such was the rapacity of their forays against shipping that the British first intervened in 1820, and ultimately during the 19th century all the states became British protectorates. This situation lasted until 1971, when the British withdrew east of Suez. Plans for the seven sheikhdoms to federate with nearby Qatar and Bahrain (also British protectorates) fell through but, in 1972, they formed the United Arab Emirates. When I was there they were known as the Trucial States.

Dubai, the first port of call, is a sort of Little Venice. A wide creek separates the town into two parts, one newer than the other. At that time (before the massive offshore oil finds of the early 1970s in which Jacques Cousteau played a part),

Dubai was the entrepôt of the Trucial States. Trade and fishing flourished, particularly pearl fishing. The town was full of low mud-walled houses and narrow lanes. Everywhere were tall, square wind towers that trapped the slightest breeze and funnelled it to the living quarters below. The only school was in the Emir's Palace, women wore the *burqah* (a stiff beak-like mask, the Koranic verse "Men are in charge of women" was strictly observed), and donkeys were the common means of transport. (I have since been back to Dubai, and it has all changed. Now there are air-conditioned skyscrapers, fast roads, cars of every known make, new port facilities, hospitals, schools, mosques, and even fountains in the squares—where water was once very scarce! One of the most modern, but so far underused, television stations in the Middle East has been built there. Coca-Cola and Fanta are sold everywhere. And women sometimes go without the *burqah*.)

The same story is true of Abu Dhabi, a bit further along the coast. It had been like Dubai except perhaps for more *barastis* (shanties of palm fronds), situated near a maze of creeks and islands. But oil was found there the year after I first visited the town, and now it has an international airport, broad tree-lined boulevards (nourished at enormous expense), a modern communications system, and all the rest that goes with high-tech 20th-century state-of-the-art (including a pervasive smell of sewage).

It was in Abu Dhabi that I got my next cabin-mate. After having walked around the town, I returned to the ship to find a large black man in Arab dress standing in front of the cabin door and holding a scimitar in a purposeful sort of way. My access was barred, so I went to get an officer. He called the purser, a Goan who spoke some Arabic, and together we went back to my cabin. I was now to share it with a sheikh, the purser explained. The sheikh, it transpired, was having a beer (the Koran only forbids wine) in the saloon and had left his servant to guard his belongings. All this was satisfactorily sorted out and the servant even let me examine his scimitar.

That evening when I retired to my cabin the servant was inside sitting on the floor. His master was lying on the lower bunk and drinking beer out of a bottle. He greeted me, and I took the opportunity to have a good look at him. About twenty-five, I decided, slightly built, good features, a small pointed beard and sallow skin.

I clambered into the upper bunk and prepared to sleep. The problem was that there was only one light in the cabin, almost right above me. When it appeared the Arab had no intention of turning it out, I waited a while and then did so myself. Whereupon the servant switched it back on. So I rolled over to face the wall and tried to sleep. What seemed like hours went by. The light still remained on. Gradually I became aware the sheikh was standing by my bunk, and I turned to see him looking at me with a curious expression on his face. He put his thumb in his mouth and sucked it. With a sinking feeling I realised what he wanted. I shook my head. Whereupon he took off his watch and gave it to me—a Patek Philippe. I shook my head again. He spoke to his servant, who approached, holding the scimitar. I leapt from the bunk, but the servant barred my way.

By the cabin door was a bell. I pushed the button as hard as I could and kept my finger on it. After an interminable time the officer of the watch appeared and wanted to know what the problem was. I spent that night and the next sleeping on one of the sofas in the saloon.

The following morning we were in Doha, the capital of Qatar. More primitive than Abu Dhabi, it was a small impoverished village even though oil had been struck in Qatar as early as the 1940s. (Now, I believe, it has 100,000 people living there with motorways, a desalination plant for fresh water, and many of the other trappings of modernity.) On the second morning the purser woke me in the saloon. We were in

Manama Harbour, Bahrain, and the sheikh had already disembarked. He had left a gift for me, however—the Patek Philippe watch. I didn't have that very long as it was stolen on the train from Basra to Baghdad.

Bahrain is a complex of low-lying islands off the coast of Saudi Arabia. The first of the Persian Gulf states to acquire oil wealth, it had a much more relaxed air about it. Women went unveiled, for instance, and worked alongside men. There were bars and clubs, a racetrack, and a golf course. Industry was more diversified. All in all, Bahrain was a reasonably civilised place and I quite liked the feel of it. (Since I was there they have built a huge oil refinery, an aluminium smelter, and a shipyard, doubtless insurance against a future when the oil reserves run out.)

Of the rest of that voyage there is nothing much to tell. We called at Kuwait (then a British protectorate but to become independent in 1961) and at Abadan in Iran. Kuwait was a bustling, affluent place with construction going on everywhere. Even the ubiquitous soft-drink stands had air-conditioners before which their proprietors crouched! However, no one with a Bahraini stamp on his passport was allowed ashore at Abadan. This was because Iran laid claim to Bahrain. So I leant over the ship's rail and stared at the refinery—all there was to see, I was told, so I don't think I missed much.

Finally we arrived at Basra, 120 kilometres up the Shatt-al-Arab waterway, formed by the historically significant confluence of the Tigris and Euphrates rivers. Basra (later to become the scene of fierce battles in the Gulf War) is perfectly flat and surrounded by luxuriant date groves (there are forty different varieties of date). Canals run through the city and are overlooked by elegant two-storied houses with flat roofs and balconies running the entire width of the upper storey. Along the Shatt-al-Arab there is a fashionable corniche road where the wealthy took the evening air.

Some hundred kilometers north of Basra, where the two great rivers join, is the legendary location of the Garden of

Eden. It is also said that the Tree of Knowledge is there, nowadays surrounded by a low mud-brick wall with a cafe nearby where one can be served dates and yoghurt. In this part of the world they claim that Eve tempted Adam with the succulent date, not an apple, as I had always been led to believe.

But a month later, in London, the apple I wanted to eat was Fleet Street. I was down to my last £10 and hadn't been able to crack this Street of Journalistic Dreams, so in desperation I took a job as sub-editor in the office of the Australian company Truth and Sportsman Ltd. (so help me). This really consisted of little more than wielding a large pair of scissors nightly, cutting out items from the first editions of the London morning papers that would be suitable for newspapers back in Sydney.

On the night of Wednesday, July 24, I was going through these first editions about 10 P.M. The lead story in all the papers was: WAR IN MUSCAT. I read the reports very carefully and realised that no one had a correspondent in Muscat itself because of the Sultan's Non-Objection Certificate. The closest one worked for the *Daily Express*, which by-lined its story from Bahrain, while journalists for other papers were reporting from Kuwait, Baghdad, and Karachi. The farthest away from the action was the *News Chronicle*'s man, in Beirut, so I called the *News Chronicle* and asked to speak to the Foreign Editor.

"I have just been in Muscat," I said, fudging the fact that it was seven weeks before, "and I know all about the war there, its origins, the plans of the Sultan's commander-in-chief, and so on."

"You interest me," said the Foreign Editor, whose name was Sylvain Mangeot (a nice man, I later discovered, of French extraction though born in London). "Can you come and see me?"

I rushed over and, for the very first time, was able to get past the doorman of a Fleet Street newspaper. Mangeot listened to me quietly, then said, "I want you to go into that room over there and I'll get a journalist to take your story down."

"Wait a minute," I replied. "I'm a journalist. I can write the story myself."

"In that case I'll give you a typewriter."

The piece was run on the foreign page the next day. The *News Chronicle* billed me as "Our Man on the Spot" and gave me a poster headline: INSIDE MUSCAT.

That afternoon the editor himself rang me. "I would like to meet you," he said. "Maybe we can offer you a job."

I was in. Two days later I started at the *News Chronicle* (a great liberal paper that Charles Dickens once edited, by the way). My career in British journalism had begun. In Malcolm Muggeridge's felicitous phrase I had become a Fleet Walker. And it was all due, in a way, to Martin Wynne, the Sultan's Governor of Gwadar, the man who read the classics.

20

Zanzibar / The Comoro Islands

━━━━━━━━━━━━━━━━━━━━━━━━━━━━━

ISLANDS OF PERFUMES AND POLITICS

My first visit to Zanzibar was full of ignominy. With my arms twisted behind my back by a policeman, I was frog-marched onto the tarmac at Zanzibar Airport and put into an ancient De Havilland bound for Tanga on the Tanganyikan mainland. Just some hours before, I had arrived on the same shuttle from Dar es Salaam. Having been refused entry to the People's Republic of Zanzibar (as it had been renamed), I locked myself in the airport lavatory, and it was only after the plane had taken off again for Tanga that I was discovered.

The date was January 19, 1964, and things were confused in Zanzibar. A week earlier a hitherto unknown group led by the self-styled Field Marshal John Okello had stormed two police armouries and the local radio station. Nine hours later the Sultan had fled on the royal yacht, the government had collapsed, and Field Marshal Okello was exhorting its members to "come out of hiding and give yourselves up to be shot." The Zanzibari opposition leaders were caught completely unprepared by Okello's coup. Even my old friend Babu (Abdul Rahman Mohammed), founder of the Umma

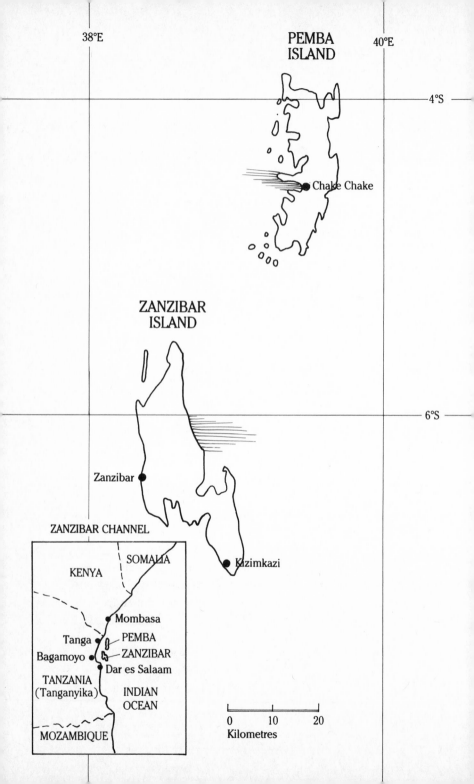

("Masses") Party, was in self-exile in Tanganyika and had to paddle an outrigger canoe back to Zanzibar.

Our film crew had been working in Kenya but was hurriedly ordered to go to Dar es Salaam, as were most British journalists and television teams in the area. Some travelled to the island by dhow only to be arrested and imprisoned on the spot. Among them was Clyde Sanger, formerly of the *Manchester Guardian* and an erstwhile colleague. Others did as I did and suffered a similar fate; these included the British talk-show host Michael Parkinson, then working for the London *Daily Express*.

Okello went his erratic way—sentencing people to 155 years' imprisonment, holding summary courts right in the streets, and plastering Zanzibar with his own weird "ten commandments," such as:

- Avoid personal enjoyment, drink, dances, and idleness
- Give up your association with your wives
- Do not eat cold or leftover food
- Do not evacuate your bowels in a field
- Never wear another person's clothes
- Do not eat the head of a fish or accept a drink of water in the street

Perhaps unsurprisingly, the Field Marshal would later spend some time in a mental asylum, but not before Zanzibar joined Tanganyika on April 24, 1964, to become the Republic of Tanzania—a union modelled, curiously enough, on that of the United Kingdom of Great Britain and Northern Ireland (President Nyerere of Tanganyika became President of Tanzania and President Karume of Zanzibar became Vice-President).

Shortly after this date, Babu extended an invitation to me to return to Zanzibar. The Revolutionary Council ruled the island (it still does), and Babu, an intelligent, educated, and kindly man was the third most important political figure.

The President, at the time, was Abeid Amani Karume, a former dockside worker and virtually an illiterate, and the Vice President was Abdalla Kassim Hanga, a rather sinister-looking man who had studied in the Soviet Union, had a Russian wife, and was said by the Europeans to live up to his name.

Next to the comparatively huge island of Madagascar, Zanzibar and its neighbour Pemba are the largest islands off the East African coast. About 60 kilometres apart from each other, they lie some 40 to 60 kilometres from the mainland. Zanzibar is the bigger island, being almost 100 kilometres long and 40 kilometres wide (compared to Pemba's 60 by 30 kilometres). There are other differences. Zanzibar is flat with an even coastline whereas Pemba is very indented and hilly (and it's on Pemba that the bulk of the cloves for which the islands are famous is grown).

For well over a century the very name Zanzibar has borne romantic connotations for the English-speaking world. Perhaps this has something to do with the fact that Dr. David Livingstone set off from there (one can still see his house near the harbour) on his final expedition to Capricorn Africa. And it was also the departure point for other explorers: John Speke, who discovered Lake Victoria and the source of the Nile; Richard Burton, who discovered Lake Tanganyika (and the sensual delights of the Bantu bottom); and H. M. Stanley, who "found" Dr. Livingstone. Almost every novel about East Africa seems to begin or end in Zanzibar, not to mention its appeal as an exotic setting for various old Hollywood movies—there was even a *Road to Zanzibar* (1941) in the Bob Hope–Bing Crosby–Dorothy Lamour series of "Road" pictures.

The original inhabitants of Zanzibar were undoubtedly mainland Africans, but the first immigrants to arrive on a more or less regular basis were Persians. From the 9th century on, they came from the coastal regions of the Persian Gulf contiguous to Shiraz, the ancient heartland of Persia.

They readily intermarried with the Africans, and to this day the indigenous people of Zanzibar call themselves Shirazis.

The most persistent relationship through the centuries, however, has been with Arabs from the opposite side of the Persian Gulf (and most particularly with those of Oman), who established colonies all along the East African coast—Mogadishu, Malindi, Mombasa, and Kilwa as well as Zanzibar. These communities developed a distinctive civilisation called Swahili (Arabic for "Man of the Coast") and a lingua franca, KiSwahili ("language of the coast people"), a modified Bantu tongue with a heavy infusion of Arabic words and constructions. Many KiSwahili terms have come into English or are familiar because of their use in Hemingway's African stories or Robert Ruark's novels: *bwana* ("master"), *safari* ("journey"), *simba* ("lion"), *jambo* ("hello"), *uhuru* ("freedom"), *askari* ("soldier"), and *shamba* ("cultivated field").

The Arabs also brought Islam with them and, throughout the entire period of their colonisation, there was a steady influx of Indians, mainly from Surat and Kutch. Unlike the Arabs the Indians remained culturally aloof and, in the end, controlled all commerce. The Arabs became a leisured landowning aristocracy and monopolised political power. The Africans remained the hewers of wood and drawers of water, as usual.

The Portuguese appeared on the scene at the beginning of the 16th century, and by the end of the third decade they had become the masters of all the Arab settlements along the East African coast from Mogadishu to Mozambique. They even seized Muscat itself, the capital of Oman. The Omanis, however, eventually ousted them in 1649 and, under a series of vigorous and aggressive sultans, set about reconquering the East African colonies. The most important, Mombasa, was finally captured in 1698, but the Portuguese made several efforts to regain it (the last being in 1728) before they retreated permanently to Mozambique.

Dynastic struggles in Oman led to Mombasa's breaking free, and Sultan Seyyid Said then transferred his entire court to Zanzibar so he could be closer to the action. This was not the only reason for the move. A growing slave trade was developing in East Africa at the same time that a market had emerged in the Persian Gulf, and Oman was in a position to exploit this situation. Furthermore, cloves had been introduced to Zanzibar and were to prove very lucrative (in the 1850s Zanzibar was producing three-fourths of the world's crop). Thus, from about 1830 on, Zanzibar was to all intents and purposes an independent sultanate. This was more or less confirmed in 1856 when Said died. His sons in Muscat inherited the sultanate of Oman, his sons in Zanzibar the sultanate of Zanzibar.

Britain became interested in Zanzibar in the 1840s and prevailed upon the sultan to sign a treaty forbidding the export of slaves to India. This, however, did not stop the slave trade, which went on for decades until, under more British pressure, Sultan Bargash closed the infamous Zanzibar slave market in 1872 (an Anglican cathedral was later built on the site). That slowed the slaving business but failed to stop it altogether.

At Bagamoyo in Tanganyika, some 60 kilometres northwest of Dar es Salaam and opposite Zanzibar Town, I met the last surviving slave of this particular trade (slaving still goes on, mainly in Cameroon and the Sudan). Her name was Maria Ernestina and she had been taken from her home in what is now Zaire about 1890 by Arab slavers. German colonial rule had freed her after the Brussels Act abolishing the trade came into force in 1892. She died, I believe, a few years ago. Bagamoyo was the place where the slave caravans reached the coast and where the slaves were loaded into dhows for the trip across Zanzibar Channel.

As indicated, the Germans had meanwhile become active in Tanganyika. In 1884 the explorer Dr. Karl Peters penetrated the interior. He made contact with twelve native chiefs, whose land Bismarck declared to be German territory the following year. There was still the question of the narrow coastal strip claimed by the sultan of Zanzibar. In 1890 Britain and Germany signed the Treaty of Heligoland in which Heligoland, after seventy-six years of British rule, was exchanged for a British protectorate over Zanzibar. For his ten-mile-wide strip of coast the sultan got £200,000. So Zanzibar became part of the British Empire and Tanganyika part of the German Empire.

At the end of World War I, Tanganyika was in England's hands as a British mandate, and in 1961 it became an independent member of the British Commonwealth under Julius Nyerere (he stepped down in 1985). Zanzibar received full independence from Britain two years later with the sultan as head of state. A coalition of the Zanzibar National Party and the Zanzibar and Pemba People's Party controlled the parliament even though the opposition Afro-Shirazi Party led by Abeid Karume had received more votes (*"Uhuru kwa waArabu"*—"Freedom for Arabs"—was the bitter response).

Exactly one month after independence, Field Marshal Okello launched his coup at the head of six hundred insurgents armed with sticks, stones, and axes. Okello, who was born in Uganda, had been briefly a policeman and a bricklayer in Zanzibar. His followers were either policemen discharged after independence or members of the Afro-Shirazi Youth League. The capture of the two armouries (the only ones in Zanzibar) made the Government unable to resist or retaliate, and Okello rapidly armed his "Freedom Fighters." A reign of terror was unleashed on the Arabs and perhaps 5,000 were killed. Their houses were looted, their women raped, and many fled. Weeks later Babu claimed that Okello had only been chosen for the job because his KiSwahili was Kenyan-accented (so that when he broadcast over the captured radio station, his accent would reassure the other East African governments). He dismissed Okello as a "disc jockey." In any event the Revolutionary Council had the Field Marshal declared a prohibited immigrant the following month while he was visiting Kenya and Uganda.

We stayed at the Zanzibar Hotel, an old Arab mansion that was once the sultan's guest-house. It was air-conditioned and comfortable. Most of the other guests at the time were East Germans, since East Germany had been the first government to recognise the People's Republic of Zanzibar. This created a bit of a problem when Tanzania came into existence because West Germany had an embassy in Dar es Salaam. It was decided simply to leave things as they stood, especially as the East Germans had promised to finance a slum clearance and re-housing project in Ng'ambo ("the other side" across a creek that was formerly the sewer), the African part of Zanzibar Town (the housing estate is, I understand, unbelievably ugly). We were in the section called Stone Town, which was the Arab and Indian quarter.

Most of the buildings there were, indeed, of white or white-washed stone. On a peninsula, Stone Town is a maze of narrow alleyways, shops, and bazaars. The houses have delicate wooden balconies and shuttered windows, and many of them also have ornate carved doors with brass studs. The carvings show pre-Islamic motifs—rosettes and leaves, chains, fish and wavy lines representing the sea. The piquant scent of cloves hangs over everything. Stone Town is an elegant place that gives substance to those exotic images evoked by the word Zanzibar, and it was once, in fact, *the* metropolis of East Africa. When most of the continent of Africa was a dark mystery to the world, Zanzibar was known. As a local proverb goes: Play the flute in Zanzibar, and Africa as far as the great lakes dances.

We soon discovered that we were not the only television crew at the Zanzibar Hotel. There was one from *Deutscher Fernsehfunk* (East German television), led by their Chief Reporter, Hubert Kintscher. As co-workers we all helped each other. I later travelled to East Berlin and met his family, and he also introduced me to the director of *Deutscher Fernsehfunk*. I remember Hubert with affection. Unfortunately, he died two years after that, in Vietnam.

At the Zanzibar Hotel we also made the acquaintance of Heinrich Eggebrecht, the Secretary of the Afro-Asian Solidarity Committee in the German Democratic Republic. He waved his Australian passport under my nose and talked about his internment and subsequent release there during the war.

"You know," he said, "now that we're here, the British should ask the West Germans for Heligoland back."

Although he was engaging in banter, he might have unconsciously given one of the real reasons the East Germans were so interested in Zanzibar. At the time the Treaty of Heligoland was signed there was mild opposition to it. Some thought Germany was giving away a mackerel to catch a sprat (in other words, a large territory for a smaller, less valuable one). But the Kaiser insisted. The Heligolanders were German-speaking (or, to be more accurate, Friesian) and the island did control the mouth of the Elbe, the river on which Germany's largest port, Hamburg, is situated as well as the entrance to the Kiel Canal (Kiel was the site of the big naval base).

Che Guevara was in Zanzibar at that time and I met him as well, a slight figure in black beret and green fatigues and smoking a huge cigar—a sort of punk Fidel Castro. I had a few words with him but he hardly struck me as the charismatic leader he was painted. Still, he did give me a cigar on parting. I also met Eduardo Mondlane of FRELIMO (*Frente Libertação de Moçambique*) and his successor Samora Machel, both of whom are now dead. All in all, it was quite a gathering of the clans including some rather unusually scrutable Chinese. They were dancing much farther away than the African great lakes to the tune the Revolutionary Council was playing.

The members of that body were fairly amiable, or at least

as amiable as their personalities allowed. After all, I *was* a friend of Babu. Karume took a noncommittal stance and Hanga seemed devious, but others in that circle—Ali Sultan, Salim Rashid, Badawi Qualatein—were friendly enough.

They had taken over the English Club as their headquarters. It was near the harbour, the interior was lined with tiles and the club rooms had a view over the white sails of dhows. Today it is called Afrika House. One night we were drinking there with members of the Revolutionary Council when I saw Karume get up and go to one of the bookcases. He took a book down, tore out a couple of the pages and spat into the paper. He then wadded them up into a ball and threw it out the window. No one said a word.

I went over to the bookcase and looked through the titles.

"What about these?" I asked, holding up four volumes of *The Memoirs of William Hickey*, the great diarist of 18th-century Calcutta.

"You have them," Ali Sultan said—and I still do. They had originally been published by Hurst & Blackett in 1923. Pasted on the inside front cover of each volume were the by-laws of the English Club library, of which Item 10 reads: *No book may be taken from the Library by any Member not permanently resident in Zanzibar*. Well, to quote Virgil: *Dis aliter visum* ("The gods thought otherwise").

We were able to film most of Zanzibar—the ruined city of Kizimkazi in the south, dating from the beginning of the 12th century; the Beit al Ajaib ("the House of Wonders"), Zanzibar's most famous building, erected in 1883 as a palace for Sultan Bargash; two other 19th-century palaces some distance out of town; workers' cooperatives, where they dried and sorted cloves; a few of the literacy classes in the villages; even some rehabilitated prostitutes who were being taught to do needlework. There was a lot of misdirected political activity in Zanzibar at the time. Later, in an attempt to break down what was viewed as the Indians' elitist attitudes, Karume ordered their daughters to marry Africans, which led to a number of suicides among the unfortunate girls. Karume was eventually assassinated in 1972. Babu was accused of complicity in the plot (he was in Dar es Salaam when it happened) and thrown into prison by President Julius Nyerere, but never charged. After a number of years he was released and left Tanzania.

We also spent a day on Pemba, mainly to see a bullfight. The *mchezo wa ng'ombe* ("game of the bull") is a leftover from the Portuguese occupation, but it really bears little resemblance to a *corrida de touros* at Montijo in the heart of Portugal's bull country. This one took place near the town of Chake Chake in a large grassy clearing. The three "bulls" were actually small-horned zebu (Asiatic oxen). One by one they were released from their neck ropes, and the "matadors" would cautiously approach them behind bits of white cloth or rush matting. Whenever a bull charged they broke and ran or would try to climb one of the nearby coconut trees. At last four of them banded together, tackled the bull and brought it to its knees—rather like something between a rodeo and a football game.

Before we left Zanzibar, Babu consented to an on-camera interview. "I am optimistic," he said. "The future looks bright. We have it in our hands to remold society, to re-direct it. Yes, I can be confident."

Little did he know.

Back in Dar es Salaam I saw an article in the *East African Standard*. Someone had caught another coelacanth in the Comoro Islands—the twentieth or perhaps the thirtieth (the figure must be over one hundred by now). The fish was alive and in a tank on the island of Anjouan. I cabled London and the response was: Yes, we are interested. There was plenty of film of dead coelacanths since the first one had been found by a trawler off East London in South Africa during 1938,

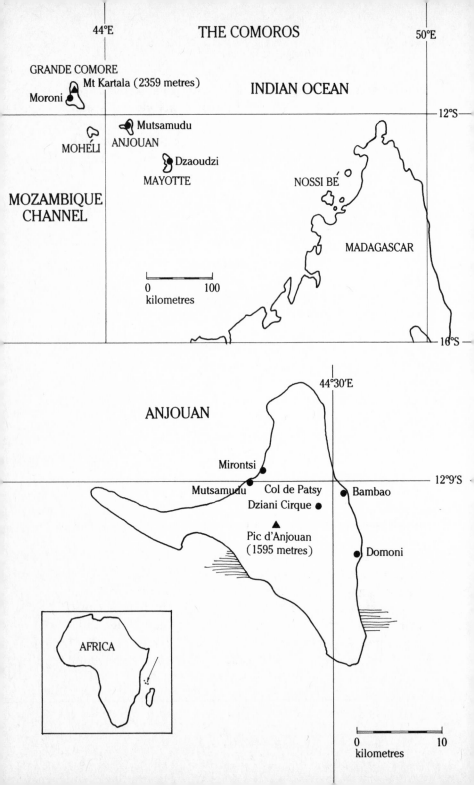

but no pictures of live ones. Air France en route from Paris to Tanzania to Madagascar put down at Moroni on Grand Comoro, so we took the two-hour flight from Dar es Salaam.

Professor J.L.B. Smith of Rhodes University, Grahamstown, South Africa, had first identified the fish, to the amazement of the scientific community. Coelacanth (the name means "hollow spine") fossils existed from the Cretaceous Period, 50 to 70 million years ago, but to find a modern specimen of a fish most had thought to be extinct was almost beyond belief. Yet this is what happened. Smith was determined to find another one and, to this end, distributed leaflets throughout the region in English, French, and Portuguese, offering a reward of £100 for any information that led to the capture of another individual of the species.

I would later meet Professor Smith in Grahamstown and be given a copy of one of the leaflets. There was a picture of the East London coelacanth with its characteristic overlapping scales (like armour plating), fins that looked like legs (the South African trawler crew referred to the coelacanth as "Old Fourlegs"), and an extra tail fin that ended in a point. The text, in the three languages, read:

> Look carefully at this fish. It may bring you good fortune. Note the peculiar double tail and the fins. The only one ever saved for science was 5 ft. (160 cm) long. If you have the good fortune to catch one DO NOT CUT OR CLEAN IT IN ANY WAY but get it whole at once to cold storage.

World War II interrupted Professor Smith's quest, but when it was over he continued his search, without result. Deciding that the coelancanth caught off South Africa must have been a stray and that the fish, instead of being from the ocean's depths, was more likely to be a reef-dweller, he looked to warmer waters farther north. On a trip to Zanzibar in 1952 he met a friendly British skipper named Hunt, who traded to the Comoros. Hunt carefully examined the leaflet and said he had seen such a fish before. A few weeks later he sent Smith a telegram: HAVE FIVE FOOT SPECIMEN COELACANTH. A fisherman had caught one some 200 metres off the coast of Anjouan. Next day he tried to sell it in the market and a schoolteacher showed him the leaflet, one of several that Hunt had distributed. Smith flew to the Comoros where the fish was preserved.

The natives of Anjouan knew the fish as *kombessa*. It was caught from time to time, generally using squid as bait. The fish was not held in very high regard as food. It was too oily and when cooked became soggy and jelly-like. It was more palatable dried and salted, and this was how they usually prepared it. They used the horny scales to roughen bicycle tubes when mending punctures.

Today at least ninety coelacanths are preserved in museums and institutes around the world. The fish has remained unchanged for a longer period than any other vertebrate now living, and its rediscovery was hailed as "the most interesting and important zoological find of the century." It is also the closest relative to the immediate ancestor of all vertebrates (including man), the Eusthenopteron, which fossil evidence indicates crawled out of the sea about 10 million years ago.

Then in November 1954 the first live (and the first female) coelacanth was caught at Anjouan. The fisherman managed to tow it behind his pirogue (dug-out canoe) into the tiny harbour of Mutsamudu. There it was placed in a small whale boat that had been sunk in shallow water, and a net was fastened across the top. An account announcing the catch in the February 1955 issue of *Nature* said: "The greenish-yellow luminescence of its eyes was very pronounced . . . and the colour of the fish was dark greyish-blue, recalling that of the steel of a watch-spring. . . . The pectoral fins in particular can move in almost any direction and showed themselves capable of assuming practically every conceivable position." Unfortunately, the fish died after a few hours. When it was cut open, it was found to contain clusters of eggs at all stages of development "such as are observed in oviparous sharks."

The Comoro Islands lie across the throat of the Mozambique Channel midway between the northern tip of Madagascar and the African mainland (oil tankers from the Persian Gulf pass between them *en route* to Europe). There are four of them: Grand Comoro, Mohéli, Anjouan, and Mayotte (now known as Mahoré). All are volcanic and each can be seen from two of the others (Mohéli and Anjouan). They stretch for 220 kilometres in a northwesterly to southeasterly direction, but their total area (2,236 square kilometres) is comparatively small—a little less than the island of Oahu in Hawaii. Still, they are home to some 300,000 people, living mainly in villages around the coasts. Moroni on Grand Comoro is the capital and the biggest town in the group.

The people appear to be African with a substantial Arab and Malagasy admixture. The Africans probably came from Mozambique, the Arabs from the Persian Gulf, and the Malagasy from northwest Madagascar. The language, Comorian, is a sister tongue to KiSwahili. The dominant religion is Islam.

France claimed control of Mayotte, the southernmost island nearest to Madagascar, in 1841. The French had been around Madagascar since the middle of the 17th century. How they came to Mayotte is not quite clear, though it seems likely the sultan there was seeking some form of insurance against his rivals. Initially France ruled Mayotte through an administrative union with the Madagascan island of Nossi-Bé. Then in the 1880s she seized the other three islands, mainly because the British and Germans were showing signs of interest. Even so, the French were largely concerned with Mayotte, the only island with a sheltered lagoon that provides one of the best anchorages in the Western Indian Ocean.

During World War II the islands were occupied by South African forces (who built the airstrips) but, at the end of the war, reverted to France and were declared an Overseas Territory. In 1961, a year after Madagascar was granted independence, the Comoros were given internal autonomy. A referendum on independence was held in 1974 and the majority on three islands voted for independence while the inhabitants of Mayotte preferred a continuation of French rule. This caused some re-thinking in Paris and it was decided to let the three islands become independent but to make Mayotte a "special collectivity," something that was neither a Department nor an Overseas Territory (the two categories into which France puts what's left of its colonial empire). And, as France is prone to do in such circumstances (vide Guinea), all aid and technical assistance was withdrawn from the three independent islands, so from being poor they became pitifully poor. Their per capita income ($65 per annum) is among the lowest in the world, and there is virtually no press and only one secondary school. Independence has not been a success. The first president of the Federal and Islamic Republic of the Comoros, Ahmed Abdallah, was deposed within a month. The second, Ali Soilih, established a dictatorship, expelled all French citizens, unveiled the women, banned political parties, turned towards the socialist bloc, and abolished the public service (there were no funds to pay them in any case). Soilih, in his turn, was overthrown in a coup in which foreign mercenaries were used, and Ahmed Abdallah was restored to power. He had Soilih shot. At the time of our visit, however, the Comoros were an Overseas Territory of France.

The main export is essence of ylang-ylang (the yellow-green flowers of the fragrant musk tree), which is the base for some of the world's best perfumes. The Comoros supply 70 percent of the requirements of the French perfume industry. The ylang-ylang blooms all the year round, and 30 to 50 kilograms of flowers yield a litre of essence. Most plantations are owned by French companies. But also cultivated are jasmine, neroli (bitter orange), cassia, tuberose, rock alyssum, cloves, basil, palmarosa, combavas, and patchouli; their essential oils are either extracted in steam alembics or by solvents. It is said that one can smell the lush fragrances of the Comoros as far as 30 kilometres out to sea. Indeed, the government guidebook refers to them as *"l'archipel des parfums."*

We landed at Moroni, which means "lava flow" in Arabic, and it is no misnomer—there was even one right across the runway. The lava comes from Kartala, a volcano 2,359 metres high (7,738 feet) that dominates the island of Grand Comoro. Kartala has the largest active volcanic crater in the world (300 metres in diameter) and has erupted five times this century: in 1918, 1948, 1965, 1972, and 1977. According to one legend, an expedition from the Persian Gulf came to Grand Comoro in the 10th century B.C. to recover the Queen of Sheba's throne, which had been engulfed by Kartala's crater. Before leaving Moroni, we climbed to the summit of Kartala, said to be the windiest place in the Indian Ocean. Looking down into the crater with its seething lava, we felt it could be the most dangerous as well.

Moroni itself was a white-walled town with a large two-storey arcaded mosque on the waterfront. At the time we were there it was the only capital in the world to have no street lights. When they were later installed, I was told, the citizens walked the streets all night long admiring them.

After a few hours' wait, we boarded an Air Comores plane for Anjouan. As soon as we were airborne, we could see the Pic d'Anjouan (Peak of Anjouan) rearing nearly 1,600 metres (5,248 feet). A short time later we were in Mutsamudu, the chief town of the island. Mutsamudu huddles on a little strip between the sea and wooded hills. It is a jumble of flat-roofed buildings amid a labyrinth of narrow tunnel-like streets under an imposing citadel, very Arab or Moorish in appearance. Outside Mutsamudu we found the Hotel al Amal, a charming small establishment, festooned with creepers and surrounded by palm trees. The hotel is situated on the peninsula of Mirontsi where it catches the passing sea breezes. Here we made arrangements for a car to drive us to Domoni on the other side of the island where the coelacanth was.

Anjouan used to be known to English seamen as Johanna. During the 17th century it was a centre for pirates and corsairs who preyed on Mogul, French, and Dutch shipping in the Indian Ocean. They preferred Johanna to the other Comoros because, as one navigator of the time commented, "The women go practically naked and are very free-minded. Even their husbands are not shocked by their wantonness." Anjouanais were hired on as sailors by the British and some learnt English. Many adopted the names (usually taken from the nobility) bestowed on them by their officers, so even today one can meet Cecils, Stanleys, Dudleys, and so on.

Captain Quail of the corsair *Seahorse* (sponsored by Charles I) looted £20,000 in one year, and the corsair *Roebuck* (fitted out by a syndicate of London merchants) £30,000. The first-mate of the *Roebuck*, incidentally, was Davy Jones, who supposedly gave his name to the sailors' sea devil. Even notorious Captain William Kidd of the *Adventure* was in the Comoros around 1695 and 1696. Perhaps part of the treasure he is reputed to have buried on a number of islands off the east coast of America—the Florida Keys, Coney Island (Nantucket), Charles Island (Connecticut), among others—may have come from the years he spent on Johanna.

Arabs are the elite in Anjouan as they were in Zanzibar before the revolution. Indians are the merchants. The polygamous Comorians are the impoverished, and one thing that contributes to this is their custom of the "big wedding." This is a feast given by a groom some ten or fifteen years after his first marriage (it usually takes him that long to save the necessary money). To be accepted socially, a "big wedding" is obligatory. We went to one that had been going on for a week—a week of feasting, dancing, singing, and a little drinking (unlawful for Muslims, but still everyone knows that when *tembo* or coconut wine passes the lips of a true believer it turns to water). There was much gaiety and a bit of inno-cent flirtation. All the guests were colourfully dressed, the men in *kandzous* or long white robes with red fezzes, the women in patterned *chiromanis* or full dresses and wearing the scarf-like *lesso* (for instant veiling in front of strangers).

Then it was up the winding road out of Mutsamudu past plantations of ylang-ylang and orderly rows of russet-coloured clove trees to the Col (Pass) de Patsy at 650 metres (2,132 feet), where there were stony plots devoted to subsistence crops like cassava, rain rice, and pigeon peas, and down the other side of the mountain range to the Cirque (Amphitheatre) of Dziani where there were gardens of rock alyssum, tuberose, and jasmine. Soon the perfume distillery at Bambao came both into view and into stunning olfactory range, to be followed by Domoni, the former capital, dating from the 12th century.

Here the coelacanth awaited us in a large trellis-work cage that was hauled up from the depths. I observed its slow and measured movements, its primitive appearance, its sharp hooked teeth. Most of all I was conscious of its eyes. Definitely not your usual opaque fish eyes. These were alert, watching, waiting. The eyes of a predator, the eyes of man's ancestor.

21

Ladakh

━━━━━━━━━━━━━━━━━━━━━━━━━

WHAT THE ORACLE FORETOLD

It was Tarzie Vittachi who first made me think about Buddhism. I was staying with him at the time in Bambalapitiya, a suburb of Colombo on the beach south of the city. One of the best-known journalists in Sri Lanka, as editor of the *Ceylon Observer*, Tarzie was a balding, slightly brooding Sinhalese who later became a columnist for the Asian edition of *Newsweek*. Now he is dead.

But then (back in 1956) he was in his late thirties. One day he asked me to come with him to a temple, the Subodharmaya at Dehiwela. We sat silently for a while in front of an impressive statue of the Buddha. The Russian mystic Peter Ouspensky called it "the Buddha with the sapphire eyes" (Tarzie was a follower of Ouspensky also), but in fact the *pol-thel* (coconut oil) lamps gave the whole statue an eerie bluish glow.

Tarzie picked up a frangipani blossom (the Sri Lankans call them temple flowers) which had fallen to the floor and held one petal in his fingers.

"This is the question the Buddha answered," he said. "Buddhism is the philosophy of being," he went on, "a demanding doctrine and the opposite of self-deception. There are no gods in Buddhism, only the energies that are in man and can be used to transform him. The Buddha has shown one way. There are many, as many as all the petals on all the temple flowers.''

Later, in India, I had cause to ponder Tarzie's words when I visited various Buddhist sites such as Bodhgaya in Bihar, where the Buddha sat under a pipal or Bo tree and meditated his way to enlightenment, Sarnath near Benares where he preached his first sermon in a deer park, the remarkable cave temples of Ajanta and Ellora in the west of India, and the monuments at Sanchi near Bhopal.

The Buddha was a real man. His name was Siddhartha Gautama, and he was the son of the ruler of the Sakya clan. He grew up in the Nepalese *terai* or hill country on the border of India but, at the age of twenty-nine, renounced the world and its pleasures. After meditating under the Bo tree he became "Awakened" (for this is what *Buddha* means). Buddhism is the way of life of the Awakened One. Gautama died in 544 B.C. at the age of eighty. According to Buddhist tradition a Buddha appears every 5,000 years, and the names of his twenty-four predecessors were revealed to Gautama, though none was an historical personage. Some Buddhists claim that Christ was a Boddhisattva, a Buddha who, on the threshold of *nirvana*, turned away from this blissful state out of compassion for the mass of ordinary men.

By the year 1200 Buddhism had disappeared from India, but not before two central doctrines were established. The older and more orthodox is the *Hinayana* ("the small ferry boat"), in which the individual must cross the stream of life to the farther shores of *nirvana* by his own efforts alone. The later and more heterodox doctrine is the *Mahayana* ("the large ferry boat"), in which an enlightened monk conveys his cargo of souls to their release from all suffering and desire. Today the southern strata of Buddhist countries (Sri Lanka, Burma, Thailand, Laos, and Kampuchea) for the most part follow the *Hinayana* discipline while the northern strata (Tibet, Bhutan, Sikkim, China, Mongolia, Korea, Vietnam, and Japan) mostly follow the *Mahayana* discipline. The only places in India where Buddhism survives are the Darjeeling district and Ladakh. In both cases this is a result of Tibetan incursions, and the Buddhism is in the Tibetan or Tantric form. (When the Dalai Lama fled from Tibet in 1959, he went to Darjeeling.)

The Tantras (treatises) originally dealt with "the way things are" or "how it feels *to be*." This led to meditational cults and yogic practices, many of which have been adopted by individuals or groups in the West. Extensive use is made of mystical diagrams (*mandalas*) and sacred formulae (*mantras*). The best-known *mantra* is "*Om mane padme hum*" ("Praise the jewel in the lotus"), often called the six holy sounds because it has six syllables. Much of this material came from pre-existing worship in Tibet that *Mahayana* Buddhism later incorporated into its structure (including oracular priests, local nature divinities, and the notion of a divine king).

In the late summer of 1956 I was in Srinagar, Kashmir. Ever since the partition of India nine years earlier, Kashmir has been a bone of contention between that country and Pakistan. The seeds of this situation were, unhappily, sown by the British. At the close of the First Sikh War in 1846, Kashmir was given to Rajah Gulab Singh, who amalgamated his state of Jammu (predominately Hindu) with Kashmir (predominately Muslim) and Ladakh (predominately Buddhist). On partition in 1947 the Hindu Maharajah signed an Instrument of Accession to India. Pakistan refused to recognise this and occupied part of Kashmir (Azad Kashmir or Free Kashmir they called it), while Indian forces moved into the rest. After much fighting the matter was taken up by the United Nations and a ceasefire arranged in 1949. When I was there feelings on both sides still ran high (later, in 1965 and 1971, these were to erupt into other outbreaks of war).

I wrote a number of articles on Kashmir for the Australian press and gave a talk over All-India radio, which were, I suppose, mildly favourable to the Indian view. Krishna Menon, then the Foreign Minister, seized on them and quoted some extracts during one of the interminable UN debates on the matter. I entered history via the UN Hansard. The Kashmiri government was very grateful. Be our guest, representatives said. Have a holiday with us.

Provided I can go to Ladakh, I replied. Well, that presented a problem. Ladakh was a restricted zone, as it not only bordered Pakistan but also China in Tibet (indeed, hostilities were to break out in 1962 between China and India over Ladakh). A decision on Ladakh at that time could only be made by the central government in Delhi. In the meantime I was offered accommodation on one of the celebrated English houseboats scattered around the lakes in the Vale of Kashmir (connected to the River Jhelum and Srinagar by canals on which *shikaras*, a type of gondola, ply). Incidentally, these houseboats are also, in a roundabout sort of way, a product of the handing over of Muslim Kashmir to a Hindu Rajah. His heirs churlishly refused to allow the sale of land to British buyers wishing to escape the heat of the summer plains. So they built houses on panelled barges and moored them to little artificial islands planted with poplars, willows, and *chenars* (oriental plane trees). Thus, while not exactly instigating the Kashmiri tourist industry—the Mogul emperors had done that—these charming establishments at least embellished it.

While waiting for Delhi's decision, I made a number of sidetrips: to the popular summer resort of Pahalgam sitting under its pine trees; to the Cave of Amarnath, source of the Ganges; to Gulmarg ("Meadow of Flowers"), from where one can see in Pakistan the snowy peak of Nanga Parbat (8,126 metres or 26,650 feet) seeming to float above the clouds; up the Sind valley to Sonamarg ("Meadow of Gold") and to the formal gardens on the banks of Dal Lake—Nishat Bagh ("Garden of Pleasure") with its ten terraces and Shalimar Bagh ("Garden of Love," as in "Pale hands I loved beside the Shalimar," one of the *Indian Love Lyrics* by Laurence Hope, the pseudonym of Adela Florence Nicolson). Shalimar Bagh was built by the Mogul Emperor Jahangir, who lived there during the summer months with Nurjehan, the "Light of the World," to whom he would recite the famous couplet of the 10th-century Persian poet Ferdowsi: "*Agar Fardaus bar ru-i-zamin ast / Hamin ast wa hamin ast wa hamin ast*" ("If there is a Paradise on earth / It is this, oh it is this, oh it is this"). The verse is inscribed over both entrances to the Hall of Private Audience in the Red Fort at Delhi, the hall in which the Peacock Throne once stood.

At last permission came from Delhi.

Ladakh, often called Little Tibet, is the highest and most remote part of India. Its name comes from the Tibetan *La Tags* ("land of the high mountain passes"). The language, Ladakhi, is a form of Tibetan and they use the Tibetan script. Tibetans invaded Ladakh in the 8th and 10th centuries, but there are other groups in the country—Mons, the first (some say Aryan) inhabitants, and Dards, who came from Baltistan in Pakistan. The first mention of Ladakh seems to be by Herodotus, who describes it in his history as a land of extraordinary ants:

> There is found in this desert a kind of ant of great size—bigger than a fox though not so big as a dog. These creatures, as they burrow underground, throw up the sand in heaps, just as our own ants throw up the earth, and they are very like ours in shape. The sand has a rich content of gold and this it is that the Indians are after when they make their expeditions into the desert.

He goes on to say that the Indians had to fetch the gold by day when the ants were asleep because they were ferocious creatures. It is thought that the "ants" were actually marmots, the large Asiatic marmot (bigger than a fox) with a bushy tail. They are only found at elevations above 4,000 metres (13,120 feet) and, when disturbed, stand on their hind legs and whistle. The Ladakhis use their fat for medicinal purposes and believe the animal has a soul that is both malicious and mischievous. It is indeed true that marmots make their burrows on small sandy plains beside the rivers and that gold is sometimes found in these mounds.

Ladakh lies to the east of Kashmir. As the eagle flies it is only about 230 kilometres from Srinagar to the capital, Leh. But the same eagle would have to soar to an altitude of almost 4,000 metres (13,120 feet) as well in order to reach what is one of the highest inhabited regions of the world, a land the size of England consisting of high barren plains cleft by deep valleys. Cowley Lambert, an early traveller, writing in 1877, said, "The prevailing features of this country are bare, rocky mountains, bare gravel slopes and bare sandy plains."

Why did I wish to go to such a harsh place? Because it was one of the last refuges of Tibetan Buddhism and, for centuries, Tibet itself had been forbidden territory to foreigners. I wanted to see a Tibetan lama, turn a prayer wheel or two, drink Tibetan tea with yak's butter, have a look at a society where polyandry was still practised, and, perhaps, to consult an oracle.

So we were off, in a jeep. Our party included myself, a driver, and an official from the Kashmiri Government. We drove out of the lush green valley of Kashmir and up the steep winding curves of mountains to the 3,500-metre pass (12,380 feet) of Zoji La. The road was frighteningly bad, with heart-stopping thousand-metre (or more) drops to the streams below. In the distance we could see the red and brown peaks of mountains. On our way we met no other voyagers (to use the Kashmiri term it was *ghairi ghat*, "away from the river," i.e., well off the beaten track). All was silence in those high and desolate areas.

For much of its history very few people had ever visited Ladakh. Moorcroft, Trebeck, and Vigne wrote about the country in the 1840s. There had been some Moravian missionaries, an Italian or two, the occasional American or German, and of course the British resident commissioners. Today that has all changed, and Ladakh does get tourists of a sort, around 10,000 or so a year. For it is on the so-called "hippie trail," along with Goa and Katmandu. Not only do the hippies (or "dharma bums," as they are sometimes called by those who disapprove of them) throng to the country between May and November, but so do more serious students of Buddhism, often middle-aged, middle-class Europeans and Americans. Everything in Ladakh is religion-oriented one way or another, and those seeking an answer to the problems of Western societies often go there to find it. Not that a rural, superstitious population cut off from the rest of the world for centuries would seem very likely to have the answers, but this does not deter the seekers after "the Truth." Buses now ply between Srinagar and Leh in the season, and there are even hotels and guesthouses in Leh and Kargil. In my day the traveller had to be content with a dak bungalow (government rest house).

Once over Zoji La we were in the treeless, dun-coloured Ladakhi highlands. The road followed along a river in a gorge. To each side were gulches and gullies, ahead lay ring after ring of stark, turtle-backed mountains. Hours later we had crossed the Great Himalayan Range and found ourselves on the plateau that makes up Ladakh proper. Suddenly there were green, terraced fields and poplar, mulberry, and apricot trees. We had arrived at Kargil, the second biggest town. In reality it was a wretched little place.

Here we stayed the night at the dak bungalow overlooking the local bazaar. The rule at dak bungalows elsewhere in India is strictly first-come, first-served, and you must move on within twenty-four hours. But as there was no one else, we took it over. It was fairly primitive—no bathrooms, rough beds, and lamps using yak's butter for fuel. The *khansama* (the keeper) kept himself busy with the cooking. He served up some *sattu* (barley flour porridge mixed with Tibetan tea), and he showed me how to make the tea. It is brewed the day before, with a pinch of soda added, and the mixture is then allowed to simmer until it turns a pinkish colour. The following day this is put into a long, narrow churn, with salt and yak's butter added, and then it is churned, heated, and served. The drink has the consistency of cocoa but not the savour. I found it tasted slightly oily as well as being salty. But the Ladakhis drink it all the time, and it is an important part of their diet.

It was at Kargil that I learnt my first Ladakhi word, *Julay* ("Greetings"), and saw my first Ladakhis close up. They had dark tanned faces, a Mongol appearance, and a rather over-whelmingly strong smell. Later I discovered that some of them never ever bathed—on principle. The men wore a loose knee-length coat dyed a deep purplish red and tied at the waist with a white woollen sash. They had felt socks that came up to their knees, and on their feet were woollen shoes with yak leather soles. Their cap was cone-shaped with pro-jecting flaps that could be tied under the chin. The women had a similar coat but theirs was ankle-length, and over their backs they wore a goatskin cape with the hair turned to the inside.

But what made the women's costume one of the most picturesque I have ever seen was the headdress. This is called a *perak* and represents a woman's dowry (on a woman's death the *perak* goes to her eldest daughter). It is a sort of layered lozenge of red material, thickly studded with bright-blue turquoises and *kau* (filigree silver ornaments), that starts from the forehead, passes right over the head, and hangs down the back as far as the waist. On the left shoulder a long rectangle of several rows of coral is attached to the *perak*, as are stiff ear-lappets made of black astrakhan (a style invented centuries ago by a queen of Ladakh who suffered from earache). In addition, they have silver pendants which dangle from their left shoulder and necklaces of silver, turquoise, and coral. On one side of their waist is a round plaque of brass or silver perforated in the design of a *mandala*. When a Ladakhi woman walks she is always accompanied by a host of sounds from all these various little tinkling ornaments.

We continued on our way and soon were running along the Indus River on the high plateau. Although the colours of the earth were grey and ochre, there were clumps of flowers—buttercups, clematis, cornflowers, and bluebells. It was very hot and there was no shade. Almost everywhere we went—along the roadside, in the fields, on the outskirts of villages—were *mani*, piles of stone in the form of walls. Some were about 5 metres wide and 2 metres high (about 16 feet by 7), and of varying lengths, but one we saw must have been nearly a kilometre long. The stones are piled up by wayfarers and each one has the *mantra "Om mane padme hum"* written on it, by which the depositor gains merit.

Also everywhere were *chorten* or Tibetan-style stupas, which differ from Burmese pagodas in that they have a square base on which a number of smaller cubes are arranged in decreasing steps. These culminate in a large ball out of the top of which rises a long spire. At the tip of the spire is a diagram of a crescent moon cradling the sun. At the centre of this is an eye, the symbol of *nirvana*.

The countryside became more cultivated. Poplars marked off fields which had literally been scraped out of bare rock, and beyond these was the brown river. On the horizon peak piled upon spectacular peak.

We passed Mulbekh, a village nestling at the foot of a majestic rock. The small houses had gashed openings in the walls for windows and were surrounded by fences painted red. Bright-coloured paper flags flew from the roofs. As we passed, all the men, women, and children of the town stopped to watch us. About one family in ten, I had heard, was polyandrous. Thus, when the eldest son marries, his wife also becomes the wife of his brothers—and of any other man who happens to be under the same roof either permanently or temporarily. Any children are considered to be the progeny of the eldest son, thereby ensuring that the property passes from eldest son to eldest son all the time. One of the reasons usually cited for polyandry in various societies is that there are often many more men than women. But in Ladakh I felt the main reason had less to do with an imbalance in the ratio of the sexes than in the region's laws of inheritance.

As we began to climb out of the Indus gorge, the landscape

started to become dotted with *gompas*—monasteries (some call them lamaseries) looking like housing-estate tower blocks and often perched on crags—where the head lama (teacher) is known as the *rinpoche*. The monasteries own nearly all the land in Ladakh, and the peasants have to pay them a tithe. In effect the *rinpoche* rules their lives, and it is to him they go with all their problems. Indeed, the reason why so many Westerners come to Ladakh is to be able to sit at the feet of some noted *rinpoche*.

Finally we came into the long fertile valley of Leh. The town is hemmed in by the mountains of the Ladakh and Zanskar ranges, which rise to 8,000 metres (26,240 feet) or more. On a hillside above the town is the massive fortified palace of the kings of Ladakh. It is crumbling and empty. The *Gyalpo* (King) and the *Gyalmo* (Queen), monarchs in name only since all power actually lay with the *rinpoches*, lived in a smaller palace at Stok, 15 kilometres away.

Leh was a jumble of narrow, winding lanes with dilapidated flat-roofed houses, but one street was broad and lined with poplars—the bazaar street, which was centrally located and ran uphill. Leh used to be on the historic caravan route between Yarkand in Sinkiang (China) and Lhasa in Tibet, and yak trains needed plenty of room to move about. The dak bungalow was at the upper end of this street, and once again there were no other travellers in occupancy. Here we found conditions better and the arrangements more comfortable than at the one in Kargil, with two large bedrooms, a living room, and a dining room. There was also a bathroom, and I lost no time in asking the *khansama* to heat some water for me.

Feeling much better, I then went for a stroll. Part of the charm of Leh is, I decided, its implausibility, for it has a kind of *Lost Horizon* atmosphere, an irretrievable quality about it. I bought some apricots and mulberries and returned to the dak bungalow, where I was introduced to *chang* or steaming barley beer, slightly cloudy and tasting a bit like hot lemonade. Later the *khansama* treated us to another Ladakhi delicacy—*thukpa* or noodle soup with tomatoes and cabbage. And, of course, Tibetan tea.

There is really nothing much to see in Leh except the *gompa*, on a peak high above the palace. It had no windows on the ground floor (a protection against thieves), but those on the second floor were covered with fine white cloth or translucent paper. In the assembly hall were pictures of the eight Buddhist symbols: the wheel, the fish and the conch shell, the vase and the flower, the umbrella, the white prayer banner, and the woven symbol of the number eight, the *palbu*. There were also prayer wheels and prayer flags; gongs, drums, and cymbals; young lamas in clean robes; nuns in satin and brocade. And the *rinpoche*, serene, pious, slight of build. He was a Red Hat. There are also Yellow Hats (yellow being the colour associated with purity, red with authority).

Yellow Hats came into Tibetan Buddhism as a reform sect in the 15th century. It was the tantric practices of the Red Hats they wanted to reform. Their founder was Tsong Khapa ("the man from Onion Land," a reference to the eastern province of Amdo on the border of China where onions can be grown), who introduced celibacy, forbade all intoxicants and narcotics, and preached the doctrine of reincarnation at the lama level (incidentally, lamas who fall by the wayside are reincarnated as dogs). The third reincarnation of Tsong Khapa extended the influence of the Yellow Hats to Mongolia, then the most powerful country in the Far East. And the strength of the Yellow Hats in Mongolia persuaded the Mongols to conquer Tibet and install the ruling Yellow Hat as the Dalai Lama (*Dalai* being the Mongolian translation of the Tibetan *Gyatso*, meaning "Primeval Ocean"), thus combining spiritual and temporal power in one person.

The *rinpoche* of Sankar monastery, about 2 kilometres from Leh, was the head of the Yellow Hats in Ladakh. He, like his predecessors, was a politician and sat in the Kashmiri Constituent Assembly. Most of the other *rinpoches* were Red Hats and they continued their unreformed tantric ways, which included carrying the *phurbu* (the mystic dagger, one of the major symbols of demonism), drinking *chang*, fornicating, and worshipping a plethora of divinities, many with terrifying aspects.

I also visited a few of the other monasteries within easy reach of Leh, mainly to examine the paintings done by the monks on the walls of their shrine rooms. Most showed scenes from the Buddha's life. One, at Stakna, was a full-length portrait of a 17th-century guru, an old man wearing an orange robe and bathed in a green light. It was quite affecting, an ikon in its way. Although most of the monasteries were austere and shabby, I was told that they held great treasures stored away out of sight. Since the advent of tourists there are monks who have sold some of these treasures along with the usual thigh-bone whistles and silver butter-lamps.

The second day we were in Leh my guide arranged an audience with the King and Queen, an unassuming middle-aged couple ceremoniously if not regally dressed (the King, Kunsang Namgyal, died in 1974). Nothing of much interest emerged from this meeting until the King called for his *onpo*. This turned out to be his oracle, a surprisingly young man outfitted in some splendour. He had a brocaded yellow silk shirt under his burgundy coat and wore a high-peaked red hat with a brim that curled up at the sides rather like a conquistador's helmet. The *onpo* blew on his thigh-bone whistle, rang some hand bells, and beat on a small drum, all the while chanting *mantras*.

I was intrigued and asked what he was doing.

"Preparing to go into a trance," was the answer. "Then he can foretell the future."

"Can he see my future?" I enquired.

"Yes," the guide replied. "He can see the future of the whole world."

After a little while the *onpo* began to shake and tremble and went into his trance—not a violent nor an epileptic one, he just became rigid and his eyes took on a glassy sightless stare. Then he spoke in short bursts. Spittle dribbled down

317

his chin. He spoke again, and again spittle dribbled down. Suddenly it was over. He leant back and was soon his normal self. Taking his drum, his hand bells, and his thigh-bone whistle, he left the room. The guide looked uncomfortable.

"Did he say anything about me?" I asked.

"Yes," came the reply.

"What?" Perhaps unwisely, I wanted to know.

"Something not very pleasant," the guide said.

"Well, tell me," I insisted.

"You will have an accident," I was told. "He did not know what kind of accident, but you will be badly hurt. He said he saw you in a dry gorge with no shirt on and blood coming out of your head."

"Where will all this take place?"

"He did not know. He said it was in the hot season."

At the time, I dismissed it from my mind, but on the return trip down Zoji La pass I remembered the prophecy. The Ladakhis say that if you disbelieve what the oracle tells you it is doubly certain to come true. Still, nothing untoward happened—then.

However, five years later in the province of Murcia in Spain, a car I was driving failed to take a curve on a mountain road and went over a precipice. (It was subsequently discovered that the steering had locked.) I was thrown out and found unconscious by a passing Moroccan motorist, who took me to a hospital in the nearby town of Lorca. I had lost my shoes and my shirt in the accident, and all the bones on the left side of my face were broken. I was covered with blood. Although never in danger of losing my life, I was seriously injured and ill for a month. And I still carry some of the scars on my face.

As it happens, that part of Spain is very dry and it was midsummer.

22

Haiti

═ ═ ═ ═ ═ ═ ═ ═ ═ ═ ═ ═ ═ ═ ═ ═ ═

PAPA DOC—THE BLACK SHEEP

Haiti—the First Black Republic. The name means "mountainous land" in one of the Indian languages (Ciboney or Arawak). It was not so called, as one charming mulatto girl told me, "because we hate each other" (she used the rare French verb *se haïr*). But it could well have been when I was there. That was in the time of Papa Doc—François Duvalier, *Président à Vie* ("President for Life"). From 1957 to 1971 he ruled the island with capricious malevolence, and it seemed then that every man's hand was turned against his neighbour.

On the map Haiti looks somewhat like the head of a crocodile about to snap up Cuba. Unfortunately, it is the Haitians themselves who have suffered that sad, saurian fate. With the lowest standard of living in the Western Hemisphere, Haitians have the shortest life expectancy (thirty-three years). Ninety percent of the population are illiterate. Diseases like yaws and malaria are endemic, and now AIDS has become a major problem there as well. Paranoia—political, social, and religious—is an abiding feature of Haitian life. Fear has always been with the people. Fear of the *houngans* or voodoo priests, fear of the zombies (or living dead), fear of the rulers, fear of the outside world—an overriding fear of assorted ghosts, bogeymen, and malicious spirits. It is, in short, the fear born of ignorance and superstition.

The western third of the island of Hispaniola (the eastern two-thirds constitute the Dominican Republic), Haiti is a little smaller than the Netherlands and supports about 6 million people, less than half that of the Netherlands, but there the comparison ends. Haiti is a jumbled mass of mountains. There is a story, perhaps apocryphal, that an Elizabethan sea captain, when asked by the Queen to describe Haiti, responded by crumpling a sheet of paper in his fist and throwing it on the floor. (This Elizabethan sea captain got around a bit, for I have heard the same tale told of other mountainous Caribbean islands.) In any case, the mountains of Haiti rise in steps, with the highest peaks over 3,500 metres (11,480 feet). A Creole proverb says: *Dèyè morne gainyain morne* ("Behind the mountains are mountains"). The official language of the country (spoken by 10 percent of the population) is French, but the real language of Haiti is a Creole patois with strong West African structural influences.

Still, Haiti is not all mountains. There are some plains, mainly along the rivers and around the two biggest lakes, one nearly 180 square kilometres in area. Also, four islands are scattered along the coastline: Ile de la Tortue in the north, the original home of the buccaneers, who spitted their beef over a *boucan* or barbecue; Ile de la Gonâve in the jaws of the crocodile, the home of giant iguanas and also where the *Mary Celeste* ultimately foundered in 1885; Ile Grande Cayemite, to the east of the town of Jérémie; and Ile à Vaches, opposite the town of Les Cayes. The last two islands are off Haiti's southern peninsula.

If these place-names sound a little surreal, try some others—Mirebalais ("Broom sight"), Dondon ("Stout girl"), Grand-Gosier ("Big Throat"), Trou-de-Nippes ("Hiding-Place-for-Old-Clothes"), Bassin Zim ("Iron Pot Basin"), Ça-Ira ("It Shall Go On"), and Anse-à-Pitre ("Clown's Cove"). However, accompanying these curious designations are some unforgettable images. Haiti is gingerbread houses, the mottled green of cultivation and the arid brown of eroded hillsides, baobab trees, donkeys with cropped ears, distant *mornes* wreathed in mist, vast ruins, flamboyants (royal poincianas) in bloom, wild balsam, lianas, and magnificent orchids. Here can be found some of the most beautiful women in the world—mulattos with creamy white complexions, straight black hair, and green eyes. It has been said of them that they are like panthers dreaming.

But Haiti is also a hungry country with a grotesque history.

One day in December 1492 some Indians fishing in a bay in northern Haiti saw three "giant shells" floating on the water. Christopher Columbus had arrived, and on Christmas Eve he founded the first settlement in the New World, La Natividad. A handful of Spaniards stayed behind, protected by a log fort, while Columbus sailed back to Spain to report that he had at last reached the Indies, which he mistakenly believed were islands off the coast of Asia. When he returned with a new fleet he found nothing but the bones of the Spaniards. The fort was a heap of ashes. The eventual historical aftermath of this was the wholesale destruction of the Indians and, when they had virtually disappeared, the importation of Negro slaves.

Spain soon lost interest in the western third of Hispaniola when English, French, and Dutch pirates used Ile de la Tortue as a base to prey upon shipping from the ports of Veracruz in Mexico and Portobelo on the Isthmus of Darien (Panama). By the Treaty of Ryswick (1697) she granted the colony of Sainte Domingue (now modern Haiti) to France. A series of royal governors ensued who brought in their wake noblemen from France in search of colonial estates. In the beginning was sugar and rum. During the 18th century over a million slaves were imported from Africa as estates prospered and towns and country houses sprang up. Sainte Domingue became the richest colony in the world, and Les Grands Seigneurs de Sainte Domingue were the jewel in the crown of Versailles. In 1767 they exported 72 million pounds weight of raw sugar, 51 million pounds of white sugar, 2 million pounds of cotton, and a million pounds of indigo as well as vast quantities of hides, molasses, cocoa, and rum. Nor was it only in quantity that Sainte Domingue excelled. Its coffee was the equal of the best mocha, its tobacco of first-grade Havana leaf, its cocoa more acidulated and with a more delicate flavour than any other. No other part of the earth's surface yielded so much wealth proportionately.

By 1789 the slave population numbered over 500,000 blacks. There were also about 40,000 mulattos and some 30,000 whites. The French Revolution was arousing great expectations amongst the whites, who desired a greater measure of independence from France, and amongst the mulattos, who wanted equality with the whites. These stirring ideas soon spread to the slaves and in 1791 there was a slave revolt, the only successful slave revolt in history. From among the blacks emerged leaders such as Toussaint Louverture, Jean-Jacques Dessalines, and Henry Christophe, men who knew how to organise and turn a rabble into an army. And they knew how to fight. Christophe is said to have taken part with 800 other coloured volunteers in the Battle of Savannah (1779) in the American War of Independence.

Toussaint Louverture was kidnapped by Napoleon and died of starvation in a French prison, but Dessalines and Christophe, helped by the mulatto Alexandre Pétion, went on to defeat the French troops. On January 1, 1804, Dessalines proclaimed the independence of Haiti, the First Black Republic. Later he assumed the title of emperor.

As for the whites, they had all either fled or been massacred at the beginning of the revolt amid scenes of appalling cruelty. Colonists were attacked with machetes or sawn in half. Children were barbecued. Women were raped and then disembowelled. Crops and houses were put to the torch. As far away as Bermuda a glow was seen lighting the night sky for several evenings.

Dessalines was assassinated in 1806 and the country split in two. Christophe became king of the north and built an imposing citadel in the mountains behind Cap-Haïtian (formerly Cap Français) where he reigned until 1820. Pétion, in the south, was president of a republic. After Christophe committed suicide with a silver bullet, Haiti was once again united and the long dictatorship of Boyer followed. When he died a period of anarchy set in until a new dictator, Soulouque, took over. His name had been drawn out of a hat to avoid conflict among the generals, and the choice pleased them because they considered Soulouque a fool.

Soulouque had himself crowned Emperor Faustin I. He placed the crown, worth $100,000, on his head himself (no fool he). He also named 4 princes, 59 dukes, 90 counts, 200 barons, and 346 chevaliers. Soulouque, who was illiterate, spent most of his time dreaming up court rituals. He subsequently invaded the Dominican Republic but this attempt at conquest failed. (It has, however, left a residue of suspicion among the Dominicans, who are predominately white or mulatto, not black. The Dominicans are uneasily aware of this racial contrast, as they are of Haitian poverty and over-population.)

After Soulouque there was a string of presidents who came to power through coups d'état or revolutions. In 1915, after the assassination of President Sam, American marines landed at Port-au-Prince and stayed in Haiti until 1934. But from 1918 to 1922 they had to put down a revolt, the so-called Caco War, a savage campaign whose most savage act was the final betrayal to the US forces of the guerilla leader, Charlemagne Péralte. He was stripped naked and nailed to the door of the American headquarters as a warning to others who might be contemplating taking up arms against the US occupation forces.

During the American period roads were upgraded, the telephone system actually worked, and the economy improved a great deal. But after the Americans left everything slipped back into the old formula. President followed president in rapid succession, many of them lining their own pockets in the process. Finally, after a brief period of military rule, Dr. François Duvalier came out on top.

Since the time of Napoleon this extraordinary and brutal history has attracted men of letters. Victor Hugo's first novel, *Buj-Jargal*, was about the slave revolt; Alphonse de Lamartine wrote a poem in praise of Toussaint Louverture; Eugene O'Neill based his play *The Emperor Jones* on Christophe; and, more recently, there was Graham Greene's *The Comedians*, a novel that pleased Papa Doc not at all. Graham Greene, he once informed me, was both a member of the KGB *and* the CIA. He also hinted that Greene was probably possessed by the spirit of one of his (Duvalier's) enemies who had died.

My first visit to Haiti was in 1962. Generalissimo Rafael Trujillo had been assassinated after thirty-one years as the dictator of the Dominican Republic. Although the political situation there was clouded, a presidential candidate nevertheless had emerged—Donald Reid, the son of a Scots settler from Clackmannanshire, the smallest county in the British Isles (he didn't make it, Juan Bosch came to power in 1963). He proved to be an eminently suitable focus for a story we were doing about the excesses of the Trujillo regime and the uncertainties of political life in the Dominican Republic. After we filmed that we went on to Haiti, but not to do another political documentary. This one was to be strictly a travelogue though, of course, politics entered into it.

While we were there the British ambassador, who was also dean of the diplomatic corps, was expelled because he had had the temerity to protest to Papa Doc about the unlawful seizure of a British yacht by Haitian customs officials. The yacht had run into trouble in high seas off the southern coast and put into the port of Jacmel for shelter. The Haitians said the captain should have first applied for permission and so they confiscated the yacht, stole all his clothes, and deported him barefoot to Jamaica. For a few years after this there was only a chargé d'affaires at Port-au-Prince, but the British Embassy was finally closed in 1966 since there seemed little point in trying to deal with Duvalier.

We stayed at the Sans Souci Hotel, an old colonial mansion

near the centre of town. Through the owner, Georges Heraux, I met a number of people. One was Bernard Diederich, a New Zealander, founder and editor of the English-language newspaper, the *Haiti Sun*. (He was later expelled by Papa Doc and wrote a book about him in which he described the president meditating in his bath while wearing the black homburg that identified him in the Haitian mind with Baron Samedi, the god of death.) Another was his columnist, Aubelin Jolicoeur, an ingratiating little man with an ivory-handled walking stick who became the model for Graham Greene's Petit Pierre in *The Comedians*. The Haitians knew him as "The Butterfly" because he flitted from table to table at Hotel Oloffson, collecting material for his column as well as any woman (preferably white) who might succumb to his rather oily charm.

Jolicoeur took us to see the Oloffson, perhaps one of the best-known hotels in the Caribbean. It is an elaborate 19th-century gingerbread palace with a zigzag staircase entrance, ornate lacy ironwork balconies, tin cupolas, and a tower with intricate fretwork and dado. The whole structure sits imposingly on the side of a hill like a magnificent piece of wedding confectionery. Graham Greene called it a "fragile, absurd anachronism" but to Americans it was known as the "Greenwich Village of the Tropics." The suites were named after various favored guests—the author James Jones, who was married there, Marlon Brando, and so on.

With Jolicoeur as our guide we filmed in the Cabane Choucoune at Pétionville, 500 metres (1,660 feet) up the mountain behind Port-au-Prince. Pétionville is the home of the mulatto elite, roughly 10 percent of the population (the French-speakers). The Choucoune (named after that little yellow bird Harry Belafonte sings about) is built like a giant *caille*, the African-style hut with a thatched roof that is found in the countryside. Here we watched supple and elegant mulattos doing "the wooden-leg dance," the stilty, jerky *méringue*, native to the island.

And he introduced us to Haitian art as he was something

of an expert on these primitive painters (Jolicoeur now has his own gallery there). I bought a Préfète DuFaut (DuFaut is a peasant living near Jacmel). It shows a grid-like vision of the streets of Jacmel criss-crossing a landscape of cone-like mountains and is full of stick figures. The painting has no true perspective but the colours are a swirl of vivid reds, blues, greens, yellows, oranges, and browns. Art is Haiti's fourth largest export, and her painters are known throughout the world.

Jolicoeur also directed us to a voodoo session, in the poor quarter of Morne Marinette where there were many *hounfors* or temples. We went several times, each time taking a bottle of rum to help the adepts get into the right mood. Voodoo is a religion of a sort but one with no rules, no hierarchy, no scripture. Here the act, the performance of the ritual itself is everything—the rhythmic drumming, the drinking of rum, the dancing and singing, the invocation of the *loas* or gods, the use of *langage* (similar to "talking in tongues"), and the phenomenon of possession.

They say 90 percent of Haitians are Roman Catholic and 100 percent are followers of voodoo (although there are official sanctions against voodoo, they have been largely ignored). When the African slaves arrived in the New World, they brought with them their highly developed religious beliefs and attitudes toward life. The bulk of Haitian Africans came from the areas around the Gulf of Guinea. The word *voodoo* is itself Dahomean in origin, and voodoo in Haiti consists in the main of rites, beliefs, and practises that parallel those of Dahomey (now Benin) in West Africa. But there are other cults in Haiti (Ibo-Kanga, Congo, and Simbi) which are not Dahomean, and one (Pétro) is indigenous to the country. In addition, *houngans* practise black magic, deal with evil spirits, and in general fill the role of local witch doctor.

Two controversial mysteries are connected with voodoo. One concerns the notion of zombies. By using certain herbs, the *houngan*, it would appear, can seemingly destroy another person's will and induce a remarkably death-like state in him. Supposedly, the victim is subsequently revived, to a degree, and then sold into slavery. The other matter is the *cabrit sans cornes* ("the goat without horns")—human sacrifice and cannibalism. In 1863 a small girl called Claircine was killed and ritually eaten at Bizoton during a voodoo ceremony. Those involved were tried, found guilty, and executed. This is the only known documented case, but Katherine Dunham, the American anthropologist and dancer, who is a voodoo initiate and has a house in Haiti, believes there have been other instances.

We were also in Port-au-Prince during the three-day Mardi Gras festival, a rather ragged affair compared with the splendours of Rio de Janeiro or Trinidad. The floats were very modest, some sponsored by societies calling themselves Moors or Carib Indians. Various dancing teams, each under a *Roi* or "king," performed in worn costumes with tarnished spangles while a hodgepodge parade of people decked out in fancy dress, clown outfits, and so on snaked through the streets. The processional masquerade seemed mostly a blur of sensations—heat, dust, bare feet, the smell of perspiration—but over the noise and the crowd in the main street hung a portrait of Papa Doc traced out in electric lightbulbs.

After Carnival we headed for Cap-Haïtien and the Citadelle. In those days this meant an eight-hour drive over a dirt road, often with stretches washed away or littered with fallen boulders. Nowadays, I believe, thanks to French money and French engineers, there is a tar-sealed highway and the trip takes only four hours. Our route crossed the Artibonite valley between the Massif de la Selle and the Massif du Nord. Here there were straggling villages that reminded me of Africa and irrigated rice paddies becoming, as the landscape got drier, plantations of sisal and kenaf. Then we were climbing, past mangoes and bread fruit, past hibiscus and datura, past ravines and streams. Wild aloes and maguey trees grew along the roadside. Clusters of conical huts appeared and people could be seen hoeing their patches of garden, a relatively rare sight since it was popularly believed that the mountains were the haunts of zombies. Over the ranges we went, out onto the flat sugarcane fields south of Cap-Haïtien, and then into the seaside town itself, which has been described as "the most subtly beautiful city in the West Indies."

Theoretically the avenues run parallel to the waterfront from Avenue A through Avenue Q, and the streets are at right angles numbered from 1 to 30. But, like much in Haiti, this is only a vague approximation. Both avenues and streets are more usually known by the buildings that line them—Rue de Cathédrale, Place d'Armes, and so on. Although King Henry Christophe set fire to Le Cap in 1802, burning all but fifty-nine of the houses, and an earthquake nearly destroyed it in 1842, to be followed by a hurricane in 1928, it must be admitted that part of the town's charm is a result of these disasters. The houses, painted every colour of the rainbow, are built out of or right on the previous ruins, with the effect that they present a kind of colonial Cubist canvas embedded in stone and mellow red brick.

Just 16 kilometres south of Cap-Haïtien lies the village of Milot and the remains of the palace of Sans Souci, destroyed in that same earthquake of 1842. Built of stuccoed brick four storeys high, Sans Souci was meant to rival Versailles, and the grounds cover twenty acres in a valley at the bottom of a thousand-metre (3,280-foot) mountain, La Ferrière.

The palace had floors of marbled mosaic, walls of polished mahogany, and was richly decorated th. oughout with paintings, tapestries, drapes, and other luxu es imported from Europe. Beneath the floors ran conduits carrying water from a cold mountain stream (a sort of early air-conditioning) that eventually emerged in the various fountains on the grounds. Christophe held court here surrounded by his nobility—he even created a Duke of Marmalade and a Duke of Lemonade!—as well as sundry English retainers for he admired everything English (he was born on the British West Indian island of St. Kitts or St. Christopher, whence his name). All that remains today of this opulence is part of the facade, some of the flooring, a few staircases, and Christophe's chapel, where he shot himself in the head with the silver bullet. Undeniably a man of action, he had suffered a stroke some time before and had become increasingly incapacitated and depressed. His tomb lies on the ramparts of the Citadelle and bears this inscription:

Ci-gît le Roi Henry Christophe, né le 6 Octobre, 1767, mort le 10 Octobre 1820, dont la devise est; Je renais de mes cendres.
[Here lies King Henry Christophe, born the 6th of October 1767, died the 10th of October 1820, whose motto is: I am born again from my ashes.]

To get to those ramparts of the Citadelle is a two-hour climb on muleback along a steep and rocky track to the top of La Ferrière. With walls 50 metres high (164 feet) and 10 metres thick (32.8 feet), the Citadelle rears up from the mountain like a giant ship. Over 200,000 men laboured thirteen years to build it, and about 20,000 of them perished in the effort. Four gun corridors contain 365 cannon, and there is an immense storeroom full of cannonballs. Hundreds of smaller guns litter the battlements. Fifteen thousand troops garrisoned the Citadelle, which was regarded as impregnable. Christophe used to drill his squads on a parapet with no guard rails, and occasionally he would order the soldiers to march over the edge—to their deaths.

Six years were to elapse before I saw Haiti again. In the meantime *The Comedians* had been published (1966) and filmed (1967), US aid had been cut off, the tourist trade had dwindled to almost nothing, and 30,000 refugees had fled the country. Papa Doc had become, in his own words, "The Black Sheep of the Americas."

Yorkshire Television had decided to do a series on location in Central and South America with the British journalist Alan Whicker as reporter. Among the topics considered was:

329

Men Who Never Hear the Word No. Papa Doc headed the list. I approached the Haitian chargé d'affaires in London, whose name was Delorme Méhu. It was obvious he didn't think our chances were very good, but he promised to relay our request to the Haitian Ministry of Foreign Affairs in Port-au-Prince. Months went by with no reply. When the time for our departure was drawing closer, I called on Méhu once again and this time mentioned that I knew Aubelin Jolicoeur.

"Send him a cable," Méhu said. "He has a lot of influence with Dr. Duvalier."

This I did. An answer came back within a week: CONTACT THE PRESIDENT DIRECT STOP HE IS SYMPATHETIC STOP.

I wrote out another cable and then had it translated by a French friend into the most flowery French she could command. This time the response was instant: BIENVENU A HAITI STOP DUVALIER PRESIDENT A VIE STOP.

Aubelin Jolicoeur met our television crew at the airport. He was, it turned out, Papa Doc's official greeter. There was no Customs examination, no inspection of passports. We sailed through and into waiting taxis. The drivers were *Tontons Macoutes*, strong-arm men from Papa Doc's personal militia. The name means "Uncle Bagman" and accurately describes how they lived, which was by demanding goods and money from people without payment and stuffing the loot into a big carry-all bag. Our personal driver was called Racine and he had red eyes (in the voodoo pantheon red eyes are associated with gods noted for their viciousness).

We drove up the hill to the Castelhaiti Hotel, a towering white concrete block with over one hundred rooms. But it was empty. We were the only guests. That night, as we munched our solitary meal surrounded by waiters, the lights flickered and went out. This was the regular power breakdown. You could have set your watch by it.

The next day Papa Doc was making one of his rare excursions outside the Presidential Palace to open a new Red Cross centre. This was the first time I had seen him. He arrived in a black Mercedes and was carrying his own personal sub-machine gun. His wife, Madame Simone Duvalier, accompanied him (but went unarmed, as far as I could tell). *Tontons Macoutes* were everywhere. The roof of the Red Cross centre was lined with them. They were dressed in shiny blue suits with revolvers stuck in their belts or in armpit holsters; most wore steel-rimmed dark glasses, and some had military-style snap-brimmed hats on.

Papa Doc agreed to see us at the Presidential Palace the following day, in what was to be the first of a number of meetings. These occasions sometimes had their unexpected side. For example, Papa Doc had given us a laissez-passer addressed: To All Civil and Military Authorities. Usually this was enough to get us past the various sentries, guards, and *Tontons Macoutes*—but we had reckoned without the Presidential Guard. When we showed up for our second meeting, they told us they had no authority to disturb the President. They further pointed out that the laissez-passer did not stipulate a set time for our visit. Somewhat bemused, we waited patiently in an antechamber until Alan Whicker came up with a bright idea. We had seen a telex in Papa Doc's office at our previous meeting. If we could find another telex, we could send him a message saying we were waiting right outside his door! Finding a telex machine proved a bit more difficult than we had anticipated—it turned out that there were only two in all of Haiti. But we eventually did track the other one down, and the ploy worked.

In a way I became quite friendly with Papa Doc. He dearly loved to have someone to talk to, even someone who didn't always agree with him. I discovered he was a bit of a "coffee-shop philosopher" with a ragbag of ideas ranging from Plato through Vico to Hegel, Kant, and Comte. These he had summarised in a book, *Oeuvres Essentielles: Eléments d'une Doctrine*. He presented me with a copy and even signed it in a spidery hand. He also showed me some poems he had had published under the *nom de plume* of Abdurrahman.

With his owlish glasses, black homburg, and baleful grin

Papa Doc was indeed a figure to inspire fear, and I admit at times I felt an icy *frisson* approaching panic when I was with him. It was hard to remember he had once been a kindly country doctor (hence the nickname), having graduated in medicine from Cornell University in New York. He was also interested in Haitian history, particularly of the Dessalines period, and had studied anthropology. He was very fond of his family and introduced them to us.

"I delivered my daughter of her first child," he told me proudly. "I hope my son follows in my footsteps as a doctor."

His son, Jean-Claude, then a sullen seventeen years old, was more interested in cars and had a whole stable of them ("Borrowed," he said; "Commandeered," others whispered). From time to time he crashed one.

The President showed us around his quarters, then took us into the kitchen and made us each a cup of coffee.

"I can cook also," he said laughingly. "But you wouldn't like what I make. The ingredients come from my cellars."

This was a morbid reference to the often grisly stories told about him personally torturing prisoners in the cellars of the Presidential Palace. He supposedly had the head of one of them, Captain Blucher Philogènes, delivered to him in a bucket of ice and, according to the story, had sat with it for hours trying to induce the severed head to disclose the names of its colleagues.

How much truth there was in this I have no way of knowing, but I was told on good authority that most of these sensational tales were exaggerated inventions. Papa Doc encouraged the stories (as he encouraged his identification with Baron Samedi), but at least one, I know, was true. Duvalier was always curious to find out who was visiting Haiti and would ring Pan American (the only airline serving the country then) for the passenger list. On this particular occasion the man who answered the phone was especially prompt in telling him what he wanted to know. Papa Doc thanked him and asked his name.

"I remember someone of that name," he said.

"Yes," the clerk replied. "It was my father."

His father had vanished, like so many Haitians, years before. But later that day the old man returned to his home, emaciated and in ill health. He had been held in solitary confinement.

On another occasion Papa Doc introduced us to the leader of the *Tontons Macoutes*, a woman called Madame Max Adolphe and known as "Adolphine." She also presided over the *Fillettes-Lalo* ("Daughters of the Law"), the female arm of the *Tontons*. Adolphine took part in all the parades, witnessed all the executions, and was said to be particularly partial to the latter.

"You see," Papa Doc gloated. "In Haiti there's no need for Women's Lib."

One morning at breakfast there was a new guest in the hotel, a middle-aged man with a lop-sided face. When he got up to leave the table, I noticed that he was crippled. The manager told us that he was a regular visitor who came every year. He owned a garage in Pennsylvania and was of Slav extraction. Why did he choose Haiti we wondered.

"Where else can a middle-aged cripple get a different sixteen-year-old girl every night of the week?" the manager asked. Sadly, it was true that prostitution was one of the few ways a Haitian woman could manage to live. Out of a potential workforce of 3 million, only 60,000 people in the country had jobs. The average income was about $100 a year.

Papa Doc used this situation to his advantage. To begin with, the *Tontons Macoutes* received no wages. They were given instead a licence to extort—and to settle private grudges. They were extensions of a personalised predatory state. For instance, we filmed Papa Doc visiting several jewellers' shops with his wife and daughter, and they just pocketed whatever took their fancy. The shopkeepers' "payment" was a wolfish smile and a warm handshake from Papa Doc.

On another day Papa Doc took us on a tour of Port-au-

Prince. Cheering crowds chased the black Mercedes everywhere it went—for good reason. Papa Doc was throwing handfuls of money out the windows. We stopped frequently, not to admire the view but for Papa Doc to produce thick wads of banknotes which he gave to suitable candidates.

Papa Doc has gone now, gone *nan Guinée* as they say in Haiti when someone dies ("gone to Guinea"). He was succeeded by Jean-Claude, who became Baby Doc. He ruled in much the same authoritarian way as his father had, even to touring in his car, a dark-blue Maserati, and throwing money out the windows to peasants on the roadside. And, like his father before him, he salted millions of dollars away in Swiss accounts, never daring to leave the country while he ruled for fear of being overthrown in his absence. In February 1986 Baby Doc fled the country and sought uneasy exile in France. (In April 1986 Duvalier's accounts and other assets were frozen by the Swiss Government, something the Reagan Administration did not get around to doing until March 1987.) Meanwhile social unrest and political turmoil gripped Haiti, and many of the hated *Tontons Macoutes* were attacked by mobs. Adolphine went into hiding. But Aubelin Jolicoeur survives, and in a news photo of the ruling Junta taken shortly after the changeover he is standing slightly to one side, resting on his ivory-handled cane, a look of studied indifference on his face.

After our documentary film on Haiti was broadcast in the UK, Yorkshire Television submitted it for the Dumont Award, the prestigious prize for international journalism presented by Nat Dumont and the University of California at Los Angeles. "Papa Doc and the Black Sheep" won this award in 1970.

23

The British Islets

SOME OF THE 1,500

During the late 1950s and into 1960 I worked for BBC Television on the "Tonight" programme, one of the first successful news magazine programmes (and not to be confused with America's popular "Tonight Show"). Indeed, the "Tonight" programme can be said to have provided the model for all the similar television news magazine formats that came afterwards. "Tonight" had style, panache, and a weekly audience of more than 60 million.

A lot of original thought went into devising it, and even now, almost thirty years later, I can still hear the voice of the programme's "onlie begetter," Donald Baverstock, a Welsh wizard and true descendant (in the mythic sense) of Merlin: "Television is not interesting 'facts' or 'pictures' but questions stemming from them" *and* "People are not characters in the abstract but only in a context." The technique of the interview was minutely analysed ("Whatever way the subject answers, the question is before him like the peak of a mountain. He can slide down either side—onto another peak!" *and* "Feed an emotion, never a thought"). The background to every story was thoroughly and rigorously researched ("All things involve issues" *and* "Never show a thing as it is but as people imagine it to be, and *know the difference*!").

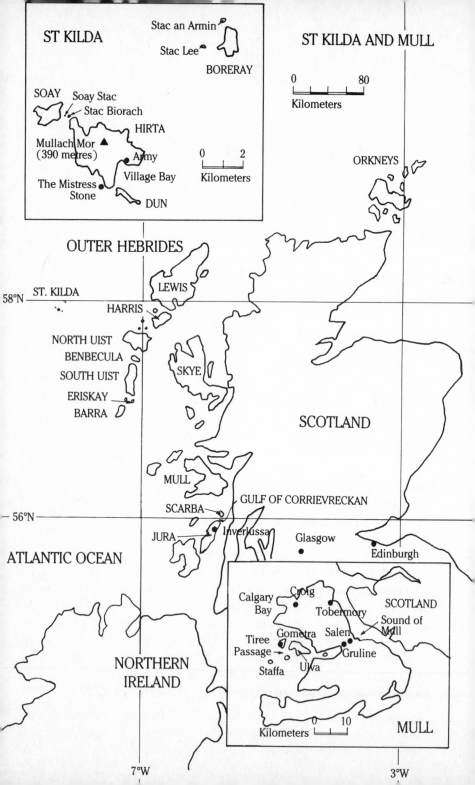

Our innovative techniques made a virtue of available light and available sound, pioneered the use of hand-held cameras and lightweight tape recorders (paving the way for *cinéma vérité*); the programme was endlessly inventive and technically sophisticated and reported on people and events in a way that had never been seen on television before or (I believe) since. Above all, the show conveyed an atmosphere of intelligence and up-to-the-minute know-how, but with a seemingly effortless, stimulating style. Among my colleagues were Alastair Milne, who became Director-General of the BBC, Antony Jay, joint writer for the acclaimed "Yes, Minister" television series, and the well-known British television reporter Alan Whicker.

Although we did many tours abroad, our main activity was closer to home filming in the British Isles. For years my routine as a director was to leave London early on a Monday morning, travel that day (and perhaps part of the next), investigate the story during the second and third days, and, if I thought it worked, call for a camera crew and film it on the fourth. On the fifth day I would return to London.

The end result of this ceaseless travelling was that I had filmed in virtually every part of Great Britain and Ireland, seen almost every town and village, driven over nearly all the roads, ridden on most of the railways, sailed on most of the ferries. And, as well, I had been in the Channel Islands, the Orkneys and Shetlands, the Inner and Outer Hebrides, and on the Isle of Man, the Isle of Wight, and Anglesey.

For the British Isles do not only consist of just the two large islands, as many people think. There are at least 1,500 smaller ones. Perhaps even more. (It all depends on what yardstick one uses for "island." The Oxford English Dictionary defines an island as "a piece of land completely surrounded by water." But a large rock in a big lake can fit this definition. A British survey in 1861 attempted to resolve the problem by stating that an island had to have enough grass to provide summer pasturage for one sheep. It can be argued that, in those latitudes, summer pasturage is itself subject to a number of factors: the fertility of the land, good weather or bad, the effect of the Gulf Stream, and so on. And what sort of sheep are being talked about? A moufflon, a Shropshire, a Southdown? They each and all have varying appetites!)

Be that as it may, I managed to visit some very out-of-the-way British Isles. Hidden nooks and crannies definitely off the beaten track. Like Lundy, for instance.

Lundy lies at the entrance to the Bristol Channel (though I prefer the more poetic name for that body of water, the Severn Sea). The island is small, barely 5 kilometres long facing due north and south and 1 kilometre wide. The exposed western side is cliffbound; the land slopes down from there to the eastern side, which is sheltered and has trees and vegetation. The cliff scenery is truly spectacular and spectacularly wild. In summer, Lundy is visited by occasional day-trippers from Ilfracombe and Bideford in Devon. Both are approximately 40 kilometres away, and the trip by boat takes three hours. This was how we travelled.

The attraction of Lundy has always been that it is, in effect, a private principality. It is one of the few places in the world where there are no taxes of any kind and no licensing laws—no income tax, no sales tax, no fees for gun or dog licences, no road taxes (no roads), no liquor licences (though there is a tavern). Since 1824 Lundy has been a free island successfully resisting the jurisdiction of the mainland magistrates. The first owner after that was W. H. Heaven and, as a result of this, it has often been called "the kingdom of Heaven." A later owner in 1929 began to print his own stamps in denominations of Puffins—one Puffin being equal to one penny (Lundy means "Puffin Island" in Norse). The stamps are still used to frank mail to the mainland, and some issues are collectors' items. When the owner tried to mint Puffin coins, however, he fell foul of the Coinage Act and was brought to trial. Notwithstanding, puffins and half puffins continue to have local circulation.

Today Lundy and its twenty-five or so inhabitants are under the control of the National Trust, but the island has had a romantic history. It was a hermitage for early Christians and a base for Viking raiders. After the Norman Conquest Lundy came into the possession of the de Marisco family but, in the 13th century on the orders of Henry III, the head of the family was hanged, drawn, and quartered for piracy. His castle can yet be seen (though castle is rather too grand a word for it).

Over the centuries Lundy changed hands and rulers many times. At one stage it was seized by Moorish sea rovers, at another by the French. For a while it was a convict settlement. And it was the last bit of England to be held for Charles I against the Roundheads. The island also has its niche in literature. Don Guzman's great ship in Charles Kingsley's *Westward Ho!* is wrecked on Great Shutter Rock, the southwest point of the island.

Lundy has a hotel, a church, a general store, a cafe, and about a dozen or so houses. For the rest it offers nothing to do except wander and look. An answer to that question raised by the poet W. H. Davies:

> What is this life, if full of care
> We have no time to stand and stare.

And on Lundy you can stand and stare at birds (over 400 species visit the island); Lundy ponies, a small hardy breed like Welsh mountain ponies; Soay sheep; grey seals; and sitka deer, who hide among the rhododendrons.

Another spot, the Isle of Man, is no private principality, however. It is a kingdom in its own right with its own parliament, laws, currency, stamps, and language. It is not part of the United Kingdom but, happily, the reigning British monarch is also Lord of Man.

The Isle of Man, in the middle of the Irish Sea between Britain and Ireland ("Latitude damp, longitude chilly," as someone once said), is 50 kilometres long and 20 kilometres across and has about 63,000 people. There's one sizeable town, Douglas, full of hotels and boardinghouses, and six smaller ones scattered around the coast. Once there used to be lead mines on Man but now the principal sources of income are farming, fishing, tourism (it is a popular resort for Lancastrians), and motorcycle racing. Also, some people come attracted by the low income tax (20 percent), the lack of death duties, and the lure of no capital gains tax. Many of these persons are retired, which has led to Man being called "God's Waiting Room."

I went to Man to interview the last native speakers of Manx. They were Mrs. Sage Kinvig, who was then 89, and Mr. Ned Maddrell, who was 82. Both are now long since dead. Perhaps only sixty or seventy people on the island have a good working knowledge of the language but they have all studied it from books. For Manx has some (albeit limited) practical value. All laws must be promulgated in both Manx and English. This is done at Tynwald, the oldest continuous parliament in the world (it celebrated its millennium in 1979), on Tynwald Day (July 5).

Manx is a Celtic tongue related to Irish and Scottish Gaelic, but unlike those two it has little literature. The first book to be written in Manx was a translation of the Book of Common Prayer in 1612 and the translator chose English orthography. So Manx looks very different from its sister languages.

Ned Maddrell was a sprightly old man, a trifle deaf but very proud of his role as one of the last native speakers. He was brought up in the remote village of Cregneeash, where "unless you had the Manx, you were a deaf and dumb man." He was illiterate but Mrs. Kinvig read the Manx Bible daily and had made many tape recordings for *Yn Cheshaght Ghailckagh*, the Manx Society, a body intent on preserving the dying language.

In the 18th century the situation was very different. "The

population of the island is twenty thousand, of whom the greater number are ignorant of English,'' reported the Society for the Promotion of Christian Knowledge. About a hundred years ago more than 13,000 people spoke Manx and by the turn of the century 5,000. So the decline has been fairly rapid. Manxmen are naturally saddened by the decay of their ancient tongue although it survives in place-names, personal names, and isolated words (scallops are called "tan rogans" in Douglas shops, and ruined abandoned houses are referred to as "tholtans" in government acts). And, of course, everyone believes in supernatural beings. *They* all have Manx names: the "buggane" or hairy giant; the "gabbal ushty" or water horse; the "phynnodderee" or leprechaun. When the Bible was translated into Manx, "satyr" in Isaiah (Chapter 13, verse 21) was rendered by "phynnodderee." This is not an isolated occurrence. The Bible translators are said to have used the word "shynnagh" or "kite" in place of "fox" whenever it occurred (there are no foxes on Man), but some dispute this reading. "Betting pools" posed a similar conundrum as did "soothsayers" to modern-day translators. But Man is not all relics of the old former speech.

The Romans never made it to Man nor did the Normans, so there is nothing from those periods. The Vikings did, however, and in 1079 united Man with the Hebrides into the Kingdom of Man and the Isles. The bishop still preserves the name of this kingdom in his title, Bishop of Sodor and Man (Sodor is *Sudreyjar*, "Southern Isles" in Norse). In 1266 the island passed to the Scottish crown and in the 14th century to the English king. He appointed the Stanley family (Dukes of Derby) as Lords of Man but in 1765 bought the regality of the island for £70,000 and took over the position himself. While the Stanleys were in control, a member of the Christian family (an ancestor of *Bounty* mutineer Fletcher) was governor. There are two other links with the *Bounty*. William Bligh was married on the island at Kirk Onchan and thereby became a relative of Fletcher by marriage. And Peter Heywood, a midshipman on the *Bounty* and only fourteen at the time of the mutiny, was the son of a Manx "deemster" or judge. He was left at Tahiti, where the Royal Navy found him. On his return to England he was tried and condemned to death but later reprieved.

Apart from that the Isle of Man can offer bare, heathery hills, sandy little coves, the heavy smell of yellow gorse in bloom, white-walled cottages with fuchsia hedges, and the easy-going Manx. "*Traa dy-liooar*," they say to most things ("Time enough"). To be truthful there *is* a 19th-century air to the place. For example Douglas has horse-drawn trams. And there is a steam railway dating from the last century that still has the same locomotives (not to mention an electric tramway and an electric mountain railway from the same period). Also unique are the Loghtan sheep, a breed with four horns, and of course the famous Manx cat, which has no tail—all aspects of the isolation of species. As are the remnants of the unique language. An 18th-century "carval" or devotional song puts Man's predicament rather curiously but not without force: ". . . *jeh bioys skee / myr yn pelican syn aasagh*" (". . . weary of life / like a pelican in the desert").

Another Norse name for the *Sudreyjar* is *Havbredey*, "the isles on the edge of the sea"—otherwise, the Hebrides. Several times we went to the Inner Hebrides: to the Isle of Skye, not only for the connection with Bonnie Prince Charlie and the Scottish Jacobite heroine Flora MacDonald ("Carry the lad that's born to be king over the sea to Skye," as Sir H. E. Boulton put it in his well-known *Skye Boat Song*), but also to film the golden eagle as this is one of the last places in the British Isles where they can be seen nesting; to Rum, Eigg, and Muck (the Small Isles), mostly just because of their comical names; and to Jura, the wildest and emptiest Hebridean isle, where George Orwell wrote *Animal Farm* in a croft near the northern tip. Some people there still remembered him, mainly because he was nearly drowned in Corrievreckan, a whirlpool in the narrow channel between Jura and Scarba. Not only do they have long memories on Jura, they have long lives, if local markings are to be believed. There's a stone at Craighouse commemorating one Gillouir MacCrain who saw "180 Christmases" before dying in 1645. In Inverlussa churchyard lies another member of the same family, Mary MacCrain, who died in 1856 aged 126.

And we went to Mull, where yet another attempt was being made on the Tobermory Treasure. This is supposed to be 30 million ducats lying in the wreck of the *Almirante de Florencia*, a ship of the Spanish Armada which anchored in Tobermory Harbour for shelter and provisions in 1588. When it became obvious the Spaniards were about to leave without paying for anything, Donald MacLean, the Laird, went aboard to try and settle the matter. For his trouble he was captured and imprisoned, but he managed to escape to the ship's powder magazine and blow it up. Since the early 17th century there have been numerous salvage ventures, but apart from some cannon and a few silver goblets, some pieces of eight and one gold chain, nothing of value has yet been raised.

When on Mull I took the opportunity to visit Salen, some 15 kilometres from Tobermory. It is a small place on a wide bay, founded in 1809 as a model village by a most remarkable man, Lachlan Macquarie. The son of an impoverished farmer on Ulva, an island to the west of Mull, he joined the British army at the age of fifteen, saw action in India, Persia, and Russia, and rose through the ranks to become a general. In 1808 he retired and bought Jarvisfield Estate on Mull. Then, in 1810, he became Governor of New South Wales for eleven years and can justly be called "The Father of Australia." Certainly he left his mark on my country—from the ground plan of Sydney to the Lachlan and Macquarie rivers, from Port Macquarie to Macquarie Harbour and the five towns he founded some 60 kilometres west of Sydney on the banks of the Nepean River (the Macquarie Towns as they are known). His tomb lies 3 kilometres from Salen at Gruline, where he is buried with his wife and his Indian servant George.

Staffa, a tiny island 10 kilometres southwest of Mull, also has an Australian connection. It was "discovered" in 1772 by Sir Joseph Banks, who was fresh from his voyage with Cook on the *Endeavour* and on his way to Iceland. When he first came to the island there was only one inhabitant (today there is no one). Other visitors soon followed—Sir Walter Scott, John Keats, William Wordsworth, and Felix Mendelssohn. What brought them there was Fingal's Cave. Mendelssohn was so inspired by it he wrote "Die Fingalshöhle" or the "Hebrides Overture." Because of this piece it is probably the best-known Hebridean island. To get there we sailed on a small boat from Croig, a little port in the northwest of Mull, past the sweep of Calgary Beach (after which Calgary in Canada is named) and Gometra, an island west of Ulva, into Tiree Passage.

The cave itself, which is partly flooded by the sea, is about 65 metres (213 feet) long, 14 metres (45 feet) wide, and 20 metres (65.5 feet) high. The walls are quite vertical and composed of black hexagonal pillars split transversely every 40 cm or so (about 16 inches). To quote Queen Victoria, who visited Staffa in 1833, it is "a great vaulted hall." As the sea rises and falls in the cave musical sounds come from the pillars, something that may have given Mendelssohn his original idea.

There was once a memorable "Tonight" tour of the Outer Hebrides. A boat was hired, and the television crew and reporter (Fyfe Robertson, a tufty-bearded Lowland Scot with a face like an Old Testament prophet) lived right on board. Most of the islands were filmed: Lewis and Harris (actually different ends of the largest island), where the tweed comes from; the Uists (North Uist, Benbecula, and South Uist); Eriskay (home of the *Eriskay Love Lilt*, perhaps the most hauntingly beautiful of the traditional Gaelic love songs); and Barra, where the film *Whisky Galore!* (1948) was made (after the book of the same name by Compton Mac- kenzie).

The Outer Hebrides are the last stronghold of Scottish Gaelic. They are also the last place where you can see a *tigh dubh* or black house, though these are now being carefully preserved. Black houses were once common throughout the Highlands. They are long, windowless houses with thick stone walls and roofs of thatch weighted down with stones. They have one room with a rammed earth floor, where ani- mals and people lived together. Usually there was a peat fire in the middle of the room but no chimney, and the thatch roof was therefore blackened by the smoke. Withal, I was told, they were warm and comfortable.

The islands have been the scene of many a failed project. The most spectacular (for being the most costly) was that of Lord Leverhulme, founder of Unilever. He wanted to turn Lewis and Harris into the greatest fishing centre in Europe. He spent more than three-quarters of a million pounds, but the dream died with him in 1925. The slump that followed forced over one thousand able-bodied men to emigrate to North America (some of whom returned during the Great Depression). There have been other notable failures. In 1844 Lewis was bought by Sir James Matheson for £190,000. He was a *taipan* or merchant prince in Shanghai (and his com- pany, Jardine Matheson, is still a power to be reckoned with in Hong Kong), and he invested £500,000 earned in the China trade for improvements, draining the land, financing indus- tries, etc. But it came to nothing and, in an effort to alleviate the misery of his tenants, he waived all debts and encouraged emigration by offering free passages to Canada.

The islanders have always walked a thin line between pov- erty and prosperity. The land is hard. It is, in fact, Lewisian gneiss, "the oldest known fragment of Europe." Something else sets the islands apart from the rest of Scotland—the light. It has a quality of luminosity that heightens colours and gives a sharp edge to everything. This is because it is reflected off clear seas. At times the islands appear bathed in rays the colour of pistachio.

And parallelling the bleak, uncompromising landscape is a bleak, uncompromising faith—the United Free Presbyterian Church, the sternest Calvinist sect in the world and centred on Lewis (the other islands are mainly Roman Catholic). Here Lord's Day Observance strictly means what it says—everything closed, no transport, no working, no cooking, no lighting fires, no washing, no playing, no watching television, no listening to the radio or to music, no conversation, no reading or writing. Only church-going, and even there no hymns are sung. Visitors are definitely not welcome.

Of all the 500-odd Hebridean islands there was one I dearly wanted to see—St. Kilda. Perhaps because the most remote society in Britain had existed there for almost 2,000 years in complete isolation until contact with the outside world brought about its decline and resulted in the evacuation of the remaining thirty-six inhabitants in 1930. Perhaps because of a picture I had once seen of a dozen or so men standing in front of a row of thatched stone cottages, men with beards wearing homespun clothes, Tam o'Shanters on their heads and pipes in their mouths—the St. Kilda Parliament.

There are actually four islands: Hirta, Soay, Boreray, and Dun as well as several stacks. All rise steeply from the sea and are ringed with breathtaking cliffs 300 metres high (984 feet), the most magnificent in the British Isles. As Wordsworth says:

> Breaking the silence of the seas,
> Among the farthest Hebrides.

They lie 85 kilometres due west of Lewis and Harris and nearly 200 kilometres from the Scottish mainland. Where the name St. Kilda came from is a bit of a mystery. There is no such saint. The nearest possibility might be from the name of a spring on Hirta—Tobar Childa (Childa's Well). Some scholars have suggested that the name comes from the Gaelic word for hermit or saint, *culdee* (*céle dé*, "companion of God"), others that it represents the islanders' pronunciation of Hirta as Hilda (since they habitually replaced the Gaelic *r* with an *l*).

Today St. Kilda is the property of the National Trust, but it also has a permanent garrison of forty men to maintain a missile tracking station on Mullach Mor, one of Hirta's peaks. The British army has a radar station, a signals centre, a power generator, and all the usual amenities including a cinema. Communication is maintained by helicopter, and it was on one of those that we arrived from the firing range in South Uist. The army is a community on but not of St. Kilda. The old way of life has gone forever. Each summer, though, the National Trust sends working parties to restore the houses (we stayed in one) and cleits (small dry-stone, turf-roofed structures used for storing the dried birds that were the St. Kildans' staple diet).

Traditional crofting activities included fishing, tending the stock, cutting peat, harvesting, shearing (they called it "roo'ing" and either plucked the wool or cut it off in small tufts with a penknife), spinning and weaving. The men also collected thousands of birds and birds' eggs. They worked in pairs, and using horse-hair ropes they scaled the cliffs and stacks in their stockinged feet. Accidents, though rare, did happen as they caught gannets, puffins and, most importantly, fulmars, which provided oil for their lamps. St. Kilda has the largest gannet rookery in the world (37 percent of the world's gannet population is estimated to be found there). Other seabirds, though not so numerous, are equally well-represented.

One species is unfortunately no longer there. On a July day in 1840 two men were climbing the rock known as Stac an Armin, at the northern end of Boreray. It was misty and suddenly they came upon a giant bird. They clubbed it to death. So perished the last great auk in Britain. It was not unlike a penguin, about 75 cm high (2 feet, 6 inches), black in colour and flightless (it used its wings as paddles). Four years later on another island off Iceland the last known great auks were similarly killed.

So important was fowling to the St. Kildans that a young man had to prove himself by scaling Stac Biorach in Soay Sound, a climb of 73 metres (239 feet) and regarded as the most difficult in the island group. And just before a young man's marriage (or funeral), he had to balance on one foot on the edge of The Mistress Stone (an archway with a sheer drop of 80 metres—262 feet—to the sea below) while holding his other foot in his hands!

The population was a healthy one and remained relatively stable (it declined from a peak of 180 in 1697 to between 70 and 100) until last century when contact with the mainland began. In 1851 the population was 110, but the following year 36 St. Kildans emigrated to Australia. They boarded the barque *Priscilla* in Liverpool, but on the voyage smallpox broke out among them. When the barque reached Melbourne on January 19, 1853, it was quarantined for five weeks in the bay that later was named for the passengers' home island. Only 16 survived, and one of these eventually returned to St. Kilda. He was Ewen Gillies, a man who had quite an adventurous life. He looked for gold in Australia and New Zealand, went to America and joined the Union Army in the Civil War, then went back home, where he tried to improve the deteriorating lot of his fellow islanders. In the end he gave up in despair and emigrated to Canada.

John Bull's other island, Ireland, does not have so many isles around it. But like Britain most of them are to be found in the north and the west: boomerang-shaped Rathlin, within sight of the Mull of Kintyre in Scotland where Robert the Bruce took refuge in a cave after his defeat at Perth in 1306 and was inspired by a spider (it had tried six times to swing across a web and failed five times) to regroup his forces and eventually win the Battle of Bannockburn (1314) that drove the English out of Scotland; Tory Island, off the coast of Donegal; and Achill and the islands in Clew Bay, County Mayo. Then there are the Blaskets off Dun Slea in County Kerry. I have stood on Dun Slea and looked at the Blaskets (''the next parish to America''), but they are no longer inhabited. Through field-glasses one can see the derelict stone houses and the outlines of gardens. Life was primitive. There was no church, no pub, no shop, though one old woman's house was known as the *dáil* or ''talking place.'' In the evenings people entertained themselves by telling stories that their ancestors had related for more than one thousand years. Some wrote down an account of their lives, and one book, *An t-Oileánach* (translated into English as *The Islandman* by Tomás Ó Criomhthainn (Thomas O'Crohan), is an Irish classic.

Probably the best-known islands of Ireland are the Aran Islands in Galway Bay (there are three small, barren islands—Inishmore to the northwest, Inishmaan in the middle, and Inisheer to the southeast). These are famous partly because they are the setting for John Millington Synge's play ''Riders to the Sea'' and Robert Flaherty's documentary film *Man of Aran* (1934). But, in addition, the Aran Islands contain the greatest concentration of prehistoric, early Christian and pagan monuments to be found anywhere in Europe. Chief among them are the Duns or great dry-stone Iron Age forts that line the cliffs facing the raw Atlantic. Dun Aengus, on Inishmore, is the most impressive. It is horseshoe-shaped, with the open end facing the cliff and a drop of about a hundred metres (328 feet) to the restless sea. Dun Aengus has three rings of defence, the central one reinforced with a line of jagged limestone uprights (about 24 hectares—59 acres—are enclosed). There are also cromlechs (circles of monoliths), cashels (stone-walled enclosures around a fort or church), clochans (beehive huts), round towers, storehouses, and early stone churches founded by monks, as well as ring forts,

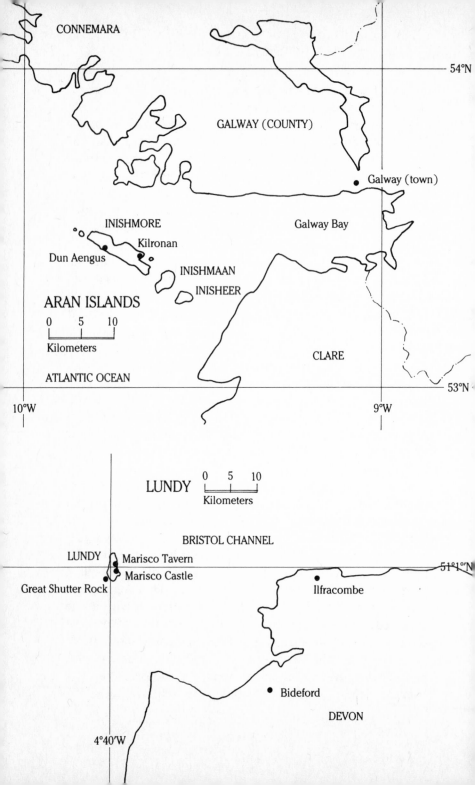

CONNEMARA

54°N

GALWAY (COUNTY)

Galway (town)

INISHMORE

Galway Bay

Kilronan

Dun Aengus

INISHMAAN

INISHEER

ARAN ISLANDS

0   5   10

Kilometers

ATLANTIC OCEAN

CLARE

53°N

10°W

9°W

LUNDY

0   5   10

Kilometers

BRISTOL CHANNEL

LUNDY

Marisco Tavern

51°1′0″N

Marisco Castle

Great Shutter Rock

Ilfracombe

Bideford

DEVON

4°40′W

oratories, and grave slabs—all in all, a happy hunting ground for the archaeologists.

But the people of Aran have other concerns, such as earning their living. Life has never been easy on these islands. Two or three times a week a steamer leaves Galway for Kilronan on Inishmore. That was how we came there. Kilronan is the principal town on the northeast coast of the island. It does not have much to offer except accommodation of sorts. What was of interest to us was the house Flaherty had built for *Man of Aran* (a film not looked upon with much favour in the islands). The house is well situated. It overlooks on one side a little land-locked bay with a secluded white beach, where all the sequences with curraghs (keelless small boats made by stretching tarred canvas—in ancient times hide—over a framework of lathes) were filmed. On the other side the ground rose to Dun Aengus. The house itself, where all the interior shots were done, has a large skylight on the roof that faces north. According to the locals, the scenes showing the hunting of the basking sharks were faked and Flaherty brought in Connemara men to act the part of Aran Islanders. One always hears these kinds of stories about film-makers (though a contemporary review by E. V. Lucas in *Punch* tended to agree. It read: "In so far as it is a rendering of the efforts of the Atlantic to overwhelm and demolish a wall of rock it is magnificent but the human note is inadequate"). Similar things were said about Synge, and it was even claimed that his Irish was not really very good and that he mistranslated a lot of expressions (the most often voiced objection seemed to be that "the wonder of the Western world" should really have been put into English as "It's the most unusual thing in the world"—which I hardly think matters). Synge, for his part, said the islanders were shut inside "a world of individual conceits and theories."

The women of the islands fear the sea as it constantly claims lives. But in addition to fishing, the islanders grow potatoes. They till the potato patches, and because the islands are so stony the fields have to be built up. Alternate layers of sand and seaweed are placed on the rock base, and any crevices are filled with stones. It is back-breaking work.

Knitwear also contributes to the islands' economy. Aran "ganseys" (sweaters and cardigans) are in great demand not only in Dublin but also in London, and I have even seen them in Sydney. Many stitches are unique to the islands and go by such names as the Tree of Life, the Crooked Road, the Carrageen Moss, and the Castle. *Crios* or gaily coloured woven belts are also made as well as *pampooties* or sandals of undressed cowhide sewn together and tied across the instep (the only practical footwear for walking on the limestone flags that make up most of the surface of the islands). The clacking of knitting or loom needles is one of the islands' most distinctive sounds. And the glimpse of piled-up cow dung for use as fuel one of the most distinctive sights.

A woman lay dying in one of the cottages. Not an old woman, but one who had had a hard life. We were asked to visit her. Everyone, it appeared, had done so and said farewell. People came from Galway and even by curragh from Inishmaan and Inisheer. It helped her. Strangers were expected to do the same.

"Don't look at me, I'm dying," she said in Irish, adding in English, "It's not difficult."

Two other people were sitting silently in the room. The bed was large and wooden, the bedclothes thick and woollen. She lay still, eyes closed.

"Suppose there is no afterlife?"

The questions tumbled from her thin lips. "Where am I going? . . . What does it all mean—life and death? . . . How will I know when I am dead?"

One of the others spoke, first in Irish and then, for our benefit, in English. "Whist. You're in the hands of God."

"He's not listening to me."

"Whist."

We were deeply moved.

Still, there is time for imagination. According to the people of Aran, the islands are all that is left of Hy Brasil, a mythical fifth province of Ireland that sank below the waves. (Celtic legends are full of such stories. The Lost Land of Lyonesse is supposed to have been submerged off the Cornish coast.) In the islanders' view, the cliff-top forts were built to defend Hy Brasil from invaders. One day, they say, Hy Brasil will rise again from the sea and will become once more a land flowing with milk and honey.

24

The Congo (Zaire)

HEART OF DARKNESS

Congo. The word doesn't exactly trip lightly off the tongue. There is a certain malevolence to it (the gutturals perhaps?). But there is also the heavy hand of history with its images of darkness, cruelty, and death. No wonder the Congolese have changed the name of both the river and the country to Zaire. Yet Zaire is only a Portuguese form of the Kikongo word *nzari*, meaning "great water." And a great water it is: the river's basin covers 3,800,000 square kilometres and drains all or parts of the modern nations of Zaire, Congo (Brazzaville), the Central African Republic, Cameroon, Gabon, Angola, Zambia, and Tanzania. Its length is 4,700 kilometres (2,914 miles), making it the fifth longest river in the world (after the Nile, the Mississippi, the Amazon, the Yangtze) with a volume second only to the Amazon.

In *Heart of Darkness* Joseph Conrad describes the river as "an immense snake uncoiled, with its head in the sea, its body at rest curving afar over a vast country, and its tail lost in the depths of the land." I have seen the tail of this snake near the village of Musofi in the province of Shaba (formerly Katanga). Here the Lualaba—the local name for the Upper Congo—arises. It is a lively stream about 30 metres (98 feet) wide, winding through marshes and meadows among low hills and yellow grassland. I have seen the body of this snake from the air, flying over the thick rain forests of Equator and Upper Zaire provinces. It slunk through the country, or as N. Vachel Lindsay says in his poem *The Congo*:

> Then I saw the Congo creeping through the black,
> Cutting through the jungle with a golden track.

I have seen the same body at its greatest width—in Malebo Pool (formerly Stanley Pool), where Kinshasa, the capital (formerly Léopoldville), stands on one bank and Brazzaville, the capital of the other Congo, on the opposite. Malebo Pool, almost a huge, shallow lake, is 25 kilometres wide and 30 kilometres long, with large islands, crocodiles, and fast-moving clumps of water hyacinth. Below the Malebo Pool are the Livingstone Falls (no doubt also renamed), which stretch for nearly 400 kilometres and are, strictly speaking, a series of turbulent rapids and violent cataracts.

And I have seen the head of this snake, where it debouches into the Atlantic near the tiny Angolan town of Santo António do Zaire (now called Mpinda). Here a tawny surf broke onto the arcing sandbar, while islands of vegetation were swept far out to sea by a current of some 9 knots; the water was sweet not salty and flowed at approximately half a million cubic metres a minute.

It was these characteristics that attracted the attention of the Portuguese navigator, Diogo Cão, when he coasted cautiously along the West African land mass below the equator. The year was 1482 and Cão was going where no European had gone before. At first he thought he had come upon a bay or inlet, but he soon realised it was the estuary of a great river. As the Portuguese chroniclers record (my translation):

> . . . it enters the sea on the Western side of Africa, forcing a broad and free passage, in spite of the ocean, with so much violence that for the space of twenty leagues it preserves its fresh water unbroken by the briny billows that encompass it on every side: as if this noble river had determined to try its strength in pitched battle with the ocean itself.

Cão sailed a short way up the Congo. He was convinced that it was a highway to the centre of Africa, so he landed and erected a *padrão* on the left bank near the site of what would one day become Santo António do Zaire. This *padrão* was torn down by the Dutch in 1614 but rediscovered centuries later. A *padrão* or standard was a round marble pillar about 2 metres long topped by a square block with a cross sitting on it. On one side of the block were carved the arms of Portugal, the famous *quinas* or five shields, each with five lozenges on them representing the Five Wounds of Christ. On the remaining sides the captain who erected the *padrão* was expected to add his name, the date, and whatever observations he wanted to make. Meant to mark a formal claim to the land by the Portuguese crown, *padrões* were an idea of King John II and Cão was the first sea captain to carry them. In time the coast of Southern Africa would have several of them sitting on prominent headlands. I have seen one that Cão erected on his second voyage of discovery at Cape Negro in the extreme south of Angola 10 kilometres north of Porto Alexandre. Though badly weathered it still stands high above the cliffs.

Cão stayed a while and discovered that the people called themselves *Bakongo* and their language *Kikongo*. He also learnt that some distance to the east was a royal city, Mbanza Kongo, where the *Manikongo* (or "Lord of the Congo") lived. Cão thought immediately of Prester John, the legendary Christian king whose kingdom was believed to be somewhere in Asia or Africa. Before continuing his voyage down the coast of Africa, Cão left four of his companions to be conducted with gifts and messages to Mbanza. On his return he put in again at Santo António do Zaire and found that the four had been detained at the *Manikongo*'s court. He seized four Africans as hostages to ensure the safety of his ambassadors and tried to explain to the local chief, who was a relative of the *Manikongo*, that his subjects would be returned within fifteen months.

So began a curious episode in Portuguese history, the

alliance between Portugal and the Kingdom of the Congo. For the first time, Africans were treated as equals by Europeans. There was no military occupation, no commercial exploitation, no administrative control. The alliance was foremost a means to spread the civilising influence of Western Christianity.

To this end the African hostages were provided with their own apartments, given wardrobes, taught Portuguese, and shown a bit of the country. They were then returned to Mbanza with rich presents for the *Manikongo* and a hope that he would embrace Christianity. The *Manikongo* proved receptive and asked for missionaries, builders, and traders to be sent to his country.

Cão, well satisfied, resolved to sail up the river and did so as far as the modern port of Matadi. At this point the Crystal Mountains rear up abruptly, and just above the city is the Cauldron of Hell (the last stretch of the Livingstone Falls). The city is perched on high hills and, as its citizens say, to live there one must know how to conjugate the verbs to climb, descend, and perspire. The atmosphere there is like a fiery crucible because the rocks in the region capture the sun's rays and reflect them (Matadi means "stone"). On some rocks at the very entrance to the Cauldron of Hell one can still see the following words engraved by Cão alongside symbols of a cross and the *quinas*:

Aqui chegaram os navios do esclarecido rei Dom João de Portugal
[This point was reached by the ships of the distinguished King John of Portugal]

King John for his part answered the *Manikongo*'s request, and in 1490 three caravels were despatched to the Congo carrying priests, skilled workers, tools, and religious objects. The expedition was peaceful, its purpose to evangelize and reorganise the kingdom along European lines. The results were auspicious. The *Manikongo*, Nzinga a Nkuwu, and his wife and eldest son, Mbemba a Nzinga, were baptised, taking the names of the king, John, his wife Eleanor, and that of the heir to the Portuguese throne, Affonso.

Mbemba a Nzinga succeeded his father in 1506 and died in the early 1540s, and his long reign as Affonso I represents the "Golden Age" of the Kingdom of the Congo. An educated man in the European sense, he spoke Portuguese fluently and was well versed in Portuguese history and literature. Not until almost the 20th century would the world see other similar successful examples of African assimilation emerging from Sierra Leone, the Gold Coast (Ghana), and Senegal— but never from the Belgian Congo.

The Portuguese still point to their relationship with the King of the Congo as the best thing in their five-hundred-year association with Africa. The principles embodied in that association—racial equality, a sincere attempt to Christianise and educate the Africans, military and economic assistance without strings attached—are, in their view, superior to those that motivated other Europeans. Critics are, however, quick to respond that, when the Congo experiment failed, the slave trade became the major Portuguese activity in the region (and in Angola). The Africans were betrayed, they say, not only by the slavers but also by the missionaries, who took concubines and entered the slave trade themselves. Some go so far as to say that this has been the fate of the Congo (and Africa) at the hands of all Europeans who have attempted to impose their ideas upon the native inhabitants. But the Congolese have done their share of betraying as well.

I first saw the Congo in 1961, entering the country from Northern Rhodesia (now Zambia). It was the time of the Katanga secession (and in commemoration of that event I still have a pile of worthless Katanga banknotes). That was when I was driven to the source of the Lualaba, about 70 kilometres along a dirt road south of Jadotville (now Likasi). It was a Welsh-born American, Henry Morton Stanley, who proved that the Lualaba was part of the Congo and followed it almost 4,000 kilometres from midway along the upper course to Matadi.

When I got back to Élisabethville (we then called it Evil, and now it is known as Lumumbashi), I couldn't put the thought of the Congo out of my mind. The *river* was the country, it seemed to me. This was long before my later visits when I would stand on the sandbar near Santo António do Zaire, long before I would be in Léopoldville, long before I would witness the shambles of Stanleyville (now known as Kisangani). On this first trip I decided to try and unravel the skein of the river.

The Lualaba, because it flowed northwards, was firmly believed by Dr. Livingstone (and most European geographers) to be the source of the Nile. That there might be any connection with the great river that exits on the west coast of Africa—the Congo—was regarded as a fanciful notion. Stanley, who would come to be regarded as the greatest African explorer, initially set out in 1875 to prove that the Lualaba was the Nile, but discovered what no one had guessed—that the Lualaba turned west-northwest and southwest across the equator in a great loop to become the Congo. In this aspect it is unique. No other river in the world crosses the equator, and the Congo does it not once but twice.

It is not navigable all the way. Apart from the Livingstone Falls, there are also the seven Stanley Falls (now called Boyoma Falls) above Kisangani and the five rapids at Kasongo as well as the famous gorge of Portes d'Enfer (the Gates of Hell) which precedes them. In Belgian times rail links were built to get around these falls, which made it possible to travel the length of the river. It can still be done, but with difficulties. The steamers tow barges behind them, where the second- and third-class passengers travel, while first-class are accommodated on the boat. After a day or two the trip palls considerably. The heat is like a sauna. Admittedly, the scenery is endlessly shifting and fascinating. There is not only the primeval forest with its troops of monkeys, there are hippopotamuses and crocodiles, passing pirogues laden with smoked fish and other provisions, riparian villages with naked children swimming in the river. But there are frequent inconvenient delays and monotonous food, and there are often thieves on the barges.

All along the river the lingua franca is Lingala, a partially Creolised Bantu language with borrowings from Arabic, French, and Portuguese (the word for Europe, for example, is *Mpoto* or "Portugal"). Lingala, which properly belongs to the Middle Congo, may have been modified by Portuguese mulattos from Mbanza trading up river in the 17th century. At least one Lingala word has crossed the Atlantic to the United States, *nguba* or peanut (Georgia is the Goober State). Lingala has become the official language of the Zairois armed forces, and today it is spreading rapidly in the region.

Back in Europe, Stanley was approached by Léopold II of Belgium to help open up the Congo basin and so he returned to the river. There he signed enough treaties with African chiefs to ensure that, by the time of the Berlin Conference in 1884-85, when thirteen European nations and the United States sat down to partition Africa, a strong case could be made for handing the Congo over to the private company formed by Léopold II. Thus, the Congo Free State, as it was known, came into the personal possession of the Belgian king.

This beginning was *not* auspicious. Nearly one-third of the area was already a field of operations for slave traders. The most notorious, a Zanzibari called Hamidi bin Muhammad, better known by his nickname Tippoo Tib, was made governor of a province. Léopold quickly discarded the sham of the private company and instead set up his own private government. Though on the northern bank, Boma on the Congo between Santo António do Zaire and Matadi was chosen to be the capital, and there Léopold sent a governor-general, an assistant, and a commander-in-chief of the gendarmerie or *Force Publique*. Then began the real rape of the Congo. Although Léopold was already a very wealthy man who had made a fortune speculating on Suez Canal shares, his pockets weren't deep enough. He decided to exploit the natural wealth of the country, which in those days consisted almost entirely of ivory and rubber.

Rubber grew wild and to harvest it the Africans had to go into the jungle and find the trees. When they had tapped the latex, they could sell it only to the monopoly held by the Congo Free State for a low price. Because there was a growing demand for bicycle and automobile tires in industrial societies, the profit margin was enormous. The Congo Free State therefore imposed ever-increasing quotas, and failure to meet these elicited a dreadful punishment—the amputation of a hand, usually the right one. Soon, the baskets of severed hands laid at the feet of the European post commanders became themselves the raison d'être for Léopold's domain. *Force Publique* soldiers began to bring them to the stations in place of latex. Hands became a kind of grisly currency; the rapacious soldiers were paid their bonuses according to the number of hands they collected! To quote N. Vachel Lindsay again:

> Listen to the yell of Leopold's ghost
> Burning in Hell for his hand-maimed host.

When news of this reached Europe, Britain initiated a campaign against the misrule and atrocities in the Congo Free State. Following a report by Roger Casement, the British Consul in Boma, international pressure forced Léopold to set up a Commission of Enquiry with lawyers from Belgium, Italy, and Switzerland to investigate the allegations contained in the Casement Report. After an on-the-spot inspection it confirmed them all, and in 1908 the Congo Free State was officially taken over by the Belgian Government. It is estimated that, during Léopold's time, between 5 and 8 million Africans either died from starvation or were tortured and murdered.

Belgian rule was paternalistic. They habitually referred to the Congolese as "children." The Belgian Congo did advance economically, however. There were vast rubber as well as coffee, palm oil, and cotton plantations. Modern industrial cities sprang up, a few with boulevards that looked as if they had lost their way from Brussels and had somehow been put down in the jungle. The mineral wealth of Katanga was exploited. Mines were opened all over Katanga plateau, and by the late 1960s the Congo was producing 8 percent of the world's copper, 73 percent of its cobalt, 80 percent of its industrial diamonds, 60 percent of the world's uranium (the fuel for the first atomic bomb came from Katanga), and many other minerals. The eight-hour day became routine, there were old-age pensions, free medical care, free housing for workers, and the Catholic missions provided primary and secondary education. The wealth of the Congo allowed Belgium to make a rapid recovery from World War II, and it gave Belgians a high standard of living.

Yet the Africans were deprived of all political rights to an extent unknown in the British or French colonies. Those who had had the benefit of a secondary education, the *évolués*, were admitted to "honorary membership" in the white race. For this there were two categories—*Immatriculation* granted equal social status with whites (but no political rights), while the *Carte du Mérite civique* completely restricted social and political rights but allowed a few limited privileges.

The Belgian Government spoke vaguely of a Belgo-Congolese community at some time in the distant future. But in 1958 an ex-brewery salesman from Léopoldville and a former postal clerk in Stanleyville (where he had once been jailed for embezzling postal funds), Patrice Lumumba, attended the All-African People's Conference at Accra in Ghana. I met him there. A tall, slightly built, softly spoken man with a little goatee beard, he had one burning conviction: The Congo must be free.

Back in Léopoldville he began to deliver some fiery speeches on this theme, and as a result riots broke out which lasted four days. Shocked out of their complacency, the Belgians promised elections for local and provincial governments. This was not sufficient. The Congolese launched a campaign of passive resistance. In a last-ditch effort to save the situation, Belgium called for a Round Table Conference in Brussels. Although there were differences of opinion among the Congolese members of the conference (Lumumba favoured a strong central government while Joseph Kasavubu and Moise Tshombé wanted a loose federation), they were nevertheless unanimous on one point—Independence Now! The Belgians caved in. Just why has never been satisfactorily explained. Perhaps they thought the Congo would fall into anarchy and they would be invited back. Perhaps the prospect of a long and costly colonial war appalled them ("Not one soldier for the Congo" was the slogan of the Belgian Socialist Party). Whatever the reason, like Pontius Pilate they washed their hands of the country.

The Congolese were totally unprepared to govern themselves. Less than a week after independence, in July 1960, the 25,000-strong *Force Publique* mutinied, and an orgy of looting, raping, and murdering Europeans followed. Whites fled the country in panic. And, in the midst of all this, Tshombé declared Katanga's secession from the Congo (to be followed a month later by Kasai Province). He asked Brussels for troops to restore order in Katanga and the Belgians responded.

Lumumba and Kasavubu appealed to the United Nations, and an international force was soon despatched to help get the Congo's administration under control. But the UN force had no intention of clashing with Belgian troops supporting Katanga's secession. So protracted negotiations were entered into with the Belgians in an effort to get them to withdraw.

Meanwhile things got worse in the Congo and another separate state was proclaimed in South Kasai. Lumumba appealed to the Soviet Union for help and the Cold War arrived in Central Africa. The government finally collapsed. Kasavubu, as president, dismissed Lumumba. Lumumba, as prime minister, dismissed Kasavubu. Joseph-Désiré Mobutu, a former sergeant in the *Force Publique*, seized power. When news of this reached Stanleyville, Lumumba's ally Antoine Gizenga declared Oriental Province (now Upper Zaire) to be independent (as the People's Republic of the Congo), and some of the provincial garrison attacked units of Mobutu's *Armée Nationale Congolaise* (as the *Force Publique* had become). Only six months after independence, the Congo was divided into four regimes, each with its own army and foreign sponsor.

Mobutu's response was to arrest Lumumba and have him flown to Élisabethville. What happened then is unclear but Lumumba was killed, either trying to escape or, more likely, on Tshombé's orders. World reaction was so strong that Mobutu was forced to resign and Kasavubu took over once again. By this time the Belgians had agreed to withdraw from Katanga, and United Nations troops were authorised to use necessary force to restore order in the province. Tshombé turned to white mercenaries for support, and a civil war followed.

That was the situation when I first went to the Congo, towards the middle of 1961. At the beginning the mercenaries were in control (they were mainly Belgian Flemings and French from Algeria with a few Rhodesians and English among them), but slowly the UN forces gained the upper hand. Tshombé offered to negotiate with Dag Hammarskjöld, the UN Secretary-General, but flying to meet Tshombé at Ndola in Northern Rhodesia, Hammarskjöld's plane crashed and he was killed. The fighting went on, continuing until January 1963 when Tshombé fled to exile in Spain.

Just before this I was in the Congo for the second time. We had been in Angola filming the war there and wanted to interview Agostinho Neto, the president of the *Movimento Popular de Libertação de Angola* (MPLA), and Holden Roberto, leader of the *Frente Nacional de Libertação de Angola* (FNLA). Both were operating from the Congo—Neto at Léopoldville and Roberto at Thysville (now Mbanza Ngunga), some 120 kilometres from Léopoldville and nearer the Angolan border, where the FNLA had a training camp (the MPLA at that stage had no guerilla fighters). So we flew, in a roundabout fashion, from Luanda to Lourenço Marques (now Maputo) in Mozambique to Johannesburg to Léopoldville. When we arrived we found hotel accomodations were at a premium, but we managed to find rooms at the Memling. Not before we had signed an agreement, though, which I still have. It reads:

> I'M authorizing the hotel direction to made my luggage and personnal effects and put them out of the room if i didn't liberated the room at 12 o'clock A.M. on the previously date of my booking.

I also took the opportunity to call on Kasavubu and Mobutu, who was once again back in his barracks. Mobutu, a round-faced, bespectacled man of medium height, offered us a jeep and an escort of soldiers for the trip to Thysville, which we gladly accepted. Although Léopoldville was fairly safe, the Lower Congo was still in anarchy.

But we discovered that it wasn't only black men with guns we had to worry about. On our return to Léopoldville we found that some laundry we had given out the day before had been returned. So we all were able to enjoy the luxury of a change of clothing after a shower. The next morning the sound recordist was worried. He took off his shirt and showed me his back and chest. They were covered with small pustules. I thought at first that he had small pox and asked him whether his shots were up to date. He assured me they were. We got the hotel management to call a doctor, who immediately diagnosed the problem.

"Each pimple," he said, "contains the maggot of a small fly, the tunbu fly."

The sound recordist protested that he had felt no bites nor had he seen any flies buzzing around him.

"Did you have any washing done?" the doctor asked. "Especially a white shirt?"

"Yes."

The doctor explained that the washerwomen usually spread the clothes out on grass to dry. These flies were attracted by the white colour and laid their eggs on the garment. Body temperature was usually enough to hatch the eggs and the maggots would burrow into the host's skin.

What could be done? Short of squeezing each maggot out, there was nothing. In London perhaps they knew some treatment, the doctor suggested. The sound recordist was flown out that night by Sabena (Belgian airlines). We couldn't get on the same plane so we had to take the ferry to Brazzaville and try our luck with U.T.A. (the French airline). The ferry across the river is always accompanied by a guard boat, just in case the engine fails (below the shallow Malebo Pool are the Livingstone Falls).

Even though the Katanga secession was over, the Congo's troubles were not. Kasavubu had arrested Gizenga but, in doing so, he did not stamp out the revolt in Oriental Province. The reins were taken over by Christopher Gbenye who, with two other men, Pierre Mulele and Gaston Soumiallot, launched the Simbas on the province in mid-1963. Simba means "lion" in KiSwahili. They were tribesmen, many of them children (the cruellest of all, it was said), armed only with spears, clubs, and arrows. Each recruit was inducted in a ceremony where magic was supposed to make him immune to bullets. If he took the precaution to wave palm branches, while looking neither left nor right and chanting *"Mai, mai"* ("Water, water"), then he believed the enemy's bullets would turn to water. In addition, they would smoke marijuana before going into battle. Then they only had to "throw their eyes" at the enemy to render him helpless.

The Simbas attacked every visible aspect of colonialism. The white population was particularly vulnerable as the Simbas killed all educated people, raped all nuns, and executed all missionaries who could not escape them. The *Armée Nationale Congolaise* melted away before them, and within twelve months they had overrun more than half the Congo. At his wit's end, Kasavubu invited Tshombé back from exile to form a government of national unity. Tshombé's solution, again, was to recruit an army of mercenaries, on this occasion mainly Rhodesians and South Africans though there were others, like Cuban refugee pilots. ("Mad Mike" Hoare, who later tried to take over the Seychelles and wound up in a South African prison, made his name at that time with his so-called "Wild Geese.") They were a deadly force, equally as savage as the Simbas, and in addition they were armed with the latest weapons. They, too, raped, looted, and committed atrocities of their own. They even shot Africans for the benefit of television cameras (notably for an Italian team). Within three months these mercenaries had driven the Simbas back through the jungle to the northeastern corner of the Congo.

Only one place remained in Simba hands by late 1964, and that was Stanleyville. The self-styled Simba Lieutenant-General Nicolas Olenga controlled the city, which had 1,300 Europeans living in it. This was the backdrop for my third visit to the Congo.

Olenga was insane. He boasted that he had personally killed thousands of Americans and accused the Belgian Government of having dropped an atomic bomb on the Congo. When Lumumba was forming his political party he had promised his followers that, come independence, they would turn white and become rich like the Europeans. Olenga said that only Lumumba's death had prevented this from happen-

UNPACKAGED TOURS

ing but, when he returned to earth, he would keep his word. The way to ensure that Lumumba would come back was to kill all the European and American hostages in Stanleyville. Gbenye sent a message to the United Nations threatening to "wear their hearts around our neck like fetishes." The Simbas referred to whites as *mateka* ("butter," from the Portuguese word *manteiga*) and said they would eat them.

While the mercenaries besieged Stanleyville, the hostages' position became increasingly perilous. Something had to be done. And it was. On November 24, 1964, six hundred Belgian paratroopers (flown from Kamina in Katanga by US Air Force transport planes) dropped on Stanleyville. At the same time, the mercenaries attacked.

The fighting lasted less than a day and the Simbas fled precipitately into the surrounding forests. They left behind them the bodies of almost a hundred whites and the corpses of thousands of blacks. Many had been killed by being forced to drink petrol and then having their stomachs cut open and their bodies set on fire.

A few days later word came that a band of Simbas was terrorising a village some hundred kilometres or so downstream from Stanleyville. A platoon of South African mercenaries was to be sent to deal with them, and we asked for permission to accompany it to film the episode. This was granted, but not before each of us had agreed to accept a pistol and brief instructions in how to use it. We set off by steamer, the jeeps and equipment towed in three barges.

The village was about a kilometre from the river and was quite small, maybe half a dozen huts in a clearing. There was no sign of activity. The mercenaries deployed in a semicircle and advanced on the huts. Suddenly Simbas appeared from the jungle and ran towards them, all the while shouting "*Mai, mai!*" They threw spears and shot off arrows. One had a gun but couldn't seem to fire it. Against the superior weapons of the mercenaries, they were picked off like flies.

While we were filming this, another group of Simbas suddenly rushed up from behind. I turned to face them and a spear creased my head (I still bear the scar). Pulling out my pistol I fired point blank at the nearest man. He was wearing a ragged shirt and a sort of kilt of monkeys' tails. His teeth were filed and I guessed his age to be about sixteen or seventeen. He fell to the ground dead and the other Simbas broke and ran. The mercenaries pursued them.

"Do it again, guv," the cameraman said. "I didn't get it on film that time."

Although the Congo was, later, pacified to a degree, neither Kasavubu nor Tshombé could control tribal and civil disruptions. Tshombé was dismissed as Prime Minister and went into exile for the second time. In 1967 a chartered plane he was travelling on was diverted to Algiers, where he was seized and imprisoned. Two years later it was announced he had died. The circumstances of his death have never been revealed, though it was widely believed to be revenge for Lumumba's death.

After Tshombé's dismissal, Mobutu (now self-promoted to Marshal) seized power again and he continues to rule. But his regime has been plagued by the same problems that dogged his predecessors. There have been some grandiose industrial projects launched, such as a multibillion-dollar hydroelectric complex to harness the power of the Livingstone Falls, and foreign-owned enterprises have been nationalised. There has also been the *authenticité* program, which not only changed all European place-names but personal first names as well (for example, Mobutu became Sese Seko or "fearless land" instead of Joseph-Désiré). As part of this drive, Western suits and ties have been banned. The everyday outfit for men in Zaire is now the *abas-cost* (literally, in French, *à bas le costume* or "down with the suit"), a sort of bush jacket. For women it is the blouse and ankle-length *pagne*, usually carrying a print of Mobutu's face on yellow or green material (the national colours).

The autocratic nature of Mobutu's rule has made him

something of an embarrassment to his Western backers (principally the United States, France, and Belgium). In 1977, Zaire's foreign debt was $300 million—the world's highest per capita at the time (today it is some $4.5 billion). The same year, some 5,000 guerillas of the *Front de Libération Nationale du Congo* (FLNC) invaded Shaba province from Angola. Mobutu's soldiers were no match for them and they were expelled only with the aid of 1,500 regular Moroccan troops airlifted by French planes. A year later the same thing happened again. This time the insurgents were defeated by French and Belgian paratroopers. *Plus ça change*, as they say. Despite his country's indebtedness and poor economic record, Mobutu has managed to siphon off sufficient funds to become one of the world's wealthiest men.

Congo. The word still has overtones of darkness and destruction. Changing the name of the country to Zaire has not dispelled them. As a Lingala proverb has it: "The leopard's heir also inherits his spots."

Afterword

▬▭▬▭▬▭▬▭▬▭▬▭▬▭▬▭▬▭▬▭▬▭▬

ON TRAVEL

When I look back on the last thirty years or so, all I seem to have done is travel. While some of my contemporaries became television executives or film directors or novelists or captains of industry or politicians or playwrights or newspaper editors or professors or even drug addicts, all I did was to voyage ceaselessly. And I sometimes ask myself: To what benefit?

Certainly my experiences have provided me with a wealth of anecdotes which I like to believe have enlivened many a party or gathering: stories about when I was in Beitelfakir, Yemen, or Tit, Algeria, or Ars, Jutland; when I first saw Timbuktu or Jan Mayen or Cape Horn; when I was imprisoned in Malange, Angola, or my car charged by an elephant in Coorg, India, or I was bitten by a snake at Iguazu Falls, Brazil; when I first ate witchetty grubs (don't ask) in Alice Springs or guinea pig in Ecuador, or dog ham in Taiwan—just to rattle off a few experiences I didn't cover in this book. I often think that Keats perhaps put my peregrinations in the best possible light when he wrote:

> Much have I travelled in the realms of gold,
> And many goodly states and kingdoms seen;
> Round many Western islands have I been
> Which bards in fealty to Apollo hold.

The word *travel* comes from the same root word as *travail*. For many centuries a journey was (and, often, still is) a day's travail. Also, the word *tour* is a form of *turn*, which is perhaps why tourists often find themselves going round in circles (the Grand Tour, incidentally, while not exactly circular, was a loop).

Francis Bacon wrote that "Travel, in the younger sort, is a part of education; in the older, a part of experience." Well, I've travelled enough to qualify in both the younger and older conditions, and I've come to believe that there is really not that great a distinction between education and experience. From a slightly different angle, popular lore says that travel broadens the mind. Well, yes, but I would be quicker to agree that travel *concentrates* the mind. Travel forces us to focus on a place and its history, to give it the attention that might otherwise be lacking in our day-to-day experience. Certainly travel can be a form of serendipity—the fascination in discovering, usually by accident, the unexpected differences between a new place and home. The differences may be as trivial as the realisation that in New Zealand the numbers of the telephone dial run counterclockwise from 0 to 1 or that in France the light switches work in the opposite direction to those in some countries—up is On, down is Off. (What—you say that that's the way the light switches work in *your* country or that's the way the telephone dial runs where *you* live? Well, there you are. The point is made.) But the experience may be more truly illuminating, like being aware of half understanding the conversations around you in Leeuwarden and then finding out that this part of the Netherlands was once one of the regions of the Anglo-Saxons—which explains why Friesian is almost English, but not quite. Or the experience can be shocking and numbing, like seeing starving children in Asia or Africa for the first time. Or it can be something you had not thought of, like the fact that Lenin's corpse has a red beard.

Some people, however, actually manage to narrow their

minds by travel. Samuel Purchas, writing in the 17th century, condemns this type for their "Apish cringes, the vanities of Neighbour Nations, without furthering of their knowledge of God, the world or themselves." Blind prejudice and wilful ignorance have a long and ignoble ancestry. Nonetheless, Veryard believed it was man's duty to travel, that nature had placed us upon the stage to be an actor and not a mere spectator. And other authors have expressed similar views on the subject.

"C'est quasi le même de converser avec ceux des autres siècles que de voyager," was how Descartes saw travel ("[Travelling] is almost the same as having a conversation with someone from another century"). My feeling is, yes if he meant seeing someone like the Rev. Ian Paisley or the Ayatollah Khomeini in action, but no if he meant that looking at ruins allows one to absorb the culture of the past. After all, Babylon now *is* just a heap of bricks, and most of Troy is in the Berlin Museum. True, some part of the Acropolis still stands today and it would be difficult to move the Pyramids somewhere else, but seeing them in their natural surroundings may not necessarily prove to be all that enlightening.

Robert Louis Stevenson is often cited on this matter: "For my part I travel not to go anywhere but to go. To travel hopefully is a better thing than to arrive." He, of course, was doing it on a donkey. These days, what with hijacked jet planes and bombs in the luggage compartments, most travellers might think it is probably better just to arrive. Travelling hopefully, though, does have its merits. Today one is usually hopeful that none of the fellow passengers is a terrorist, or hopeful that the security system at the airport is tight and running smoothly.

"Travelling is the ruin of all happiness," was English novelist Fanny Burney's view. I know some who would go along with her. My great-aunt was one. She never went farther than 20 kilometres from the farm where she was born, and she lived to be 108. I believe there must be people in, for example, Sydney's Western Suburbs who have never seen the ocean and, what's more, who never *want* to. And in fact there is probably more than a kernel of truth in what Fanny Burney says. If you see the future as represented by the USA or the USSR or Japan or China (whatever, according to your preference) and it seems to work, then travelling abroad could shatter your illusion—you may then become forever dissatisified with the present.

Quite possibly Fanny Burney was thinking merely of the discomforts of travel. The "fleas that tease in the high Pyrenees" might not be so much in evidence in these days of pest control, but there are any number of equally annoying people, obstacles, or conditions ready to fill in the gap—take your pick between the hordes of fellow travellers or the frequently long and unconscionable delays that leave many of us seething in airport lounges. In my particular case, much of my travelling has been done to and in those out-of-the-way parts of the globe where one really is more likely to encounter insects (as I've described) than other tourists. Perhaps it's making a comment on the fate of the world to say that, on balance, I think I rather prefer the insects.

One of the most penetrating comments was made to me once, many years ago, by a friend of mine (alas, now dead), who told me that the first person to shake hands with you when you got off the boat or train in a foreign country was yourself. This was in the days before air travel became widespread, yet it still holds true. Travel often does make a person come to terms with himself in strange surroundings. Travel writing should convey this kind of insight to the reader, I believe, but very little of it actually does.

Good travel writing ought to describe travel with some kind of purpose, though some of the recent travel books seem to be more properly described as travel books with a gimmick—such as how to bicycle to India or cross Australia on a camel. I suppose one could direct the same criticism against me, to a certain extent, in *Unpackaged Tours*—that going from country to country with a film crew (and all of it paid for by someone else, the best way to travel you might say) doesn't give a very in-depth portrait of each country. Which is true of course, but I didn't intend that it would. Still, I hope this overview of these lesser known or hard-to-reach places on our planet at a specific time in their development does show something about the extraordinarily astonishing diversity of the world and the power of history and geography to shape our lives.

I confess also that there is something of the collector's instinct that gave an added measure of joy to my travels. From time to time I did find myself thinking: Now I've seen all the countries in Europe. Now I've seen all the countries in the Americas. Now I've seen all the countries in Africa. And so on.

Yet I still look longingly at the atlas and those countries I've never visited—Mongolia, North Korea, Madagascar, etc. Is it possible that there is someone who has been everywhere? For all I know, there may indeed be a society of such people. But I wonder how anyone would *prove* it? Probably by spinning all those travellers' stories and anecdotes that get told at various parties and get-togethers. Which seems to bring me back where I started. Can this be all that travel gives to those who follow a peripatetic profession (or possibly obsession)?

The great travellers of the past, such as Ibn Batuta and Marco Polo, left famous accounts of their voyages. So did some of their 17th- and 18th-century successors. But by then travel seems to have largely become an English pastime, and certainly to this day travel books are firm favourites in both Britain and the United States. In Europe, too, but more often these seem to be the coffee-table variety. (Oddly, only in Australia does the popularity of travel books lately appear to have temporarily declined. Maybe a result of all the people who want to travel *to* Australia?)

There is another type of travel writing, of course—the ever-ready guide or *vade mecum*. Today we have such titles as *Europe on $5 a Day* or *With a Backpack through Asia*, but I prefer the more traditional guides, the ones that mirror the prejudices and fantasies of the publishing nation. The English Blue Guides are strong on where to get a good cup of tea abroad and whether the trains run on time. The French Michelin Guides emphasise restaurants and French-speaking pharmacies in foreign countries (essential for obtaining suppositories). German Baedekers are replete with historical and architectural details of all known ruins. Whereas American guides are usually quite explicit about the price of everything. At least this is often how these guides look to outsiders.

Such travel guides contain dreary facts and the most mundane prose. But travel has also inspired poets. Shelley and Keats were among those stimulated by the excavations that were then going on in Egypt in their time. Byron travelled in the Balkans (as has been noted). Matthew Arnold used Persian motifs, Robert Southey was taken by Arabian ones. Perhaps no one has caught the essence of travel more than James Elroy Flecker when he wrote:

> We travel not for trafficking alone:
> By hotter winds our fiery hearts are fanned:
> For lust of knowing what should not be known
> We make the Golden Journey to Samarkand.

And although I wasn't aware of it for a long time, I think this was always my credo. I travelled "not for trafficking alone," though it usually *was* trafficking that brought me to many a place in the first instance. I was and am possessed of an insatiable curiosity, a "lust of knowing what should not be known." Sadly, I have never been to Samarkand—but who knows? Maybe one day. As Flecker's poem goes on to say: "It was ever thus. / Men are unwise and curiously planned."

Life also turns out to be curiously planned. I believe travel helps us to contemplate it in a variety of permutations.

Selected Bibliography

CHAPTER 1: ALBANIA

Byron, Lord. *The Poetical Works of Lord Byron*. Edited by E. H. Coleridge. Atlantic Highlands, NJ: Humanities Press, 1972 (reprint of 1905 edn.). Oxford: Oxford University Press, 1901.

Ehrenburg, Ilya. *European Crossroads*. Trans. by A. Markov. New York: Alfred Knopf, 1947.

Fischer, Bernd Jürgen. *King Zog and the Struggle for Stability in Albania*. Boulder, CO: Eastern European Monographs (dist. by Columbia University Press), 1984.

Gardiner, Leslie. *Curtain Calls: Travels in Albania, Romania & Bulgaria*. Ottawa: Bibliographic Distribution, 1976. London: Gerald Duckworth, 1976.

Hamm, Harry. *Albania: China's Beachhead in Europe*. Trans. by Victor Anderson. London: Weidenfeld & Nicolson, 1963.

Hobhouse, John Cam (Lord Broughton). *A Journey through Albania: During the Years 1809 & 1810*. Salem, MA: Arno Press, 1970 (reprint of 1817 edn.). London: John Murray, 1817.

Lear, Edward. *Journals of a Landscape Painter in Albania*. London: Bentley, 1851.

Logoreci, Anton. *The Albanians: Europe's Forgotten Survivors*. Boulder, CO: Westview, 1978. London: Victor Gollancz, 1977.

Noli, Fan. *George Castrioti Scanderbeg*. New York: International University Press, 1947.

Pano, Nicholas. *The People's Republic of Albania*. Baltimore: The Johns Hopkins University Press, 1968.

Pollo, Stefanaq, and Puto, Arben. *The History of Albania: From Its Origins to the Present Day*. New York: Methuen, 1980. London: Routledge & Kegan Paul, 1981.

Skendi, Stavro (ed.). *Albania*. New York: Praeger, 1956. London: Atlantic Press, 1951.

Zakhos, Emmanuel. *Albanie*. Paris: Petite Planète, 1972.

CHAPTER 2: GREENLAND

Bornemann, Claus et al. *Bogen om Grønland*. Copenhagen: Politikens Forlag, 1968.

Bure, Kristjan (ed.). *Greenland*. Copenhagen: Royal Danish Ministry for Foreign Affairs, 1961.

Dronke, Ursula (ed.). *The Poetic Edda*. New York and Oxford: Oxford University Press, 1969.

Gad, Finn. *The History of Greenland* (Vol. 1). Montreal: McGill-Queens University Press, 1971, 1973, 1983 (4 vols). London: C. Hurst, 1970, 1973, 1983.

Holand, Hjalmar R. *Norse Discoveries and Explorations in America: Leif Ericson to the Kensington Stone*. New York: Dover Publications, 1969 (n.d., paperback).

Ingstad, Helge. *Land Under the Pole Star*. London: Jonathon Cape, 1966.

_____. *Westward to Vinland: The Discovery of Pre-Columbian House-sites in North America*. Trans. by Erik J. Friis. New York: St. Martin's Press, 1969. London: Jonathon Cape, 1969.

Jones, Gwyn. *The Norse Atlantic Saga: Being the Norse Voyages of Discovery & Settlement to Iceland, Greenland, America*. New York and Oxford: Oxford University Press, 1964 (1986: paperback).

Krogh, Knud J. *Viking Greenland*. Copenhagen: The National Museum, 1967.

Mowat, Farley, *West Viking*. New York: Minerva, Funk & Wagnalls, 1968. London: Secker & Warburg, 1966.

Nørlund, Poul. *De Gamle Nordbobygder ved Verdens Ende*. Copenhagen: The National Museum, 1967.

Oleson, Tryggvi J. *Early Voyages and Northern Approaches, 1000–1632*. Toronto: McClelland and Stewart, 1963.

CHAPTER 3: PARAGUAY

Bastos, Augusto Roa. *I the Supreme*. Trans. by Helen Lane. New York: Alfred Knopf, 1986. New York: Aventura, 1987 (paperback).

Caballero, Ernesto Giménez. *Revelación del Paraguay*. Madrid: Espasa-Calpe S.A., 1958.

Cadogan, Leon. *Ayvú Rapytá: Textos misticos de los Mbyáguarani*. São Paulo: University of São Paulo, 1959.

———. *La Literatura de los Guaranies*. Mexico DF: Editorial Joaquin Mortiz, 1970.

———. *Mil apellidos guaranies*. Asunción: Editorial Toledo, 1960.

Herring, Hubert. *A History of Latin America*. New York: Alfred Knopf, 1968. London: Jonathon Cape, 1954.

Kolinski, Charles J. *Independence or Death: The Story of the Paraguayan War*. Gainesville, FL: University of Florida Press, 1965.

Lane, William. *The Workingman's Paradise*. Sydney: Edwards Dunlop, 1892.

Meyer, Gordon. *The River and the People*. London: Methuen, 1965.

Pendle, George. *Paraguay: A Riverside Nation*. New York: Gordon Press, 1976 (reprint). New York and Oxford: Oxford University Press, 1967.

Souter, Gavin. *A Peculiar People*. Sydney: Angus & Robertson, 1968.

Southey, Robert. *A Tale of Paraguay*. London: Longman, 1825.

Voltaire (François-Marie Arouet). *Candide*. New York: Bantam Books, 1981 (paperback). *Candide ou l'Optimiste*. Paris, 1759.

Warren, Harris Gaylord. *Paraguay*. Norman, OK: University of Oklahoma Press, 1949.

Whicker, Alan. *Within Whicker's World*. New York: David & Charles, 1983. London: Elm Tree Books, 1982.

Zook, David H. *The Conduct of the Chaco War*. New York: Bookman Associates, 1960.

CHAPTER 4: SÃO TOMÉ AND PRÍNCIPE

Boxer, Charles R. *The Portuguese Seaborne Empire.* New York: Alfred Knopf, 1970. London: Hutchinson & Co., Ltd., 1969.

———. *Race Relations in the Portuguese Colonial Empire.* New York and Oxford: Oxford University Press, 1963.

Camões, Luís de. *Os Lusíadas.* Oporto: Porto Editora, 1960. (*See below*, Frank Pierce.)

Duffy, James. *Portugal in Africa.* Harmondsworth: Penguin Books, 1962.

Pierce, Frank (ed.). *Luís de Camões: Os Lusíadas.* New York and Oxford: Oxford University Press, 1973.

Tenreiro, Francisco. *A Ilha de São Tomé.* Lisbon: Junta de Investigacões do Ultramar, 1961.

CHAPTER 5: THE SUBANTARCTIC ISLANDS

Chilton, C. (ed.). *The Subantarctic Islands of New Zealand.* Christchurch: The Philosophical Institute of Canterbury, 1909.

Cook, James. *The Voyage of the Resolution and Adventure (1772–1775).* Ed. by J. C. Beaglehole. London: Hakluyt Society, 1961.

Eden, A. W. *Islands of Despair.* London: Melrose Press Ltd., 1955.

Eunson, Keith. *The Wreck of the General Grant.* Wellington: A. H. & A. W. Reed, 1974.

Jenkins, Geoffrey. *Grue of Ice.* New York: Viking Press, 1963. London: Collins, 1962.

Kerr, I. S. *Campbell Island: A History.* Wellington: A. H. & A. W. Reed, 1976.

Lawson, Will. *The Lady of the Heather.* Sydney: Angus & Robertson, 1945.

McLaren, F. B. *The Auckland Islands.* Wellington: A. H. & A. W. Reed, 1948.

McNab, R. *Murihiku.* Invercargill: William Smith, 1907.

Musgrave, T. *Castaway on the Auckland Islands.* London: Lockwood, 1866.

Ross, Sir James Clark. *A Voyage of Discovery and Research in Southern and Antarctic Regions, 1839–43* (2 vols). Montclair,

NJ: Augustus M. Kelley, n.d. (reprint of 1847 edn.). London: John Murray, 1847.

Wild, F. *Shackleton's Last Voyage: The Story of the Quest.* London: Cassell, 1923.

Wilson, Colin. *Enigmas and Mysteries.* New York: Doubleday, 1977. London: Aldus Books, 1976.

CHAPTER 6: GUINEA

Attwood, William. *The Reds and the Blacks.* New York: Harper & Row, 1967.

Fage, J. D. *History of West Africa.* New York and Cambridge: Cambridge University Press, 1969.

Howe, Russell Warren. *Black Africa.* Croydon: New African Library, 1966.

Laye, Camara. *The Dark Child* (*L'Enfant Noir*). Trans. by James Kirkup and Ernest Jones. New York: Farrar, Straus, 1954. Paris: Librairie Plon, 1954.

Rivière, Claude. *Guinea: The Mobilization of a People.* Trans. by Richard Adloff and Virginia Thompson. Ithaca, NY: Cornell University Press, 1977.

Thompson, Virginia, and Adloff, Richard. *French West Africa.* Westport, CT: Greenwood Press, n.d. (reprint of 1958 edn.).

CHAPTER 7: BURMA

Collis, Maurice. *Trials in Burma.* New York: AMS Press, n.d. (reprint of 1945 edn.). Harmondsworth: Penguin Books, 1945.

Courtauld, Caroline. *In Search of Burma.* Englewood Cliffs, NJ: Salem Press, 1985. London: Frederick Muller, 1984.

Kipling, Rudyard. *Collected Verse.* London: Hodder & Stoughton, 1912.

____. *From Sea to Sea: And Other Sketches. / Letters of Travel.* New York: Charles Scribner's Sons, 1900. London: Macmillan, 1900.

____. *Rudyard Kipling's Verse.* New York: Doubleday, 1940.

Klein, Wilhelm. *Burma.* Hong Kong: Apa Productions, 1983.

Maugham, W. Somerset. *The Gentleman in the Parlour: A Record of a Journey from Rangoon to Haiphong*. Salem, MA: Ayer Company Publications, 1977 (reprint of 1935 edn.). London: William Heinemann, 1935.

Orwell, George. *Burmese Days*. New York: Harcourt Brace Jovanovich, 1950 (1974: paperback). London: Secker & Warburg, 1949.

Scott, Sir J. G. (pseud. Shway Yoe). *The Burman: His Life and Notions*. New York: AMS Press, n.d. (reprint of 1910 edn.). London: Macmillan, 1882.

CHAPTER 8: SOUTH-WEST AFRICA (NAMIBIA)

First, Ruth. *South West Africa*. Magnolia, MA: Peter Smith, n.d. (reprint). Harmondsworth: Penguin Books, 1963.

Frenssen, Gustav. *Die Reise von Peter Moor nach Südwestafrika*. Berlin: Grote, 1905.

Green, Lawrence G. *Lords of the Last Frontier*. Cape Town: Howard B. Timmins, 1952.

Van der Post, Laurens. *The Lost World of the Kalahari*. New York: Harcourt Brace Jovanovich, 1977. London: Hogarth Press, 1958.

CHAPTER 9: SOCOTRA

Bent, Mabel. *Southern Arabia*. London: Longman Green, 1900.

Botting, Douglas. *Island of Dragon's Head*. London: Hodder & Stoughton, 1958.

Gurney, Jason. *Sheba's Coast*. London: Robert Hale, 1966.

Harper, Stephen. *Last Sunset*. London: Collins, 1978.

Lang, Andrew (ed.). *Arabian Nights Entertainments*. Magnolia, MA: Peter Smith, n.d. (reprint). New York: Dover Publications, 1969 (paperback). London: Longman Green, 1898.

CHAPTER 10: PITCAIRN ISLAND / THE COOK ISLANDS

Ball, Ian M. *Children of the Bounty*. Boston: Little, Brown, 1973. London: Victor Gollancz, 1973.

Becke, Louis. *The Mutineer*. Sydney: Angus & Robertson, 1898.

Belcher, Diana (Lady Belcher). *The Mutineers of the Bounty and their Descendants in Pitcairn and Norfolk Islands.* New York: AMS Press, 1976 (reprint of the 1870 edn.). London: John Murray, 1870.

Delano, Captain Amasa. *The Voyages and Travels of Amasa Delano.* Hobart: Cat and Fiddle Press, 1973 (fac. edn.).

Mackaness, George. *Life of Vice-Admiral William Bligh.* Sydney: Angus & Robertson, 1931.

Nordoff, Charles, and Hall, James N. *The Bounty Trilogy.* Boston: Atlantic Monthly Press, 1982 (one volume containing *Mutiny on the Bounty, Men Against the Sea*, and *Pitcairns Island*).

Shapiro, H. L. *The Heritage of the Bounty: The Story of Pitcairn Island through Six Generations.* New York: AMS Press, n.d. (reprint of 1936 edn.). London: Victor Gollancz, 1936 (published in England as *Descendants of the Mutineers of the Bounty*).

Silverman, David. *Pitcairn Island.* Cleveland, OH: The World Publishing Co., 1967.

Chapter 11: The Faroes

Jacobsen, Jørgen-Frantz. *Barbara.* Trans. by E. Bannister. Harmondsworth: Penguin Books, 1949.

Kampp, Aage H. *Færøerne.* Copenhagen: Alfred G. Hassings, 1967.

Severin, Tim. *The Brendan Voyage.* New York: McGraw-Hill, 1978. London: Hutchinson, 1978. New York: Avon, 1979 (paperback).

Smith-Dampier, E. M. (trans.). *Sigurd the Dragon Slayer: A Faroese Ballad Cycle.* Millwood, NJ: Kraus Reprint Co., 1969.

West, John F. *Faroe: The Emergence of a Nation.* Port Washington, NY: Paul S. Eriksson, 1973. London: C. Hurst, 1972.

Williamson, Kenneth. *The Atlantic Islands.* London: Collins, 1948.

Chapter 12: Torres Strait

Haddon, A. C. (ed.). *Reports of the Cambridge Anthropological Expedition to Torres Straits* (six vols.). New York: Johnson Reprint Co., n.d. (reprint of 1935 edn.). Cambridge: Cambridge University Press, 1904–1905.

Holthouse, Hector. *Ships in the Coral*. Sydney: Macmillan, 1976.

Huxley, Thomas H., and Huxley, Julian S. *Diary of the Voyage of H.M.S. Rattlesnake*. Millwood, NJ: Kraus Reprint Co., n.d. (reprint of 1935 edn.). London: Chatto & Windus, 1935.

Idriess, Ion L. *Isles of Despair*. Sydney: Angus & Robertson, 1947.

_____. *The Wild White Man of Badu*. San Francisco: Tri-Ocean Press, n.d. (reprint). Sydney: Angus & Robertson, 1950.

Lawrie, Margaret (ed.). *Myths and Legends of Torres Strait*. New York: Taplinger, 1972. Brisbane: University of Queensland Press, 1970.

MacGillivray, J. *Narrative of the Voyage of H.M.S. Rattlesnake*. London: Boone, 1852.

Moore, David R. *Islanders and Aborigines at Cape York: An Ethnographic Reconstruction Based on the 1848–1850 "Rattlesnake" Journals of O. W. Brierley*. Atlantic Highlands, NJ: Humanities Press, 1979. Canberra: Australian Institute of Aboriginal Studies, 1979.

Singe, John. *The Torres Strait: People and History*. New York: University of Queensland Press, 1980. Brisbane: University of Queensland Press, 1979.

Walker, D. (ed.). *Bridge and Barrier: The Natural and Cultural History of Torres Strait*. Canberra: Australian National University Press, 1972.

CHAPTER 13: ARMENIA

Arlen, Michael (senior). *The Green Hat*. London: Cassell & Co., 1924. Chicago: Academy Chicago Publishers, 1983 (paperback).

Arlen, Michael J. (junior). *Passage to Ararat*. New York: Farrar, Straus & Giroux, 1975. London: Chatto & Windus, 1976. New York: Ballantine, 1976 (paperback).

Hartunian, Abraham. *Neither To Laugh nor To Weep*. Boston: Beacon Press, 1968 (paperback).

Javakhishvili, A., and Gvelesiani, G. (eds.). *Soviet Georgia: Its Geography, History and Economy*. Moscow: Progress Publishers, n.d.

Khatchatrian, A. *L'Architecture arménienne*. Paris: Guenthner, 1948.

Lang, David Marshall. *Armenia: Cradle of Civilization.* New York: Allen & Unwin, 1978 (2nd edn.). London: Allen & Unwin, 1970, 1978, 1980 (3rd edn.).

Pasdermadjian, H. *Histoire de l'Arménie.* Paris: Librairie Samulian, 1964.

Rustaveli, Shota. *The Lord of the Panther-Skin* (also published as *The Knight in the Panther's Skin*). Trans. by R. H. Stevenson. Albany, NY: State University of New York Press, 1977. Tbilisi: Sabchota Sakartvelo, 1968 (this edn. trans. by Venera Urushadze).

Toynbee, Arnold (ed.). *Treatment of Armenians in the Ottoman Empire* (documents). London: H.M. Stationery Office, 1916.

Werfel, Franz. *Forty Days at Musa Dagh.* New York: Viking Press, 1934. New York: Carroll and Graf, 1983 (paperback).

CHAPTER 14: THE GUIANAS

Bacon, Margaret. *Journey to Guyana.* London: Dobson, 1970.

Behn, Aphra. *Oronooko; or the Royal Slave.* Salem, MA: Ayer Company Publications, n.d. (reprint). London: The Folio Society, 1953. New York: Norton, 1973 (paperback).

Bresson, Marcelle. *La Guyane.* Paris: Les Éditions du Cygne, 1929.

Daly, Vere. *A Short History of the Guyanese People.* London: Macmillan, 1976.

Devèze, Michel. *Cayenne, Deportés et Bagnards.* Paris: Julliard, 1965.

Dew, Edward. *The Difficult Flowering of Surinam.* The Hague: Martinus Nijhoff, 1978.

Doyle, Arthur Conan. *The Lost World.* Buccaneer Books, n.d. (reprint). London: John Murray, 1960.

Hudson, W. H. *Green Mansions.* New York: AMS Press, n.d. (reprint of 1923 edn.). New York: Barnes, 1944. New York: Airmont, 1987 (paperback).

Lichtveld, Lou. *Suriname.* Paramaribo: Radhakishun, 1959.

Londres, Albert. *Au Bagne.* Paris: A. Michel, 1925.

Newman, Peter. *British Guiana: Problems of Cohesion in an Immigrant Society.* New York and Oxford: Oxford University Press, 1964.

Niles, Blair. *Condemned to Devil's Island*. London: Jonathon Cape, 1930.

Rout, Leslie B. *Which Way Out? A Study of the Guyanese-Venezuelan Border Dispute*. East Lansing, MI: Michigan State University Press, 1971.

Seznec and Sylviane. *Notre Bagne*. Paris: Denoël, 1950.

Stedman, John G. *Expedition to Surinam, 1772–1777*. Ed. by C. Bryant. London: The Folio Society, 1963.

____. *Narrative of an Expedition Against the Revolted Negroes of Surinam*. Ed. by R. A. Van Lier. Amherst, MA: University of Massachusetts Press, 1972.

Waugh, Evelyn. *When the Going Was Good*. Westport, CT: Greenwood Press, 1976 (reprint). London: Gerald Duckworth, 1947.

CHAPTER 15: JUAN FERNÁNDEZ

Defoe, Daniel. *Robinson Crusoe*. New York: Bantam Books, 1981 (paperback). London: W. Taylor, 1719.

De Val, Maura Brescia. *Mares de Leyenda*. Santiago: Talleres Gráficos Garcia, 1979.

Dillingham, William B. "The Encantadas," in *Melville's Short Fiction*. Athens, GA: University of Georgia Press, 1977.

Mégroz, R. L. *The Real Robinson Crusoe: Being the Life & Strange Surprising Adventures of Alexander Selkirk of Largo, Fife, Mariner*. Philadelphia: R. West, 1973 (reprint). London: The Cresset Press, 1939.

Melville, Herman. *Billy Budd, Sailor: And Other Stories* (includes "The Encantadas"). New York: Penguin, 1968 (paperback).

____. *The Enchanted Isles*. London: Constable & Co., 1923 (Standard Edition).

Rogers, Captain Woodes. *A Cruising Voyage Round the World*. Magnolia, MA: Peter Smith, n.d. (reprint). New York: Dover Publications, 1970 (paperback).

CHAPTER 16: THE BRITISH MAIN

Caiger, Stephen. *British Honduras: Past and Present*. London: Allen & Unwin, 1960.

Coe, Michael D. *The Maya.* New York and London: Thames and Hudson, 1984 (3rd rev. edn.; paperback). London: Thames and Hudson, 1966.

Cook, Lt. James. *Remarks on a passage from the river Balise in the Bay of Honduras to Merida, the capital of the province of Jucatan in the Spanish West Indies.* London: Published for C. Parker, 1769.

Davidson, William J. *Historical Geography of the Bay Islands, Honduras: Anglo-Hispanic Conflict in the Western Caribbean.* Birmingham, AL: Southern University Press, 1974.

Floyd, Troy S. *The Anglo-Spanish Struggle for Mosquitia.* Albuquerque, NM: New Mexico University Press, 1967.

Gregg, A. R. *British Honduras.* London: H.M. Stationery Office, 1968.

Henry, O. *Cabbages and Kings.* London: Hodder & Stoughton, 1916.

Luke, Sir Harry. *Caribbean Circuit.* London: Nicholson and Watson, 1950.

Thompson, J.E.S. *Maya Archeologist.* Norman, OK: University of Oklahoma Press, 1975. London: Robert Hale, 1963.

CHAPTER 17: THE CANARY ISLANDS

Cuscoy, Luis Diego. *The Book of Tenerife.* Santa Cruz de Tenerife: Ediciones Izaña, 1957.

De Espinosa, Alonso. *The Guanches of Tenerife.* Trans. by Sir C. Markham. London: The Hakluyt Society, 1907.

Macbeth, Madge. *Three Elysian Islands.* Las Palmas de Gran Canaria: Imprenta Lezcano, 1958.

Mason, John, and Mason, Anne. *The Canary Islands.* New York: Hippocrene Books, 1976. London: B. T. Batsford, 1976.

CHAPTER 18: TRISTAN DA CUNHA

Booy, Derrick. *Rock of Exile.* Old Greenwich, CT: Devin-Adair, n.d. (reprint). London: J. M. Dent & Sons, 1957.

Brander, J. *Tristan da Cunha, 1506–1902.* London: Allen and Unwin, 1940.

Housegood, Nancy. *The Glass Island*. London: Hodder & Stoughton, 1964.

Mackay, Margaret. *Angry Island*. London: Arthur Barker, 1963.

Munch, Peter. *Crisis in Utopia*. New York: Thomas Y. Crowell, 1971.

CHAPTER 19: THE PERSIAN GULF

Dutchess of St. Albans. *Where Time Stood Still: A Portrait of Oman*. Boston: Charles River Books, 1982. London: Quartet Books Ltd., 1980.

Hawley, Donald. *The Trucial States*. New York: Irvington, 1971 (paperback). London: Allen & Unwin, 1970.

Heard-Bey, Frauke. *From Trucial States to United Arab Emirates*. New York and London: Longman, 1982.

Morris, James. *Sultan in Oman*. London: Faber and Faber, 1957.

Phillips, Wendell. *Oman: A History*. International Book Center, n.d. (reprint). London: Longman, 1967.

Searle, Pauline. *Dawn Over Oman*. New York and London: Allen & Unwin, 1979.

Storrs, Sir Ronald. *Orientations*. London: Nicholson and Watson Ltd., 1937.

Zahlan, Rosemarie Said. *The Origins of the United Arab Emirates: A Political and Social History of the Trucial States*. New York: St. Martin's Press, 1978. London: Macmillan, 1978.

CHAPTER 20: ZANZIBAR / THE COMORO ISLANDS

Ayany, Samuel G. *A History of Zanzibar: A Study in Constitutional Development, 1934–1964*. Totowa, NJ: Rowman & Allenheld, 1970. Nairobi: East African Literature Bureau, 1970.

Clayton, Anthony. *The Zanzibar Revolution and Its Aftermath*. Hamden, CT: The Shoestring Press, 1981. London: C. Hurst, 1981.

Douglas, Alexander. *Holiday in the Islands*. Cape Town: Purnell & Sons (S.A.) Pty. Ltd., 1976.

Guide to Zanzibar. Zanzibar: Government Printer, 1949.

Kerr, Alexander (ed.). *The Indian Ocean Region*. Nedlands: University of Western Australia Press, 1981.

Lofchie, Michael. *Zanzibar*. Princeton, NJ: Princeton University Press, 1965.

Middleton, John, and Campbell, Jane. *Zanzibar: Its Society and Politics*. Westport, CT: Greenwood Press, 1971 (reprint of 1965 edn.). New York and Oxford: Oxford University Press, 1965.

Morley, Robert, and Morley, Sean. *Islands*. Philadelphia: Chilton Book Co., 1970.

Okello, John. *Revolution in Zanzibar*. New York: International Publications Service, 1967. Nairobi: East African Publishing House, 1967.

Ostheimer, John M. (ed.). *The Politics of the Western Indian Ocean Islands*. New York: Praeger Publishers, 1975.

Smith, J.L.B. *Old Fourlegs*. London: Longman Green, 1958. London: Pan Books, 1958 (paperback).

CHAPTER 21: LADAKH

Danielli, Giotto. *Buddhists and Glaciers of Western Tibet*. London: Kegan Paul, Trench & Trubner, 1933.

Douglas, William. *Beyond the High Himalayas*. London: Victor Gollancz, 1953.

Harvey, Andrew. *A Journey in Ladakh*. Boston: Houghton Mifflin, 1983 (1984: paperback). London: Jonathon Cape, 1983.

Moorcroft, William, and Trebeck, George. *Travels in the Himalayan Provinces of Hindustan*. London: John Murray, 1841.

Ouspensky, Peter D. *Tertium Organum: A Key to the Enigmas of the World*. Trans. by Peter D. Ouspensky and E. Kadloubovsky. New York: Random House, n.d. (paperback). Cape Town: Stourton Press, 1961 (an abridgement by F. Hall).

Smith, Nicol. *Golden Doorway to Tibet*. Indianapolis, IN: Bobbs-Merrill, 1949.

Vigne, Godfrey. *Travels in Kashmir, Ladak and Iskardo*. London: Henry Colburn, 1842.

CHAPTER 22: HAITI

Bitter, Maurice. *Haiti*. Paris: Éditions du Seuil, 1970.

Cave, Hugh B. *Haiti: Highroad to Adventure*. New York: Henry Holt, 1952.

Courlander, Harold. *The Drum and the Hoe: Life and Lore of the Haitian People*. Berkeley, CA: University of California Press, 1960 (n.d., paperback).

Diederich, Bernard, and Burt, A. C. *Papa Doc: Haiti and its Dictator*. London: Bodley Head, 1969.

Dunham, Katherine. *Island Possessed*. New York: Doubleday, 1969.

Duvalier, François. *Eléments d'une Doctrine (OEuvres Essentielles, Tome 1)*. Port-au-Prince: Collections OEuvres Essentielles, 1968.

Fermor, Patrick Leigh. *The Traveller's Tree*. London: Arrow Books, 1961.

Heinl, Robert Debs, and Heinl, Nancy Gordon. *Written in Blood: The Story of the Haitian People, 1492–1971*. Boston: Houghton Mifflin, 1978.

James, Cyril L. *The Black Jacobins: Toussaint L'Ouverture and the San Domingo Revolution*. New York: Random House, 1963 (n.d., Vintage paperback).

Métraux, Alfred. *Haiti: Black Peasants and their Religion*. Trans. by Pierre Lengyel. London: George C. Harrap, 1960.

____. *Voodoo in Haiti*. Trans. by Hugo Charteris. London: Andre Deutsch, 1959. New York: Schocken, 1972 (paperback).

Nicholls, David. *From Dessalines to Duvalier: Race, Colour and the National Independence in Haiti*. New York and Cambridge: Cambridge University Press, 1970.

Rodman, Selden. *Haiti: The Black Republic*. Greenwich, CT: Devin-Adair, 1961 (1984: 6th rev. edn.).

Rotburg, Robert. *Haiti*. Boston: Houghton Mifflin, 1971.

CHAPTER 23: THE BRITISH ISLETS

Booth, David, and Perrott, David. *Islands of Britain*. London: Guideway Windward, 1981.

Chapman, R. W. (ed.). *Johnson's Journey to the Western Islands of Scotland and Boswell's Journal of a tour of the Hebrides with Samuel Johnson LLD*. New York and Oxford: Oxford University Press, 1965 (1984: Penguin paperback).

Crookstone, Peter (ed.). *Island Britain*. London: Macdonald & Co., 1981.

Etherton, D., and Barlow, V. *Tempestuous Isle*. London: Lutterworth Press, 1950.

Johnson, Samuel. *See above*, Chapman, R. W.

Kinvig, R. H. *Isle of Man: A Social, Cultural and Political History*. New York: Charles Tuttle (reprint of 1975 edn.). Liverpool: Liverpool University Press, 1975. Atlantic Highlands, NJ: Humanities Press International, 1978 (3rd rev. edn., paperback).

Langham, Anthony, and Langham, Myrtle. *Lundy*. New York and Newton Abbott: David & Charles, 1970 (new edn., 1984).

MacGregor, Alasdair Alpin. *The Farthest Hebrides*. London: Michael Joseph, 1969.

Maclean, Charles. *Island on the Edge of the World: The Story of St. Kilda*. New York: Taplinger, 1980. London: Tom Stacey Ltd., 1972.

Macnab, P. A. *The Isle of Mull*. New York: David & Charles, 1974. Newton Abbott: David & Charles, 1970.

Mason, T. H. *The Islands of Ireland*. London: B. T. Batsford, 1936.

Murray, W. H. *The Hebrides*. London: William Heinemann, 1966.

Stenning, E. H. *Portrait of the Isle of Man*. New York: International Publications Service, 1975 (3rd edn.). London: Robert Hale, 1972 (published as *The Isle of Man*).

Synge, John M. *The Aran Islands*. London: Allen & Unwin, 1961 (Library Edn.).

____. *Collected Works of John Millington Synge*. Ed. by Robin Skelton. Washington, DC: The Catholic University of America Press, n.d. (Vol. 1: *The Poems*, paperback). New York and Oxford: Oxford University Press, 1962–68 (4 vols.).

Thompson, Francis. *St. Kilda and Other Hebridean Outliers*. Newton Abbott: David & Charles, 1970.

CHAPTER 24: THE CONGO (ZAIRE)

Anstey, Roger. *King Leopold's Legacy: The Congo under Belgian Rule*. New York and Oxford: Oxford University Press, 1966.

Brausch, Georges. *Belgian Administration in the Congo*. New York and Oxford: Oxford University Press, 1960.

Clarke, Stephen J. *The Congo Mercenary*. Johannesburg: South African Institute of International Affairs, 1968.

Colvin, Ian. *The Rise and Fall of Moise Tshombé*. London: Frewin, 1968.

Conrad, Joseph. *Heart of Darkness*. In *The Collected Works* (vol. 5). London: William Heinemann, 1919. New York: Penguin, 1984 (paperback).

Diallo, Siradiou. *Zaire Today* (*Zaire Aujourd'hui*). New York: International Learning Systems, 1977. Paris: Éditions Jeune Afrique, 1977.

Forbath, Peter. *The River Congo: The Discovery, Exploration, and Exploitation of the World's Most Dramatic River*. New York: Harper & Row, 1977. London: Secker & Warburg, 1978. New York: Dutton, 1979 (paperback).

Gérard-Libois, Jules. *Sécession au Katanga*. Brussels: CRISP (Centre de Recherche et d'Information Socio-Politiques), 1963.

____. *Nineteen Sixty-four: Political Documents of a Developing Nation* (in French). Compiled by B. Verhaegen (CRISP Series). Princeton: Princeton University Press, 1966.

Heinz, G., and Donnay, H. *Patrice Lumumba: Les Cinquantes derniers jours de sa Vie*. Brussels: CRISP (Centre de Recherche et d'Information Socio-Politiques), 1966.

Lindsay, Nicholas Vachel. *Collected Poems*. New York: Macmillan, 1955.

Meredith, Martin. *The First Dance of Freedom: Black Africa in the Postwar Era*. New York: Harper & Row, 1985. London: Hamish Hamilton, 1984.

Reed, David. *111 Days in Stanleyville*. London: Collins, 1966.